Cultural History and Education

D0162159

Cultural History and Education

Critical Essays on Knowledge and Schooling

Edited by
Thomas S. Popkewitz
Barry M. Franklin
Miguel A. Pereyra

ROUTLEDGEFALMER
New York and London

Published in 2001 by
RoutledgeFalmer
29 West 35th Street
New York, NY 10001

Published in Great Britain in 2001 by
Routledge Falmer
11 New Fetter Lane
London EC4P 4EE

Copyright © 2001 by RoutledgeFalmer
RoutledgeFalmer is an imprint of the Taylor & Francis Group

Printed in the United States of America on acid-free paper
Design and typography: Jack Donner
Cover illustration: Christine E. Alfery

All rights reserved. No part of this book may be reprinted or reproduced or utilized in any
form or by any electronic, mechanical, or other means, now known or hereafter invented,
including photocopying and recording or in any information storage or retrieval system without permission in writing from the publishers.

Library of Congress Cataloging-in-Publication Data

Cultural history and education: critical essays on knowledge and schooling :
    edited by Thomas S. Popkewitz, Barry M. Franklin, Miguel A. Pereyra.
        p.   cm.
    Includes bibliographical references and index.
    ISBN 0–415–92805–2 — ISBN 0–415–92806–0
        1. Education—Histriography. 2. Culture—Histriography. 3. Education—Research—
Methodology Social Aspects—Cross-cultural studies. 4. Education—History—Cross-cultural
studies. 5. Comparative Education. 5. Postmodernism and education. I. Popkewitz, Thomas
S. II. Franklin, Barry M. III. Pereyra, Miguel A., 1950–

LB45 .C838 2000
306.43—dc21   00–042500

Contents

Acknowledgments

The preparation of this book has involved working across continents and with numerous people who have made this manuscript possible. We would like to thank Lynn Fendler, who worked with the earlier drafts of this manuscript, and Dar Weyenberg, who followed Lynn in helping to edit, check references, and all those things that make it possible to bring a manuscript to publication. In addition to their hands-on-assistance, their knowledge of the field helped to clarify the book as a whole. We also need to thank Chris Kruger of the Department of Curriculum and Instruction at the University of Wisconsin-Madison. Her intelligence and understanding of scholarly work has eased the burdens of getting the manuscripts ready for publication and in keeping contact with the various authors at different phases of the publication process. All three, in different but complementary ways, help keep academic life somewhat sane in an environment that often threatens to turn otherwise. We also wish to thank Christine Alfery for her cover illustration on the book jacket, and Lynn Marie Franklin for proofreading the final manuscript.

We also need to thank the University of Wisconsin-Madison's Tinker Foundation Fellowship, which enabled Miguel A. Pereyra to work on the manuscript during the Fall 1999 semester; the Fulbright Fellowship at the University of Helsinki in Winter 2000, which enabled Tom Popkewitz to work on completing chapter 1, and editing the remainder of the manuscript; and the Office of the Vice President for Research at the University of Michigan for providing a publication subvention grant to support the translations of several chapters of the book.

Two of the chapters appearing in this book have been published previously: Thomas S. Popkewitz (1997), "The production of reason and power: Curriculum history and intellectual traditions," *Journal of Curriculum Studies* 29(2): 131–64; and Thomas S. Popkewitz (1998), "Dewey, Vygotsky, and the social administration of the individual: Constructivist pedagogy as systems of ideas in historical spaces," *American Educational Research Journal* 35(4): 535–70. The former has undergone revision; the latter appears as it was originally published; both appear with permission of the original publishers.

Finally, we would like to thank Heidi Freund, editor for Routledge, for her continual support; and Karita France dos Santos, who assumed editorial responsibility for this book and with whom we have enjoyed our many conversations during the publication processes.

Preface

Banished to the sidelines during the last two decades by a flurry of interest in the methods of social history, the study of ideas is enjoying something of a resurgence these days among historians and critical researchers of education. Appearing on the scene under the rubric of cultural history, this scholarship involves cross-disciplinary approaches to historical studies and is attached to broader intellectual movements in social and political theory and critical studies. The approaches depart from the practices that have typically characterized the work of intellectual historians. Cultural historians are not interested in identifying the key ideas that are thought to characterize a particular period or age. Nor do they wish to investigate the so-called great ideas of the past and the individuals who championed them. With diverse intellectual interests and theoretical approaches, cultural historians bring to bear a particular connection with theories of knowledge and language as they rethink the problems and methods of historical studies.

Internationally, these cultural historians have integrated German traditions of conceptual history and French traditions in the history of science and genealogical studies into a dialogue with American historical methods and topics. Employing methods identified with such labels as the "linguistic turn," the "new cultural history," and "postmodern history," cultural historians have joined critical traditions concerned with the relation of knowledge, power, and social change.

What distinguishes cultural history from traditional intellectual history, then, is a concern with knowledge as a field of cultural practices and cultural reproduction. For cultural historians, history is the study of the historically constructed ways of reason that frame, discipline, and order our action and participation in the world. The purpose of the investigation into systems of knowledge (or the rules of reason) is to understand how the "common senses" of social and cultural life are invented and *make* the objects of the action that order the possibilities of innovation and change. We use the word *make* in chapter 1 to emphasize the ways in which the world and "self" are fabricated, that is, as fictions but also as the result of making that has actual and material consequences. The historical narratives of a cultural history pay particular attention to change or "ruptures" in knowledge and how these changes order, intern, and enclose social, cultural, and political action. When considering educational history, the concern is how ideas construct, shape, coordinate, and constitute social practices through which individuals "reason" about their participation and identity.

In an important sense, a cultural history is not about "culture," but about dissolving the divide between the "social" and "cultural" in modern theories. In this sense of "culture," then, the study of knowledge is not only about the past, but also about the present. Without falling into the trap of a presentism that often plagues the field of contemporary history, the contributors of this book ask about the changing systems of ideas and principles of reason through which we have come to think, talk, "see," and act in the world. This focus on the rules and standards of reason provides a way to understand the present, that is, how current social policy and educational policies are related to and/or discontinuous with past configurations.

This current volume draws on a number of leading scholars from different national contexts whose work may be new to an American audience. The contributing authors are people who are doing work in cultural history with varying intellectual approaches and who constitute the cutting edge in the field of historical studies in education.

The discussion of cultural history that takes place herein provides an important departure from the historicism that has dominated the field of historical studies in the United States. That historicism has focused on the movement in time of events and "actors" without paying attention to how that knowledge frames and organizes action and *produces* its acting subjects. The intellectual departure of this book is in its challenge to the ways in which explanations of change are ordered through the chronological structuring of events and actors to "tell" the stories of the past and the present. The focus on knowledge also provides a way to rethink the problem of social change and the politics of knowledge that were previously considered through "revisionist history" or the "hidden curriculum" literature.

This focus on the construction of knowledge introduces a way of considering the politics of knowledge and the problem of change in education. Attention is given to how the forms of reason in schools construct the agents of history as an effect of power. The focus is on systems of knowledge as embedded in social transformations and the structures of power. School knowledge about the individuality of the "child," the "teacher," the "community," is viewed as related to and productive in particular social, cultural, and political conditions. The methodological consequence of this approach, it is argued in this volume, is to denaturalize the rules for social and individual "problem solving," making those rules susceptible to critique and thus opening additional possibilities for action through the dislodging of the ordering principles that intern and enclose the identities of the acting subject.

Finally, while our central and common interest is to explore a field of scholarship that has been generally unacknowledged in American history of education studies, this volume brings into proximity two otherwise different intellectual trajectories. One is a particular social science discourse on postmodernism in the United States, and the other is a broad band of scholarship that has been actively reshaping the fields of history, humanities, and social sciences over the course of recent decades. In focusing on this broader historical context of intellectual production, we have been generally dismayed by the myopic and provincial quality of much American educational research (as well as the Spanish researchers that follow American trends) when it comes to the historical and global connections and networks through which contemporary researchers of different political ideologies work. As the essays of this book suggest, a complete and accurate picture of "postmodern" scholarship in the United States reveals that much important work is taking place in a context whose international dimensions encompass far more than a French invasion theory alone.

Organization of the Book

The essays are divided into four sections. The first part, *History, the Problem of Knowledge, and the New Cultural History of Schooling: An Introduction*, explores the more general intellectual fields in which a cultural history has emerged and its relation to the study of education. Written by the editors, the chapter locates a cultural history in a historical reading of the different intellectual trajectories that make possible this book and its contributions.

The second section, entitled *Rethinking the Discipline of History*, provides explorations of the history of the history of education. The chapters in this section examine recent theoretical and methodological questions about the history of education. Employing their experience in active historical research programs in, respectively, Portugal, Germany, and Brazil, the authors of the chapters in this section consider the challenges of rethinking the history of education in broad terms, while turning to particular historical studies to illustrate the potential directions and possibilities of a cultural history. The authors discuss the implications of the "linguistic" and "pictorial turns" in the writing of history as well as the importance of developing a critical perspective toward the study of educational knowledge that dissolves the distinction between the cultural and the social.

The third section, *Constructing a Cultural History*, focuses on two major considerations in the new history. One is the rethinking of the epistemologies that order historical studies through the notion of genealogy. Pointing to different modes of interpretation through which genealogy is deployed, the chapters in this section provide ways to think about different sets of assumptions and methods for conducting historical research. At the same time, the chapters draw on the authors' research in the United States, Spain, and elsewhere to consider the idea of genealogy. Finally, the section gives attention to curriculum history through a discussion of the knowledge of schooling as "systems of reason" that can be investigated as an effect of power.

Where the first three sections of this volume are concerned with examining the contours of a cultural history through interrelating theoretical and empirical/historical analysis, the fourth and final section, *Schooling as Fields of Cultural Practice*, looks at cultural history from a different direction. The chapters in this section explore particular historical problems related to studies of literacy, school, and teacher education reform to changing patterns of knowledge associated with schooling. The purpose of the section is to provide exemplars of a cultural history–based understanding of schooling.

Together, the different sections can be read as a landscape of cultural history in which to consider its different intellectual trajectories and possibilities. By no means do we feel that we have exhausted the range of possibilities, nor is this book intended as an all-encompassing survey of the field.* The contributions to the book also provide a way to consider U.S. (and possibility British) studies in relation to a broader European and Latin American intellectual context. We say this more fully in the first chapter, but the popular focus on what has been thought of as "the French influence" in postmodern social theory in the United States reflects a lack of historical understanding of a more cosmopolitan and longer-term development of intellectual traditions that transverse, among others, Germany, France, Portugal, Spain, Iceland, and Latin America. This book is an attempt to challenge the myopic communal sense of "self" of many U.S. educational researchers and historians as well as to broaden the ways in which critical studies of education can be understood.

With that said, the contribution of the book is fourfold: First, it brings together major American, European, and Latin American writers to explore the implications of cultural history for understanding the emergence and implications of the modern school. The European and Latin American authors included in this volume have made important contributions to educational history yet may be less well-known in English speaking contexts because they have rarely, if ever, been published in English.

Second, the chapters provide unique and challenging perspectives to the heretofore commonsense understanding of the historical development of the school and the problem of educational change. They do this through engaging in a conversation that interrelates historical, archival studies of education with social, cultural, and political theories of knowledge.

Third, the book engages Anglo-American traditions of historical research in education with German, French, Iberian, and Latin American historical traditions.

Fourth, the book is unique in its systematic focus in bringing together cultural, social, and historical theories into a conversation about the politics of schooling, teaching, and knowledge.

The book is designed for a variety of graduate courses in educational history, educational philosophy, educational research methods, and curriculum studies. The book can serve as a primary or supplementary text in many of the curriculum, foundations, and policy courses found in most departments and schools of education.

Thomas S. Popkewitz
Barry M. Franklin
Miguel A. Pereyra

Note

* For those interested in further reading in this area, a recent volume that compliments this one is S. Cohen (1999), *Challenging Orthodoxies: Toward a new cultural history of education*. New York: Peter Lang.

part 1

History, the Problem of Knowledge, and the New Cultural History of Schooling:

An Introduction

History, the Problem of Knowledge, and the New Cultural History of Schooling[1]

Thomas S. Popkewitz, Miguel A. Pereyra, and Barry M. Franklin

History is perpetually suspicious of memory, and its true mission is to suppress and destroy it.

—Pierre Nora, 1984

"What is knowledge" in a preliminary way is the social meaning of human-made symbols, such as words and figures, in its capacity as means of orientations. In contrast to most nonhuman creatures, humans have no inborn or instinctive means of orientation. When growing up, humans have to acquire through learning sets of social symbols with their meaning and thus parts of a social fund of knowledge from their elders. Access to wider knowledge, to better and more comprehensive means of orientation increases the power potential of human groups.

—Norbert Elias, 1984

History becomes "effective" to the degree that it introduces discontinuity into our very being as it divides our emotions, dramatizes our instincts, multiplies our body and sets it against itself. "Effective" history deprives the self of the reassuring stability of life and nature, and it does not permit itself to be transported by a voiceless obstinacy toward a millennial ending. It will uproot its traditional foundations and relentlessly disrupt its pretended continuity. This is because knowledge is not made for understanding; it is made for cutting.

—Michel Foucault, 1977

Have we wrestled with the problem of the changes in the mediations of language, analysis, image and voice in the world around us and introduced problematics derived from that intellectual effort into our investigation of the past? . . . At this time the discipline of history needs new cognitive maps, new strategies of analysis, and new thought experiments.

—Mark Porter, 1997

This book emerges out of a long-term pursuit to understand the *present* of schooling as historical practices in producing ways to think, act, feel, and "see." While it is easy and almost clichéd to say that the past is in the present and that we need a historical understanding of schooling, the placement of our "self" in time and space is a difficult and profound task. History is not the movement toward some form of reliable representation. Rather, historical thought is part of the present. It is conveyed in the very structures of representation that provide the narratives that construct memories of the present. As Huyssen (1995:3) argues, "The past is not simply there in memory but it must be articulated to become memory. Memory is *recherché* rather than recuperation."

History, in the sense that we use it in this chapter, is an understanding of the present and of collective memory as the weaving together of multiple historical configurations that establishes connections that make for the common sense. A history of the present thus makes possible "the suspension of history itself"; that is, it makes visible what is assumed through the narratives that join time, space, and the individual (Tessitore 1995: 33). For us, an understanding of the past in the present is an ironic undertaking to suspend history itself.

A cultural history as a *history of the present* considers reason as a field of cultural practices that orders the ways that problems are defined, and possibilities and innovation sought. But this concern with knowledge and reason, what is sometimes narrowly called "the linguistic turn" in the social and historical sciences, is not only a concern with text and discourse but with the relation of knowledge and the social. Its methodological approaches aim at dissolving the boundaries between what has previously been viewed as distinct—discourse and reality, text and the world—divisions that are residues of modernity. Thus, while we use the term "cultural history," our interest is in a history of the present that dissolves the textual, real, cultural/social distinctions.[2]

The history of the present, as Walter Benjamin (1955/1985) suggests, is where each generation encounters the past in a new way through a critical encounter in which the fragments of the past meet the present. This approach to historical studies is a counter to what Benjamin calls *an empty history*: the picturing of a universal, boundless human progress associated with ideas of an infinite perfectibility, an additive viewpoint whose illusions are of a seemingly continuous movement from the past to the present, and whose methods have no theoretical armature. To write history is to rethink the possibility of history as a reliable representation of the past and to engage in a critical conversation where previously, Benjamin argues, there was only a present emptied of history. The past is not the point that culminates in the present from which people "learn" about their domestication and that provides a temporal index for their future. Benjamin argues, as do we, that history is the critical engagement of the present, by making its production of collective memories available for scrutiny and revision.

This history of the present that we call "cultural history" also stands against an old and unfruitful tendency in the U.S. academy. That tendency rejected any idea that history is related to the situation of contemporary life. The argument was that if history is of the present time, then *history does not exist*. On the contrary, a self-understanding of the present, we believe, is a historical orientation that challenges the making of "the past into an aesthetic refuge for the pressing problems of the present" (Rüsen 1993: 182).[3]

This task of writing cultural histories is made easier by a wide range of English-language literature that has emerged in multiple disciplines over the past few decades (see, e.g., Bonnell and Hunt 1999; McDonald 1996; Jenkins 1997; Cooper and Stoler 1997; Schram and Neisser 1997; Neubauer 1999; Bentley 1999; and Wilson 1999). Cultural history is made possible through the important translations of the pioneering work of Michel Foucault and Norbert Elias, although neither used the term "cultural history" in his writing. Both thinkers, in distinct yet at times overlapping ways (see Smith 1999), focus on how systems of knowledge organize our *being* in the world through the construction of rules of reason, the ordering of the objects of reflection and the principles for action and participation. Traditions of the German conceptual historians have also been brought into the U.S. context to help shape some of these thoughts about the change of concepts over time and the social conditions that relate to those changes (see, e.g., Koselleck 1985; Hampsher-Monk, Tilmans, and van Vree 1998). Thus, a major task of this book is to examine a broad band of theoretical strategies and methodologies that move across the educational research of Europe, Latin America, and North America to form what we call a "cultural history."

But while our initial interest is to explore a field of scholarship that is generally unacknowledged in U.S. educational history,[4] the very epistemological and methodological frameworks of a cultural history that we speak about intersect with the intellectual trajectories associated with postmodernism in the United States (see, e.g., Rosenau 1992; Popkewitz 1997; Porter 1997, Bentley 1999). This book enables a consideration of postmodernism within the broader arena of the active reshaping of the humanities, the social sciences, and particularly the field of scientific history that has been taking place for at least the last three decades in both the English and non–English-speaking worlds. In this context, educational critics of postmodernism in the United States (and Spanish followers of the trends in American research) have too narrowly conceived the resulting scholarship by misrecognizing the historical and global connections and networks through which contemporary researchers of different political ideologies work.[5] As the essays of this book suggest, what is called "postmodern" scholarship in the United States draws from a broad international context of scholarship, and is much more than the fruits of French scholarship brought to American shores.

This chapter initially considers all strands of current historical work as historicist, a general outlook of modernity that is concerned with understanding the past through dimensions of temporality. We then proceed to differentiate between various approaches to historicism. We first discuss social and intellectual history, focusing on the approach to the writing of history that is subservient to a philosophical structure of an a priori and (ironically) *ahistorical* subject that shapes and fashions the meanings and images of historical narratives. The following section draws attention to cultural history, which makes knowledge a central concern of inquiry. We again differentiate between social and intellectual history and cultural history by revisiting the Spencerian question that has dominated curriculum history ("What knowledge is of most worth?"). Our purpose in this discussion is not to summarize the individual contributions to this book but to engage the specific historical arguments made by the authors in a broader context of rethinking educational research.

Changing the Subject: Historicism, History, and Knowledge

We focus on how the general attitude of historicism is made concrete through social and intellectual histories that focus on social regulation and social control. This historicism, which we relate to "the hidden curriculum" tradition in U.S. research, has an ironic quality. It takes for granted the knowledge of the school and thus, we argue, inscribes an ahistorical subject through which the narratives of the past are structured in the present. That structure of historical narratives, even when seeking critique, embodies salvation stories that denude it of a critical stance.

We Are All Historicists, Or Are We?

This first section begins our journey to think broadly about a contested idea in historical studies, that of historicism.[6] We can think of historicism as a product of the modern imagination that assumes that history will always be made new and in need of rewriting in each generation. Ancient and medieval cosmologies conceived a closed universe in which nothing new or unfamiliar was allowed to become real. But modern historicism reconfigured reality through a change in the concept of time that enabled discussions of difference and continual change.

> The modern concept of reality is related to the rise of historicism, because it depends upon a changed notion of temporality opposed to that of the ancient and medieval world. The modern concept of time implies that events ... take place not only in history but through history, and temporality has become a component part of reality. ... [As such,] historicism, a product of modern imagination, assumes that history will always be made. As a result, the history of historicism is marked by perpetual claims to newness. (Thomas 1991: 32)[7]

We can state here, early in our discussion, that all modern historical studies are historicist through the interest in temporality. Kracauer (1993a; 1993b), for example, insightfully argued in the first decades of the twentieth century that photography and historicism could be understood as having a certain parallelism (see Frisby 1986). For Kracauer, historicism was the photography of time.

On the whole, the advocates of historicist thinking believe that they can explain any phenomenon purely in terms of its genesis. That is, they believe at the very least that they can grasp historical reality by reconstructing the series of events in their temporal succession without any gaps. Photography presents a spatial continuum; historicism, the complete mirroring of a temporal sequence, simultaneously contains the meaning of all that occurred within that time. (Kracauer 1993a: 424–25)

This conception of temporality saturates the "new histories" of the first third of the twentieth century and those of the 1960s and 1970s (from Lamprechtian cultural history, adopted by the American progressive historians to the French historical school of the *Annales* and the different Marxist and *Annaliste*-oriented social histories). The focus on temporality is also embodied in the *"'new' new histories"* that emerge with postmodern thought.

Further, historicism, with its various trajectories, embodies the Enlightenment's commitment to reason in the search for progress. Knowledge, it is believed, is how we have contact with the world, the means by which we assume the security and stability of our place in it, as well as the guarantor in the pursuit of our commitments toward social betterment. This commitment is, at one level, one of the general legitimating "truths" of modernity and modern social and historical studies, including the cultural studies discussed in this book. But to talk about a legitimating truth of the Enlightenment, we will continually have to differentiate between the different trajectories taken in working through this modern commitment to social and historical inquiry.

In this way of thinking, all historical work shares the view that knowledge "constitutes" the reality that is studied (Olábarri 1995: 10). Friedrich Meineche, a founding figure of modern history, notes that historicism, as a *way of looking* (a *Denkart*) in an independent and scientific discipline, was a strategy to construct the "historization [sic] of all our knowledge and experience of the cultural world."[8] As such, "[i]t is not intended to suggest that historical forces somehow condition the orientation of the knower, but rather that the knower imposes an historicizing mode on the explanations that constitute scientific knowledge and on the understandings that constitute the wise experience of historical reality" (Page 1995: 27).

If we use a broad concept of historicism, *we are all historicists.* But most of the time, historians are unaware of the challenge embodied in their reflections about how the knower imposes a historicizing mode on "data" and events. But to differentiate between the particular historicism of social and intellectual history and that of a cultural history, we will refer to the latter as a *historicizing* approach that entails a history of the present. As António Nóvoa argues in his chapter, the nineteenth-century invention of historicism linked the field of experience with the horizon of expectation through which progress was envisioned. Such a linking in history and social science made possible new ways of governing through a chronological and linear sense of time. This notion of time, Nóvoa continues, created new spaces to define our references, affiliations and identities that have become extended and accelerated and are in need of renegotiation.

To reaffirm that all modern history is historicist, we can turn to a form of foundationalism that locates the knowledge of contemporary histories as epistemologically post-Kantian. The equilibrium conceived by Kant between the *mundus intelligibilis* (the world approached in the empirical thought of Bacon and Newton) and the *mundus idealistic* (knowledge produced by a priori ideas drawn from Cartesian thought) is inscribed in the intellectual matrix of the most influential modern schools. The matrix is found in the historical inquiry of the contemporary *Annaliste* mentors, from Comte, Spencer, and Durkheim, to François Simiand, Lucien Febvre, and Marc Bloch. The epistemological basis of the overall modern historical inquiry leaves aside, as Foucault argued, the distinctive Hegelian attachment of historicism that has a totalizing vision of history related to an evolutionary and normative conception of progress.

Knowledge "Wars" to "Cultural" Wars

Once it is said that all modern history is historicist, we can trace changes from the turn of the century to locate different trajectories that are not evolutionary but do mark shifts in foci and strategies. Reacting against the hegemony of political history, a scientific tradition of social history emerged in the second half of the nineteenth century and the first decades of the twentieth whose institutionalization related to the formation of the modern nation-states and the triumph of liberalism in Europe.[9] Social history in these early intellectual traditions was incorporated in universities as a modern system of science based on research-oriented projects. Beginning in the 1960s, a diverse range of theoretical issues based on Saussurean structuralism, Marxist, psychoanalytical and, later, anthropological and feminist knowledge was brought into the discipline of history to challenge a second generation of social history. This social history rejected political history by focusing on institutions and "mentalities." Central was the French historical school of the *Annales*.[10]

One of the distinguishing features of that social history of the 1960s was the bringing of historical inquiry nearer to the social sciences, to what was also called "scientific history." The "new" social history emphasized methodological innovations in the development of a verifiable, quantifiable knowledge. History was to be guided by particular regulative models drawn from structural-Marxism, the ecological-demographic research program of the French *Annales* school, and cliometric history, prominent in the United States at that time (Stone 1981). An intense debate ensued about theory, the methodologies and the nature of historical knowledge, and its political implications. This debate occurred as a discussion about the "procedures of the social sciences," that is, about the primacy of "quantitative documentation" from one side, and from another about the movement of historical approaches that looked at people "from the bottom" rather than from the perspectives of political and social elites (see Porter 1997). This debate about science and who to study arose in the social sciences as well as in the field of history.

The importance of these debates was that they helped to consolidate a historical sociology that sought to find a path away from positivism. New journals and associations were created, such as the *Journal of Social History* in 1977, which focused on an interdisciplinary approach to historical studies and were part of the institutionalization process. The debates about a historical sociology coexisted with and were part of important structural changes manifested in the U.S. civil rights movement, changes in the global economy, and the worldwide students protests of the era (see Smith 1991, for a discussion of these changes). In that context, the revisionist movement in the history of education emerged and thrived through the beginning of the 1980s.

We can think of the debates of the 1970s and 1980s in which a "revisionist" history was instituted in historical and educational historical discussions as the *theory or knowledge wars*, as does Jay (1998). With a bit of playfulness, Jay suggests these were "the years when Foucauldians, Habermasians, Althusserians, Gadamerians, and the like engaged in mortal combat (or least a struggle for top billing at the bulletin of the MLA)" (1998: 17). Today's debates evolve around cultural wars (see Burke 1994, 1997). These wars involve a constellation of aesthetic, moral, class-based, and gender values in which *culture* is a major vehicle for scrutinizing the unresolved problems of what some call "late modernity" or "postmodernity."[11] Without losing sight of the Enlightenment idea of progress, we might conclude that the postmodern historical inquiry "such as related to Foucault, Barthes, Derrida, Lyotard among others" is both "a sophisticated mixture of *modernity* (an ideological struggle to liberate oppressed men and women) and *post modernity* (rejections of master stories, interest in the role of language, adoption of vision of the world as representation)" (Olábarri 1995: 20, italics ours).

A milestone for the shift in orientation of historical inquiry was the publication of Hayden White's *Metahistory: The Historical Imagination in Nineteenth-Century Europe* (1973a).[12] White, who calls himself both a Marxist and a cultural historian trained in medieval history, viewed his work as a *"rebellion against positivism."* He stressed the existing link between literature and rhetoric—the poetic function conceived in a linguistic mode—in the making of historical explanation. White argued that history had a double face —a scientific one and an artistic one through its literary construction. In addition to literary theory, White drew on Jakobson's structuralism for thinking about discourse, and French poststructuralist thought before it was fashionable in U.S. intellectual circles. He thought that Foucault provided a new way to think about the history of ideas that had profound implications for the writing of history that was an "antihistory."[13] White viewed Foucault's work as antihistory in the sense that Foucault's history went against the then mainstream practices of historicism through its insistence on going beyond language as resemblance, bringing in a certain brand of structuralism known at that time as poststructuralism. White's *Metahistory* can be understood as a move into a postmodern theory to reshape historical inquiry to reflect on the project of historians (see Bonnell and Hunt 1999: 2; Eley 1992: 207; White 1999).[14]

It is not surprising that White's *Metahistory* has never been reviewed by any journal associated with the field of history of education in the English-speaking world,[15] indeed from 1979 to 1998 there were only sixteen articles published in the field of education that cite White's work. We say that we are not surprised because U.S. educational historians (as well as much of its educational science community) tend to avoid reflection on the epistemology of science and the sociology of knowledge that characterize their field.[16] There are only three American historians of education, for example, that we have identified as referring to White's *Metahistory* in the *History of Education Quarterly*: Clarence H. Karier, Richard Angelo, and Sol Cohen.[17] Cohen is a particularly interesting figure in the American academic field of history of education, one who has been challenging the orthodoxies of a social history while pursuing a cultural history (see Cohen 1999). Cohen's interest is in a configuration of historical inquiry in education that would involve a "new radical revisionism ... more self-reflective, provisional, and unafraid of philosophical introspection and not just conceived as a strategy for surpassing the marginal position of history of education in the professional programs of teacher education everywhere" (1999: 59). Through the appearance of his work in *Paedagogica Historica*, the oldest European journal of history of education, Cohen's ideas have had more impact in Europe than in his home country.[18]

Social History, Educational Knowledge and Social Regulation:
The "Hidden Curriculum" Traditions

One of the hallmarks of "revisionist" social histories and historical sociology was the concern with social regulation.[19] A major focus was on the knowledge of schooling as performing regulatory functions of social control, such as with the "hidden curriculum" arguments. In this focus, knowledge is explored as "something" that articulates social interests and forces rather than as a productive practice in the construction of power itself—the latter being a central concern of a cultural history. As we will argue in subsequent sections, the shift from knowledge as an epiphenomenon in social regulation and control to knowledge as a field of cultural practices and cultural reproduction leads to different problematics for the study of schooling.

Regulation is certainly not an unfamiliar issue for educational historians. During the 1960s and 1970s, the so-called revisionist historians of education in the United States placed the issue of social regulation and control at the heart of their scholarly work. Challenging the scholarship of an earlier generation of educational historians who celebrated the public school as the agency of progress and democracy, the revisionists presented a decidedly different picture of the American educational enterprise. They saw the American public school as an agency of social control from its origins in the mid-nineteenth century through to the present day. The history of public schooling was viewed as one of regulation, imposition, and repression. It perpetuated the power and privilege of the nation's upper and middle classes over and against those of ethnic and racial minorities, the working class, and the urban poor. As the revisionists tell the story, the historic role of America's public schools is inextricably linked to a host of curricular and pedagogical practices that serve to differentiate the educational experience of the rich from the poor. The ultimate effect of this differentiation is to channel rich and poor children to different and unequal life destinies, the former to affluence and leadership and the latter to economic subordination (Greer 1972; Karier, Violas, and Spring 1973; Katz 1968, 1975; Spring 1973).

In the 1980s a growing number of educational historians began to challenge this account. As these scholars see it, it is too simplistic to assume that there is a one-to-one correspondence between the organizational and administrative practices of schools and the work and citizenship requirements of the larger society. Embracing the Gramscian concept of hegemony with its less coercive and more subtle understanding of the universal forces of regulation through which repression and domination occur, these educational historians have offered a more nuanced explanation of how schools regulate and control. As they see it, the socializing message of schooling has never been all that consistent. Like other societal institutions, American public schools have throughout their existence embraced contradictory and conflicting goals that have resulted in inconsistent and unclear outcomes. Drawing on conflict theories with a Hegelian dialectic of origin and evolution, these historians view schools as sites of contestation and conflict in which efforts at regulation are more implicit than explicit, rely more on suasion than coercion, and are as likely to be resisted as embraced (Kaestle 1976; Reese 1983; Warren 1987). It is, they argue, naive to assume that schools simply serve to reproduce the existing culture or to believe that minorities and the poor simply accept the efforts of the educational professions to mold them in the image dictated by the nation's political and social elite.

It is at this point that we can focus on educational historians who write about the curriculum as part of the explanatory frameworks of social regulation. Knowledge serves as a framework to understand social interests that are brought into schooling to produce inequities and injustices. Such efforts include explicit social control interpretations that explore how processes of curriculum selection, organization, and delivery differentiate curriculum content along class and racial lines and impose that content on children in ways that channel these different children to different and unequal occupational and citizenship roles (Franklin 1986). These efforts include explanatory frameworks to not only depict the regulative role of the curriculum in less deterministic ways and recognize the contradictory purposes of public schooling, but also to emphasize the conflict surrounding its workings and stress the uncertainty of its results (Labaree 1988).

The notion of regulation, however, inserts a particular conceptualization vis-à-vis power and salvation themes of an inevitable progress. Regulation is related to a repressive notion of power, such as how curriculum, for example, differentiates children in conformity with some a priori structures or ahistorical "unconsciousness" whose consequence is to produce advantage and disadvantage in society. Class has been the most prevalent concept, although more recently concepts of race and gender are incorporated either as privileged concepts or as parallel concepts that stand as foundational to explore unequal relations. To define change in a more elaborated way that is not seen as deterministic, concepts of voice and resistance have been introduced; concepts that are structural as they are positioned in relation to predefined forces or a foundation of dominance and repression.

Empty History/ An "Ahistorical" Historical Unconsciousness

The social history of regulation in schooling embodies the particular subservient relation to philosophy in which an a priori structure, or an ahistorical "unconscious" is posited as fashioning and shaping the meanings and images of history. That "unconsciousness," again in its nonpsychoanalytic sense, has different structures. It travels on the surface of narratives as the "nature" of individuality through which life is given meaning, or as the "nature" of social life that organizes the structure of events and the "knowing of people." Knowledge is not, in and of itself, a practice but something that is used in social practices to affect some outcome. The common phrase "knowledge is power" captures this idea of knowledge as useful or available to be used to effect intent. The narrative of history gives an order to how people and individuals "use" concepts and ideas to effect purpose and intent in social action.

This subservient relation to philosophy is a particular unquestioned and unarticulated assumption of U.S. educational historians (and social and educational research as well, see, Popkewitz 1997). The locus of change is the inscription of the actor who enacts cultural interests and produces a collective authority in the plotting of time and change. In the prior studies of schooling, for example, the problem of regulation embodies a philosophical a priori subject. The central premise is that knowledge is an epiphenomenon to other forces, structures, or groups that exercise control over the ideas and organizational arrangements of schooling. This particular doctrine of historicism, across its variations, focuses on such things as the establishment of hegemony (a structural concept brought into education studies through readings of Gramsci).

The narrative strategy of history and the social sciences inheres to the subservient relation to a philosophical unconsciousness. Social and intellectual histories in the United States, for example, assume the a priori identification of stable actors to affirm the flow in the narrative of historical and sociological studies of schooling. The assumption is that the actor is the agent in history who makes that history. Studies of schooling, for example, view ideas as expressive of individual purpose (such as intellectual histories of John Dewey), view institutional development as a pluralist competition among social interests, and view particular ruling groups as actors who dominate and oppress others. If power is discussed, it is located in the actors who rule and who are ruled. Change is measured according to rational, chronological time in which actors configure a history that establishes, or challenges the privileged position of particular groups of actors. The telling of the change is a telling of the stories of the flow of events, the changes in the organizations, the operational systems of rules and relations between actors and actions, or the progression of connections or networks of actors. Change is the activity that differentiates social practices over time with the philosophical unconsciousness—the actor—given to that story.

The commitment to the a priori subject also becomes an ordering principle in the construction of methods. It becomes possible to make the archival text and the positive event the given context in which to chart and make visible the flows of actors. The archives and events become the naturalized space for the actor's actions.

In contemporary research, it is almost impossible to "think" and reason about the world, the self, and change without the ahistorical, philosophical unconscious. It is the doctrine of modernity in thinking about the Enlightenment itself. When the actor is seen as absent in social and historical investigations, that research is seen as antihumanistic and the world as deterministic and without the possibility of change.

The linking of the idea of Enlightenment to the a priori constructed actor of history is itself a recent invention. The introduction of the a priori actor was a radical departure as the locus of truth was moved from a divine subject and transferred to the human creative subject. Previous notions of a transcendent entity, of a world fixed by placement by birth, and of human beings as subjects of fate or Divine Will are supplanted by a move to the earthy city of human intervention in worldly fates. Taylor argues that:

> Through a dialectical reversal, the creator God dies and is resurrected as the creative subject. As God created the world through the Logos, so man creates a "world" through conscious and unconscious projection. In different terms, the modern subject defines itself by its *constructive* activity. Like God, this sovereign

subject relates only to what it constructs and is, therefore, unaffected by anything other than itself. What seems to be a relationship to otherness—be that other God, nature, objects, or subjects—always turns out to be an aspect of mediate self- relation that is necessary for complete self-consciousness. The absolute knowledge made possible by the phenomenological reduction of difference to identity in subjectivity's full knowledge of itself realizes Western philosophy's dream of enjoying a total presence that is undisturbed by absence or lack. (Taylor 1986: 3)

But to engage in such a historicism can denude schooling of its historicity, producing what Benjamin called an empty history. The historicist tradition embodied in social and intellectual history inscribes a universalized knowledge in which the a priori subject can be emancipated. But this notion of emancipation is not emancipatory in a universal sense as its universalism of "human" and "inalienable" rights are products of particular historical formations and power relations (Mehta 1997).

The very foundation of the modern systems of knowledge embodied in the idea of historicism is a relic of social and cultural transformations. The early university institutionalization of the history of education took place in the German-speaking countries during the first third of the nineteenth century. History of education was a knowledge included, first, in the training of *Gymnasium* teachers, and later, elementary school teachers, in a frame of theological training for future teachers with the right consciousness for producing the next generation in the modern nation (see Oelkers 1999; Gonon 1999).[20] Steedman (1998), for example, considers the construction of the historical archive as the construction of memory and hope. She gives attention to the archive as a particular way in which history came into being in the nineteenth century through the construction of an identity of the historian as both alone and at home. But this identity involved important shifts in the objects that historians constructed through their gaze. Whereas in the eighteenth century, "there was a gap between things and their meaning . . . in the nineteenth century we see all sorts of historians strive for a representation in which there was no gap between the thing and its image; in which representation *was* the thing that 'actually happened'"(Steedman 1998: 73).

In contemporary social and educational inquiry, the expression of contingencies ironically embodies a foundational faith in the virtue of knowledge to empower and liberate, popular political and academic phrases that leave little room for contingency. History is subservient to some prior universal that leaves little choice even when there are ideas about diversity, flexibility, and multiplicity of viewpoints that populate political and academic conversations. The school context becomes a constant, timeless physical space where the actions of the teacher and the student move in a continuous series of events. What everyone "knows" is transported along the surface that "tells" of the past and that moves from the past to the present as the marching "order" for the future-defining teaching as responsive, schools as relevant, and children as self- fulfilled. The common sense of knowledge provides the stable markers or monuments from which to think about *normalcy, achievement,* and *competencies.*

This historicism is not only characteristic of the historical profession but also of the social and psychological sciences that tell the stories of schooling and of the future good life for teachers, children, and society. The historicism is an erasure of how the objects of the school and the narratives of the child are constructed within particular historical patterns as the reason of the philosophical unconsciousness. The inscription of the completely self-conscious a priori actor, as Popkewitz's chapter on curriculum history argues, is related to the philosophy of consciousness whose modes of reflection occur at a conjuncture of the emergence of modern liberal thought, the modern state's concern with articulating the collective will, and mass schooling (see also Varela's chapter). This erasure is another irony of both the social and historical studies of schooling. There is a denial of the historicity of the historical knowledge and conditions of schooling.

Michel de Certeau's approach, summarized in a recent paper on the "new historiography," is meaningful here:

> since historical texts can no longer be seen as transparent windows that allow full sight of the past "as it was," historians must substitute for the naïve mimeticist reading method fostered by such a view, one that is centered upon textual silences and blind spots, both of which are signals of the text's "unconscious." In such a reading method, textual signs do not refer unproblematically to something outside the text; they are rather concrete materializations of a number of mechanisms of production that made these texts possible (Pieters 2000: 36).

The ironic emptying of history-in-history is the challenge of this book. Our interest is in a historical imagination in the study of schooling that focuses on knowledge as a field of cultural practice and cultural production. It is to historicize what previously was subservient to a philosophical "unconsciousness," that is, the objects and events that stood as the monuments of schooling that projected its moral imperatives and salvation stories. This historicizing does not reject commitments but considers how commitments are interned and enclosed through the making of the objects of interpretation, reflection, and possibility (see, e.g., Hamilton 1989; also see chapters by Dussel, Chartier and Hébrard, Hamilton, and Popkewitz in this book).

Educational History, Memory, and Salvation Stories

The emptying of history has other implications that we can touch upon in this chapter. One is the insertion of particular doctrines of a historicism whose narratives are not able to provide a critique of the conditions of knowledge in which it works. Related to this insertion of its contemporaneous frameworks is the production of salvation stories of the school told through the progressive narratives of the child and the teacher.

What is important in the above analyses is that a particular doctrine of the historicism is inserted as a set of principles drawn from the Enlightenment. A set of cultural rules about the organization of a linear and universal time was inserted as the ahistorical a priori of the narrative of schooling. Embodied was a particular "civilizing" impulse that sustained the cultural rules of "time" even as a critique was being mounted. The insertion of a linear time reproduced the very framework of its own contemporaneity that the critique was intended to challenge.

This issue of reproducing the very framework of contemporaneity is taken up in historical studies in Bender's (1992: 63) examination of the historicism of the eighteenth century Enlightenment.

> [U]ntil recent revisions of critical methods by feminism, new historicism, a cultural materialism, Anglo-American investigation of eighteenth-century literature proceeded largely within deep-rooted postulates "within a frame of reference" that fundamentally reproduced Enlightenment assumptions themselves and therefore yielded recapitulation rather than the knowledge produced by critical analysis.

Bender continues that if knowledge is to escape tautology and not to conserve its own systems of reference and contemporaneity, there is a need for a critical analysis that can challenge the postulates and assumptions that are found in political arenas. The content of knowledge cannot be taken as representing social and personal intent; rather there is a need to make the internal cognitive structure of knowledge an object of social inquiry and a productive element in the ongoing practices of social life (see also Armstrong 1994).

The view that the content of knowledge represents social and personal intent, Callewaert (1999) has argued, also makes research (and the researchers) the new prophets of modernity. It does so through inserting the project of research as "action" that takes past and present narratives as prescriptions for planning. This prescription, Callewaert continues, is a political strategy of intellectuals that needs to be questioned both epistemologically and ideologically. Such "action research" focuses on the relation of power in the projects of researchers who position their research (and themselves) as the overseers of the present and the future. When historical narratives inscribe the actors who produce change, they obscure the fact that the technologies of emancipatory projects involve tensions between colonialism and postcolonialism with respect to the governing of individuals (see, e.g., Mehta 1997; Young 1990; also

Spivak 1999).[21] These narratives efface is the historical relations among policy, policing and research that emerged in the nineteenth century.

The significance of epistemological rules that conserve their own system of reference lies in the production of memory/forgetting that we referred to earlier. Steedman has pointed out that "History, inside and outside the academy, is an important (though not the only) location of Memory" (1998: 66). History is a process of ideation, imagining, remembering, and also a place of dreams. Dussel in this volume argues, for example, that school uniforms fabricate a memory of the laws and codes of culture on the body of the child and the teacher. This occurs through the systems of moral and political classifications and categories that order school dress.

But this process of ideation, imagining, remembering, this place of dreams, has itself a particular configuration within schooling. This link is to the production of salvation stories that Meyer, Boli, Thomas, and Ramirez (1997) argue organize the formation of national school systems. The modern school functions to reterritorialize the individual through stories that link the development of the child to that of the nation. The salvation stories of the curriculum produce a collective authority that places diverse peoples, languages, and prior customs into a seemingly seamless whole, that of the nation-state. The individual becomes the agent who enacts the collective purpose embodied as the nation-state.

Social histories, when critiquing the salvation stories of the school, have tended to focus on the school curriculum, what we previously considered as the "hidden curriculum" in which the histories of the nation link the development of the individual to the images and narratives of nationhood. The salvation stories, as told in teacher education, were not only about the curriculum but also about the teacher and the developing child. Warde and Marta Carvalho's chapter in this book argues, for example, that the Brazilian history of education provided a narrative for teachers about the civilizing processes associated with Christianity. This formation of a historical narrative is in the same vein as the one elaborated upon earlier that indoctrinated teachers in Europe starting from the second half of the nineteenth century, and is still practiced today with an updated rhetoric, related to developing a "professional ethics."

The salvation stories that connect the teacher, the child, and the nation are not only in the narratives about the child, the nation, and the citizen. What is also inscribed in the construction of salvation stories is a particular rationalized order of a chronological time, one that goes unnoticed according to the principles of action theories. Warde and Carvalho's chapter, for example, focuses on the Brazilian professionalization and rationalization of processes of teaching as incorporating a European "sacredalization" of time that was linear, continuous, and universal. This particular conceptualization of time, Warde and Carvalho argue, was apparent not only in the celebration of the moral imperatives of teaching but also in Brazilian critical analyses that in the 1970s drew on Gramsci to alter the narratives of history and in current reforms to govern and regulate relations between the state and the teacher. The inscription of salvation stories in the epistemological conditions of knowledge rather than in the subject matter or "content" of history becomes important when we return to the discussion of social regulation and control in social histories of the U.S. school. A Gramscian concept of hegemony is also inscribed in these studies. Warde and Carvalho's analysis suggests that we might look to how the knowledge conditions of such histories can produce an erasure of critique through a particular universalizing and "sacredalization" of time and space.

Here we return to the idea of an ahistorical consciousness that operates along the surface of the salvation stories of the child, the teacher, and the nation told in social history. Embedded in the salvation stories of the school, Meyer, Boli, Thomas, and Ramirez (1997) argue, are action theories that inscribe the a priori structure of an agent whose individuality is linked to the collective saga of the nation as a particular rationalized and moralized ordering of time. The memory produced through the systems of representation and differentiations as history is also a forgetting. Caspard (1998), for example, argues that the history of the Western European school has been constructed as an image and vindication of itself, its ideals, and missions. What is at stake in this representation of the school requires a critical examination of the collective memory as it constitutes political, social, cultural, and economic practices in education.

One can think of a cultural history in light of these critiques. While historicist in its general commitments, our focus on a cultural history aims to establish a critical enterprise through historicizing the systems of reference and the framework of its contemporaneity. The questioning of the a priori subject in historicism is not to forego the use of reason or action for social change, but to make the common sense of historicism the problematic. It is also to construct a historical method that does not resort to the a priori structure of the actor that is explanatory and that writes about culture around the "spirit," the "mind," and the "consciousness" of peoples, their civilizations (beliefs, arts, morals, laws, customs), and their "philosophy of life."

We can think of a critique of the a priori subject as itself a strategy of change. This is expressed by Rose who argues that the task of inquiry is to disturb "that which forms that groundwork of the present, to make once more strange and to cause us to wonder how it came to appear so natural" (1999: 58; also Popkewitz 1991). To show the contingency of the arrangements that we live by is to show how thought has played a part in holding those arrangements together and to contest the strategies that govern the human possibilities. But to critique the a priori subject is also to consider how cultural and social dimensions overlap with the political. As Nóvoa's chapter emphasizes, this notion of the political is continually brought into focus in questions about language, that cannot be dissociated from issues in which power is engaged and contested.

Changing Ways of Thinking:
From Modernist to Postmodernist Historical Inquiry

The historicizing that we speak about as a cultural history is different from the ideas of regulation and control common to most social histories. These social histories of control, as Popkewitz notes in his chapter on curriculum history, embody a sovereign notion of power as something that someone holds. There are actors whose sovereignty enables them to act in their own interests and develop a collective authority. The historical study of regulation and social control that we spoke about earlier expresses this sovereignty notion of power. Social histories plot the processes of domination and repression that structure events. But as the chapters in this book attest, power and historical narratives can be ordered differently, namely without a search for the origins of sovereignty and without the ahistorical a priori subject inscribed in actor-centered social histories. Regulation and governance can be thought about historically as the imposition of order through knowledge. Through this sense of knowledge as regulation and governance we can approach a cultural history of schools without an epistemology of a constantly unfolding progression and a subservient relation to philosophy.

Knowledge as a Regulating and Governing Practice:
The Decentered Subject

One point of departure is to think of regulating and governing as a productive rather than a repressive force. Central to this consideration of regulation is Foucault's focus on the productive qualities of the rules and standards of reason. Knowledge, he argues, regulates and governs through the principles in which options are made available, problems defined, and solutions considered as acceptable and effective. Social history focuses on regulation through theories of action (and actors) that effect reason; however, knowledge can also be understood as "making" the world and individuality by interning and enclosing possibilities.

Foucault's ideas about power as a productive element related to knowledge are central to a number of multiple chapters in this book. Inés Dussel argues that school dress, often today seen as either inconsequential or uncritically placed in debates about individualism, is in fact part of the moral economy and the production of identity and difference. Moving from semiotics studies of dress to its performative functions, she examines the move from Christian pedagogy in the seventeenth century to new technologies of the eighteenth and nineteenth centuries that inscribed the laws and codes of culture related to the bourgeois revolution and changes in the military discipline onto children's bodies and school populations. With the uniformizing of children's clothing came a dedifferentiation—the simultaneous individualization of children and the universalization of their relations. Nóvoa argues for a broader idea of Foucault's disciplinary power, stressing the important role of vision and images in "telling the truth." He argues that we need to investigate the role of knowledge not only as a strategy of surveillance (as proposed in Foucault's famous discussion of Bentham's panopticon) but also as one of the spectacle, with the two regimes of power coinciding through the consumption of images.

The focus on knowledge as productive power involves the epistemological *decentering of the subject*. Decentering of the subject considers the historical production of principles as fabrications, in the double sense of fictions and of the making of agents in historical narratives. This approach considers the construction of the child as having a childhood and the discursive practices through which parents become a calculable object of scrutiny and reflection (Popkewitz and Brennan 1998). This strategy to focus on knowledge and reason is not to rid ourselves of the subject itself, but to dislodge the ordering practices that enclose the boundaries established for thought as action.

Foucault elaborates an understanding of Kant and his quest for the meaning of *Aufklärung* or the Enlightenment that can be read as a commitment to change through the decentering of the subject. Foucault affirms his criticism of the present through an examination of "the historical workshops" (*atteliers historiques*), a truly meticulous historical construction of the genesis of social practices and discourses that create multiple forms of subjectivity (see Foucault 1984). Historicity for Foucault meant a rejection of a historicism that looks for origins: "what is found at the historical beginning of things is not the inviolable identity of their origin; it is the dissension of other things. It is disparity" (1977: 142). Foucault's energetic refusal of historicist knowledge produced by academic historians was not a rebuff to history itself "and not even to the historical erudition" but to the primacy of its contents and uses, to its practices.

> ... one cannot fail to be struck by the impossibility of our culture of raising the problem of history of its own thought. It's why I have tried to make, obviously in a rather particular style, the history not of thought in general but of all that "contains thought" in a culture, of all in which there is thought ... (1998: 267)
>
> If history possesses a privilege, ... it would play the role of an internal ethnology of our culture and our rationality. (1998: 293)

Foucault felt the pressing need to revise the traditional liberal paradigm of historical inquiry by building alternative conceptions of making history through challenging the constraints of this discipline by way of seeking relationships with other forms of knowledge production and discipline ascriptions.

Decentering as a notion, however, is not unique to cultural histories but is found also in Marx, and carried forward in the writings of Durkheim and Weber. It is given particular methodological distinctions in the work not only of

Foucault, but postmodern feminism, among others. Julia Varela's chapter positions cultural history in a long tradition of critical thinking in the social sciences. She suggests that the decentering of models of consciousness was argued by Marx in challenging the idea of a constantly unfolding and progressive history.

While the decentering of the subject produces a particular methodological focus on knowledge, the intent is not to inscribe the cultural in opposition to the social, with its variations of text versus reality, theory versus practice. António Nóvoa and Heinz-Elmar Tenorth point to the overlapping of the social and the cultural through a turning from the "linguistic turn" to the "pictorial turn." They seek to understand how language and "culture" give intentionality through the logic that they inscribe for subjects to act and transform their worlds. The focus on the images of the school, Nóvoa argues, positions the spectator who enters a game of images, illusions, suspicions, and contested narratives that complement but cannot be reduced to texts. Tenorth, by comparison, compares earlier cultural studies in Germany that focused on the life histories of everyday people with current studies that link history to literary criticism, media studies, and anthropology, such as Clifford Gertz's discussion of "thick descriptions." He illustrates this shift methodologically through a discussion of how the representations of school photographs can illuminate pedagogical meaning, forms, and structures.

The use of photographs in the writing of history is itself an old occupation of historians, as we argued earlier. But Nóvoa and Tenorth place the study of images in a set of theoretical configurations of the grammar of schooling that have different and innovative possibilities. In this respect, we believe that the use of photography is as Michel Foucault (1982) said in commenting on Duane Michals' calligraphy on photographs as creating *new ways of seeing:* "a knowledgable form of reconciling the instantaneity of photography with the continuity of times for telling a story" (Foucault 1994: 250).

This overlapping of the cultural and social through a decentering strategy is also explored in the chapter by Anne-Marie Chartier and Jean Hébrard. They first distinguish between the history of science concerned with the ways in which scientific knowledge is created and developed, the history of education concerned with the political aspects of the development of school systems, and a cultural history concerned with the history of interactions between spoken and written cultures and the acquisition of "mental tools," (a concept from the French historical school of the *Annales*). In their essay, a number of their different research projects are brought together in a discussion of reading and writing as historical inventions that played an important role in the diffusion of intellectual tools and underlay cultural transformations related to the church, the bourgeoisie, and the new state during the ancien régime and after the French Revolution. They argue that even in the Treaty of Trente the school was considered as an institution whose purpose was the passing on of the science of salvation through ensuring that all Christians were literate. The teaching of writing was an innovation related to civilizing people's customs and minds. But the idea of reading was not constant, as its focus shifted from the catechism (memory writing), to tool writing (the reckoning of tradesmen and shopkeepers), to its modern aims as moralizing narratives and "reading for the sake of reading." Chartier and Hébrard's historical discussion of literacy problematizes commonsense assumptions about reading and writing, and thus dissolves the distinction between the social and the cultural.

Genealogy and Cultural History

One important strategy in cultural histories is genealogical, an approach offered by Nietzche and re-visioned in the work of Foucault. In one fashion, genealogy is a way to consider how systems of reason change over time as cultural practice. Central is how problems of social and individual life become constituted as they do, and change so as to effect the conditions in which we live. Thus, a genealogical approach provides a way to locate change in the systems of knowledge that organize the "self" through the effects of power.

> Genealogy is not, as it sometimes seems to be, a new method of doing history with its own rules and principles; it is rather an effort to take history itself very seriously and to find it where it has least been expected to be. Genealogy takes as its objects precisely those institutions and practices which, like morality, are usually thought to be totally exempt from change and development. It tries to show the way in which they too undergo changes as a result of historical developments. And it also tries to show how such changes escape our notice and how it is often in the interest of these practices to mask their specific origins and character. As a result of this, genealogy has direct practical consequences because, by demonstrating the contingent character of the institutions that traditional history exhibits as unchanging, it creates the possibility of altering them. (Nehamas 1985: 112, cit. by Payne 1997: 28)

Historical practice as defined by genealogy is not only an interpretative analysis, and a critical hermeneutic of the complexities of historical processes as engendered in social sources. It is also a practice of analytical work that Foucault conceived as a product of "patience and a knowledge of details and depend[ing] on a vast accumulation of source material" (1977: 140).

But while providing some orientation to the problem of history and the present, genealogy has moved in different ways through different theoretical and methodological connections. Varela, who studied with Foucault, introduces the idea of genealogy as a method with which to consider the interrelation of material and symbolic processes that cuts across the formation of knowledge and which brings to light their social functions in their institutional development. Drawing on the work of Foucult and of Norbert Elias, Varela brings us to consider how and why the structure of the social fabric changes at the same time as the individual. To return to our earlier discussion about the inscription of the philosophy of consciousness and theories of action in social and intellectual history, Varela explores how this became a historical fact. She argues that the formation of individual personalities, individual subjects, and the idea of society as composed of isolated individuals became necessary at the precise historical moment when the legitimacy of power was being based on the idea of a general "will."

Antonio Viñao and Ingólfur Ásgeir Jóhannesson's chapters also develop a genealogical method but by integrating Bourdieu's idea of a social field. Viñao's chapter, for example, draws on Bourdieu's (see, e.g. 1984) notions of intellectual field and *habitus* to consider social dimensions that relate to intellectual dimensions. Viñao's historical project is to consider the academic professorate through an examination of the texts of school courses, the selection processes for academics, the inspectors and inspector systems, and the distribution of time and work in school. It is a study of the history of the cultural and academic elite through its methods of training, means of selection and admittance into the group, as related to varying modes of power, both collective corporate and individual. He rejects ideas of individual agents determining thought and action and methodological individualism that sees belief systems as the sum of discrete and explicit positions that can be traced to a single original source. Instead Viñao examines the sociology of the institutionalization of teaching and the anthropology of ordinary life to understand schools as a broad landscape from which multiple trajectories emerge to form the Spanish teacher and the educational academic disciplines.

Ingólfur Ásgeir Jóhannesson also develops a genealogical method, one that seeks to integrate Bourdieu's idea of a social field and Foucault's interest in the cultural practices of knowledge. His study historicizes the post–World War II educational reforms in Iceland, providing a way to rethink the patterns of governing, a theme that we return to later.

While David Hamilton does not explicitly use the concept of genealogy, his analysis examines the interrelation of the knowledge of schooling as a cultural practice that changes over time as it overlaps with social and institutional practices. Specifically, Hamilton examines the amalgamation of ideas, institutions, and technologies through which the notions of educational method and order "make" for the genesis of the modern school. He studies the transformation of the school from a more nomadic space to that of a bounded territory space having a variety of uses and functions that are productive, symbolic, and disciplinary. The institutionalization and systematization of schooling in the seventeenth century occur in relation to the development of the ideas of method and discipline that relate to a number of cross currents of the Renaissance and Reformation—Calvin's notion of double grace, the constructions of building as schools and the use of desk and file lockers—that overlap with the broad intellectual highway connecting a Christian heritage of church orders, school orders and political orders. The "territory" that Hamilton discusses is not a geographic place but a discursive space that folds together multiple different practices and processes.

Hamilton argues that the school, as the title of his essay suggests, "comes from nowhere," in that it is not borne out of a continuity from something previously existing nor from a singular historical trajectory or origin, but rather exists in a dialogue between the present and the past. Schooling, like a Russian doll, is largely constituted by a layered series of inner spaces hidden from the outside. Hamilton's manner of historicizing the school goes against the grain through a discomforting and self-conscious challenge to the working assumption of ancestry that stands as the monument of schooling. To approach school as not having an ancestry is, Hamilton argues, liberating as it releases the investigation of modern schooling from directed, linear, one-thing-before-another theorizing.

We can think of the historical practice produced by genealogical work as implying an interventionist concept of history, the one that Foucault named "effective history," itself a kind of knowledge (see also Dean 1994). It is a knowledge "made for cutting" rather than promoting continuity with evolutionist approaches to change. Genealogy is work with the aim of producing "knowledge as perspective," of understanding and explaining the present, a knowledge that it is itself openly judgmental and value-laden but not in the positivist sense of "bias" that once dominated sociology and the history of social science.

Regulation, Governing, and the State

We can further develop the idea of a cultural history by focusing on distinctions of regulation and governing in the notion of the state. The idea of the state has been introduced in social histories in order to rethink the functionalist histories of curriculum differentiation that dominated the field in the 1960s and 1970s. Functionalism sought to explain how numerous specialized courses of study and conceptual notions, for example, vocationalism, in the first decades of the century, channeled students into occupational and citizenship roles based on their background and ability (Callahan 1962; Krug 1969). Although contested, the differentiated curriculum made the schools an instrument of social control to preserve the political and economic power of the upper and upper-middle classes at the expense of the working classes, particularly the urban poor and racial and ethnic minorities (Hogan 1985; Carnoy and Levin 1985; also see discussions of contradictory demands on differentiations in schools in Angus, Mirel, and Vinovskis 1988; Tyack 1974; Kliebard 1995; Labaree 1988).

These explanations tended to make the regulation of schooling a problem of social control. The explanations focus on the origins of regulation as the result of economic social pressures or institutional developments. The search for origins itself bound inquiry to an a priori structure that fashions and shapes the meanings and images of history. What was thought missing from all these accounts was a consideration of the governing mechanism through which curriculum differentiation was embraced.

One solution to this problem is to be found in the recent interest of sociologists in theories of the state. Rooted in the classic sociology of Max Weber and the more recent work of such scholars as Theda Skocpol, this explanatory framework focuses on state bureaucracies and their managers as key players in political and social reform (Weber 1946, 1968; Skocpol 1985). In a state-centered interpretation, the state or the agencies and individuals in the public sphere who hold obligatory authority over others are autonomous actors functioning at their own behest to enact reform, often independently of other groups and classes, to attain the administrative capacity they require to address pressing problems. The state, in other words, can possess its own goals and take its own initiatives to attain those ends. Although its programs and policies often support the long term interests of dominant social classes, the state is not simply a vehicle through which these classes pursue their particular interests (Skocpol 1992; Finegold and Skocpol 1995; for a productive appraisal of the issue of the state after the cultural turn, which challenges previous approaches, see Steinmetz 1999).

A central premise of this social history is that a major characteristic of twentieth century American political reform has been state building. Within this theoretical context, the regulative initiatives of schools are thought of as a part of state building. One can understand, for example, the establishment of special education programs as an effort by early twentieth century urban school administrators to create the administrative capacity to deal with a number of pressing problems (Franklin 1994). Special classes and schools offered urban school administrators a way to maintain their historic commitment to the common universal ideal of school accessibility in the face of early twentieth century enrollment growth and diversity that also introduced "troublesome" children to teach. Likewise, the establishment of special education provided the administrators with a professional ideology that celebrated their technical expertise and consequently their standing as part of a distinct professional specialty within the schools.

The idea of the institutional development of professional administrative practices and state legal-administrative practices are also dimensions to cultural history, as argued in the chapters of Viñao, Ingólfur Ásgeir Jóhannesson, and Hamilton, although each chapter emphasizes different theoretical orientations to the relation.

But the emphasis in these chapters is on moving the social and cultural into closer proximity with each other so as to dissolve the distinctions themselves.

In his state-centered history of special education, Franklin (1994) notes that school administrators did not simply create special education programs *de novo*. Such programs appeared as the reasonable, appropriate, and natural solution to the problem of enrollment growth and diversity as a result of changes in ways in which Western intellectuals talked about deviance. In fact, according to Franklin, a fundamental shift in our discourse about deviance that was underway since the mid-eighteenth century and involved a medicalization of the concept of deviance represented a prerequisite condition for schools to be able to assume responsibility for the kind of children who would be accommodated through special education (Franklin 1994). What, in other words, is missing from explanations of regulation derived from theories of the state is a consideration of how knowledge is a field of practices that intervene as a part of social life. It is this topic that stands at the center of our understanding of cultural history.

From this we can return to the state without redeploying the distinctions between the text and practice, the social and the cultural, and the opposition of government to the private or the personal. We can give attention to the state, as did Foucault (1979), through giving attention to the assemblage of practices that aims at the governing of capacity for action (Popkewitz 1996, 2000b). Taking our cues from postmodern theory about discourse and "reason" as governing practices, we can think of a cultural history as directing attention to the networks, exchanges, and relations among a range of public, private, and voluntary organizations through which regulative and governing practices are produced.

This focus on the assemblage of practice as forming the principles of governing is central to Katharina Heyning's discussion of teacher education reforms. Employing what she calls an archaeological approach, she examines the formal minutes from departmental meetings at the University of Wisconsin-Madison. Rather than see the seemingly bureaucratic grammar of these documents as without meaning, she focuses on how they embody multiple other texts. Her historicizing is a method that considers how to read the present texts and others not present as a relational field. She explores how certain historical discourses are mobilized in the documents to construct a system of supervision and surveillance, and, at the same time, a productive practice through generating principles of action in the narratives and images of the teachers.

Popkewitz's chapter on the reading of Vygotsky and Dewey in contemporary educational reforms also provides a way to rethink the concept of the state as the art of governing. Popkewitz's concern is the historical configurations of the past and the present constructed by the texts that remake what is possible and plausible to "reason" about education. He argues that there is no "real" reading of the ideas, no one "true" meaning of Dewey's notion of "community" or Vygotsky's "zone of proximal development." Rather, the task is to understand how these texts were part of an intertextual and institutional context that made the texts "reasonable" for governing interpretations. This historicizing of "reason" and "the reasonable person" is not one of truth but of power relations that overlap not only with education, but with broader social and cultural arenas. Popkewitz argues that this amalgamation of ideas, institutions, and technologies are today different from when Vygtosky and Dewey wrote in the last century, embodying new patterns of governing and power.

This rethinking of the state as a governing practice through principles of knowledge is embodied in the chapter by Ingólfur Ásgeir Jóhannesson. He examines the rupture of discourse in Icelandic education in the 1970s and 1980s. Educational reforms were introduced to rationalize and professionalize teaching, but these ideas and practices rubbed against previous discourses: an amalgamation of rural traditions, a congregational pedagogy that related state and religion, a storytelling tradition of literature, religion, and discourses about intelligence, excellence, and achievement that connected with the colonial rule of Denmark. The genealogy places the conjuncture as an intermediate gray area in which the rules, capital, and values are uncertain.

This brings us back again to an important distinction of contemporary scholarship that a cultural history seeks to break. That distinction is between the social and cultural, a distinction that takes different forms as in the dichotomy between text and reality, but also in the distinction between the context of policy formulation and the context of policy realization. These different layers of differentiation carry a particular epistemology that inscribes a perceived break between what people say (discourse) and what people actually do. This distinction between theory and practice is itself a legacy of the philosophy of consciousness and theories of action that "make" knowledge something "used" by specified agents. But the theory-practice distinction renders ideas and discourses as ahistorical phenomenological artifacts, either dependent on the mental structures of individuals or dependent on material determinations that are outside of the ways in which ideas or discourses construct (and construe) the world (Hunt 1989; Chartier 1988). We argue, in contrast, that economic and social relations are not prior to or determinant of cultural ones; they are themselves fields of cultural practice and cultural production that cannot be explained deductively by reference to an extracultural dimension of experience or to structural forces that have an ontological status separate from the ordering principles of knowledge itself. Knowledge constitutes what appears as the norms that "are already there," that is, what serves in social contexts as foundational and "preexisting facts that seem to live beyond them, often surviving empirical refutation" (Schram and Neisser 1997: 5). As Chartier (1988) has argued, there can be no decoding and situating of oneself as a historical "being" without a discursive structuring of language that defines historical experience or interest in the first place. The representations of the social world themselves are the constituents of social reality.

Historicizing as the Interweaving of the Past and Present

We can bring the previous discussion about a cultural history together by focusing on a question that has dominated the U.S. field of curriculum theory and curriculum history. That question has been called the Spencerian question: "What knowledge is of most worth?" This question has appeared in different forms in American historical and educational research in reference to the debates, the dilemmas, and the directions taken by schools. We will argue for a reordering of that question as well as engage one of the most important challenges to a cultural history, that posed in the work of the German-American historian Georg G. Iggers.

Rethinking the Spencerian Question: Toward a Cultural History

The Spencerian question assumes a certain philosophical, ahistorical a priori. That prior assumption is that a foundational knowledge can be identified, at least in principle, that can lead to the essential purpose or normative function of the school. With the right method or ideology, the knowledge of most worth can be identified (even if that absolute is only an ideal that is not thought realized in practice). Further, the Spencerian question inserts theories of action that inscribe the agent who is to bring progress through that absolute knowledge. In this sense, we can think of the Spencerian question as a performative reiteration of an absolute ideal that stands as an unmitigated good to measure the progress and the progressiveness of schooling. Knowledge becomes an object that is used to effect purpose rather than one that forms purpose and intent.

The Spencerian question can be considered, in contrast, as a monument to how people are to tell the "truth" about society, themselves, and their routes of salvation. It is not to ask what knowledge is of most worth, but how that worth is produced as a cultural field of practices. What counts for knowledge at any given moment is embodied in the conflicts over who can speak, and according to what criteria of truth. The discourses through which principles of action are generated are interrogated to consider how they are given affectivity and authorization.

Our historicizing is redirected to reason rather than to accept the categories of thought as stable entities. It provides a way to examine the particular expressions that link reason to the problem-solving rationalities of science and, as discussed earlier, the actor who is identified as the agent of change. In this sense, our attention is directed to the systems of reason (images, narratives, and discourses) through which the objects of schooling are classified and ordered over time, providing a way to think about change.

Thus, the modern curriculum becomes caught in its doubleness. It is an expression of the Enlightenment toward the child as a participant in the construction of the world. But it is also a linking of nineteenth-century science, morality, and political notions of progress to the individual through the acquisition of knowledge. Modern curriculum is a governing practice concerned with the administration of the child through forms of knowledge that would order the sensibilities and feelings of the individual. Once we view knowledge in this manner, it is not a hidden aspect of the curriculum but part of its surface appearance that goes unnoticed.

For our purposes here, then, curriculum is a practice of regulation and governance through the reason generated for organizing action (and actors) and establishing purposes (structurally or individually). Knowledge provides the principles through which options are made available, problems defined, and solutions considered as acceptable and effective. Knowledge is a practice that fabricates worlds and individuality (with fabrication having its dual meaning of fiction and making) and thus can be understood as material, turning Marx's interest in labor into one of knowledge itself.

Culture and the Social

One of the most frequent criticisms of the historicism that we speak of (and more generally criticism related to postmodernism) is that such scholarship does not "see" culture within social processes. This question was given attention by the German-American historian Georg G. Iggers. In his last work, *Historiography in the Twentieth Century: From Scientific Objectivity to the Postmodern Challenge*, Iggers uses a historicist framework to critique the work of authors associated with the reshaping of historical inquiry, such as Clifford Geertz, Hayden White, Michel Foucault, Jacques Derrida, and Dominic La Capra, among others. Iggers views the linguistic turn as a set of semiotic or linguistic approaches that do not "see the culture within the framework of social processes and methodologically results in an irrationalism [since t]he interpretation of symbols cannot be tested empirically." In his interpretation of Foucault's dictum that "reality does not exist, that only language exists," linguistic theory and the philosophy of language, he says, lend themselves "better to literary criticism than to historical writing" (1997: 125, 132).[22]

The postmodern challenge that appears in the subtitle of his book is not for him a challenge for historical inquiry, although he recognizes the necessity to "take the postmodernist critique of historiography very seriously" and his "position is probably somewhere between the postmodernist position and a more conservative one" (see Domanska 1998: 100).[23] Iggers is interested in a reconstructionist/constructionist historiography (the writing of history) that gives emphasis to the centrality of the meaning and the interpretation, but with the empirical, archival evidence related to understanding of the continuity and development over time of the processes, forces, and circumstances, as he says, "historically understood." For Iggers, to observe that "history does not use scientific vocabulary, does not mean that it cannot deal with the historical past," but "the interpretation of meaning" must be "an attempt to get back at *reality*" (1997: 105, italics ours).

Various ideas produced in the debates about the "linguistic turn " are acknowledged in several chapters of the present volume such as those by Nóvoa and Viñao.[24] It seems clear that there is an oversimplification of so-called postmodern thought in Iggers's critique. (See Iggers 1999, for a most recent and by some means sympathetic outlook of postmodernism or histiography.) Understanding postmodernism through its focus on literary theory, as expressed often in poststructural analysis, does not make sense as we have continually argued by focusing on the relation of a variety of different trajectories related both to postmodern theory and cultural history.[25] Instead we can turn to Derrida's textualism, which locates literature at the center but reads both science and philosophy as forms of literary genres. Here we find another orientation, as that created by Foucault, that takes as a key category the networks of knowledge/power. In this case, the social body is conceived and constructed as a heterogeneous whole (scientific theories and systems of reason, philosophical conceptions and multiple rationalities, laws and regulations, governmentality and actor strategies).

It is this configuring of knowledge as part of an amalgamation of social structures, processes, and practices that makes hisorical studies more than merely talking about textual or semiotic considerations. Postmodern thought (which is not just literary or text analysis but also critical ethnography in what Popkewitz calls a social epistemology in his contributions to this book) involved a radical break with the major assumptions of modernist historicism.[26] It made this break by introducing a deconstructing reading of the use of language in "history's content as well as the concepts and categories deployed to order and explain historical evidence through our linguistic power of figuration" (Munslow 1997: 181). Further, while this argument seems to speak of knowledge as socially embedded, we also need to be careful in using the term "socially constructed" which in many cases represents an unreflective rhetoric, as Latour (1999) has pointed out with respect to the sciences (also see Hacking 1999).

A leading cultural historian, Roger Chartier, has perceived this challenge of historical knowledge in the following way.

> One cannot—or can no longer—accept an epistemology of the correspondence or duplication between the historical discourse and the events or realities that are its objects, as if the discourse were mere cartography, a faithful copy of the past. Historians today are fully aware of the gap that exists between the past and its representation, between the vanished realities and the discursive form that aims at representing and understanding them. Narrow is the way, therefore, for anyone who refuses to reduce history to an untrammeled literary activity open to chance and worthy only of curiosity, yet also refuses to define its scientific character based on the one model of knowledge concerning the physical world. (1996: 27)

If we continue using modernist versus post modernist historical inquiry as illuminating research ideal types (see Bauman 1987, and also Outhwaite 1999), we could return to Iggers' strategy to "get back to reality," in order to see how it distinguishes postmodernist historical thinking from modernist historical thinking. Postmodernism, "as represented by Foucault and Derrida, but also by Roland Barthes, raises the possibility that there is no truth at all. . . . What remains then for them is the text, and the text can be interpreted in many ways. . . . This basically means that we can't reconstruct the past" (see Domanska 1998: 195). This does not mean that there are not better ways to tell the truth, but that our ways of constructing truth and memory are always of contingent foundations, as feminist scholarship continually reminds us, and in need of a historicizing for their potential dangers. Iggers, although an outstanding epistemic individual among modernist historians, retains his ties with a historicism that inscribes a subservience to a philosophical a priori by maintaining the central feature of that historiography: "trust as the unmediated relation of the historian to the past" (see Porter 1997: 4).

What Do We Mean by Cultural History?

Our bringing together a number of European, Latin American, and U.S. researchers who are interested in the history of the school is a strategy to encourage thought about the study of education that extends beyond the field of history. While we noted earlier a relation between a cultural history and a field of U.S. cultural and political research that is sometimes called postmodernism, we do not intend to collapse the diverse intellectual trajectories in this book under that rubric. Just the opposite. Our purpose is to underscore that this conversation overlaps with German, French, Latin American, and British traditions that existed prior to the recent "naming" of postmodernism in the United States. Further, the questions raised about knowledge and power have continued to play a part in current debates about history, social science and the humanities. Cultural history is, in many respects, a configuration in historical inquiry after the late eighties that transverses not only the academic community of historians but also the social sciences (see Evans [1999] for a characterization of historical inquiry at the present as a multicultural domain; Burke [1994] for the varieties of cultural history in today's historiography; and Hunt [1989], Kelley [1996], and Burke [1997, chapter 1], for a history of cultural history and its traditions and varieties). It is part of a more complex process produced inside the life of the academic community of social sciences where fragmentation, recombination, and hybridization of disciplinary fields have intersected during the past few decades, creating and legitimizing "new" fields and specializations (see Dogan and Pahre 1990; Gibbons et al. 1994).

At the same time, in recognizing the reconfigurations presently occurring, we have sought to keep our distance from the imposition of narrative as a mere fiction through a number of different intellectual strategies. We continually focus on the need to dissolve the relation of the social and culture, the text and reality, and to view knowledge as a productive aspect of power. We are also aware of the values of a "poetics of knowledge" ("the set of literary procedures by which a discourse escapes literature, gives itself the status of science, and signifies this status" [Rancière 1994: 8].[27] Instead of the traditional historicist view of the "rational" transparency of language in historical representations, we have thought of narrative as "an arena in which meaning takes form, in which individuals connect to the public and social world, and in which change therefore becomes possible" (Bonnell and Hunt 1999: 17). In this sense, we also reject the new historical inquiry (and certain cultural studies and post-colonial thought) that seeks to revive a self-explanatory narration in which the new stories of the nation and people reinstitute the traditional pattern of making history, with its adherence to logical time, fixed space, and universal salvation narratives such as those of nationhood (for critiques of these tendencies, see, e.g., Cooper and Stoler 1997; Gupta and Ferguson 1997; Spivak 1999; Adler and Hermand 1999).

In this discussion, we have sought to highlight the following points of a cultural history:

The concern with knowledge is a central object of study. This approach considers language as more than giving information or getting information, but also as disciplining, ordering, and dividing a field of cultural practices. As the essays in this book suggest, making knowledge a central focus of study involves considering different trajectories of integrating social and political theory, different views of historiography, and different ways of thinking about culture in the study of human affairs.

A cultural history is a history of the present. But cultural history is not presentist; it does not position history in a programmatic moral role to identify the absolute, transcendent values for society and inscribe them in schooling. The history of the present aims to grasp the conditions concerning what is possible to say as "true," and to consider the present configuration and organization of knowledge through excavating the shifting formations of knowledge over time.

Cultural history entails systematic and continuous interdisciplinary interaction. Throughout this essay, we have tied the study of history to anthropology, sociology, literary studies, and philosophy, among others. As a result, the normal disciplinary boundaries dissolve.

A notion of change is built on the politics of knowledge. To elucidate the impositions of knowledge is a strategy that makes visible the principles that intern and enclose consciousness, thus opening up different possibilities and alternatives.

It dissolves the divides of knowledge and practice, and of the dichotomy between what people say (discourse) and what people *actually* do.

Noting that culture is the bedrock of the essays in this book, there are also different approaches taken toward cultural history, as Nóvoa outlines in his chapter. There are overlapping agendas and a cautiousness about "new" itineraries, no matter how attractive and seemingly reassuring (and, for some, spiritually uplifting at a time of unstable epistemologies). That cautiousness is both historical and political and means to avoid the expression of a new totalizing project. As William Scott remarked, the editor of the new journal *Rethinking History*, in a review of one of the leading theoretical work of today's French cultural history,[28] while *culture* seems at issue everywhere—in economics, social practices, the study of signs and symbols, and is expressed in diffuse sensibilities—there is a particular need for a disciplined and methodologically rigorous conduct of historical research that, and this is our proviso, requires a vigilant self-reflectivity.

The destabilizing strategy to dislodge the ordering principles that intern and enclose action is a strategy to produce the possibility for other actions and possibilities. As Varela argues, power and freedom cannot be understood in opposition but rather in terms of distribution of one and the other. The essay by Dussel also seeks to dissolve the opposition between freedom and repression as they are intertwined historically through disciplining of the body—with the liberties of the body, Dussel argues, are always implied new responsibilities that are part of the consolidation of power.

We have also argued that change is the making of the rules for "telling the truth" contingent, historical, and susceptible to critique. While we have argued that a cultural history provides different priorities, epistemologies, and a politics of knowledge important to the present, we deploy this argument with a certain hesitation. This hesitation is a historical recognition that knowledge has its own doubleness. The shifts in interpretive means of disciplined knowledge are not only responses to disciplinary struggles about the questions of knowledge, but also shifts of the power relations through which disciplinary constructions are formed and made possible (see, e.g., Rose 1999; Popkewitz 1997; Wagner 1994). While talking about a cultural history, it is important to keep this doubleness of knowledge in mind. The reconfiguring of social and historical inquiry is embedded in fields of practices and relations, never outside of them.

Notes

1. In the writing of this chapter, we benefited from the comments and critiques of Mary Bauman, Inés Dussel, Lisa Hennon, Ruth Gustafson, Dar Weyenberg, and the Wednesday Group at the Department of Curriculum and Instruction, University of Wisconsin-Madison.
2. There is an ironic quality in using the term culture to deconstruct its opposition,

in that this the social, in that this may reinscribe the distinctions. Our hope is for this not to happen; "cultural" is viewed here as a convenient term to think about the configurations and connections of collectively mediated aspects of the world and knowledge, in its broadest sense. For a discussion of the relation of cultural and social history, see Frijhoff (1998).

3. "Configurable comprehension" is a metaphor coined by the late Louis O. Mink, a constructivist who helped provide for the "linguistic turn" in the historical inquiry with his philosophy of history (see Mink 1987: 56–57).

4. We do find some British and American educational historians who explore the implications of a cultural history (Cohen 1999), but most of the intellectual scholarship is being done outside the formal disciplinary field of educational history in the curriculum field (see Popkewitz and Brennan 1998; Baker 2000).

5. There is also a tendency for the educational critics to have read only secondary sources and to take the rhetorical announcements as the substantive intellectual arguments being brought forward. For a general discussion, see Popkewitz and Brennan (1998); on comparative education, Popkewitz (2000a).

6. The meaning of historicism is contested, with some arguing a broad view of its temporality, as here, and others a more restricted view (see Szacki 1979, chapter 11; and Schnädelbach 1984, for comprehensive analysis of the variety of historicisms following the German pattern; see the forum published by *History and Theory* 34(3), 1995, on "The Meaning of Historicism and Its Relevance for Contemporary Theory," Wittkau 1994; and Oexle and Rüsen 1996; Pieters, 2000 for the most recent debates) For our purposes, we will talk about the social historians as providing a particular form to historicism that is explained later in the section.

7. Thomas's discussion follows the German historian of ideas Hans Blumenberg (1983).

8. The Rankean *Geisteswissenschaften*, consolidated by a cognitive alliance between historicism and positivism, successfully institutionalized and professionalized the modern system of science. In the present, the crisis of the liberal and scientific paradigm of history that formed in the cognitive alliance has more clearly distinctive features than it did a century ago.

9. One can also trace such a celebratory history in Latin America through Warde and Carvalho's chapter on Brazil.

10. This was called "the new social history" as a way of differentiating the social historical traditions that developed in the early part of the twentieth century, what the British historian George Mauclay Trevelyan called "history with the politics left out" (see Simon 1983, for a review of its impact in history of education).

11. Others have used such terms as "advance liberalism," and "the second crisis of modernity." We use late modernity and postmodernity not to take sides here, but only to signal that significant changes are occurring that require new interpretive approaches.

12. See *History and Theory* 37(2), 1998, for a complete monograph on this work and its twenty-five years of influence.

13. White was the first American historian to provide a positive and lengthy review of Michel Foucault's work in the field of history (1973b; also 1978), the same year of Metahistory's appearance (also see Domanska 1998). In his systematic treatment of Foucault as a "historian," White described Foucault as being in "praise of historicism" through his demonstration of "relentlessness of historicity." White thought that "[un]like the conventional historian, who is concerned to clarify and thereby to 'refamiliarize' his readers with the artifacts of past cultures and epochs, Foucault seeks to 'defamiliarize' the phenomena of man,

society, and culture which has been rendered all too transparent by a century of study, interpretation, and conceptual over-determination." For White, Foucault's writing also represented a "[h]eady stuff, to be sure. And it is quite understandable that Foucault has been the object of attack of almost everyone who has not been simply puzzled by him." (White 1973: 50, 44) (See Brieler 1998; also Burke 1992; O'Farrell 1989; Goldstein 1993; Noiriel 1994; and Vázquez García 1997, for contested questions of Foucault as historian).

14. If we examine the broader impact of *Metatheory* we find that from 1987 to the end of 1999 the Web of Science (from the Institute for Scientific Information) registers 602 different articles that cite it.

15. The entire renovation of historical practice in education produced after the fifties in the United States and later in Europe and Australia was thought as the fullest incorporation of history of education in the disciplinary field of history (see Lowe, 2000, for an overview and selection of main papers published in the last decades in several American and European journals). Sol Cohen cogently demystifies this view as a mirage, using a biographical narration of his tutor Lawrence Cremin, the leading historian of education for decades whose ambitious project was writing a "universal history" of American education within a distinctive historicist program (1999: 273–99; see also chapters 1 and 2).

16. While there seems to be more spaces for theoretical history or for assuming the role played by theoretical constructs in the structuring of historical narration, that idea of theory tends to harken back to a notion of a middle ground theory, an idea rooted in the traditional Mertonian sociology of knowledge (see, eg., Kaestle 1992: 202; or Kaestle 1999 for a more recent methodological landscape of history of education based on modernist approaches, but which any reference to postmodern social historical inquiry). What is ignored in educational historians' discussions is the long-term debates about the interplay of theory narrativity and method in history, such as in the work of Topolski (1987, 1991, 1999). If in the professional field of history during the past few decades we find more space for theoretical history or for assuming the role played by theoretical constructs in the structural making of historical narration, we are not referring to the use of direct theoretical arguments, or to an exercise of testing theoretical hypotheses: in fact, it is amazing how lacking in the academic history of education of this kind of reflection and literature. The German academic community has paid more attention to these issues, although little theory of science has been applied to educational historiography. See von Prondczynsky (1999) for a recent account and approach (although his reading and reservations of postmodern historiography are too restricted).

17. Angelo is currently not involved in the field of educational history. Karier was the first American educational historian to acknowledge White's *Metahistory*, which he did in his 1978 Presidential Address to the History of Education Society, strategically called "The Quest for Orderly Change: Some Reflection." In this paper, he asked his colleagues to look for the "meta-structure of history," as White did, to provide a new and illuminating perspective "to *imaginatively* enter the world of the dead from a living present" (Karier 1979: 160; italics ours).

18. See the monograph on "History of Education in the Postmodern Era" (vol 32(2): 1996) edited by Cohen in conjunction with the journal's editor, Marc Depaepe.

19. We can differentiate the two here. Historical sociology is often related to discipline of sociology where secondary as well as primary sources are used. It is not a fixed rule but one used if only to demarcate disciplinary boundaries.

20. In the case of the United States, see Chambliss (1979) for an account of the nineteenth century and Depaepe (1983), Hiner (1990), and Lagemann (2000, ch. 3 and 6) for the twentieth century

21. Spivak is instructive here: "Postcolonial studies, unwittingly commemorating a lost object, can become an alibi unless it is placed within a general frame, Colonial Discourse studies, when they concentrate only on the presentation of the colonialized or the matter of the colonies, can sometimes serve the production of current neocolonial knowledge by placing colonialism/imperialism securely in the past, and/or by suggesting a continuous line from the past to our present"(1999: 1).

22. Iggers seems not to have read Foucault's discussion of the systems of thought. Iggers (1997) refers to secondary sources. However, Iggers does not reject Foucault in the overdetermined way a number of historians do. A prime example of that sort of response to Foucault is the one expressed by the distinguished analytical philosopher of history Arthur C. Dalton in the recent, superb survey of contemporary historiography by Ewa Domanska, who interviewed some of the world's leading theorists and philosophers of history. For Dalton, Foucault "is one of the scariest human beings I know, and one of the most dangerous" (see Domanska 1998: 182). Foucault is the second most mentioned figure by the interviewees, noted by Alan Megill in the introduction to Domanska's book (the first mentioned is Hayden White with 232 mentions, followed by Foucault with 80, Richard Rorty with 46, and Jacques Derrida with 36).

23. This use of the term "postmodern" as an evil to be fought against modernism is a rather frequent rhetorical device (see, eg., Masemann and Welch 1997).

24. See Eley (1992) for a complete review of the "linguistic turn," and also Cohen (1999, chapter 3) from a perspective from the field of educational history.

25. One counter argument is also that it is not possible to escape from the "text" because there is nothing outside of it (see Callinicos 1989, for a criticism)

26. Gabrielle Spiegel (1990) coined the phrase "semiotic challenge" to argue that the historical inquiry produced in the most recent epoch is unthinkable without this linguistic turn.

27. Watten (1996:221) suggests that this is at the heart of the modernist substance of historical inquiry, that is to say *narrativity* ("historical thought [traditionally] located, intellectually considered, near the suppression of the nonnarrated") is reconfigured as next to the nonnarrative and nonrepresentational content through (re)textualization.

28. *Pour une histoire culturelle*, edited by Jean-Pierre Rioux and Jean-François Sirinelli (1997) Paris: Editions du Sevil.

References

Adler, H. and Hermand, J. (1999). *Concepts of culture*. New York: Peter Lang.

Angus, D. L., Mirel, J. E., and Vinovskis, M. (1988). Historical development of age stratification in schooling. *Teachers College Record* 90: 211–36.

Armstrong, D. (1994). Bodies of knowledge/knowledge of bodies. In D. Jones and R. Porter (Eds.), *Power, medicine, and the body*. London: Routledge.

Baker, B. (in press). *In perpetual motion: Theories of power, educational history, and the child*. New York: Peter Lang.

Baumann, L. (1987). Legislators and Interpreters: On Modernity, Postmodernity, and Intellectuals. Ithaca, NY: Cornell University Press.

Bender, J. (1992). A new history of the enlightenment. In L. T. Damrosch (Ed.), *The profession of eighteenth-century literature: Reflection on an institution* (62–84). Madison: University of Wisconsin Press.

Benjamin, W. (1955/1985). Theses on the philosophy of history. In *Illuminations, essays, and reflections* (ed. by H. Arendt; trans. by H. Zohn) (253–64). New York: Schocken Books.

Bentley, M. (1999). *Modern historiography: An introduction.* London: Routledge.

Blumenberg, H. (1983). *The legitimacy of the modern age* (trans. by R. M. Wallace). Cambridge, MA: MIT Press.

Bonnell, V., and Hunt, L. (Eds.). (1999). *Beyond the cultural turn: New directions in the study of society and culture.* Berkeley: University of California Press.

Bourdieu: (1984). *Distinction: A social critique of the judgment of taste.* (R. Nico, trans.) Cambridge, MA: Harvard University Press.

Brieler, U. (1998). *Die Unerbittlichkeit der Historizität. Foucault als Historiker.* Köln-Weimar-Wien: Böhlau.

Burke, P. (Ed.). (1992). *Critical essays on Michel Foucault.* Aldershot: Scolar Press.

———. (1994). Varieties of cultural history. *Geschichte und Gegenwart* 13: 48–53.

———. (1997). Varieties of cultural history. Ithaca, NY: Cornell University Press.

Callahan, R. E. (1962). *Education and the cult of efficiency: A study of the social forces that have shaped the administration of the public schools.* Chicago: University of Chicago Press.

Callewaert, S. (1999). Philosophy of education: Frankfurt critical theory and the sociology of Pierre Bourdieu. In T. Popkewitz and L. Fendler (Eds.), *Critical theories in education: Changing terrains of knowledge and politics* (117–44). New York: Routledge.

Callinicos, A. (1989). *Against postmodernism: A Marxist critique.* Cambridge: Polity Press.

Carnoy, M., and Levin, H. M. (1985). *Schooling and work in the democratic state.* Stanford, CA: Stanford University Press.

Caspard, P. (1998). The school in crisis, crisis in the memory of school: School, democracy and economic modernity in France from the late middle ages to the present day. *Paedagogica Historica* 34(3): 691–710.

Chambliss, J. J. (1979). The origins of history of education in the United States: A study of its nature and purpose, 1842–1900. *Paedagogica Historica* 19: 94–131.

Chartier, R. (1988). *Cultural history: Between practices and representations.* Ithaca, NY: Cornell University Press.

———. (1996). History between narrative and knowledge. In R. Chartier (Ed.), *On the edge of the cliff: History, language, and practices* (13–38). Baltimore: Johns Hopkins University Press.

Cohen, S. (1999). *Challenging orthodoxies: Toward a new cultural history.* New York: Peter Lang.

Cooper, F., and Stoler, A. (1997). *Tensions of empire: Colonial cultures in a bourgeois world.* Berkeley: University of California Press.

Dean, M. (1994). *Critical and effective histories: Foucault's methods and historical sociology.* New York: Routledge.

Depaepe, M. (1983). L'Apport de l'Histoire de l'Educacion a la Définition der Politique Éducatives. Quelques Réflexions méthodologiques. In W. Frijhoff (Ed.), *L'Office d'Ecole/The Supply of Schooling* (15–31). Paris: INRP.

Dogan, M. and Pahre, R. (1990). Creative marginality: Innovation at the intersections of social spaces. Boulder, CO: Westview Press.

Domanska, E. (1998). *Encounters: Philosophy of history after postmodernism.* Charlottesville and London: University Press of Virginia.

Eley, G. (1992). De l'histoire sociale au 'tournant linguistique' dans l'historiographie anglo-américaine des années 1980. *Genèses* 7: 163–93.

Elias, N. (1984). Knowledge and power: An interview by Peter Ludes [held in 1982)]. In N. Stehr and V. Meja (Eds.), *Society and knowledge: Contemporary perspectives on the sociology of knowledge* (251–92). New Brunswick and London: Transaction Books.

Evans, R. J. (1999). *In defense of history*. New York: W. W. Norton.

Finegold, K., and Skocpol, T. (1995). *State and party in America's new deal*. Madison: University of Wisconsin Press.

Foucault, M. (1977). Nietzsche, genealogy, history (original version appeared in 1971). In *Language, counter-memory, practice: Selected essays and interviews* (ed. by D. F. Bouchard) (138–64). Ithaca, NY: Cornell University Press.

———. Governmentality. *Ideology and Consciousness* 6: 5–22.

———. (1984). What is enlightenment? In P. Rabinow (Ed.), *The Foucault reader* (32–50). New York: Pantheon.

———. La pensée l'emotion. In Dits et écrits 1954–1988: Vol. IV 1980–1988 (243–250). Paris: Editions Gallimard.

———. (1998). *Aesthetics, method, and epistemology: Essential writings of Foucault 1954–1984 (Vol. 2)* (ed. by J. D. Faubion). New York: The New Press.

Franklin, B. M. (1986). *Building the American community: The school curriculum and the search for social control*. London: Falmer Press.

Franklin, B. M. (1994). *From "backwardness" to "at-risk": Childhood learning difficulties and the contradictions of school reform*. Albany: State University of New York Press.

Frijhoff, W. (1998). Conceptual history, social history, and cultural history: The test of "cosmopolitism." In I. Hampsher-Monk, Tilmans, and F. van Vree (Eds.), *History of concepts: Comparative perspectives* (103–28). Amsterdam: Amsterdam University Press.

Frisby, D. (1986). *Fragments of modernity: Theories of modernity in the work of Simmel, Kracauer, and Benjamin*. Cambridge, MA: MIT Press.

Gibbons, M., Limonges, C., Nowotny, H. (1994). *The new production of knowledge: The dynamics of science and research in contemporary society*. London: Sage.

Goldstein, J. (Ed.) (1993). *Foucault and the writing of history*. Chicago: Chicago University Press.

Gonon, P. (1999). Historiographie als Erziehung. Zur Konstitution der pädagogischen Geschitsschreibung im 19. Jahrhundernt. *Zeitschrift für Pädagogik* 45(4): 521–30.

Greer, C. (1972). *The great school legend*. New York: Basic Books.

Gupta, A. and Ferguson, J. (Eds.). (1997). *Culture, power, place: Explorations in critical anthropology*. Durham, NC: Duke University.

Hacking. I. (1999). *The social construction of what?* Cambridge, MA: Harvard University Press.

Hamilton, D. (1989). *Towards a theory of schooling*. London: Falmer Press.

Hampsher-Monk, I., Tilmans, K., and Van Vree, F. (Eds.) (1999). *History of concerts: Comparative perspectives*. Amsterdam: Amsterdam University Press.

Hiner, N. R. (1990). History of education for the 1990s and beyond: The case for academic imperialism. *History of Education Quarterly* 30(2): 137–60.

Hogan, D. J. (1985). *Class and reform: School and society in Chicago, 1880–1930*. Philadelphia: University of Pennsylvania Press.

Hunt, L. (1989). *The new cultural history*. Berkeley: University of California Press.

Huyssen, A. (1995). *Twilight memories: Marking time in a culture of amnesia*. New York: Routledge.

Iggers, G. G. (1997). *Historiography in the twentieth century: From scientific objectivity to the postmodern challenge*. Hanover and London: Wesleyan University Press.

———. (1999). Historiography and the challenge of postmodernism. In B. Stråth and Nina Whosek (Eds.). *The postmodern challenge: Perspectives East and West* (281–302). Amsterdam: Rodopi.

Jay, M. (1998). *Cultural semantics. Keywords of our time.* Amherst: University of Massachusetts Press.

Jenkins, K. (Ed.). (1997). *The postmodern history reader.* New York: Routledge.

Kaestle, C. (1976). Conflict and consensus revisited: Notes toward a reinterpretation of American educational history. *Harvard Educational Review* 46: 390–96.

———. (1983). *Pillars of the republic: Common schools and American society, 1780–1860.* New York: Hill and Wang.

———. (1992). Theory in educational history: A middle ground. In R. K. Goodenow and W. E. Mardades (Eds.), *The city and education in four nations* (195–204). Cambridge: Cambridge University Press.

———. (1999). Historical methods in educational research. In J. P. Keeves and G. Lakomski (Eds.), *Issues in educational research* (121–131). Amsterdam: Pergamon.

Karier, C. H. (1979). The quest for orderly change: Some reflections. *History of Education Quarterly* 19(2): 159–77.

Karier, C. H., Violas, P., and Spring, J. (1973). *Roots of crisis: American education in the twentieth century.* Chicago: Rand McNally.

Katz, M. (1968). *The irony of early school reform: Educational innovation in mid-nineteenth century Massachusetts.* Boston: Beacon Press.

———. (1975). *Class, bureaucracy, and schools: The illusion of educational change in America* (Expanded edition). New York: Praeger.

Kelley, D. R. (1996). The old cultural history. *History of the Human Sciences* 9(3): 101-26.

Kliebard, H. (1986). *Struggle for the American curriculum, 1893–1958.* London: Routledge & Kegan Paul.

Koselleck, R. (1985). *Future past: On the semantics of historical time.* Cambridge, MA: MIT Press.

Kracauer, S. (1993a). Photography. *Critical Inquiry* 19: 420–37.

———. (1993b). *The mass ornament.* Cambridge: Cambridge University Press.

Krug, E. A. (1969). *The shaping of the American high school, 1880–1920.* Madison: University of Wisconsin Press.

Labaree, D. F. (1988). *The making of an American high school: The credentials market and the central high school of Philadelphia.* New Haven, CT: Yale University Press.

Lagemann, E. C. (2000). *An elusive science: The troubling history of education research.* Chicago, IL: University of Chicago Press.

Latour, B. (1999). *Pandora's hope: Essays on the reality of science studies.* Cambridge, MA: Harvard University Press.

Lowe, R. (2000). *History of education. Vol. I: Major themes.* London: Routledge.

McDonald, T. (1996). *The historic turn in the human sciences.* Ann Arbor: University of Michigan Press.

Masemann, V. and Welch, A. (Eds.). (1997). *Tradition, modernity, and postmodernity in comparative education.* Dortrecht and Hamberg: Kluwer Academic Publishers and UNESCO Institute for Education.

Mehta, U. (1997). Liberal strategies of exclusion. In F. Cooper and A. Stoler (Eds.), *Tensions of empires: Colonial cultures in a Bourgeois world* (59–86). Berkeley: University of California Press.

Meyer, J., Boli, J., Thomas, G., and Ramirez, F. (1997). World society and the nation-state. *American Journal of Sociology* 103(1): 144–181.

Mink, L. O. (1987). *Historical understanding* (ed. by B. Fay, E. O. Golob and R. T. Vann). Ithaca and London: Cornell University Press.

Munslow, A. (1997). *Deconstructing history.* London: Routledge.

Nehamas, A. (1985). *Nietzsche: Life as literature*. Cambridge: Cambridge University Press.

Neubauer, J. (Ed.). (1999). *Cultural history after Foucault*. New York: Aldine de Gruyter.

Noirel, G. (1994). Foucault and history: The lessons of a disillusion. *Journal of Modern History* 66(4): 547–68.

Nora, P. (1995). Between memory and history: *Les Lieux de Mémoire* (originally published in 1984). In J. Revel and L. Hunt (Eds.), *Histories: French constructions of the past* (632–36). New York: New Press.

Oelkers, J. (1999). Die Geschichte der Pädagogik und ihre Probleme. *Zeitschrift für Pädagogik* 45(4): 461–83.

Oexle, O. G. and Rüsen, J. (Eds.). (1996). *Historismus in den kulturwissenschoftin: Geschichtrkonzepte, historische Einrchützungen, brundlagen probleme*. Köln: Böhlau.

O'Farrell, C. (1989). *Foucault: Historian or philosopher?* New York: St. Martin's Press.

Olábarri, I. (1995). "New" new history: A longue durée structure. *History and Theory* 34(1): 1–29.

Outhwaite, W. (1999). The myth of modernist method. *European Journal of Social Theory* 2(1): 5–25.

Page, C. (1995). *Philosophical historicism and the betrayal of first philosophy*. University Park: Pennsylvania State University Press.

Payne, M. (1997). *Reading knowledge: An introduction to Barthes, Foucault, and Althusser*. Oxford: Blackwell.

Pieters, J. (2000). New historicism: Postmodern historiography between narrativism and heterology. *History and Theory* 39(1): 21–38.

Popkewitz, T. S. (1991). *A political sociology of educational reform: Power/knowledge in teaching, teacher education, and research*. New York: Teachers College Press.

———. (1996). Rethinking decentralization and the state/civil society distinctions: The state as a problematic of governing. In T. Popkewitz (Ed.), *Educational knowledge: Changing relationships between the state, civil society, and the educational community* (173- 200). Albany: State University of New York Press.

———. (1997). A changing terrain of knowledge and power: A social epistemology of educational research. *The Educational Researcher* 26(9): 5–17.

———. (2000a). National imaginaries, the indigenous foreigner, and power: Comparative educational research. In J. Schriewer (Ed.), *Discourse formation in comparative education* (261–94). Berlin: Peter Lang Verlag.

———. (2000b). *Educational knowledge: Changing relationships between the state, civil society, and the educational community*. Albany: State University of New York Press.

Popkewitz, T. and Brennan, M. (1998). Restructuring of social and political theory in education: Foucault and a social epistemology of school practices. In T. Popkewitz, and M. Brennan (Eds), *Foucault's challenge: Discourse, knowledge, and power in education* (3–35). New York: Teachers College Press.

Porter, M. (1997). *Cultural history and postmodernity: Disciplinary readings and challenges*. New York: Columbia University Press.

Prondczynsky, A. von (1999). Die Pädagogik und ihre Historiographie. Umrisse eines Forschungsfeldes. *Zeitschrift für Pädagogik* 45(4): 485–504.

Rancière, J. (1994). *The names of history: On the poetics of knowledge*. Minneapolis: University of Minnesota.

Reese, W. (1983). Neither victims nor masters: Ethnic and minority studies. In J. H. Best (Ed.), *Historical inquiry in education: A research agenda* (230–50). Washington, DC: American Educational Research Association.

Rose, N. (1999). *Powers of freedom: Reframing political thought.* Cambridge: Cambridge University Press.

Rosenau, P. (1992). *Post-modernism and the social sciences: Insights, inroads, and intrusions.* Princeton, NJ: Princeton University Press.

Rüsen, J. (1993). *Studies in metahistory.* Pretoria: Human Sciences Research Council.

Schnädelbach, H. (1984). *Philosophy in Germany, 1831–1933.* Cambridge: Cambridge University Press.

Schram, S. F. and Neisser: T. (Eds.). (1997). *Tales of the state: Narrative in contemporary U.S. politics and public policy.* Totowa, NJ: Rowman and Littlefield.

Scott, W. (1999). Cultural history, French style. *Rethinking History* 3(2): 197–235.

Simon, J. (1983). The history of education and the "new" social history. *History of Education Review* 12(2): 1–15.

Skocpol, T. (1985). Bringing the state back in: Strategies of analysis in current research. In P. B. Evans, D. Rueschemeyer, and T. Skocpol (Eds.), *Bringing the state back in* (3–37). Cambridge: Cambridge University Press.

———. (1992). *Protecting soldiers and mothers: The political origins of social policy in the United States.* Cambridge, MA: Harvard University Press.

Smith, D. (1991). *The rise of historical sociology.* Oxford: Polity Press.

———. (1999). The civilizing process and the history of sexuality: Comparing Norbert Elias and Michel Foucault. *Theory and Society* 28(1): 79–100.

Spiegel, G. (1990). History, historicism, and the social logic of the text in the middle ages. *Speculum* 65(1): 59–96.

Spivak, G. (1999). *A critique of postcolonial reason: Toward a history of the vanishing present.* Boston: Harvard University Press.

Spring, J. (1973). *Education and the rise of the corporate state.* Boston: Beacon Press.

Steedman, C. (1998). The space of memory in an archive. *History of the Human Sciences* 11(4): 65–83.

Steinmetz, G. (Ed.). (1999). *State/Culture: State formation after the cultural turn.* Ithaca, NY: Cornell University Press.

Stone, L. (1981). *The past and the present.* London: Routledge and Kegan Paul.

Szacki, J. (1979). *History of sociological thought.* Westport, CT: Greenwood Press.

Taylor, M. C. (1986). Introduction: System . . . structure . . . difference . . . other. In M. Taylor (Ed.), *Deconstruction in context: Literature and philosophy* (1–34). Chicago: University of Chicago Press.

Tessitore, F. (1995). *Contributi alla Storia e alla Teoria dello Storicismo. Vol. I. Tra Storicismi e Storicità.* Rome: Edizioni di Storia e Letteratura.

Thomas, B. (1991). *The new historicism. And other old-fashioned topics.* Princeton, NJ: Princeton University Press.

Topolski, J. (1987). Historical narrative: Towards a coherent structure. *History and Theory* 26(1): 75–86.

———. (1991). Towards an integrated model of historical explanation. *History and Theory* 30(3): 324–38.

———. (1999). The role of logic and aesthetics in constructing narrative wholes in historiography. *History and Theory* 38(2): 198–210.

Tyack, D. (1974). *The one best system: A history of American urban education.* Cambridge, MA: Harvard University Press.

Vazquez García, F. (1997). Foucault y la Historia Social. *Historia Social* 29: 145–59.

Wagner: (1994). *The sociology of modernity.* New York: Routledge.

Warren, D. (1987). New business in the history of education. *Educational Studies* 18: 34–37.

Watten, B. (1996). Nonnarrative and the construction of history. In J. Herron et al. (Eds.), *The ends of theory* (209–45). Detroit, MI: Wayne State University Press.

Weber, M. (1946). *From Max Weber: Essays in sociology* (ed. and trans. by H. H. Gerth and C. W. Mills) New York: Oxford University Press.

———. (1968). *Economy and society: An outline of interpretive sociology* (ed. by G. Roth; trans. by C. Wittich, E. Fischoff, et. al.). New York: Bedminister Press.

White, H. (1973a). *Metahistory: The historical imagination in nineteenth-century Europe*. Baltimore: Johns Hopkins University Press.

———. (1973b). Foucault decoded: Notes from underground. *History and Theory* 12(1): 23–54.

———. (1978). *Tropics of discourse: Essays in colonial criticism*. Baltimore: Johns Hopkins University Press.

———. (1999). *Figural realism: Studies in the mimesis effect*. Baltimore, MD: Johns Hopkins University Press.

Wilson, N. J. (1999). *History in crisis: Recent directions in historiography*. Upper Saddle River, NJ: Prentice Hall.

Wittkau, A. (1994). *Historismus: Zur Gerchichte der Begriffs und der Problems* (2nd ed.). Göttingen: Vandenhoeck and Rupprecht.

Young, R. (1990). *Colonial desire: Hybridity in theory*. London: Routledge.

part 2
Rethinking the Discipline of History of Education

2

Texts, Images, and Memories

Writing "New" Histories of Education

António Nóvoa

Today, we are facing a time marked by the consciousness of our limits for interpreting and making sense of the world's complexities. We know that we need to ask new questions, search for different meanings, imagine other histories. This is not a new feeling, and other generations have been confronted with it. But it has acquired peculiar contours and it is influencing our quest for understanding. In the historical field, an effort must be made to bring multiple and diversified points of view together; or, in the words of Cornel West:

> [t]o thrash the monolithic and homogeneous in the name of diversity, multiplicity, and heterogeneity; to reject the abstract, general, and universal in light of the concrete, specific, and particular; and to historicize, contextualize and pluralize by highlighting the contingent, provisional, variable, tentative, shifting, and changing. (1990: 93)

In this chapter, I struggle with the complexities of historical research in education. I acknowledge the diversity of methodological approaches used by historians, underlining that "the way to deal with that complexity is not to ignore it but to sophisticate our analytical repertoire, ever improving our ability to uncover the ways that power works, personality is produced, disciplinary matrixes are legitimated, and objectivity is defined" (Kincheloe 1991: 243).

The chapter is organized in three sections:

- In the first section, *Rethinking history and history of education after the linguistic turn*, I direct my attention to a group of authors and a set of arguments that are opening new ways of working with "texts," incorporating their analysis in the historical inquiry.
- In the second section, *"Memories of Seeing": The pictorial turn and the construction of educational histories*, I look to the importance of "images," not so much as primary sources, but as forms of saying and seeing that change our historical understanding.

- In the last section, *"Remembrance" and "Imagination" in the historical writing of education*, I address issues of "memories" (reminiscences of the past and projections of the future) and the need to redefine space-time relationships in order to build new historical approaches.

The chapter is a montage of several pieces linked by an intention of contributing to a reconceptualization of the educational history field. I know that our epistemological reflection is much more complex than our theoretical understandings or methodological practices. With Bronislaw Baczko (1978), I remember that famous painting by Goya in which two men fly in the direction of a "promised land." They are fired on from below, from the earth that they try to escape. Let us avoid the "optimism" (to praise the utopia of the action) or the "pessimism" (to criticize the crazy act), and let us take the painting as it is: it places the "flying man" in the foreground and attracts our vision to him.

Rethinking History and History of Education after the Linguistic Turn

The *text* is at the center of the "new" historiographical modes that focus not only on the organization of discourses over time but also on the elucidation of how discourses have constructed and reconstructed people's lives and social realities. At present it is impossible to ignore the ideas and the arguments brought by the authors connected with the linguistic turn. Historians are compelled to redefine the foundations of their work, even if they remain hesitant to accept the integration of the notion of *discourse* or to assume their act as essentially *poetic*: "New models (Ricoeur, Habermas, Foucault, Derrida, etc.) authorize new ways of looking at texts, of inscribing texts within discourses and of linking both texts and discourses to their contexts" (White 1987: 185). The main argument is that history "interprets" and "molds" facts, more than discovering and finding them. Consequently, the historian's reconstruction of the past as a narrative inevitably has a constructive dimension that links history to literature rather than science's narrative past.

Such an argument is thoroughly developed by Paul Ricoeur (1994) when he compares the parallel intellectual operations of rhetoric and history: the *inventio* of rhetoricians and the documental research of historians; the *dispositio* and the explanation stage; the *elocutio* and the writing of history. From his perspective, this comparison is legitimated by the current dilemmas faced by history in order to articulate an epistemological approach that both underlines the scientificity of documentation and analysis and a literariness concerned mainly with narrative styles. In view of these dilemmas I stand against the opposite extreme which would erode the "scientificity" of history and collapse all *reality* into *discourse*. I agree with Martin Jay (1991) when he suggests that instead of trying to isolate the text from the world or explain the text by the world, it is useful to dissolve the boundary between the two.

Foucault's work is a good illustration of the turn from social to cultural history, from social topics examined through quantitative methods toward cultural ones interpreted through their rhetorical signatures (Hutton 1991). Foucault proposes to look at texts as objects on their own terms, and not as manifestations of subjective realities:

> To be brief, let us say that history, in its traditional form, undertook to "memorize" the *monuments* of the past, transform them into *documents*, and lend speech to those traces which, in themselves, are often not verbal, or which say in silence something other than what they actually say; in our time, history is that which transforms *documents* into *monuments*. (1972: 7)

As David Harlan states, "it is difficult, after Barthes, Derrida, and Foucault, to continue approaching our texts as objects that *should* be transparent, as signs of something else, as masks concealing something held in reserve, something that will, in the end, be revealed as whole and primary and essential, a *perfect presence*" (1989: 592). Language must now be seen as a system that constitutes rather than reflects, that prescribes as well as it describes.

There are different theoretical traditions and methodological approaches within the "new" theoretical movements. One can say that there is no field of cultural history, but only historians working in a cultural mode (Hunt 1989). Considering only French intellectuals, it is possible to group these traditions in three main tendencies (Licht 1992):

- The *pure deconstructionist* approach, just as it is practiced by someone like Jacques Derrida, well illustrated by his assertion that "there is nothing outside a text" or, in other words, "there is no absolute extra-text."
- A less radical position, close to a *symbolic structuralism*, held by philosophers like Michel Foucault who argue that cultural productions do not exist outside relations of interdependence with other works and documents.
- A *sociocultural perspective*, present in some of Roger Chartier's recent writings, in which culture is seen as a deliberate product that cannot be understood without paying closer attention to the relations between practices and discourses, nondiscursive systems and enunciative facts.

These different traditions have different implications for historical work. Excepting the pure deconstructionist approach, the other two refer to social conditions and tensions. The questions they raise are essentially "historical," and not "literary." They affirm the importance of language, but they do not state that a linguistic reasoning exhausts the whole "being" (Jay 1991). Their objective is not to replace context with text or a social interpretation with a linguistic one. The world can be viewed neither as language—*textual imperialism*—nor can language be understood as merely a reflection of the world—*contextualism* (Childers 1989).

In fact, an important difference separates the rationality that organizes the production of discourses—worded, logocentric, hermeneutic—and the rationality that informs all the other regimes of practice. Nowadays, it is important to recognize that historical research involves first, an extension of the traditional inquiry of the intellectual history in order to include the collective representations and beliefs; and second, an assertion of the impossibility of reducing the nondiscursive practices to the discourses that, in several ways, are supposed to legitimize, condemn, represent, control, or organize those practices (Chartier 1992).

The transition from "History" to "histories" implies a reconfiguration of the field, ceertainly as far as the habitus of its occupants is concerned. Historians of education are face to face with a paradigmatic shift. They feel the urgency to reconceptualize their work, and to adopt a more comprehensive approach that helps to enable a shift from a *social history of culture* to a *cultural history of society* (Chartier 1989).

It is pertinent to emphasize the new attention paid by historians to some groups traditionally absent from the historical narrative. I am thinking, for instance, of the way feminist critics put women's educational experience, their lives and subjectivities in perspective: "The questions having to do with gender and gender relations which feminist critics bring to historical investigation suggest the lines along which those of us concerned with history of education can rethink what significant education events in fact *are* and how historical periods might be newly delimited" (Leach 1990: 461).

Traditionally, questions of gender had been largely absent from the concerns of educational historians. The adoption of some issues of the feminist agenda has led to a reconsideration not only of the objects of inquiry but also of the theoretical frameworks. The feminist rupture induced the emergence of new ways of thinking, building historical arguments, and providing intellectual explanations. Moreover, feminist theory has problematized dualistic accounts of gender and challenged the privileging of biology/reproductive function as a basis for drawing distinctions in society. More than a "new" object of study, the feminist critique elucidates how certain categories and languages have been socially constructed as forms of power, inside and outside the school space, mainly through pedagogical discourse (Luke and Gore 1992). This turn implies not only a greater presence of women in the historical inquiry but also an analysis of sexual and gender differences in relation to mechanisms of power, which implies a rethinking of political, cultural, and educational history (Burstyn 1990; Canning 1994).

Experience

These transitions lead history of education to a rediscovery of *experience*, allowing an understanding of how people and groups of people have interpreted and reinterpreted their world, how representations circulate in individuals, how the experience of schooling has different meanings for different people. Modernity dispossessed educational actors from their subjectivities through the imposition of a structural logic and a populational reasoning. People were classified as categories (the teachers, the learners, etc.) and managed as *populations*. After having regarded the world as structure and representation, historians need to see the world as experience, which implies a new "epistemology of the subject." As Nikolas Rose writes: "Subjectification is not to be understood by locating it in a universe of meaning or an interactional context of narratives, but in a complex of apparatuses, practices, machinations, and assemblages within which human being has been fabricated, and which presuppose and enjoin particular relations with ourselves" (1996: 10).

The concept of experience does not refer only to a mere "living through events," but also encompasses the way in which "people construed events as they were living through them" (Sewell 1990). As Kathleen Canning (1994) holds, by dissolving the myth of "natural" divisions between public and private, between women and men, women's history prepared the way for the shift toward a self-conscious study of gender as a symbolic system or a signifier of power relations. There is a strong appeal for a theory that allows us to elucidate the complex cultural construction of people's lives and experiences.

Writing about experience is not a strategy to avoid power issues; conversely, it is the best way to show how language and silence work in the reconstruction of personal and professional lives. In spite of their differences, the commonalities between critical and feminist pedagogical discourses show how issues of power and experience relate to one another. Both discourses emphasize student experience and voice, assert the objectives of self and social empowerment toward broader social transformation, speak about teachers' authority and struggle with the contradictions inherent in the notion of authority for emancipation, and are linked to political and social movements that seek to erase multiple forms of oppression (Gore 1993).

Language issues cannot be dissociated from the ways in which power is engaged, contested, deflected and appropriated (Cooper 1994). New conceptions of *subject* and *experience* are essential to educational history because they allow a new attention to be paid not only to living experience but also to the way people elaborate it. The production of counterhegemonic narratives is crucial to shape emancipatory identities; doing so "we decolonize our minds and our imaginations" (hooks 1992: 346). It is not a question of returning to individualism, but instead of establishing new relations inside social spaces and consolidating new affiliations and belongings. In this sense, the concept of *experience* must be seen not only at an individual level, but also in its collective dimension, which is characterized by a redefinition of identities through the presence in different communities of meaning.

Educational historians need to understand relations of power, not only as a totalization but also as an individualization to the extent that it ties the individual to a particular identity leading to the submission of subjectivity. Following Foucault, this debate needs to examine the "technologies of the self" and the processes of governmentality: the complex of notions, calculations, strategies, and tactics through which diverse authorities – political, military, economic, theological, medical, and so forth – have sought to act upon the lives and conducts of each and all in order to avert evils and achieve such desirable states as health, happiness, wealth, and tranquility (see Rose 1996).

School Culture

It is useful to take note of the growing comprehensiveness of the research accomplished by educational historians: "They now study children as well as adults, learners as well as teachers, the weak as well as the powerful, and education outside schools as well as within them. And they are renewing a traditional emphasis on education in an international framework" (Hiner 1990: 144). The internal functioning of the school, the curriculum design, the formation of the school knowledge, the organization of everyday school reality, teachers' and students' lives and experience are some of the issues that need a closer look.

We can give different answers to the question of why historians have considered the history of the classroom so unimportant. For the moment, I am interested in one of these answers that is directly related to the concept of *school culture*, following the definition given by Dominique Julia (1995): school culture is both an ensemble of norms that organize the branches of knowledge and behaviors that must be brought into schooling and an ensemble of practices that allow the transmission of such knowledge and the integration of such behaviors. In this sense, Julia advocates a refocusing of educational history aimed at a broader understanding of what happens inside schools.

It is possible to identify some current tendencies of historical research that try to meet this challenge by providing a deeper analysis of organizational and curriculum issues, school subjects and day-to-day school realities. The way in which Thomas Popkewitz and Marie Brennan use the concept of "social epistemology" clarifies the theoretical and historical approaches of these questions:

> Social epistemology locates the objects constituted as the knowledge of schooling as historical practices through which power relations can be understood. . . .
> When teachers talk about school as management, teaching as producing learning, or children who are at risk, these terms are not merely words of the teacher, but are part of historically constructed ways of reasoning that are the effects of power. A social epistemology studies speech as effects of power. (1998: 9)

A book edited by Ian Grosvenor, Martin Lawn, and Kate Rousmaniere focuses on the "silence" in the history of education about the practice, meaning, and culture of classrooms in the past. Assuming that their goal is to ask questions about how historians can begin to piece together "the silent social history of the classroom," they clarify their own approach:

> Schools and classrooms, we began to realize, are not static points, but whole series of events and social relations over time, rich with personal dynamics. Teachers come in and out of classrooms, hanging posters, contributing an extra bookcase or table. Students run in and out of classrooms, make marks on desk tops, leave shredded paper in their books. . . . The classroom seeps in and out of the everyday lives of children and adults. . . . What is the valid story of the past, if teachers and students remember their classrooms through the veil of their own histories? . . . The very silences of classroom history can in fact speak very loudly. (1999: 6–7)

Another interesting research trend is characterized by the close interrelationship between management and organization on the one hand and pedagogical change on the other. The way organizational factors affect pedagogical life is one of the questions asked nowadays by historians. Furthermore, several authors are voicing the need to deconstruct a "natural" history of curriculum, problematizing curriculum as *text* and historicizing its evolution over time. Finally, it is useful to point out a research trend concerned with the history of school subjects. The complex alchemy that changes academic subjects (integrated in their own social spaces) into school subjects (integrated in the schooling arena) is an important issue that needs to be made clear. Marc Depaepe and Frank Simon argue that "the real educational activity inside and outside the family, within the school borders as well as in the classroom, has indeed remained the *black box* of the pedagogical historiography" (1995: 10).

Discourse

The more important change in the posture of educational historians refers, to the rethinking of the history of pedagogical ideas through the concept of *discourse*. The history of pedagogical ideas dominated historical studies in education for a long time. It was a history devoted to a neverending search for origins, influences, and causes in an attempt to interpret the ideas of the "great" educators of the past. The "new" cultural history of education, in contrast, is interested in the production, diffusion, and reception of educational discourses throughout time and space. Therefore, the research focus has shifted to the *discursive practices* that regulate schooling, especially when there is rupture or conflict.

Language cannot be seen only as a rhetorical signature. It needs to be taken as a *text* that redefines subjectivities and identities, that ascribes rules and behaviors, that configures meanings and beliefs. Reading a text is comparable to reading a discourse-practice:

> Texts in the discourses-practices of education include textbooks, research papers, monographs, curriculum guidelines, and assessment tests. Research designs, observational data, experimental interventions, statistical tests, and inferences are also texts as well as discourses-practices. Their meaning depends upon other texts that are related to still other texts. The intertextuality of discourses and practices constitutes and structures our social and educational worlds. (Cherryholmes 1988: 8)

In opposition to a "traditional" history of ideas, several authors are calling for a historiography of conceptual structures, not of "origins," for an analysis of the historical emergence of fields and problems, not of "ideas" (Charbonnel 1988). It is useful to understand how educational discourses define categories that are central not only to our interpretation of actions and contexts, but also to our perception, definition, and construction of subjectivities.

This approach is decisive for analyzing the role played by pedagogical experts in the definition of "legitimate" or "scientific" interpretations of school realities. It is at the same time useful to study the historical foundation of educational sciences as a form of *governmentality* and not as a narrative of scientific progress. Adapting the words of Nikolas Rose to historical research in education, it is possible to identify an array of questions that need to be asked: the ways in which certain aspects of the conduct of persons (teachers, students, etc.), individually or collectively, have come to be problematized at specific historical moments, and the forces, events, or authorities that have rendered them problematic; the ways in which debates and strategies concerning the exercise of political power (and pedagogical power) have delineated the proper relations between the activities of political rule and different zones, dimensions, or aspects of this general field of conduct (for example, the ways in which the management of virtue and vice has been contested and divided between theological, pedagogic, medical, and political authorities); the ways in which knowledge, ideas, and beliefs about society, authority, morality, and subjectivity have engendered these problematizations and the emergence of different strategies, tactics, and programs of government (namely in the education field) (Rose 1999: 20–21).

The analysis of educational "knowledge" obliges us to take into consideration the warning of Daniel Hameline (1986): we can say that education is the least understood "thing," the worst understood, precisely because it is assumed to be the most clearly and univesally understood. In fact, all people "know" about education, which invites us to look at the different discourses that circulate in this arena, the ways they interact and conflict, the forms of governing that they carry on. It is not simply a question of identifying different "ideas," but also understanding the rise of expert systems of knowledge: "The power of such expert knowledge is that it is not only knowledge. Ideas function to shape and fashion how we participate as active, responsible individuals" (Popkewitz 1998: 5).

"Memories of Seeing": The Pictorial Turn and the Construction of Educational Histories

> What has been called "the pictorial turn" bids fair to succeed the earlier "linguistic turn" so loudly trumpeted by twentieth-century philosophers. The model of "reading texts," which served productively as the master metaphor for post-objectivist interpretations of many different phenomena, is now giving way to models of spectatorship and visuality, which refuse to be redescribed in entirely linguistic terms. The figural is resisting subsumption under the rubric of discursivity; the image is demanding its own unique mode of analysis. (Jay 1996: 3)

Reflection about images is vast and often inconsistent. The visual, the iconographic, and the pictorial cross with the analysis of images (graphic, mental, verbal) and give rise to symbolic, metaphorical, and conceptual links (among many others). We end up with a mixture of ideas that tend to confuse rather than clarify. What is interesting is to understand the ways in which images in the strict or literal sense are related to notions such as social imagery, or social construction of images, and the concept of society as an image and as a maker of images (Mitchell 1986).

It is impossible to produce any explanation outside a linguistic frame, because images are displayed and interpreted in social, institutional, and political fields that are discursively saturated. But, at the same time, it is necessary to acknowledge the irreducibility of image to text (and vice versa). That is why the linguistic and the discursive have not been "simply replaced by the pictorial and the figural but rather in complicated ways infiltrated by them," and "viewing texts" and "reading pictures" are now chiasmically intertwined (Jay 1996: 3).

After working in the first section of this chapter on the consequences of the *linguistic turn* for the historical research in education, I would like to draw attention to the importance of the *pictorial turn*:

> Whatever the pictorial turn is, it should be clear that it is not a return to a naive mimesis, copy or correspondence theories of representation, or a renewed metaphysics of pictorial "presence": it is rather a postlinguistic, postsemiotic rediscovery of the picture as a complex interplay between visuality, apparatus, institutions, discourse, bodies, and figurality. It is the realization that *spectator-*

ship (the look, the gaze, the glance, the practices of observation, surveillance, and visual pleasure) may be as deep a problem as various forms of *reading* (decipherment, decoding, interpretation, etc.) and that visual experience or "visual literacy" might not be fully explicable on the model of textuality. (Mitchell 1994: 16)

In his remarkable book, *Downcast Eyes*, Martin Jay (1994) explains the denigration of vision in twentieth-century Western thought. The central theme of his argument can be transposed onto the historical debate, as for example in the manifestations of hostility to visual primacy in the work of successive generations of historians. Jay argues that the long tradition of ocularcentric bias—patently obvious in the linkage between lucidity and rationality that gave the Enlightenment its name—culminated in a profound suspicion of vision and its hegemonic role. This idea may seem surprising, but its interpretative consistency is generated precisely from its paradoxical character.

Martin Jay examines the antiocularcentric discourse in detail, defining it as an often unsystematic, sometimes internally contradictory texture of statements, associations, and metaphors that never thoroughly cohere. Hence, we see in Western culture, simultaneously, a hypertrophy of the visual—the modality of the visible is always present, not merely as perceptual experience, but also as a cultural trope—and its denigration.

The construction of a "civilization of the image" from the nineteenth century onwards leads to a general lack of confidence in the value of the image in furthering scientific knowledge. We look at an image as something of lesser value, a reproduction, a poor imitation of reality: "the word *image* is looked upon poorly because we believe a design to be a tracing, a copy, a secondary object, and that the mental image is nothing more than a design of the same mold kept in our private bric-a-brac" (Merleau-Ponty 1964: 23). At the same time, images nourish all kinds of imagination and fantasies, creating the illusion of an open field of meanings and interpretations.

Western thinking wanted to be the inheritor of a unique "truth," denying the plurality of meanings (and readings) of images. It is fundamental to highlight the paradox of a civilization that promotes enormous development in techniques of production, reproduction, and communication of images, yet, at the same time, never lets go of an endemic iconoclasm. The image cannot be reduced to a formal "true" or "false" argument, and so is devalued as a tool of furthering understanding (Durand 1994).

Jonathan Crary explains the history of this process well, demonstrating that the dissociation of touch from sight occurs within a pervasive "separation of the senses" and industrial remapping of the body in the nineteenth century:

This autonomization of sight, occurring in many different domains, was a historical condition for the rebuilding of an observer fitted for the tasks of "spectacular" consumption. Not only did the empirical isolation of vision allow its quantification and homogenization but it also enabled the new objects of vision (whether commodities, photographs, or the act of perception itself) to assume a mystified and abstract identity, sundered from any relationship to the observer's position within a cognitively unified field. (1992: 19)

The achievement of that kind of optical neutrality, the reduction of the observer to a supposedly rudimentary state, was a condition for the formation of a "new" observer: "The visual culture of modernity would coincide with such techniques of the observer" (Crary 1992: 96).

This argument is crucial for the understanding of history and its formation as a nineteenth-century discipline. On one hand, historians fulfill the role of *observers* of past facts, legitimizing their work as an objective exercise that separates the "true" from the "false." The eye of the historian looks to be neutral and exterior, recording only what is there. To achieve this, it is necessary to ignore the historian's very position as observer—that is, the historian's own beliefs, opinions, and ideas—, to pretend that the "grand narrative" of which s/he is the bearer is to be constructed under the register of objectivity and universality. The metaphor of the historian as a *photographer of the past* fits well into this concept. But to achieve this, it is necessary to reduce the photographic image to a mere cliché and believe in a teleology of history.

The historian of the nineteenth century refused to enter into the game of images, into the game of multiple interpretations and of contested narratives. S/he does not accept the polysemy, the plurality of viewpoints. S/he does not look at images as "producers of meanings," but only as mere "register of facts" or a "portrait of reality."

Nowadays this attitude is difficult to sustain. If postmodernism teaches anything—as Martin Jay says—it is to be suspicious of single perspectives that, like grand narratives, provide totalizing accounts of a world too complex to be reduced to a unified point of view. In the case of postmodernism and vision, no monocular, transcendental gaze will do: "postmodernism may be understood as the culminating chapter in a story of the (enucleated) eye. Or rather, it may paradoxically be at once the hypertrophy of the visual, at least in one of its modes, *and* its denigration" (1994: 546). Instead of calling for the exorbitation of "the eye," it is better to encourage the multiplication of a thousand eyes, in what we could designate as a multifaceted dialectics of seeing (Jay 1994: 591).

A good example of this change can be taken from looking at the theoretical issues surrounding the Rodney King incidents. The whole trial of the Los Angeles policemen who assaulted Rodney King was based on the exhaustive viewing of a video that lasted about one minute. Over several months, two distinct and contradictory arguments were constructed, not as a consequence of ignoring the video, but rather of reproducing it within a racially saturated field of visibility. This showed that the visual field is not neutral to the question of race but that, quite the opposite, is itself a racial formation, an episteme, both hegemonic and forceful (Butler 1993: 15–17). The video itself has no evidentiary status, it is not an "objective" proof: "Both the perception of the tape as showing a 'reasonable exercise of force' and the perception of the tape as showing 'racist brutality' depend, not simply on the physiology of visual perception, but rather on *interpretation*, on the mediation of perception with background narratives that give visual images meaning" (Crenshaw and Peller 1993: 66).

In moving from the singular "eye" to the plural "eyes," a change is undertaken from the singular vision of panopticism, with its idea of an objective vision of control through visibility, to the stereoscopic vision of more pluralistic techniques of observation that have emerged in the twentieth century: "These techniques of the observer suggest that perspective can be multiple" (Dumm 1993: 186). This is equivalent to saying that surveillance and spectacle cannot be as clearly separated as someone like Foucault would wish, and that the objectification of the viewed subject is the product of a *discipline* of observation that has its own history as well. As stated by Jonathan Crary, Foucault's opposition of surveillance and spectacle seems to overlook how the effects of these two regimes of power can coincide: "Using Bentham's panopticon as a primary theoretical object, Foucault relentlessly emphasizes the ways in which human subjects became objects of observation, in the form of institutional control or scientific and behavioral study; but he neglects the new forms by which vision itself became a kind of discipline or mode of work" (Crary 1992: 18).

That is why the opposition between "surveillance" and "spectacle," as presented by Michel Foucault, is not accurate for providing a fruitful understanding. The consolidation of a "civilization of the image" in the twentieth century invites us to look at the development of "spectacular surveillance," as well as emerging forms of "surveillant spectacles." On the one hand, surveillance is exercised through an exposure (a surexposure) of images that provokes a visual inflation and the emergence of a "market of the eye." On the other hand, spectacle is submitted to rules of surveillance and control (indicators, standards, rates, etc.) that define its own characteristics on the basis of the consumption of images.

Games of showing and hiding are not different, but include processes that create illusions and suspicions. In this sense, it is interesting to remember the thesis of Pierre Bourdieu: "Image is literally the negative of the presence" (1965: 295). But we cannot forget that images can always be recycled and reused and therefore are open to an infinity of meanings and interpretations. There is no harmony in this "world," but vision and visuality in their rich and contradictory variety "can still provide us mere mortals with insights and perspectives, speculations and observations, enlightenment and illuminations, that even a god might envy" (Jay 1994: 594).

New analysis of images needs to be theoretically grounded, and cannot avoid a sophistication of methods and approaches. The will to look and to show is inseparable from the will to know, and it is necessary to establish a cartography of vision if we wish to apprehend the production/reproduction of images in the field of visuality.

This is what we are confronted with, leading to the need for a theory that allows us to understand that "images are not just a particular kind of sign, but something like an actor on the historical stage, a presence or character endowed with legendary status, a history that parallels and participates in the stories we tell ourselves about our own evolution from creatures 'made in the image' of a creator, to creatures who make themselves and their world in their own image" (Mitchell 1986: 9).

Recently, I was engaged in a research project about public images of teachers (Nóvoa 2000). I have organized an "archive" gathered from different countries, collecting together designs and pictures, cartoons and photographs, engravings and drawings, paintings and book illustrations. I looked for banal everyday images, and considered mainly their expressive dimensions. The purpose was to indicate the importance of this visual source for historians because the caricaturist usually intends to reach a large viewing public and, hence, favors the understanding of relationships: the relationship of the image with the public; the relationship of the public with portrayed situations.

It was not my intention to compare such disparate examples, but this miscellaneous and heterogeneous array constitutes a kind of *metapicture* that was fundamental to my understanding of teachers' images (Mitchell 1994): the images produced, accepted or rejected, returned, negotiated, and transformed by the teachers; the public images displayed (presented, promoted) by the teachers and their organizations; the images with which they feel comfortable or uncomfortable; the images produced by the press, opinionated or humorous; the question of knowing *why* certain images exist, the conditions that lead to their production, and the functions that they carry out.

A glance at the corpus of images collected enabled three general ideas to be put forward. The first illustrates the permanence of the images of teachers that have been transmitted since at least the seventeenth century. Despite all the changes that have taken place, the teachers often appear portrayed in the same way, at least up until the twentieth century. It is true that they are situated in a scene (the class) that is undergoing constant change, in particular with the introduction of simultaneous teaching. However, it is possible to detect the continuation of the same "grammar of schooling": the secondary school teachers often appear associated with their respective school subjects and the function of pupil assessment; the primary school teachers are more marked by the relationship with their pupils, very often with scenes of unusual violence. Through the analysis of the images, it is difficult to identify the ruptures constructed by the historiography of education, established chiefly through the study of texts of the educators and school reform laws.

The second idea signals the production of images at moments of pedagogical renovation, arising from political reforms in education or from the introduction of new teaching methods. In contradiction to a certain common sense
that associates these moments with great upheaval and disorientation, the
images tend to transmit serenity and organization. They function as strategies
of "propaganda" that aim to soothe consciences and suggest a more "radiant"
and "responsible" future. The designs that show the New Education, particularly post–World War I, take this tendency to the limit, eradicating the teacher
from the images: harmony reigns in the classroom, even with the absence of
the teacher. An "absence" that constitutes, needless to say, an extremely strong
presence.

The third is the existence of worldwide images of education that reinforce
the thesis of mass schooling as a "normative principle" and an "organizational
reality" permeating, in different ways, all countries and regions. It is the same
caricatures, the same cartoons that circulate, confirming that education is
probably one of the most powerful worldwide institutions. There is the same
intent and the same relationship between images and teachers (and vice versa),
even if the "picture" appears in a different context and, at times, with evidence
of local artifacts or national icons. Our historical thinking, almost always
embedded with national references, needs to open itself to the worldwide diffusion of the school model, which has been in place a long time, before we
begin to talk about the process of globalization.

The images exist and are part of the configuration process of the teaching
profession. Images of poverty alarm teachers. The ridicule contained in many
caricatures shows them to be also unbearable for society. Images of authority
are more comfortable for teachers and also for the pupil's families. The narratives "mix themselves up" and give rise to new questions. There is a crossing of
autonomous and comparative readings of the text and the images, which mark
here and there the search for knowledge. The images give new forms to the
messages and enable us to bring to light other angles of knowledge. What
interested me with regard to the images of teachers was neither the exotic nor
the exceptional; it was, on the contrary, the banal, the usual, the everyday. Or,
to say it in other words, the way in which images of teachers are subject to an
"alchemy" that is always fabricating "new" teachers' identities.

In sum, I want to underline that the elaboration of a historical approach to
the analysis of images needs to take into account the theoretical issues opened
by the "pictorial turn." A myriad of possibilities can be imagined by historians,
even if we need to be cautious against any dissolution of historical thinking in
"discourse" or in "image." In this sense, as Roger Chartier affirms, "it is
important to vigorously assert that history is commanded by an intention and
a principle of truth, that the past that it has as an object is an exterior reality to
the discourse and that its knowledge can be controlled" (1998: 16). Today it is
difficult to speak in the singular, but even so we must be able to mark the

boundaries of the "acceptable," the "likely," and the "verifiable." Recognizing that history contains a narrative dimension (literary or graphic) does not mean denying the establishment of truth(s), even if provisional and contextualized.

"Remembrance" and "Imagination" in the Historical Writing of Education

The meaning of historical writing has to be found in the light of two movements: on the one hand, the *remembering-imagining* pair that establishes new relations in historical time; on the other hand, the definition of space (although often a virtual space) as an essential reference of historical work. The excess of images gains importance as the excess of memory (and forgetfulness) and the excess of places (and non-places) are revealed. Never before in the history of humankind has there been such a strong sensation that we are the "producers of history." A history that is not the devolution of a unitary past, but a reconstruction of the past in order to propose an intelligibility of people's actions and beliefs. The speed and closeness of news makes us accomplices in a world of "sounds" and "images" in which we include our own "voice" and "portrait." It is of little surprise therefore that our society is impregnated with an excess of meanings or, more precisely, an excessive search for meanings.

This is what defines the "turn" produced by linguistic and pictorial approaches as they have been conceptualized in the previous sections of this chapter. Looking at "texts" and at "images" allow us to transform memory into an object of historical inquiry. If history was constituted as a nineteenth-century discipline through a rupture with memory, nowadays memories (individual and collective) are one of the most important "documents" for historical research (Pomian 1999). Not only as "sources," but mainly as ways of building new understandings of historical time and new emplacements of people in historical space. I am talking about a conception of history that relates, primordially, with the "present," and not with the "past." Or, to put it in other words, "historical time is a realisation of the present" (Lepetit 1999: 277). The reconceptualization of memories and the reframing of space-time relationships are contributing to the writing of new and stimulating historical works.

In a text originally written in 1967, Michel Foucault talks of history as the great discovery of the nineteenth century, adding that the current epoch tends to turn itself to space: "We are in the epoch of simultaneity, in the epoch of juxtaposition, in the epoch of closeness and distance, side by side, of dispersion. . . . Nowadays emplacement substitutes extension that, in turn, had to be substituted by localization" (1994, vol. IV: 752). In this perspective the "mirror" is defined as a utopia (a place without place), but also as a heterotopia: "the mirror becomes the place that I occupy, absolutely real, in connection with the space that surrounds me, and absolutely unreal, given that its perception is only possible by moving to a virtual point that is on the other side" (Foucault 1994, vol. IV: 756).

This quotation allows me to clarify the spatial sense of historical research, in a juxtaposition of times that raise doubts about some deep-rooted convictions of historians. The reference to the *imagined communities* related by Benedict Anderson consolidates this option: "In fact, all communities larger than primordial villages of face-to-face contact (and perhaps even these) are imagined. Communities are to be distinguished not by their falsity/genuineness, but by the style in which they are imagined" (1983: 6). Thus, collective beliefs and convictions are grouped together, merged by conflicting representations and juxtaposed layers of historical times.

This is very important for educational historians, in the sense that we are encouraged to extend the historical inquiry to global and local levels, liberating ourselves from exclusive national explanations. As a matter of fact, theories of globalization contain new explanatory potentialities that need to be joined with national-scale inquiries. Anthony Giddens talks about the dialectic of the local and global, saying that "one of the distinctive features of modernity is an increasing interconnection between the two extremes of extensionality and intentionality: globalizing influences on the one hand and personal dispositions on the other" (1991: 1). But the strongest call for a reconsideration of the "nation" as the main focus of the historical has been made by Benedict Anderson:

> For a fair part of the past two hundred years, narrating the nation seemed, in principle, a straightforward matter. Armies of historians, good and bad, helped by folklorists, sociologists, statisticians, literary critics, archaeologists, and, of course, The State, produced a vast arsenal of work to help existing or future citizens imagine the biography, and the future, of their political communities. There could be every conceivable difference in method, approach, data base, and political viewpoint, but these historians typically understood their texts as *documents of civilization,* or stories of progress, however meandering, because the nation was always, and without much question, regarded as historically factual and as morally good. (1998: 333)

Remembering-Imagining

The relationship between texts, images, and memories needs to be stressed, in as much as both seek a balance between "reproduction" and "construction," between passive surrender to the facts and active reshaping of them into a coherent picture or story. In this sense, it is eventually possible to rephrase and to "complete" the formulation of Hayden White (1999), saying that history is not only an object that we can study, but also the way we study it; it is also and even primarily a certain kind of relationship to the past mediated by a distinctive kind of written or *visual* discourse.

It is interesting to look at the pair "remembering-imagining" (or to the processes of "remembrance" and "imagination") to define the historical writing. A history of the present deals with memories and reminiscences, as well as with prospects and projections. I am thinking in the double definition of "projection": an anticipated course of action (future) that is told *today* and something that portrays a (past) situation being projected *today*. One needs to relate the origin of the so-called civilization of images with the consolidation of a historical thinking and an educational society. These three realities were born and developed in the same time period, as is clearly shown with an attentive analysis of the definitions given in the famous *Buisson Dictionary*, published in France in two main editions (1880–1887 and 1911). You have only to cite, for instance, the excerpt written by one of the emblematic figures of this time, Gabriel Compayré, who defines representative imagination as the faculty to produce images/memories, or the entry written by Georges Dumesnil where he proposes the concept of *imaginative memory*, linking the "field of experience" and the "horizon of expectation." This is what reveals the emergence of a conception of history that, as Michel Foucault explains, breaks from a cyclical vision to adopt a philosophy of progress.

An important reorganization of the observer occurs in this period, originating from new disciplinary techniques of the subject that evolve as a consequence of the fixing of quantitative and statistical *norms* of behavior (Crary 1992). The formation of an *educated subject*, the project that is to be undertaken by pedagogy, one shoulders as a governing of the self, but also as a process of social regulation: "The new patterns of governing in the 19th century, in contrast, focused power on persons in everyday life. Social policy and expert knowledge focused on the regulation of individual self-reflection, self-examination, and consciousness" (Popkewitz 1998: 23). That is to say—as Nikolas Rose puts it—we are inhabitants of regimes that act upon our own conduct in the proclaimed interest of our individual and collective well-being, "we are governed in our own name" (1999: 284).

In the nineteenth century, this triad—images, history and education—is the bearer of a linear conception of time that situates the subjects in a permanent logic of remembering-imagining. The chronological perspective of time is used to build the historical science in a past-present-future sequence. Does this perspective remain useful to us in thinking about historical work at the end of the twentieth century?

Space-Time Relationships

I am convinced that we have to introduce more complex conceptions to historical reflection that will allow us to understand the coexistence of distinct dimensions of time. "History is not a time period, it is a multiplicity of time periods that are linked to and contain each other. It is necessary to substitute the old notion of time with the notion of multiple duration" (Foucault 1994, vol. II: 279). Our discipline cannot fail to take into account the enormous developments that this debate has seen in recent decades. We are witnessing at the end of the century a compression of space and time, with the world within easy reach in an increasingly instantaneous moment time: "The present being dramatized as much as the past seems a cause without effect and the future an effect without cause" (Santos 1998). One of the main tasks of the historian is to make an effort to unfold space and time, opening up vision to new understandings.

Harold Silver (1991) is right when he states that the history of education looks to imagine past alternatives at the same time as it reflects on forms of thinking for the future. It is basically a question of overcoming the gulf between *experience* and *expectation*, conceiving historical research as a constant production of meanings. Or, in other words, as an immense playing field defined by the necessity to produce sound and rigorous statements, and, at the same time, open to an infinity of interpretations. That is why one of my concerns is to identify the ways in which the future is presented in the present.

The question has already been put forward by Reinhart Koselleck, in his work on *The future past*, where he raises as a hypothesis that, in determining the difference between past and future (or between experience and expectation), we create conditions to perceive the *time of history*: "We saw throughout the centuries a time construction of history, that led to this singular form of acceleration that is characteristic of the current world" (1990: 20–21). This comes about as there is past in the present, not only as a "before" and as an "after," but as a "during" that resides in the present of several modes. It does not reside as a "physical action," but as a complexity of memories and projects that builds senses of identity.

Today, we have to think of historical work in the framework of a shattering of traditional conceptions of the space-time relation. Space does not refer, fundamentally, to physical dimensions, but to the multiple occupations that move/relocate our references, affiliations, and identities. A fixed vision of space is contradictory to the "interpretative theories" that attempt to understand the subjective nature of reality and the sense that diverse people give to it. Time is no longer defined as an organized sequence of events, but as an individual or collective appropriation of a set of coordinates that position us in the world. The predominance of "chronology" prevents the opening up of historical research for questions that are not marked by the rigidity of temporary frames.

Adopting a different approach, Zaki Laïdi talks about a collective renegotiation of our relation to space and to time: "a space that is being extended and a time that is being accelerated" (1999: 10). Historians are asked to take into consideration not only "geographical" spaces, but mainly "spaces of meaning" (Laïdi 1998). Historians are placed in a social and conceptual environment where the "instant" (immediateness) is linked with a deeper understanding of the very long duration of origins and universes. In this sense, historical time is also compressed and extended, underlining the limits of our interpretations.

These changes are accompanied by a new vision of the historical object. It is no longer the reconstruction of the past, but precisely the opposite, of understanding the way in which the past is brought to the present, influencing our way of thinking and speaking. Attention is switched to the construction of meanings, to the amalgamation of performances and discursive practices that define a particular knowledge, historically formed, that consecrates certain ways of acting, feeling, speaking, and seeing the world.

I arrive at the end of my reflection, addressing one of the main consequences of the linguistic and pictorial turns for historians and historians of education: to articulate the discursive construction of the social with the social construction of the discourse (Chartier 1998; Hacking 1999). I mean *discourse* in the widest sense of the word, not only in its written or verbal forms. Nowadays everybody knows that it is not the *facts* but the *historians* who dominate the debate. They are tireless producers of coherence and meanings that compose a kind of "fiction" on the basis of "true" elements (Boia 1998). This does not mean that history is only a "fiction-making operation," to use the expression of Hayden White, but—and this *but* is extremely important—that it is dependent on rigorous processes, on consistent proofs, and on adequate conceptualization. The writing of history nears the "literature genre" but does not dissolve, nor does it exhaust itself, in literature. Historians are seekers of a "workable truth" communicable within an "improvable society": "The democratic practice of history here advocated needs a philosophical grounding compatible with its affirmations. We find that grounding in a combination of practical realism and pragmatism, that is, in an epistemological position that claims that people's perceptions of the world have some correspondence with that world and that standards, even though they are historical products, can be made to discriminate between valid and invalid assertions" (Appleby, Hunt, and Jacob 1994: 283).

In *Figural Realism*, Hayden White puts clearly the question of historical emplotments and the problem of "truth." He asserts that narrative accounts do not consist only of factual statements (singular existential propositions) and arguments; they consist as well of poetic and rhetorical elements by which what would otherwise be a mere list of facts is transformed into a story:

> For traditional historical discourse, there is presumed to be a crucial difference between an interpretation of the facts and a story told about them. This difference is indicated by the currency of the notions of a real story (as against a imaginary story) and a true story (as against a false story). . . . Considerations such as these provide some insight into the problems both of competing narratives and of unacceptable modes of emplotment. (1999: 29)

Recognizing this interconnection between different story-meanings and modes of emplotment, historical research needs also to define what kinds of story can be *properly* told. This must be remembered, in a time where history is the object of new public interest. The present calls for a style of investigation that is modest: "It encourages an attention to the humble, the mundane, the little shifts in our ways of thinking and understanding, the small and contingent struggles, tensions and negotiations that give rise to something new and unexpected" (Rose 1999: 11).

The historian's social function is to understand how peoples and communities construct (deconstruct/reconstruct) memories and traditions, affiliations and attachments, beliefs and solidarities. The elucidation of this process of imagining and governing identities is at the center of historical research. Education is also something we imagine. It is something we talk about, something we must talk about. Imagining education is one way of taking control of future events. Memories are part of a whole imaginary that defines our relationship with the past, building up our own way of talking about schools and education.

References

Anderson, B. (1983). *Imagined communities—Reflections on the origin and spread of nationalism*. London: Verso.

———. (1998). *The spectre of comparisons—Nationalism, Southeast Asia and the world*. London: Verso.

Appleby, J., Hunt, L., & Jacob, M. (1994). *Telling the truth about history*. New York: W.W. Norton.

Baczko, B. (1978). *Lumières de l'Utopie*. Paris: Payot.

Boia, L. (1998). Histoire et imaginaire. In J. Thomas (Ed.), *Introduction aux méthodologies de l'imaginaire* (261–64). Paris: Ellipses.

Bourdieu, P. (1965). *Un art moyen: essai sur les usages sociaux de la photographie*. Paris: Les Éditions de Minuit.

Buisson, F. (Ed.). (1880–1887). *Dictionnaire de pédagogie et d'Instruction primaire*. Paris: Librairie Hachette, 4 vols.

———. (Ed.). (1911). *Nouveau dictionnaire de pédagogie et d'Instruction primaire*. Paris: Librairie Hachette.

Burstyn, J. N. (1990). Narrative versus theoretical approaches: A dilemma for historians of women. *History of Education Review* 19(2): 1–7.

Butler, J. (1993). Endangered/Endangering: Schematic racism and white paranoia. In R. Gooding-Williams (Ed.), *Reading Rodney King/Reading urban uprising* (15–22). New York: Routledge.

Canning, K. (1994). Feminist history after the linguistic turn: Historicizing discourse and experience. *Signs—Journal of Women in Culture and Society* 19(2): 368–404.

Charbonnel, N. (1988). *Pour une critique de la raison éducative*. Berne: Peter Lang.

Chartier, R. (1989). Le monde comme représentation. *Annales* 44(6): 1505–1520.

———. (1992). Les historiens et les mythologies. *Liber* 11, 5–8.

———. (1998). *Au bord de la falaise: L'histoire entre certitudes et inquiétude*. Paris: Albin Michel.

Cherryholmes, C. H. (1988). *Power and criticism: Poststructural investigations in education*. New York: Teachers College Press.

Childers, T. (1989). Political sociology and the "linguistic turn." *Central European History* 22(3–4): 381–393.

Cooper, F. (1994). Conflict and connection: Rethinking colonial African history. *American Historical Review* 99(5): 1516–45.

Crary, J. (1992). *Techniques of the observer: On vision and modernity in the nineteenth century.* Cambridge, MA: MIT Press.

Crenshaw, K. and Peller, G. (1993). Reel time/Real justice. In R. Gooding-Williams (Ed.), *Reading Rodney King/Reading urban uprising* (56–70). New York: Routledge.

Depaepe, M. and Simon, F. (1995). Is there any place for the history of "education" in the "History of Education"? A plea for the history of everyday educational reality in and outside schools. *Paedagogica Historica* 31(1): 9–16.

Dumm, T. (1993). The new enclosures: Racism in the normalized community. In R. Gooding-Williams (Ed.), *Reading Rodney King/Reading urban uprising* (178–95). New York: Routledge.

Durand, G. (1994). *L'imaginaire—Essai sur les sciences et la philosophie de l'image.* Paris: Hatier.

Foucault, M. (1972). The archaeology of knowledge and the discourse on language. New York: HarperColophon Books (trans. A. M. Sheridan Smith).

Foucault, M. (1994). *Dits et écrits* (4 vols.). Paris: Gallimard.

Giddens, A. (1991). *Modernity and self-identity.* Cambridge: Polity Press.

Gore, J. M. (1993). *The struggle for pedagogies—Critical and feminist discourses as regimes of truth.* New York and London: Routledge.

Grosvenor, I., Lawn, M., and Rousmaniere, K. (Eds.). (1999). *Silences & images—The social history of the classroom.* New York: Peter Lang.

Hacking, I. (1999). *The social construction of what?* Cambridge, MA: Harvard University Press.

Hameline, D. (1986). *L'éducation, ses images et son propos.* Paris: Éditions ESF.

Harlan, D. (1989). Intellectual history and the return of literature. *The American Historical Review* 94(3): 581–609.

Hiner, N. R. (1990). History of education for the 1990s and beyond: The case for academic imperialism. *History of Education Quarterly* 30(2): 137–60.

hooks, b. (1992). Representing whiteness in the Black imagination. In L. Grossberg, C. Nelson, and P. Treichler (Eds.), *Cultural studies* (338–346). New York and London: Routledge.

Hunt, L. (Ed.). (1989). *The new cultural history.* Berkeley: University of California Press.

Hutton, P. (1991). The Foucault phenomenon and contemporary French historiography. *Historical Reflections/Réflexions Historiques* 17(1): 77–102.

Jay, M. (1991). The textual approach to intellectual history. *Strategies—A journal of theory, culture and politics* 4(5): 7–18.

———. (1994). *Downcast eyes: The denigration of vision in the twentieth-century French thought.* Berkeley: University of California Press.

———. (1996). Vision in context: Reflections and refractions. In T. Brennan and M. Jay (Eds.), *Vision in context: Historical and contemporary perspectives on sight* (1–12). New York: Routledge.

Julia, D. (1995). La culture scolaire comme objet historique. In A. Nóvoa, M. Depaepe, and E. Johanningmeier (Eds.), *The colonial experience in education—Historical issues and perspectives* (353–82). Gent: Paedagogica Historica.

Kincheloe, J. L. (1991). Educational historiographical meta-analysis: Rethinking methodology in the 1990s. *Qualitative Studies in Education* 4(3): 231–45.

Koselleck, R. (1990). *Le futur passé: Contribution à la sémantique des temps historiques*. Paris: Éditions de l'École des Hautes Études en Sciences Sociales.

Leach, M. (1990). Toward writing feminist scholarship into history of education. *Educational Theory* 40(4): 453–61.

Laïdi, Z., (1998). Géopolitque du sens. Paris: Desclée de Brouwer.

——— (1999). La tyrannie de l'urgence. Montreal: Éditions Fides.

Lepetit, B. (1999). *Carnet de Croquis—Sur la connaissance historique*. Paris: Albin Michel.

Licht, W. (1992). Cultural history/social history. *Historical Methods* 25(1): 37–41.

Luke, C. and Gore, J. (Eds.). (1992). *Feminisms and critical pedagogy*. New York and London: Routledge.

Merleau-Ponty, M. (1964). *L'Oeil et l'Esprit*. Paris: Gallimard.

Mitchell, W. J. T. (1986). *Iconology: Image, text, ideology*. Chicago: University of Chicago Press.

———. (1994). *Picture theory: Essays on verbal and visual representation*. Chicago: University of Chicago Press.

Nóvoa, A. (2000). Ways of saying, ways of seeing—Public images of teachers. *Paedagogica Historica*.

Pomian, K. (1999). *Sur l'Histoire*. Paris: Éditions Gallimard.

Popkewitz, T., (1998). *Struggling for the soul: The politics of schooling and the construction of the teacher*. New York: Teachers College Press.

Popkewitz, T. and Brennan, M. (Eds.). (1998). *Foucault's challenge: Discourse, knowledge, and power in education*. New York: Teachers College Press.

Ricoeur, P. (1994). Histoire et rhétorique. *Diogène*, 168, 9–26.

Rose, N. (1996). *Inventing our selves—Psychology, power, and personhood*. Cambridge: Cambridge University Press.

———. (1999). *Powers of freedom: Reframing political thought*. Cambridge: Cambridge University Press.

Santos, B. (1998). No verão com exposcópio. *Visão*. August 13.

Sewell, W. (1990). How classes are made: Critical reflections on E.P. Thompson's theory of working-class formation. In H. J. Kay and K. McClelland (Eds.), *E. P. Thompson: Critical perspectives* (50–77). Philadelphia: Temple University Press.

Silver, H. (1991). Existe un futuro en el pasado? *Revista de Educación* 296: 7–21.

West, C. (1990). The new cultural politics of difference. *October*, 53.

White, H. (1987). *The content of the form—Narrative discourse and historical representation*. Baltimore and London: Johns Hopkins University Press.

———. (1999). *Figural realism: Studies in the mimesis effect*. Baltimore: Johns Hopkins University Press.

3

"A New Cultural History of Education"

A Developmental Perspective on History of Education Research[1]

Heinz-Elmar Tenorth

Around the world, history of education research has undergone a stormy process of development in the last twenty years. There is no question that history of education research has been improved in the process, in terms of the basic structures of its sources, the methods employed, and the selection and application of theories. The international standard of history of education research today, a far cry from what it still was only twenty years ago, not only addresses schools and universities, educational policy and educational reform plans, educational philosophies and the ideas of great thinkers as the range of subjects for investigation, but a whole host of varying themes (Compère 1995; Böhme/Tenorth 1990; Bibliographie Bildungsgeschichte 1995 ff.).

Regarding human life processes, historically inspired and systematically stimulating studies on the history of childhood and youth have been conducted, but there are also examinations of adult learning (albeit more from an institutional perspective). We no longer, for example, unquestioningly think along the lines provided by Philippe Ariès when he taught us to rediscover the history of childhood (Finkelstein 1996; Fend 1988). Furthermore, we are not by any means only concerned with the normative developmental paths of adolescents. Quite the contrary: minorities, excluded individuals and groups, and the disabled are now important themes of history of education research. At the same time, they are understood as the objects and victims of not only pedagogical institutions but of fundamental pedagogical views of humanity and the world (Lane 1984, 1992; Dörner 1969; Kaufmann 1995; Hansen 1998).

Regarding the forms and institutions of socially organized education, there are presently a wealth of studies, utilizing a broad variety of methodologies (descriptive, idea-oriented or quantifying, comparative or idiographic), in which the educational system is investigated, beginning with premodern times, in all of its stages and patterns, not only with respect to the school as such but also pertaining to occupational training or social work. Such approaches have already appeared in individual studies that take a comparative-anthropological approach to those cultures in which education is not yet excluded from the socialization process.

Regarding the themes and effects of socially organized education there is, for example, a broad range of regional and even local comparative work concerning the patterns and possibilities of promoting literacy, the effects of schooling on social status, and the linking of educational opportunity to social status. There are even studies, if only in the early stages, on the effects of general education on self-perception and the construction of life careers among individuals and collective groups. Historical studies, then, can increasingly finely differentiate among the effects, for example, of gender or religious denomination, economic or political framework conditions, in epochal or national typing. Even today, studies are carried out that show the importance of education for the promotion and improvement of cleanliness and the pedagogical machinery of disinfection (Cohen and Depaepe 1996; Sarasin 1996). As has always been true, this recent work is still accompanied by studies on *the ideas and plans, and the intentions and possibilities* of education. Even the old history of ideas has been modernized, however, through the inclusion of new questions, new terminology, and new methods of analyzing ideas and discourses.[2]

Naturally, such processes of innovation always run parallel to developments that then also demand criticism. Above all, it is along the lines of such criticism and alternative constructions that I would like to organize the following discussion. In so doing, I am solely concerned with combining a systematic consideration of the consequences of the postmodern debate for historical educational research with certain programmatic considerations in terms of how the object is to be understood and the theme of historical educational research. The starting point for these considerations is a series of recently published articles dedicated to this same theme. In terms of outlining a program, rather than presenting a detailed discussion, these works call for a "new cultural history of education" as a consequence of their considerations. I am primarily concerned with calling attention to certain—in my view—innovative, but not yet sufficiently heeded developments in the sources, methods, and theories of history of education research, and to discuss them in terms of their efficacy. In this I must ask for forbearance, as I employ as a rule mainly German examples, for they are the ones most familiar to me and will allow me to be critical without any false reserve.

The question of whether the debate over postmodernity can have significance for history of education research was raised in 1996 by the editors of *Paedagogica Historica*—Marc Depaepe in cooperation with Sol Cohen—who immediately published various answers (Paedagogica Historica vol. 2/1996).[3] Both their questions and their answers are organized according to the no-longer new philosophical and time-diagnostic debate over the forms and consequences of so-called postmodernity, as conceived above all in the United

States and France, and carried out worldwide (Popkewitz 1998), but are also connected with the general debate on methods in history (Hardtwig and Wehler 1996; Conrad and Kessel 1998).

Parallel to this discussion, the authors of the *Paedagogica Historica* volume also begin with the observation that the present time of our (pedagogical) modernity is above all characterized by the experience of discrepancy, further accompanied by disappointing diagnoses. The discrepancies between claim and reality, between ambition and possibility, and between theory and practice are characteristic for the experience of education in modernity. The modern education of the human race has not improved morals or contributed to equality, nor has it promoted the shaping of the world according to rational criteria. This experience is a disappointment because the promises of the Enlightenment have so obviously not been kept. It is difficult to speak of the "advanced formation of mankind." There is little cause to believe in pedagogy's concrete promise of contributing to making people more moral and civilized, and the general pedagogical idea of modernity, that humans only really become human through education, inspires little confidence in the face of developments since the Enlightenment. Instead of educated, wise, morally behaving individuals, the history of modernity has—at best—given rise to ambivalences. At worst, but not rarely, it has in other cases produced totalitarian monsters, willing executioners, uncritical fellow travelers—as one can summarize from the comments of Cohen and Depaepe.

For the historian of education, this discussion is not only significant in that the great metanarratives, above all the tradition of the Enlightenment, have lost their order-endowing power, but rather in that the concrete, detailed narratives such as the pedagogical history of the construction of maturity lose even their validity, in any case their self-evidentiality. In terms of ideal type (most significantly developed in the writings of U.S. metahistorian Hayden White, known for having strongly accentuated the nearness of historical research to literary narrative, especially the novel, and making the aspect of the form of historical narrative into a central term of metahistorical analyses [White 1973, 1987, 1991; Lenzen 1993]), not only the plea for methodological self-reflection, but also for skepticism and objective detachment regarding old claims of history of education research now also governs, therefore, in the preliminary remarks and some of the contributions to this issue, such as that of Roy Lowe or Agostín Escolano (Lowe 1996; Escolano 1996).

Other authors, likewise, consistently demand an ironic attitude (Richardson 1996; Cohen and Depaepe 1996: 304), and stronger detachment regarding the principles of form according to which educational historians previously organized their narratives for history of education research. Sol Cohen himself, for example, opts for the use of sequences and symbiotically open linking ("both–and") instead of the application of dichotomies ("either–or"), thus rejecting the old pairings (e.g., progressive vs. traditional). The debate over historiographic narrative patterns, metaphors, and ordering principles, only just begun, can then further nourish itself on this source—itself a metaphor! (de Haan 1993)

Of course, if one looks at the consequences that come with a paraphrase of the general postmodern diagnoses for history of education work, then, along with attention to the aspect of the form of historical analysis—which is directly plausible and important—totally concrete demands on history of education work again do indeed dominate (Lenzen 1993; Tenorth 1993). They are in no way resolved in a plea for the novel or the fiction. The criticism and the new sensibility for the constructive character of all research, rather, translates into the expectation that history of education will be empirically and theoretically, historical-comparatively, and casuistically reorganized in new ways, but will not itself be destroyed. Cohen and Depaepe, for their part, see the developmental trend toward a "new cultural history of education," then, in close connection to the development of the historical disciplines themselves, stimulated in reaction to the older, no longer modern social history from the United States and taken up intensively in the other western sciences (Böhme and Tenorth 1990: 117 ff.; Hardtwig and Wehler 1996; Conrad and Kessel 1998; Welskopp 1998).

In the results, therefore, it is also visible that the general premises—philosophical, political, theoretical, social—as they are currently (and today already obsoletely?) included in the postmodern discourse (and previously affected other metadebates),[4] could in fact be stimulating for history of education research, except for the fact that they do not at the same time inspire or direct new studies concretely enough. My falling back upon concrete innovations in the basic structures of sources, methods, and theories of history of education research is, therefore, also based upon and motivated by such experiences. It is only in the practice of history of education research that its progress can occur, not simply in the ideology and program of the research. My central question, therefore, is what can be understood by the "new cultural history of education" that Cohen and Depaepe see as the outcome of the postmodern debate— without themselves revealing this "new cultural history of education." My answer to this question is oriented in part, in terms of program and criticism, on earlier German attempts at "cultural history." On the other hand, my approach focuses on more recent publications that take images and pictures as sources for historical educational research. While the German tradition can demonstrate the variety as well as the risks of "cultural history," studies of pedagogical iconography enable a view at the specific subject matter of historical educational research. They begin to reveal the contours, then, of the unique character of "pedagogical culture."

Clarifying the usefulness of "cultural history" must begin with confronting the meaning of the term "culture" itself. Therefore, it is no secret that the term "culture" (Williams 1958; Daniel 1993; Bruch et al. 1989)[5] and, correspondingly, that of "cultural history," are only seldom precisely defined and are applied very broadly, almost diffusely. Opposing terms such as "culture" on the one hand and "society" on the other may be close to one another in explanatory intent, but they prove to be insufficient at the very least when one takes into consideration other oppositions that are similarly applied. These may include "life world" (Lebenswelt) versus "culture," for example, or culture as life world, or the opposition of subject history and everyday history, as patterns of cultural history to be set up against the system histories and social histories (Mergel 1996; Gilcher-Holtey 1996; Sarasin 1996; Raphael 1996).

The situation becomes completely muddled when the already practiced or previously spread forms of "cultural history" are brought into the explanation. In Germany, according to Hardtwig and Wehler, "the term cultural history" still has "a pejorative aftertaste."

> On the one hand, one associates it with the second-hand form of a cultural history, as it was mostly kept on the margin or totally uncoupled from professionalized science or the study of history in the nineteenth and twentieth centuries. On the other hand, it is connected to holistic outlines of an oppositional historical science, not theoretically and conceptually far afield, to which a certain impulse-giving function is not disputed, but which do not allow any explicit linkage. (Karl Lamprecht, Kurt Breysig) (Hardtwig and Wehler 1996: 7)

If these general comments concerning the tradition of cultural history are applied to pedagogical historiography, a range of varying precursors come to light. In the context of so-called humanities or "cultural pedagogy," a "true cultural history" is explained as the methodologically and theoretically desirable alternative to the old historiography of pedagogy (Spranger 1920/1925).[6] The main theme of this was, for example, according to Eduard Spranger in 1920—in astonishing anticipation of recent personal life–oriented research— the attempt to pursue "the actual results of historical educational systems on the lives of the generations they educated. How successful did the pietistically, the philanthropically, the romantically raised and trained generation prove to be in cultural work?" Spranger also considered a "history of family education" as one of the themes and tasks of this "cultural history," even a "history of the child." It had yet to be written, but would promise "the most interesting results for cultural history as a whole" (Spranger 1920/1925: 155).[7]

While Spranger took up themes and the formulation of questions which absolutely had topical relevance and could stand alongside the great exemplary models of the early twentieth century (Huizinga 1919/1987; Berg 1960), the practice of writing cultural history in pedagogy was much less creative. Here, it was not questions of social history or the history of effects that dominated, but work categorized under the very conventional heading of "high culture." As an example, Michael Elzer, who interpreted "educational history as cultural history," sees culture as the scholarly tradition of education, the school, and universities and the pedagogical ideas and programs (Elzer 1965, 1967). Elzer's main focus is to show "the historical and societal potential of the intellect"; his "cultural history," therefore, is a history of pedagogical ideas and pedagogical self-understanding in its own, autonomous history. This approach almost completely ignores social structures and political references; not even the history of schooling is comprehensively present (Engelbrecht 1982–1988; Fertig 1984).[8] To again take up this model of cultural history today would be a step backward from the current state of theories and methods in pedagogical historiography.

But what does the specific approach of cultural history consist of, if Spranger's definition encompasses the history of childhood and family as much as biographies and the history of the effects of institutions? Of course, Hardtwig and Wehler, who deal with this theme in the realm of the historical sciences, do not primarily contribute to the clarification of the term (and this is quite intentional), but make clear the weaknesses of a precise definition. They use the term to cover quite varying approaches in recent historiography, from historical anthropology and the history of mentalities (in the French tradition) to intellectual and everyday history. Cultural history is essentially understood in opposition to a social history that is concerned with systems and functions, society, economy, and institutions and that (in terms of methodology) relies on the use of quantification. Instead of a new, unified theoretical conceptualization, much less a new method, this version of cultural history is nearer to the "dense descriptions" of ethnologists in the mode of Clifford Geertz (Geertz 1987; Sahlins 1981). Interaction with ethnology, anthropological research, and the humanities—as important as it might have been—may have provided the critical impulse and the role model for other work, but has encouraged unity as little as it has supported the recourse to the linguistic constitution of the world, visible in the historian's "linguistic turn," as the central piece of data of historical reconstruction (Jelavich 1993). Overall, a clarity regarding the term "cultural history" still does not exist today, not even through such dichotomizing or opposition to social history—such dichotomizing itself being a relapse. Pedagogical historiography in Germany does have the older traditions of cultural history, but is hardly able to directly utilize them for updating its own theoretical program.

In view of this unclear theoretical situation, I do not begin with a definition but with the practice of educational research. Beginning with examples of a new "cultural history–based" utilization of sources, methods, and theories, I seek to show what appears to me to be the typical aspects of this approach to the history of education. As my starting point, I refer to new sources: pictures. This is because, in a particularly significant way, pictures allow me to show the meaning and significance the term "culture" can—and perhaps has to—gain in the area of education.

Regarding pictures, it is of significance for the German discussion that Klaus Mollenhauer, whose background is in the traditions of the humanities, already pointed out for the first time in the early 1980s the "forgotten contexts," which occupied his attention intensely from that point until his death (Mollenhauer 1980, 1983; articles in Herrlitz and Rittelmeyer 1993). Mollenhauer's central, guiding concept is "culture," clearly confined or made precise at the level of higher culture.[9] He renews, then, the claim of classical educational theory, working from the subject and the subject's capacity for being depicted in pictures outward. He attempts to show how the subject educates pictures itself, and which caesura in European history are to be observed in this respect.

The sources that Mollenhauer employed for this are pictures, paintings from the high culture of Western art. They are first and foremost—for the discussion of human history caesura—pictures from the Renaissance. Mollenhauer's comrades-in-arms interpret the formulation of the questions similarly, starting from comparable sources. In the context of the construction of identity, Rembrandt's self-portraits (Michael Parmentier) or the self-portraits by Cézanne (Gottfried Boehm), Philipp Otto Runge's pictures of children (Konrad Wünsche) are studied alongside Jean Baptiste Chardin; even Otto Dix remains scarce (Dieter Lenzen; all in Herrlitz and Rittelmeyer 1993; Parmentier 1997).

One could, then, assume that such pictures in fact expand the sources utilized in the history of education. At the same time, however, they restrict the sources to high culture, primarily to the category of *Bildung,* and even further to such large themes as the construction of identity. They reach out to the epochal caesura of Western cultural history, but still primarily reinstate limits and restrictions. Some of these works may appear to do just this, and then question whether the "historian and the picture," as formulated in a renowned study by Francis Haskell, actually succeed in cooperating (Haskell 1995; Hardtwig 1998).

An answer to this question can only be found, of course, if one can clarify the precise source value that "the pictures" convey, in general and with respect to the history of education. Historians incline toward taking pictures predominantly as illustrations for what the texts have already told them. They read them as a confirmation, then, of what they find in sources that are trustworthy. But then one could also dispense with the pictures. Art historians, on the other hand, always seek new pictures and teach how to understand them. They have shown us, by way of contrast, that the old idea of the educated classes "that art is the best seismograph for the condition a society is in," that it "uncovers hidden truths better than the speculative and than scientific reason . . ." (Hardtwig 1998: 305, 316 f., 320), is in no way a mistaken belief.

One must simply learn to see the truth, as in the example of the iconographical method as it has been developed by Erwin Panofsky (Mietzner and Pilarczyk 1998; Talkenberger 1997: 11–26), among others, in order to understand the significance of pictures for decoding a culture. The historian can then learn that the tradition of the fine arts is not in fact a "document" in the usual sense, but an "invention" that transports, however, res fictae its own truth, the history of imaginations of reality, of "dreams, illusions, imaginations" (Hardtwig 1998: 321). If these sources achieve little, then they can at least guide the historian to achieve detachment to the routine processes of science ... to the thought and linkage imperatives of research that is more professional, but thereby also fixed to certain *Denktopoi* ... finally, "to achieve detachment to the value horizons and thought horizons of the particular present in general." Great art, clearly, should at least be capable of this!

The provocative—and productive—fact is now that the development of history of education work no longer restricts the extension of its source basis from including the pictures of high art, but takes into view the whole of graphic, figurative tradition. These include chalkboard drawings in the school, holy pictures in the church, pictures in Enlightenment writings, photographs, the emblems of the premodern era, as well as children's drawings or caricatures. At the same time, the term "culture" also gains comprehensive significance as the designation of a practice in which growing up occurs, which is accompanied by pedagogists, and which simultaneously demonstrates and reflexively organizes itself in its own practice.

With the profitable yield of such an expansion of sources, the interpretation problems that a new class of sources create in a methodological sense, of course, increase proportionally. It is no wonder, then, that a relevant reconsideration of methodology has already begun to occur not only among historians but also within the history of education discussion in Germany (Schmitt et al. 1997). Along with case studies on the utilization of various graphic forms as sources, the methodical problem of the interpretation of pictorial sources has been discussed extensively. Within this context, it is fitting that the 1998 International Standing Conference for the History of Education (ISCHE) organized their conference around the theme "Imagine, all the education ... ,"[10] pushing the image into the center of their considerations. Incidentally, it confirms the value of this source that we had no trouble arranging a relevant symposium in Berlin in which ethnologists, historians, photographers, art historians, museum experts, and educationalists could gather at one table and connect ideas on an iconography of pedagogy with an intensive discussion of the possibilities of a visual anthropology (Tenorth 1997).

What do pictures and images reveal to the historian of education, and which methods are to be applied? Quite simply, pictures deliver information on various levels (Tenorth 1997; Mietzner et al. 1996),[11] from the superficial all the way to the deeper structures of an image. These levels can then be understood as layers of pedagogical practice itself. For this practice, as well, encompasses a variety of meaning dimensions, forms, and structures. The presence of varying levels requires, then, a variety of theoretical means and interpretations for adequately understanding them and their contexts.

One could call the first level "realities studies," for it refers to the real objects depicted in a certain picture (such as rooms, people, and materials). These objects can be analyzed in their communicating power for the epochs and the particular picture-context—if one understands the realities and the contexts, the superficial pedagogical worlds, or learns to understand them with the help of the picture (an act that itself takes historical research for granted). The next level no longer concerns only that which is depicted but the quality, the uniqueness of the depiction itself—the style and the form, the historical shapes of education and their regulations and institutionalization, but also an image's symbolism, which can also be read as the counterbalance of a meaning-oriented practice. Based on the iconographic methods developed by Panofsky and the sources typical for these methods, at first the business of the art historian and his experience in the classification of contexts, symbols, meanings, and questions of form and style govern here. These investigations can be connected with studies on the functions—sociohistorical, political, religious—of pictures and symbols, and to further interpret these functions in the context of different theories, from semiotics to psychoanalysis. It then becomes possible to discuss the text and subtext, the surface and the deeper structure of a picture and its message. Reception analyses can, finally, help to examine the assumptions concerning context and function, as well as the overall effect of the picture.

What can be learned from such pictures for the history of education? First of all, one does learn to be careful in interpreting, for nothing is more seductive than the appearance of the image and of the authentic. Even a photograph, supposedly the result of a mechanical and chemical process, is a construction. It is not a flat depiction or document, but includes a perspective by its anticipated use, and is structured by ordinary or latently available ways of seeing. Therefore, photographs reflect first and foremost the socially accepted images of education[12] and only secondarily the interests of photographers—between state and autonomous youth culture, for example—and the expectations of the client or customer. Nevertheless, images simultaneously transport messages about the historical contours, the process of change and the resistance of the pedagogical and of the subjects in the face of the pedagogical, as do photos, even ordinary pictures of the lay public (and along with realities studies and the perspectives of the photographers).

The particular achievement of photographs as sources, as opposed to text, for example, appears to consist of the fact that they do present constructions and interpretations of reality. These constructions, furthermore, simultaneously preserve the intended and the unintended, the accidental alongside the planned and staged. They pass along the unreflected reality, the unrecognized or not yet problematized angle on a phenomenon—along with the behavior, even the suffering of the object viewed—that becomes the subject of the photographic operation and of the documenting look. In Berlin, we ourselves have learned something about the "inertia of the pedagogical form"—above all for the history of education under the conditions of dictatorship—and about its self-logic in the face of changing political or institutional conditions, about the relative independence of the form versus the intention, and about the differences between what appear to be the same—for example, about the variation in practices of indoctrination that can (but do not necessarily) exist between a national-socialist and a state-socialist banner.

Today, the gradually emerging iconography of the pedagogical thus leads first and foremost to questions that one cannot yet precisely answer, such as how historical-anthropological patterns and tenses of change in pedagogical communication react to patterns and tenses that show to advantage the pedagogical profession or policy, schools or parental homes, the classroom or the peer age group. The stability and dynamics of pedagogical relationships, a hypothesis that must at least be examined according to the results that are only now available, clearly follow tenses other than politics or economics (Siegenthaler 1993). Pedagogical patterns of time are apparently also less dynamic, and therefore "slower" than other patterns of social change. They are also apparently more dependent on internal as well as external factors, as we once thought in times in which the assumption reigned quite unquestioned that the dynamics of education were already sufficiently encompassed by the term "politicization." Not that the photos denied the role of politics, but that they also relativize them where no relativization was expected, and also there where the texts, still suggest uninterrupted politicization. This is characteristic of their independent source value. Pictures and images do indeed unmistakably show, in the dimensions or "layers" in which they represent their reality, the time of their creation. However, interpreting them in series, and over long periods of time, they show just as well the self-logic of the pedagogical form and the persistence of the practice in which humans are raised and educate themselves by dealing with the world around them.

Does the "cultural history of education" have anything to do with "culture"? It is very likely, but only if one understands the educational relationships themselves as a particular kind of culture, neither dissolving them into high culture nor confusing them with the everyday experiences of children, youth and professional pedagogists. While the first may occasionally be committed in the form of art history-oriented observation, those historians who are primarily inspired by the narratives of the actors tend to view the stories told and the world reflected in them as the complete truth. But the narratives which historians demand of their subjects, concerning their world or their memories, inherently and simultaneously interpreting as subject-oriented, are themselves constructions which require correction. For example, pictures may depict the incidental along with the historical perspective, seeming to accidentally record the apparently meaningless.

Another way of seeing, one that is compatible with the discrepancy between intention and form, between memory and description, and between subjective construction and structural determination—a view, in other words, which sees reality as culture to the extent that it understands it as generated-generating practice—the fruits of such a perspective can be studied if one uses pictures. One turns from one's own dominant, self-evident way of seeing and at least occasionally ascertains a view from outside educational relationships, the kind that ethnologists are accustomed to. They have a term for culture, which—very generally—doesn't have as its origin the mechanisms and products but primarily the practice and the cultural production. At the same time, however—in contrast to the functionalist and Marxist reduction of practice—this view understands production not economically but culturally and intentionally, is directed from the subject outward. This is to say that it is seen as a practice which is simultaneously the subject of a structural assumption and the result of the subject's own activity (Sahlins 1981; Bourdieu 1997). A short formula for this reality and its function for humans, then, is that it represents a "self-spun fabric of meanings" in which the human is "entangled" and entangles him and herself (Geertz 1987).

What can the historian of education learn about such fragile words by trusting the texts written by ethnologists over such realities? Stated generally, the educational historian makes sure of the "logic" of pedagogy without reducing it to the intention of the pedagogists or identifying it with the structure of the institution or equating it with the sorrows of the subjects. An excellent example of a related study was recently produced by the sociologist Herbert Kalthoff in an investigation of life in boarding schools; analogous studies can be found in Anglo-Saxon work on school practice (Kalthoff 1995, 1997).

It is decisive for these studies that they make the self-evident conditions that we mostly assume without discussion in the analysis of the pedagogy of institutions (or only critically deny, if we apparently ideology-critically expose them as secret agendas and believe we can do away with them) understandable, even treating them as preconditions and results of the institutional interaction. These conditions include the forming of space (Yamana 1996) and time, the processing of materials, patterns of communication, the logic of assessment, and, as a consequence, the construction of the self through participation in the construction of a societally molded form of pedagogical reality, beyond the apparent dichotomy of self-regulation and other-regulation, embedded in a precise mechanism of the pedagogical construction of the world and of humans that is so effective because it encompasses and signifies in the same manner socialization and self-socialization. The practice of pedagogy—as one could articulate by way of Pierre Bourdieu's theory—is then understood as a symbolically constituted and subjectively produced reality that creates the subjects in that the subjects reproduce it. Not only is the structure of the society and the effect of the institution visible in the disposition of the actors, then, but the activity of the subject him and herself, which reproduces such structures in that they reproduce them as subjects and simultaneously assert themselves in their autonomy—if also beyond all subject-theoretical emphasis.

Does anything remain, then, of the pedagogical intentions and the old claim to autonomy in the face of the sober, sometimes even cold view of the observer? Yes, and stronger than before, for that is what the concept of culture was to show, that the educational reality we are dealing with is only adequately grasped as a culture in the ethnological sense. From the perspective of German tradition, then, I recall that one such hypothesis was also the starting point of humanistic pedagogy—however, this is not important to this discussion.

In the face of the expectations that we all connect with the new cultural history of education, I would prefer to say that here, in this field, the new productive tasks await (without making studies in the context of "society" or "economics," oriented on "structures" or "systems" superfluous). We should learn to understand the reality of education and the reflection that accompanies it as a culture that obeys its own laws, generates its own effects, settles in its own sources, and the analysis of that requires its own particular methods. Contrary to what the (monopolizing) structural term suggests, intentions are of importance for this. Contrary to what the history of ideas assumes, they are, of course, embedded in the logic of a form that achieves its own inertia precisely by virtue of the fact that the subjects actively acquire them and thereby transform as well as confirms them. If one, as a historian, relies on texts alone, on the standard sources of our work as if they were laws and regulations, or only follows the narratives that the actors themselves pass on, one fails to see this reality. This reality is also not found in the objective results of educational practice, which document serial data such as lists of pupils or graduates, and descriptions of social statistics or financial flows. The educational historian also requires the pictures, the images that are authentic constructions and at the same time "solidified intentions" and embodied pedagogy, for the analysis of educational reality. The search is, then, not for the culture in general but the culture of the pedagogical as a particular kind of culture.

I don't know whether the new cultural history of education can already be what I expect of it. I don't know whether Sol Cohen and Marc Depaepe will agree with my comments on their *Programmwort*. I do know that it would be worthwhile to work on these themes, and this is what I intended to verify with this discussion.

Notes

1. An earlier version of this paper was presented as a lecture in Budapest, June 2, 1998 Translated from the German by Michael Halverson, Humboldt-University, Berlin.
2. For this reason, the Deutsche Forschungsgemeinschaft [German Research Association] also sponsors a focus program "Neue Geistesgeschichte" [New Intellectual History]

3. Compare Cohen/Depaepe's introduction in vol 2/1996 of Paedagogica Historica, as well as the contributions by Lowe, Escolano, Tenorth, Richardson, Cohen and Depaepe/Simon.
4. In Germany, for example, the renewal of history of education research at the end of the 1960s and beginning of the 1970s was clearly fed on the criticism of German historicism, the inspirations of critical theory and the epistemology of critical rationalism (Compare the contributions in Böhm/Schriewer 1975).
5. Oexle (1989) also sees here, around 1900, the premises which are to be taken up in order to clarify the concept of cultural history and to take leave of the humanities and its main terminology, such as "spirit" and "life"
6. Spranger criticizes a writing of pedagogical history which is content to collect "only the peculiar opinions of dead authors and school regulations of the past" (1925: 154).
7. To the best of my knowledge, the "social history of the child" which Spranger awaited from his colleague at Leipzig, Ernst Schultze, was never completed.
8. Helmut Engelbrecht's monumental study (1982–1988) takes as a starting point when using the term "culture" With Ludwig Fertig (1984), "culture and social history" are to be connected, but in his conclusions the author follows rather a "museum-padagogical" approach (IX), an analysis more along the lines of important details rather than cultural or social theory.
9. In Herrlitz and Rittelmeyer 1993 (in the contribution from Christian Marzahn), one also finds an indice for the inflating of the term culture: "Drogen-Kultur als Bildung des Geschmacks" [Drug Culture as the Training of Taste]—which hints that culture linked with random contexts degenerates to a decorative epithet for all and everything
10. XXth Session of the International Standing Conference for the History of Education, 15 to 18 August 1998, Katholieke Universiteie Leuven, Belgium
11. My sorting of the levels follows, on the one hand, the comments in Talkenberger 1997: 11–26, and, on the other hand, the methods-oriented work in our own research project "Umgang mit Indoktrination" [Dealing with Indoctrination], in which we especially use photographs as sources (Mietzner, Pilarczyk, Tenorth, and Wünsche 1996).
12. Cohen and Depaepe 1996 show this very well based on films, especially "Dead Poet's Society."

References

Berg, J. H. (1960). *Metabletica. Über die Wandlung des Menschen. Grundlinien einer historischen Psychologie.* Göttingen: Vandenhoeck und Ruprecht.

Bibliographie Bildungsgeschichte. (1996–3/1998). *Ed. Deutsches Institut für internationale pädagogische Forschung.* Baltmannsweiler: Schneider Verlag Hohengeeren.

Böhm, W., and Schriewer, J. (Eds.). (1975). *Geschichte der Pädagogik und systematische Erziehungswissenschaft.* Stuttgart: Klett-Cotta.

Böhme, G., and Tenorth, H.-E. (1990). *Einführung in die Historische Pädagogik.* Darmstadt: Wissenschaftliche Buchgesellschaft.

Bourdieu, P. (1997). *Praktische Vernunft. Zur Theorie des Handelns.* Frankfurt a.M.: Suhrkamp.

Brinkmann, W. and Renner, K. (Eds.). (1982). *Die Pädagogik und ihre Bereiche.* Paderborn: Schöningh.

Bruch, R., Graf, F. W. and Hübinger, G. (Eds.). (1989). *Kultur und Kulturwissenschaften um 1900. Krise der Moderne und Glaube an die Wissenschaft.* Wiesbaden: Franz Steiner Verlag.

Cohen, S., and Depaepe, M. (1996). History of Education in the Postmodern Era. *Paedagogica Historica* XXXII(2): 301–450.

Compère, M.-M. (1995). *L 'histoire de l'éducation en europe*. Bern u.a.: Peter Lang.

Conrad, C., and Kessel, M. (Eds.). (1998). *Kultur and Geschichte. Neue Einblicke in eine alte Beziehung*. Stuttgart: Klett-Cotta.

Daniel, U. (1993). "Kultur" und "Gesellschaft": Überlegungen zum Gegenstandsbereich der Sozialgeschichte. *Geschichte und Gesellschaft* 19: 69–99.

de Haan, G. (1993). Vom Gedächtnis zur Historiographie: Die vielen Geschichten über die DDR-Pädagogik. *Lenzen*: 133–64.

Dörner, K. (1969). *Bürger und Irre. Zur Sozialgeschichte und Wissenschaftssoziologie der Psychiatrie*. Frankfurt a.M.: Europäische Verlagsanstalt.

Elzer, H.-M. (1965, 1967). *Bildungsgeschichte als Kulturgeschichte. Eine Einführung in die historische Pädagogik. Vol. I: Von der Antike bis zur Renaissance. Vol. 2: Von der Renaissance bis zum Ende der Aufklärung*. Ratingen: Henn.

Engelbrecht, H. (1982–1988). *Geschichte des österreichischen Bildungswesens. Von den Anfängen bis zur Gegenwart* (5 vols). Wien: Deuticke.

Escolano, A. (1996). Postmodernity or high modernity? Emerging approaches in the new history of education. *Paedagogica Historica* XXXII(2): 325–42.

Fend, H. (1988). *Sozialgeschichte des Aufwachsens*. Frankfurt a.M.: Suhrkamp.

Fertig, L. (1984). *Zeitgeist und Erziehungskunst*. Darmstadt: Wissenschaftliche Buchgesellschaft.

Finkelstein, B. (1996). Revealing childhood, adolescence, and youth in the history of education: Approaches in the 1990s. *Paedagogica Historica* XXXII(2): 453–74.

Geertz, C. (1987). *Dichte Beschreibung. Beiträge zum Verstehen kultureller Systeme*. Frankfurt a.M.: Suhrkamp.

Gilcher-Holtey, I. (1996). Kulturelle und symbolische Praktiken: das Unternehmen Pierre Bourdieu. In Hardtwig, W. and Wehler, H.-U. (Eds.), *Kulturgeschichte heute* (111–30). Göttingen: Vandenhoeck und Ruprecht.

Hansen, L. A. (1998). Metaphors of the mind and society: The origins of German psychiatry in the revolutionary era. *Isis* 89: 387–409.

Hardtwig, W. (1998). Der Historiker und die Bilder. Überlegungen zu Francis Haskell. *Geschichte und Gesellschaft* 24: 305–22.

Hardtwig, W. and Wehler, H.-U. (Eds.). (1996). *Kulturgeschichte heute*. Göttingen: Vandenhoeck und Ruprecht.

Haskell, F. (1995). *Die Geschichte und ihre Bilder*. München: Beck.

Herrlitz, H.-G. and Rittelmeyer, C. (Eds.). (1993). *Exakte Phantasie. Pädagogische Erkundungen bildender Wirkungen in Kunst und Kultur*. Weinheim and München: Juventa.

Huizinga, J. (1919/1987). *Herbst des Mittelalters. Studien über Lebens—und Geistesforen des 14. und 15. Jahrhunderts in Frankreich und den Niederlanden*. Stuttgart: Kroener.

Jelavich, P. (1993). Poststrukturalismus und Sozialgeschichte—aus amerikanischer Perspektive. *Geschichte und Gesellschaft* 19: 259–89.

Kaemmerling, E. (Hrsg.). (1979). *Bildende Kunst als Zeichensystem*. Köln: DuMont Taschenbuch.

Kalthoff, H. (1995). Die Erzeugung von Wissen. Zur Fabrikation von Antworten im Schulunterricht. *Zeitschrift für Pädagogik* 41: 925–39.

———. (1997). *Wohlerzogenheit. Eine Ethnographie deutscher Internatsschulen*. Frankfurt a.M.: Campus.

Kaufmann, D. (1995). *Aufklärung, bürgerliche Selbsterfahrung und die "Erfindung" der Psychiatrie in Deutschland, 1770–1850*. Göttingen: Vandenhoeck und Ruprecht.

Lane, H. (1984). *When the mind hears: A history of the deaf*. New York: Knopf.

———. (1992). *The mask of benevolence: Disabling the deaf community*. New York: Knopf.

Lenzen, D. (Ed.). (1993). *Pädagogik und Geschichte*. Weinheim: Deutscher Studienverlag.

Lowe, R. (1996). Postmodernity and historians of education: A view from Britain. *Paedagogica Historica* XXXII(2): 307–24.

Marzahn, C. (1993). Drogen-Kultur als Bildung des Geschmacks. In Herrlitz, H.-G. and Rittelmeyer, C. (Eds.), *Exakte Phantasie. Pädagogische Erkundungen bildender Wirkungen in Kunst und Kultur* (69–82). Weinheim and München: Juventa.

Mergel, T. (1996). Kulturgeschichte—die neue "große Erzählung"? In Hardtwig, W. and Wehler, H.-U. (Eds.), *Kulturgeschichte heute* (41–77). Göttingen: Vandenhoeck und Ruprecht.

Mietzner, U., Pilarczyk, U., Tenorth, H.-E., and Wünsche, K. (1996). Umgang mit Indoktrination: Erziehungsintentionen, -formen und - wirkungen in deutschen "Erziehungsstaaten." In D. Benner, H. Merkens, and F. Schmidt (Eds.), *Bildung und Schule im Transformationsprozeß von SBZ, DDR und neuen Ländern* (11–32). Berlin: Freie Universität and Institut für Allgemeine Pädagogik.

Mietzner, U. and Pilarczyk, U. (1998). Die Bildungsbewegung im Medium Fotografie. In S. Hellekamps (Ed.), *Ästhetik und Bildung* (129–44). Weinheim: Deutscher Studienverlag.

Mollenhauer, K. (1980). Streifzug durch fremdes Terrain: Interpretation eines Bildes aus dem Quattrocento in bildungshistorischer Absicht. *Zeitschrift für Pädagogik*, 30: 173–94.

———. (1983). *Vergessene Zusammenhänge. Über Kultur und Erziehung* (2nd ed.). Weinheim and München: Juventa.

Oexle, O. G. (1996). Geschichte als historische Kulturwissenschaft. In Hardtwig, W. and Wehler, H.-U. (Eds.), *Kulturgeschichte heute* (14–40). Göttingen: Vandenhoeck und Ruprecht.

Parmentier, M. (1997). Das gemalte Ich. Über die Selbstbilder von Rembrandt. *Zeitschrift für Pädagogik*, 43: 721–38.

Popkewitz, T. (1988). US-amerikanische Erziehungswissenschaft und die Normierung sozialer Untersuchungen: Postmoderne Diskurse und das Konstrukt des Neuen Lehrers. In A. M. Stroß and F. Thiel (Eds.), *Erziehungswissenschaft, Nachbardisziplinen und Öffentlichkeit* (253–77). Weinheim: Deutscher Studienverlag.

Raphael, L. (1996). Diskurse, Lebenswelten und Felder. Implizite Vorannahmen über das soziale Handeln von Kulturproduzenten im 19. Und 20. Jahrhundert. In Hardtwig, W. and Wehler, H.-U. (Eds.), *Kulturgeschichte heute* (165–88). Göttingen: Vandenhoeck und Ruprecht.

Richardson, T. (1996). Ambiguities in the lives of children: Postmodern views on the history and historiography of childhood in English Canada. *Paedagogica Historica* XXXII(2), 363–94.

Sahlins, M. (1981). *Kultur und praktische Vernunft*. Frankfurt a.M.: Suhrkamp.

Sarasin, P. (1996). Subjekte, Diskurse, Körper. Überlegungen zu einer diskursanalytischen Kulturgeschichte. In Hardtwig, W. and Wehler, H.-U. (Eds.), *Kulturgeschichte heute* (131–64). Göttingen: Vandenhoeck und Ruprecht.

Siegenthaler, H. (1993). *Regelvertrauen, Prosperität und Krisen. Die Ungleichmäßigkeit wirtschaftlicher und sozialer Entwicklung als Ergebnis individuellen Handelns und sozialen Lernens*. Tübingen: Mohr.

Spranger, E. (1920/1925). Die Bedeutung der wissenschaflichen Pädagogik für das Volksleben. In E. Spranger (Ed.), *Kultur und Erziehung* (138–58). Leipzig: Quelle and Meyer.

Talkenberger, H. (1997). Historische Erkenntnis durch Bilder? Zur Methode und Praxis der historischen Bildkunde. In H. Schmitt, J. W. Link, and F. Tosch (Eds.),

Bilder als Quellen der Erziehungsgeschichte (11–26). Bad Heilbrunn: Klinkhardt.

Tenorth, H.-E. (1982a). Erziehung und Geschichte. Zur Theorie und Methodik erziehungsgeschichtlicher Untersuchungen. In Brinkmann, W. and Renner, K. (Eds.), *Die Pädagogik und ihre Bereiche* (237–54). Paderborn: Schöningh.

———. (1982b). Pädagogik als Wissenschaftstheorie der Erziehungswissenschaft. In Brinkmann, W. and Renner, K. (Eds.), *Die Pädagogik und ihre Bereiche* (71–93). Paderborn: Schöningh.

———. (1993). Wahrheitsansprüche und Fiktionalität. Einige systematische Über-legungen und exemplarische Hinweise an der pädagogischen Historiographie zum Nationalsozialismus. In Lenzen, D. (Ed.), *Pädagogik und Geschichte* (87–102). Weinheim: Deutscher Studienverlag.

———. (1997). Das Unsichtbare zeigen—das Sichtbare verstehen. Fotografien als Quelle zur Analyse von Erziehungsverhältnissen. *Fotogeschichte* 55: 52–56.

Welskop, T. (1998). Die Sozialgeschichte der Väter. Grenzen und Perspektiven der Historischen Sozialwissenschaft. *Geschichte und Gesellschaft* 24: 173–98.

White, H. (1973). *Metahistory: The historical imagination in nineteenth-century Europe.* Baltimore and London: Johns Hopkins University Press.

———. (1987). *The content of the form.* Baltimore and London: Johns Hopkins University Press.

———. (1991). *Tropics of discourse: Essays in cultural criticism.* Stuttgart: Klett-Cotta.

Williams, R. (1958). *Culture and society, 1780–1950.* London: Chatto and Windus.

Yamana, J. (1996). Die Struktur der Übersichtlichkeit des Landerziehungsheimes Haubinda. Zur Interpretation des "Schulstaat"—Konzepts von Herrmann Lietz. *Zeitschrift für Pädagogik* 42: 407–24.

4
Politics and Culture in the Making of History of Education in Brazil

Mirian Jorge Warde and
Marta Maria Chagas de Carvalho

Cultural History and History of Education

In Brazil, educational research in the academic field has undergone displacements since the second half of the 1980s. In this article we focus on the displacements occurring in historiographical research on education.

The first signs of change came from outside historiographical studies in the form of research that sought to look deep into intergroup relations and everyday life of school. As the grounds for these kinds of studies, in the second half of the last decade, ethnographic studies started to circulate along with other studies based on the so-called new sociology of education.[1] Except for topics related to teacher education and practice, this type of research did not produce much in the way of objects or analytical procedures for historiographical studies.[2] Their more visible effects are related to procedures that legitimated the return to pedagogical issues and the consideration of facts deemed previously as *sans prestige*.[3]

More indirectly, the field of interests and the epistemological insertion of the sociology of education had a curious outcome: the status of the historiographical production in the field of research on education was redefined, setting the history of education free from acting as subsidiary knowledge in that field. Such redefinition favored a reflection on methodological and conceptual issues—sedimenting practices of historiographical discussions on topics, issues, and procedures—and produced a certain disciplinary tradition cultivated by the education historians. Issues such as those associated with the documental status of sources and the production of written history became central. In this process, the relationship between educational historiography and its sources was increasingly debated (see Nunes and Carvalho 1993), taking the role of main driver of changes. Rooted in the debates of the Work Group on History of Education at the National Association of Post-Graduation and Research on Education (ANPEd), by the end of the 1980s, this new way of looking at things included "issues related to the widening of the concept of sources—in the emphasis given to supporting materials as, for example, photography—as well as issues associated with procedures to constitute the sources as documents and delimit the documental role of those sources" (Nunes and Carvalho 1993: 35–36).

Initially, this movement made possible a widening of the themes addressed by the field of history of education, giving rise to new interests and removing the crystallization of representations that shaped this field. This expansion of topics put "in evidence the necessary interrelation between the historical studies on education and the contributions from fields such as anthropology, psychology, linguistics, philosophy, etc." (Nunes and Carvalho 1993: 36–37). As a result, new procedures and new criteria of historiographical rigor substantially turned into research practices that attempted to address "the symbolic location of the construction of the subject and his/her practices, implying in the incorporation of theoretical references to watch the historical processes of constitution of the objects investigated" (Nunes and Carvalho 1993: 37).

As detailed later on this paper, the history of education was originally a formative of discipline, an integral part of the pedagogical culture of teacher education. This strict link between the discipline and teacher education programs was coincident with its configuration as history of pedagogical ideas, understood as part of "mankinds' moral legacy" to be transmitted to the future teacher. As a result, the goals of the courses on the history of education and the philosophy of education often merged, something that even today can be seen in the titles of many graduate programs, college courses on pedagogy, and the contents of high-school courses intended for teacher education.[4] While the emphasis on the history of education as history of pedagogical ideas has waned, the stress on the formative possibilities of the discipline persists, and now, in fact, it is expected that it will develop great syntheses that will contextualize a broad range of educational ideas and initiatives. Such syntheses, it is hoped, will enable teachers and school professionals, to become "aware" of educational problems on a national scale. With the institutionalization of postgraduation courses on education in the 1970s, research on history of education was energized. But the interest in developing this field of investigation was, initially, relatively small with the expectation that the discipline would work as a subsidiary field of other studies of higher prestige among education professionals prevailed. The vast majority of academic theses produced in the field until at least the mid-1980s assumed this subsidiary nature, for the field of history of education. These investigations took the path of history to provide the "context" or the "origin" of the object to be investigated, thus generating a type of production homologous to what could be called "introductory history" (Nóvoa 1997).

This subordination of the discipline, either to the imperatives of intelligibility and finding a theoretical solution to contemporary educational problems, or to the imperatives of the strategies of teacher education, resulted in a kind of naturalization of the field of history of education. As it was not defined by an internal logic capable of ensuring the constitution of issues, investigation topics, and procedures, the discipline begins to configure itself in a matter strictly dependent upon its object, which is reified and then naturalized. The stiffening of the investigation field was reinforced by the canonization of some pioneer works in the area. The lack of a sedimented tradition of procedures for a documental critique determined a way of reading these works that formed a historical version within an account that established the meaning of the actions reported, prescribing what was relevant to be included as history. Among these pioneer works, one in particular should be highlighted: *A Cultura Brasileira* (The Brazilian Culture), by Fernando de Azevedo, originally published in 1943 by the National Press. This book is still today one of the main references for the researcher on the history of education and has served as a framework for many studies, producing what one could call "the history of intending to fill up blanks." Azevedo's text was not understood as a discourse in perspective or pragmatically positioned. It was perceived as the work of an intellectual with a marked action as a reformer of the public education system, who had produced an account whose purpose was to defend the educational policies he had implemented. This perception generated a type of production in which rigid a priori schemes acting as frameworks for the objects investigated prevailed. This reinforced the tendency toward the naturalization of the discipline.

From the end of the 1980s on, however, freed from its subordination to the hegemonic disciplines in the field of educational research, and associated with the effort to return to primary sources, the history of education has engaged in a profitable dialogue with contemporary historiographical production. Since then, in the disciplinary map of educational researches, it is the history of education that has effected the strongest changes in the previously mentioned disciplinary framework inherited from the 1930s.[5] The changes may be observed in several areas: in investigation projects submitted to the governmental financing agencies; in the national and international congresses; in publications; in the redesign of university departments; in the attempts to create scientific societies. Starting in the 1990s, the prestige achieved by the discipline has attracted to historiographical research an increasing number of scholars, including a great contingent that, until then, addressed the pedagogical arrangements and action devices as well as those dedicated to philosophical studies.[6]

The process of reconfiguring educational historiography was accompanied by an intense conceptual and methodological reflection. Several studies dealt with those issues and, using different approaches, mapped and critiqued historiographical topics, objects, and procedures, unleashing a broad discussion. The simple occurrence of this type of reflection was very useful, as it addressed the major weakness of the discipline—the lack of discussion on its procedures and its object—and reinforced the effort to break the ties that gave the discipline its status of subsidiary knowledge in the field of education research. Perhaps this is the most significant consequence of the changes that have been redesigning the field and reconfiguring the objects of historical investigation on education. Its effectiveness, however, is widely dependent on its ability to sediment practices of historiographical reflection that produce a disciplinary tradition shaped around the procedures of historiographical research and remove the crystallization of representations that configured the discipline in its previous outline.

The new approaches and the new topic outlines that have been redesigning the field and reconfiguring the objects of historical investigation on education in Brazil have not yet turned into a well-articulated corpus, with clearly defined trends. But such reconfiguration is already evident enough to justify the attempt to draw its profile. To do this, it will be necessary to examine the issue in the context of the new interests that have reconfigured the field of educational research (see Carvalho 1997).

To get into the schools' "black box," touching on the school's organizational devices and the everyday life of its practices; to take into account the perspective of the educational agents; to incorporate the categories of analysis—such as gender; and to outline topics—such as teaching as a profession, teacher education, curriculum, and practices of reading and writing—delimiting fields of study, are some of the new interests that have been reconfiguring the history of education and redefining the relationship between the discipline and other areas of research on education. The convergence of interests around topics and perspectives of analysis makes new room for the historiographical investigation in the field of educational research. An enormous capacity to revigorate themes and instigate new ways of looking currently marks the present history of education in the field of educational research (see Carvalho 1999).

One of the main routes taken by historiographical analysis of education in Brazil has involved an interlocution with French historiography. In this dialogue, the issue that Roger Chartier adopts from Pierre Bourdieu becomes central: "What do people do with the models imposed on them or with the objects that are distributed to them?" (Chartier 1987). The emphasis on the different uses of cultural objects or models moves the education historians to turn from the pedagogical models (or laws, regulations, rules of conduct, and doctrines) toward the distinctive practices of appropriating such objects and models. This is the displacement that makes the education historian stop asking about the internal intelligibility of pedagogical systems and start looking at the multiplicity of material devices where they are inscribed, as defined cultural products, and at their use. This new way of looking means the death of the old history of pedagogy, which moves the historian's interest from the great pedagogical systems to the material processes of their circulation and appropriation. Thus the old history of pedagogical ideas is reconfigured, as interest wanes in the study of ideas disembodied from the materiality of the devices that put them into circulation and the practices of the agents who produce them or take them for their own. The field of a cultural history of pedagogical lore is beginning to come into focus, with an interest in the materiality of the processes of production, circulation, imposition, and appropriation of this lore.[7]

This emphasis on the materiality of practices, objects, and their uses produces a new way of looking at and questioning the available sources, reconfiguring the history of pedagogy in its traditional version and providing solid support to a cultural history of the pedagogical lores. In this process not only the old history of pedagogical ideas is reconfigured but also the history of school as an institution. School is now conceived of as a historical product of the interaction between devices of pedagogical normatization and the practices of the agents that apprehend them. The concepts of school *form* and *culture* are mobilized, focusing on the practices that make the sociality of schools and a certain mode of cultural transmission, as well as the devices that normatize them—devices that organize school time and school space, that normatize the lore to be taught and the conducts to be inculcated. A multiplicity of new actors—teachers, inspectors, school principals, students—and their tactics of *appropriation* also come into play (see De Certeau 1994). The school setting can be more easily perceived when a multiplicity of school materials come to fill it up, materials whose usage must be determined.

New interests, new interrogations, and new criteria with which to treat the archive have thus led to a rehistoricization of the school by particularizing the devices that make up a school *model* or *form* (see Vicent 1980) as well as its multiple appropriations in the tactics of *know-how to do* (see De Certeau 1994). Under the impact of these changes, *school* as an object is denaturalized and the language of the sources and the conceptual tools acquires historicity. The *school model* of education is then understood as a historical construction resulting from the intersection of several scientific, religious, political, and pedagogical devices, which defined modernity as a society of schooling. In this way, the anachronistic procedures that, in the previous era of historiographical production in the histories of schools, fade away. What fades away is the persistent progressive idea of the Enlightenment which has certain drawbacks for peripheral counties.

Along with these changes, the rigid borderline that previously divided the field of history of education into two are suppressed, so that the history of school institutions is disconnected from the history of pedagogical thought. Bridging the old dividing line between the history of ideas and the history of school institutions, there is a growing, multifaceted field of investigations into pedagogical texts. These investigations provide solid support for a cultural history of the pedagogical lores concerned with the materiality of the processes that spread and impose those lores and in the materiality of the practices that appropriate them. Stressing the material supports of the production, circulation, and appropriation of the pedagogical lores, these investigations include studies on a variety of texts and assemblies of texts intended for the pedagogical realm: teaching books, school manuals, education periodicals, school libraries, collections intended for teachers, and so forth. Under this new perspective, such texts are no longer a source merely of historiographical information. They are of interest as objects, in the double meaning of object of investigation and material object. The materiality of these objects becomes the support of a questionnaire that guides the investigator in the study of practices that are formalized as they are used by the school.

This is how the emphasis of the new historiography on the materiality of practices, objects, and their usage produces a new way of looking at and questioning the available sources. A new pattern of visibility makes it clear that the representations crystallized in the educational historiography led to the invisibility of what was previously not said and, therefore, was not exposed. If something needs not to be said, in the speech where such representations are intertwined, it's because it needs not to be seen. Crossing this border in and out and shuffling its delimiting lines, history of education tends to specialize in a variety of domains—history of school disciplines, history of teaching as a profession, history of curriculum, history of the learning book etc. Curiously, this trend hasn't yet been strong enough to open paths of research clearly delimited. One can see, somehow, the scattering of the disciplines field, in which researches of markedly different epistemological roots live together in apparent harmony. Unified by the purpose of providing a perspective for the historical account according to the standpoint of the actors in the processes investigated, these researches drew attention to the *representations* that certain agents have about themselves, their practices, the practices of other agents, the institutions—such as the school—and the processes that make them up. The apparent coincidence in these various approaches is however only a language coincidence. The word *representation* has been used in very different ways.

The large circulation of the concept of *representation* in recent historiographical production may make one feel that this production shares, in its entirety, theoretical references of the same epistemic extraction. It is necessary to change this impression. Under the common label of a new educational historiography, radically opposed conceptions now live side by side. In the theoretical references of some of the routes taken by this historiography, the concept of representation is forged in opposition to any kind of philosophy of consciousness; in others, this notion resets the domain of the subjectiveness. This is the case, for example, with a variety of studies whose themes are teacher education and practice.

This tendency leads to a field of research area that has taken a peculiar path since the 1980s. Due to the abandonments of Althusser-inspired approaches, ethnographic studies and the sociology of education have fueled studies that reposition the teacher in the center of school practices, as the subject that inaugurates them and is the ground for them. Based on that perspective, a suitable field has been established for a contemporary restatement of the teacher as the epicenter of school changes, particularly in the area of curriculum proposals, since the teacher is the expression, within the school, of the emerging "new subjectiveness." Foreign to the emphasis on this "subjectiveness-box" that presents itself as the key, the target, and the limit of decipherment for a hermeneutics of the living experience of the subjects, is the concept of representation developed by Roger Chartier, which has been the object of multiple appropriations in recent educational historiography. Growing out of the tradition of Mauss and Durkheim, this concept anchors the supremacy of a perspective that displaces the polarity structures/ subjectiveness by affirming a cultural history of social life "which takes as an object the understanding of the forms and the reason—or, in other words, the representations of the social world—which, against the will of the social actors, translate the positions and interests objectively confronted and, at the same time, describe society as they think it is, or they would like it to be" (Chartier 1990: 19).

The conceptual field that models the way Chartier apprehends Durkheim and Mauss is marked, as he pointed out in an interview (Chartier 1994: 139), by the interest in opposing the concept of collective *representation* to "a form of philosophy of the consciousness," to designate "the incorporation within each individual of the very structures of the social world." Mauss and Durkheim are of interest to him as they "conceive the systems of collective representation as a way the individuals internalize, incorporate the social structure itself and, thus, the creation of schemes of perception and judgment that are the basis of thinking, acting, et cetera" (Chartier 1994: 139). If one takes into account that the way Chartier appropriates the concept of collective representation is an operation that incorporates the new lores of the sign that, after Saussure, discard the instrumental conception of the language that confine the discursive practices of representation in the fragile space of the ideal relations between thought and word or word and object designated,[8] one will still be distanced from the uses of the concept of representation that institute themselves as the highest eulogy of this "new subjectiveness." But it is mainly the emphasis given to the *formality of the practices* or to the *meaning of the forms* that indicates how specifically Chartier uses the concept of *representation*. Not allowing acts of speech to be reduced to "the ideas that they state or the topics that they address" *(qu'ils portent)* (Chartier 1989: 1517), such emphasis postulates that *representation* is *practice* in which the form determines the meaning (cf. Chartier, A-M. and Hèbrard 1988), which makes it impossible to reinstall the kingdom of subjectiveness by dissociating it from the practices in which and through which the subjects constitute themselves as determined subjects (see Carvalho and Hansen: 1996).

However, no matter the conceptual differences and the thematic and vocabulary kinship, it is certain that, in the movement of these conceptual and methodological changes, the territory in which the historians of education traditionally moved has been redesigned and their research practices reoriented. The widening of topics and the reflection on procedures are, no doubt, challenges for a field of research with scarce disciplinary tradition. It is not possible to know the extent to which these changes are incorporating a process of reflection on the practices that previously configured the discipline, incorporating new interests and theoretical references into new procedures to construct the object of investigation, and effectively developing new approaches to old objects, refiguring them (see Nunes 1992). One can assume—and there are strong indications of earlier paradigms being redeveloped—that these changes are taking place on the margins of the previous production, leaving their old objects, topics, and problems untouched. History that reached its apotheosis in the nineteenth century on the forms of political history that is subservient to the cause of the advancement of the state; it is the refusal of a history that is the last refuge of "transcendental humanism,"[9] and the basis for the optimistic belief in the ceaseless advancement of mankind.

The History of Education: Discipline and Morals

In Brazil, history of education as a school discipline was included in the courses intended for the education of elementary teachers and school professionals in the 1930s. The curricula for these courses (on both the high-school and college levels) were organized by setting side-by-side two apparently exclusive cognitive standards.

The first was brought forward from previous decades by means of the *education renovators* who had been working extensively with the precepts of the so-called "new school."[10] Although it is clear that very different positions were grouped under this name, it is also known that in the process of internationalization of the new-school movements, a high degree of homogenization was achieved. Thus, among the new-school precepts that significantly marked the curriculum organization in the teacher education courses was the privilege given to a so-called scientific education based in psychology and educational sociology. In the beginning of the decade, a group of leading intellectuals— Binet, Caplarède, Dumas, and others— had legitimated the curriculum and discipline choices. Psychology would be a lasting source of legitimacy at the top of the hierarchy of educational lores. As for educational sociology, the Brazilian renovators turned especially to Durkheim for support: in the beginning of the 1930s, his work had already been translated, published, and widely circulated among students in normal school.[11]

On the other hand, the teacher formation curricula ensured room for the disciplines aimed at the moral instruction of future teachers. In this light, the history and philosophy of education were understood as one single discipline. History of education was an appendix to philosophy of education, the former adopting from the latter its topics and approaches; in this relationship, history of education was included in the curriculum as one of a number of specializations of philosophy of education, and it had to perform a programmatic role, in the moral sense: philosophy and history of education were intended to set forth the purposes of education, based on the absolute and transcendental values that human societies would have, in successive ages, striven to achieve. Today, the history of education still carries this original mark: its usefulness and its effectiveness measured by what it provides in terms of justifications for the past and as a guide for the construction of the future (see Warde 1990c).

This kind of "presentism" marks the origin of the discipline in Brazil, and is a result of the institutionalization process that found its place in the construction of the pedagogical field. The history of education was not thought of as a specialization of history, but as an approach to education. Thus, Brazilian history of education was subtracted from history. At the same time, in the hierarchy and composition of the educational lores, it was put in a subsidiary position in favor of sociology, psychology and, as a result, biology, which gained the status of ruling sciences (see Carvalho 1998; Warde 1990b).

Surveys conducted since the 1930s on the teachers that were assigned philosophy and history of education classes in the teacher education institutions indicate that a vast majority of them did not take a specific path in determining the content of the discipline (Warde 1998b). This is not the case with psychology and educational sociology, which early on acquired a more specific profile: in the 1930s, the selection process for these disciplines already demanded some professionalization from their teachers. In the case of educational psychology, this requirement was clearest, deriving from the fact that it was meant to be the source of pedagogical modernization starting in the nineteenth century;[12] from that moment on, a number of works in the field were translated or written for Brazilian publication, European experts were invited to assist in the processes of pedagogical innovation, and many laboratories and studies for psychological experimentation were created.

Conversely, the philosophy and history of education were less-professionalized pedagogical disciplines from the beginning. No specific requirements were established for the recruitment of teachers into these disciplines; that is, there was no demand for the mastery of distinct contents or specific methodological skills. In fact, very often, teachers recruited for other disciplines were requested to teach philosophy and history of education classes as temporary permanent replacements for official teachers. Professionalism in its modern meaning—as a mastery of practical skills, the capacity of material control of the objective world—was not required from the teacher of philosophy and history of education. Instead, subjective skills and mastery of words were the exemplary skills for the future teacher or pedagogue.

Although the presence of teachers educated and with a strong orientation of the Catholic Church has always been very high in the pedagogical field (Warde 1998a and b), their concentration in the discipline of philosophy and history of education was particularly great for almost the entire period from the 1930s through the 1980s, noticeably ebbing only in the 1990s. The relationship with the Catholic Church can be observed in primary and secondary schooling at religious schools and also in the training of priests and seminarians. But since the 1930s, male teachers educated in philosophy and theology at religious institutions have exercised control. This religious presence did not decrease in the following decades, as courses on philosophy at nonreligious institutions remained for a long time under the control of cadres directly or indirectly connected with the Catholic Church.

One fertile area for analysis concerns the academic path taken by the male leaders of the *renovating* movement—the new-school followers that called themselves "pioneers of the new school"—which was the rejection of control by the Catholic Church over national education, in defense of scientific, lay, rational teaching. Almost all were men with a religious—in particular, Jesuit—school education who retained a sense of Catholic spirituality and a commitment to the role of the shepherding of souls. Thus, as stated above, the opposition between two curriculum standards at stake in the organization of the teacher and pedagogue education courses—the lay and the religious, the modern and the romantic—was only an apparent one.

The standards adopted in the educational historian courses were clearly alien to those found in Brazilian college courses on history for the education of historians. The discipline of philosophy and history of education did not have the purpose of preparing historians, but rather teachers for elementary and secondary schools and pedagogues. For them, the history of education had a utilitarian role: gather the lessons from the past and project the future.[13] To achieve this purpose, the discipline was not required to provide skills for dealing with sources or accounts to be found in history. The teaching materials themselves did not result from investigations. The prime standard in the history of education was unmistakably inherited from religious philosophy: its aim was to shepherd the soul, to legitimate the past, with the purpose of morally educating the future teacher and pedagogue.

Thus, the Brazilian discipline had features that were very similar to those existing in the European countries where the process of bourgeois domination occurred by means of receiverships and alliances with the Catholic Church. As a discipline, the history of education mirrors the accommodations between the state and the church in the production of a perfect synthesis between the Christian and the citizen, the "priest of the nation," or as Guizot used to say, the "lay priest." Thus, the programs of the discipline acclaimed the idea of historical continuity, endless time, as part of a long tradition that Brazilians would be the heirs of, in which they should find their identity. This idea was so predominant that, even today, the pedagogue habitually looks to past periods to find the thread of historical continuity in which and from which the present can be justified. This procedure repeats what Compère (1995:36–37) recorded in her comparative study on history of education in the European countries:

> the History of Education has a legitimating role, no matter what country or political system: no program can actually be free of [a] certain amount of normatization. . . . One of the results of these genealogies may be the legitimization of the engaging commitment: one puts the history aside to justify that contemporary engagement. At the extremes, one can talk about finalism because the intended end is to make the school organization coincident with the scientific knowledge of the child and the political and social project which one adheres to.

History of Education: Cognitive Modeling

The historiographic literature on education had but a few Brazilian titles through the 1930s and 1940s. Foreign titles (either translated or not) prevailed, mostly French, alongside a few national manuals written for the normal schools (which, by and large, offered simplified versions of the popular foreign works). The Brazilian history of education was reduced to a chapter, an appendix, or an attachment. Only in the 1950s can one observe the emergence of a new type of historiographical writing, in which Brazilian education is raised to the position of an object of history. Between the 1950s and the 1970s, there is a significant increase in the number of both translated and locally produced titles; in the normal schools and pedagogy courses, the use of two or three manuals becomes the rule—the translated ones to cover the "general history of education" and the national ones to cover Brazil.

Both in the national and in the international literature, there were two topics most frequently addressed:[14] the history of pedagogies or of the pedagogical ideas and the history of school organizations/teaching systems/educational policies. Only after the 1950s, can one see an attempt to interconnect the two approaches by using the concepts of educational "reformers" and "reforms." These two concepts appear as tools to produce a relationship between the pedagogical models and the teaching systems, as if the "reformers" were the modern state product of the ancient thinker/philosopher of education who, taking over the role of leading the organization of a teaching system, would effect an approximation between their ideas and the objective conditions of the schools. The parallel schemes are kept; the third scheme—the "reforms" and the "reformers"—does not eliminate the previous schemes; it only updates them.

In the Brazilian writings from the 1950s, the new way of writing the history of education appears as the result of absorbing and modeling history from the memory of the education renovators; in particular, the publication of Fernando de Azevedo's work, *A Cultura Brasileira* (1943), taken by the renovators themselves as institutors of history and the inauguration point of the collective memory of culture and education.

The historiographical memory produced by the renovators focuses on the reconstitution of the past and projects the future that converts the renovators and the (Catholic) conservatives into the actual and single agents of history of education. This historiography accepts the renovators and conservatives as the mutually legitimated representatives of the social interests and the single postulators of those interests. For the renovators, society was unprepared for the democratic and scientific values and was, therefore, immature; as result, the state should be transformed into a rational structure that, by means of the public school, would educate society. This perspective was associated with the belief that good pedagogy acknowledges the social conditions that affect the school, but understands the necessity of leaving them outside the classroom in order to educate the new, hard-working, urban man. Thus, the tendency was to convert education into a pedagogical issue, that is, a "technical" one.

The representations about education produced by Azevedo—widely taken as "facts" about Brazilian education—serve as dense devices for modeling the history of education with which the author successfully erases the foundations of his account, of himself and his standpoint (see Carvalho 1989). Two strategies are adopted by Azevedo: first, reading the Brazilian civilizatory process as an endless struggle between the old and the new and as an ascending march and apotheosis; second, conferring visibility only on those who, in this fight, act in favor of the modernization of education, purging the political by means of the technical/pedagogical. In his work, Azevedo crystallizes the topics, selects the actors, and sets the dates that will organize the historiographical accounts of education published from the 1950s onward. When the memory of the past is linked to Azevedo's work, the renovators are able to appropriate the "facts" and these facts then are raised to the level of historical knowledge.

Avezedo's matrix accommodates Brazil in the sense of time inherited from Europe: linear, continuous time; the time of universal unity and civilizatory fraternity. It is the time that constitutes Western civilization, which decanted, in its womb, Christian time—dramatic time, man's saga on earth, long calvary leading to salvation. It is the Christian time that is concerned most with past and future, for which the present is but a feeble frontier between one and the other.[15] This conception of time ensured the sacralization of the process of professionalization and rationalization of the teaching practice.

A polished expression of this representation of time produced by Azevedo can be seen in the long historical cycle that he builds: starting with the arrival of the first Jesuits to Brazil, in 1549, interrupted by Pombal's reforms in the second half of the eighteenth century, resumed by the renovators from 1930 on. It was necessary to wait for over a century so that the renovators could come to the scene and reinstitute a national project of culture and education; with them, the country had recovered its roots, its traditions, and at the same time, had projected its modern future.

It is the academic production in the 1970s and 1980s that makes it possible to follow the discursive devices started by Azevedo as they preserve his historiographical modeling in studies with a predominantly Marxist approach.[16] These writings did not essentially challenge the definition of periods, the ways of conceiving history and time inherited from the renovators' historiography and made official by Azevedo. On the contrary, they took to the maximum the moralizing meaning of education and history.

The "triumph of the Marxist paradigm" (see Pécaut 1990) that can be seen in the last two decades covers virtually all fields of the so-called human sciences. This triumph was made possible very much by the academic response to the era of dictatorship (1964–1984), a period of strong political commitment on the part of scholars in the fight against the military rule. In the first phase (from the 1960s through the mid-1970s), Althusserian Marxism prevailed, to be replaced by Gramscian Marxism by the end of the 1980s. Both lines of thought presented themselves under the most radical expressions of formalism and doctrinairism (see Warde 1990c, 1993; Vieira 1994). As a result, social research moved between two complementary ways of analyzing historical situations within the Marxist tradition: hyperstructuralism and hypersubjectivism.

In the educational field, one cannot afford to minimize the significance of these two complementary forms of social interpretation, nor the fact—well investigated already—that in the 1970s and 1980s there arose a powerful new generation of scholars directly connected with the Catholic Church or part of its sphere of influence. This set of intellectuals pursued an accommodation between Azevedo-style and Marxist historiography. In the Gramscian phase, this accommodation gained a more radical form as a result of the centrality that Gramsci confers on the political action of intellectuals and his expansive concept of the state.[17] If in Gramsci the political centrality of intellectuals—understood as individual and collective subjects—is the result of his way of reading the new cycle of capital (in which "economical reform" is effected by means of "intellectual and moral reform"), in Brazilian historiography this analytical element took a prescriptive and voluntaristic form, such as Azevedo had conceived: subjects aware of social problems (particularly educational problems) would be able to intervene from the outside into the inside of history and redirect its route. Legitimacy would be conferred on such intervention by the social and political reading of intellectuals; its effectiveness would be measured by its ability to redirect the actions of the political society over that of the civil society.

With the partnership promoted by this new generation of scholars between the two kinds of Marxist-inspired social reading and the Azevedo interpretative matrix, the standard of historiographical production took a firm hold.

This standard was generalized in the 1970s and 1980s, at a pace and range never seen before, due to specific institutional conditions. From the beginning of the 1970s, a national post-graduate system led, in the education area, to new generations of authors, a growth of almost five times in the number of titles published, diversification of the publishing market, and redistribution of the institutional ranks. The quantitative expansion that occurred in the area as a whole was swiftly reflected in studies on the history of education. Between 1972 and 1988, 146 master's dissertations and doctorate theses were presented that dealt with the history of Brazilian education; counting these, related to the history of education is other countries, there were almost 200 in total.

The prevailing interpretative standard in the graduate programs on education started to lose strength during the mid-1980s. The end of the dictatorship cooled the activist writings, which basically criticized the state, and created favorable political conditions for the reconfiguration of the perspectives of analysis. From the 1990s on, multiple directions now appear in a variety of studies. What made the *new educational historiography* possible, however, went beyond the new political conditions and the conceptual and methodological reconfiguration in educational research that took place during the previous two decades. The new historiography results largely from broader political and institutional trends that have been redefining the relationship between intellectuals and the state (Warde 1992; see also Munakata 1984 and Chauí 1978), insulating the academic field from current educational policies.

New Political Games: Government, Intellectuals, and Academic Production

It is in an ambiguous territory, full of contradictions, where the relations between intellectuals and the state take place, that two contemporaneous operations seem to produce and accelerate the process of reconfiguring the historiographical production on education: on the one hand, the conceptual and methodological reconfiguration of historiographical and educational research, beginning in the late 1980s; on the other hand, the displacement of the older academic field from current educational policies, beginning around the same time.

The displacement of the traditional academic field from new educational policies can be noticed: (a) in the dismissal of intellectuals and scholars in favor of technicians such as assistants, consultants, implementers, and service providers recruited by nongovernmental agencies and organizations; (b) in the privilege assigned to the process of "on-the-job training," currently called "on-going education or capacitation," to the detriment of basic academic education; and (c) in the dismissal of academic's capacity to carry out a reading/diagnostic of the past/present and determine the (future) direction of policies.

The new educational policies were put into effect by the end of the 1980s; they are government policies intended to physically and administratively remodel public school systems by delegating their management to the city level and sending financial resources directly to the schools. They also affect the curriculum organization of the basic school (eight years of fundamental school and three years of high school) and so-called on-going teacher education.

In the mid-1980s, these policies were foreshadowed by a process of intensive persuasion undertaken by the federal government. Through systematic dissemination a set of assumptions was established, providing the grounds for the acceptance of these policies and the affirmation of their inevitability, including the assumption that the public school had already achieved universality. This assumption was the first and the most difficult to establish, as most academic research had long indicated substantial levels of preliminary school exclusion. Next, official documents began to set forth the complementary assumption that the quantitative distortions found in public schools did not result from obstruction of access, but from the high number of children failing in the first grades of elementary school; therefore, the underlying problem of public school was related to quality. The qualitative problems faced by public school were promptly redefined: outmoded curricula, unprepared teachers, and inadequate assessment methods.

The remodeling process was first statistical, then administrative, and then pedagogical: education would be an essential tool to carry out the economic and social leap forward that Brazil needed to take. After falling behind the pace of the developed countries, Brazil would have to find anew its developmental potential; to do so, in addition to adjustments in the economy and the system of government, it would be necessary to raise the national level of educability. The old motto of the "new man" was back, under a new name: the "new subjectiveness." This "new subjectiveness" became a favorite topic of speeches by both the defenders of the new educational policies and their critics. Consensus was reached around the issue: the changes occurring in the academic field—particularly the technological changes and the new management standards—had produced, automatically and predictably, a new subjectively available, and ready for a new molding.

The official documents and the studies that are the grounds for the contemporary educational policies do not argue logically in favor of the relationship between the "new subjectiveness," the need to institute a new standard of educability, and the adoption of pedagogical procedures based on the psychology of Piaget and Vygotsky. But this is far from being the core question, since one should not seek conceptual consistency when dealing with the political field: within and on behalf of it, a new episteme can always be inaugurated. The most intriguing aspect is the fact that, in the name of a radically new historical moment, an old form of speech is resumed: Brazil has a new cause, an engagement in a historical acceleration; to achieve this acceleration, it has to produce a new standard of educability, from which a "new subjectiveness," a "new man" will emerge.

The issue of the "new subjectiveness" restores, in a circuitous fashion, the mythology of modernity that emerged during the late nineteenth and early twentieth centuries. Then, as now, the myths supported a process of objective change supposedly incompatible with the consciousness, the morals, the attitudes, and the skills available—synthetically referred to today as "subjectiveness." If the objective world was, as it is today, incompatible with the subjective world (the consciousness, the morals, etc.), then one should, as one must today, perform the transmutation of the objective elements into contents of the consciousness (where the knowledge and the moral principles are located, being responsible for the attitudes and skills). This operation assumes the existence of an objective world ruled by laws, an available subject (a consciousness) and an (objective) truth ready to be (subjectively) grasped.

In favor of this assumption are those who see in the technological and managerial changes the metamorphosis of social relations, especially in the field of labor.[18] Their assumptions about the subject are reflected in the sacralized criticisms of those who bet on the ontological primacy of labor.[19]

Some Thoughts: The New Historiography of Education, between the Autonomy of Investigation and the New Rise of Subservience

One movement in the process of conceptual and methodological reconfiguration of educational historiographical studies is to turn to more distant historical periods. Interest in recent history among education historians is decreasing. This movement is highly promising insofar as it unveils new critical possibilities concerning the set of crystallizations that once configured traditional historiography and used to feed back its cultural and political commitments. Another positive is that this movement seeks to leave behind that kind of presentism that was one of the main features of Azevedo's historiography. But this search for the distant past—one with no apparent commitment to any broader policy agenda—takes the chance of resetting, under new forms, the condition of subservience of historiographical research to today's political interests. The apparent indifference of this new historiographical production to the educational policies currently being enacted may, in fact, be concealing a double commitment. A commitment to what these policies project for the future (even if they are promoted through an ultrapresentifying discourse, they are reforms loaded with utopian projections for the near future); and a commitment to what these reforms convey in terms of justifications about the past.

This hiding game involving the commitment between the new mode of historiographical investigation and the new educational policies certainly goes much further than the Brazilian frontiers. Narodowski says (1997:19):

> the desirable facts for the future are vacant, it is not necessary to investigate the relationship between the action to be undertaken and the facts of the past. In other words, there's no need to legitimate the present and the future through the

historical traditions. The past no longer settles the disputes, it is no more a referee in the decision making because the lack of utopias generates the absence of general and all-inclusive guidelines for the education.

The ways in which contemporary educational research complies with the new educational policies deserves special study as the central position of the teacher in the new teaching processes and in the new forms of organizing school work is reaffirmed, producing adequate justification to eliminate intermediate "inconvenient circumstances" between the state and the teacher. The teacher emerges as the demiurge of school life, as the state is the demiurge of societal life. The statement that the teacher is the holder of the "new subjectiveness" finds support in social researches of different complexions: remotely, in ethnography, in the so-called new sociology of education, and recently in the sociology of labor. In different forms, these fields have been supplying arguments in favor of restoring the old representation of the teacher as the epicenter of the school order.

The new historiography's lack of interest in today's political issues closely matches the discourse of the new governmental agents in the education field. These agents present themselves, now, as self-sufficient to produce the images (and diagnostics) of the past required to justify their policies: what the scholar might have to say about the past does not seem necessary. Apparently, there is a discursive rupture between the academic field and the new governmental field: the interpretation of the past the way it appears in the discourse that justifies and implements the reforms does not match the interpretation by traditional scholars. Also, the new historians are not opposing their specialized discourse to the political discourse that legitimates the present nor are they challenging the interpretation that the governmental agents put forward about the educational history of the country.

Besides looking back to more distant periods of time, the education historians are performing significant displacements involving concepts, methodology, objects—including the old polarity of "ideas" and "teaching systems"—institutional levels and pedagogical devices: from universal to singular; from the structures to the practices; from the subjects to the strategies and tactics; from continuous time (progress, in its modern meaning) to discontinuity. Due to the lack of clarity about the political nature of theoretical investment in these displacements, the education historians end up trapped in the mesh of meaning that is imposed on them by the government's policies. In addition, the lack of political investment in this historiographical work may cause its production to be imprisoned in the critical schemes that, by reactivating Azevedo's matrices and appropriating derogatorily the labels available (such as "postmodernism," "poststructuralism," etc.), frame them as a novelty to be execrated. Thus, it is the entire historiographical investment of cultural analysis that performs a promising insertion into educational studies.

Notes

1. Studies on everyday life have been developed in Brazil based primarily on two extra-educational approaches: Agnes Heller's (1972, 1977) and Henri Lefebvre's (1972), with an emphasis on the former. Regarding the presence of the so-called new sociology of education in Brazil, see Basil Bernstein (1988, 1996) and Jean-Claude Forquin (1993).

2. Concerning the lack of delimitation of specific objects, studies on curriculum should be highlighted, as they are at the heart of the new sociology of education; the recent historiography of education practically ignores this topic and dedicates more attention to the history of the school disciplines.

3. Expression used by Henri Lefebvre to refer to the quotidian aspects of everyday life. See Lefebvre (1972).

4. In Brazil, the education of elementary school teachers started in the first half of the nineteenth century by means of normal school courses, located at the intermediate level of schooling. This form of education persists to this day, though with deep internal changes that must be analyzed elsewhere. In the 1930s in addition to this education of elementary school teachers, another form of education was established at the university level, called *licenciatura* (licentiate), aimed at the education of secondary (high) school teachers. Finally, college courses on pedagogy were created to prepare education specialists as well as to qualify technical/administrative staff for the lower levels of teaching—elementary and secondary (high) school. These two forms persist to this day, with internal modifications.

5. The displacements found in the historiography of recent Brazilian education affected not only its status in the field of research on education; other disciplines have been and are being affected by such displacements as well. The history of education that was meant to be a discipline subsidiary to other disciplines is causing an inversion, and in fact other disciplines are now searching the history of education for objects and concepts. Two trends of this inversion can be highlighted: one is the chronicling, and thus denaturalizing of the educational objects—particularly the school objects; the other involves inserting school/educational objects into the culture, untieing them from direct relation with the economy.

6. There is no research on the profile of these academic groupings or on their recent destinations Thus, the statement that these groupings tend to dissolve their previous patterns derives from the register of participation in "hands-on" and "doctrinal" in new research groups, especially those researching history of education. Regarding the relationship with philosophy of education and other disciplines, in Brazil, see Warde (1990a).

7. Within this new cultural history, which a significant part of Brazilian educational historiography has been involved in, recent studies have replaced the old themes associated with the pedagogical lores. As an example: editorial series or periodicals of pedagogical destination are being reexamined as strategies to model the pedagogical practices; the reexamination seeks to verify how different forms of appropriation of these materials are implied in the tactics of re-creating and reinventing the normalization and normatization of teaching practices. Another example is the reexamination of the relations between the disciplinary fields of pedagogy and psychology; traditional studies emphasize these relations based on so-called frames of thought (that is, "pedagogical ideas" and "psychological ideas"), establishing in a Kantian way the borders of the two disciplinary fields, so that the next step is to denounce the colonizing invasion of psychology over pedagogy. One trend in recent research is the reexamination of these disciplinary

relations by means of the practices of control, classification, measurement, and homogenization of students that operate without any Kantian distinction between the pedagogical and the psychological.

8. It would perhaps be better to understand it as an operation that, somehow, incorporates Foucault's assumptions found in *L'ordre du discours* about the devices that "elide reality of the discourse in the [Western] philosophical thought" since Plato and the program therein enunciated of "restoring the discourse with its character of a happening" (Foucault, 1971: 53). Chartier gives indications of this incorporation when he proposes to "reintroduce at the heart of the historiographic critique the questionnaire put up by Foucault for the treatment of the series of discourses," as a "condition so that the texts, no matter what they are, that the historian constitutes as archives be subtracted from the ideological and documental reductions which destroyed them as 'discontinuous practices'" (Chartier 1989: 1517).

9. Expression used by Claude Lèvi-Strauss in his *Histoire y Dialectique* (1962). See on this subject the excellent study by Luiz Costa Lima, *O controle do imaginário* (1989).

10. The broad and diffuse "new school" movement intended to make schools up-to-date, rational, and scientific was an important presence from the 1920s through the 1940s. Although the "new school" movement was boosted by different social and political groups, it was the self-titled group of *renovators* or *pioneers* that became more visible in defending those ideas as well as the public school run and funded by the state, free and lay.

11. Beginning in the late nineteenth century, a series of local and foreign publications started to circulate in the educational milieu with the purpose of disclosing the "new sciences of education." After the 1920s, the publishing market saw the rise not only of specialized periodicals but also of editorial series intended for schoolteachers. Reviewing these publications reveals the prevalence of "psychology" in their titles. In 1931, Durkheim's *Sociology and Education*, translated into Portuguese, received wide circulation. During the 1930s, several titles in the sociology of education field were published, most of them disseminating the ideas of the new French sociology of education.

12. The reference made here is to Herbart who postulated for the first time in a systematic manner psychology as a tool to be used by general pedagogy.

13. Marie-Madeleine Compère reports that, in a survey conducted in France in 1982–1983 among students of education sciences, there was a prevalence of the measurement of "usefulness" in terms of action: "the knowledge of the past allows a better knowing of the present situation and a better preparation for the future" (1995: 34).

14. Compère focuses on the same types of university handbooks intended for the history of education in Europe: "the first major category of those manuals is formed by the generic history of pedagogy, abridged reflection of a genus that goes back to the very origin of the teaching of this discipline at the university: it was then a philosophic history, understood as an essential element of the human spirit's development, cherished by the men of the Enlightenment" (1995: 41). "The national history of teaching is the second category of the manuals used by the educational science students. In most of them, the work's framework corresponds to a historiographic tradition that links the school to the modern State: the starting date is considered a landmark in the national history (for example, the Revolution to France, the political unification to Italy); they only deal with the institutional aspects and the elementary and middle levels of teaching. In general, the school-related laws are analyzed in their main measures, the starting point is the first law that applies nationwide. The book usually links a chronol-

ogy of the school-related laws to a pedagogic characterization of the relevant period" (1995: 44).

15. For the conception of time in modernity, see Gourevitch (1975). For a particular focus on school time in this conception, see Compère (1997).

16. The academic production originates predominantly from the graduate programs; it consists therefore of master's dissertations and doctorate theses. When a graduate system was created in Brazil, starting in the 1970s, most of academic research was implemented from those programs. For the so-called human sciences, from this moment on there was a new age of investigation, as the indexes of the titles produced and the research standards changed significantly.

17. In Brazil, the "Christianization" of Gramsci is expressed rather symptomatically in the interpretation of his writings on Machiavelli; Gramsci's critique of the political action led by the Catholic Church in the light of Maquiavel is disregarded on behalf of a "Machiavellian" reading of Machiavelli. See Romano (1997) on politics according to the Catholic Church and according to Machiavelli.

18. Here we must make mention of the so-called new sociology of work. Concerning current research in this field in Brazil, see Dadoy (1984, 1987), Tanguy (1997), and Zarifian (1997). It should be noted that much of what has been performed as something "new" by these studies is a new reading of Pierre Naville.

19. The defense of the ontological primacy of work has been affirmed particularly by scholars who refer to Lukàcs and the Ontology of the social being (1979).

References

Azevedo, F. de. (1943). *A cultura brasileira.* Rio de Janeiro: Instituto Brasileiro de Geografia e Estatística.

Bernstein, B. (1988). *Poder, educacion y conciencia: sociologia de la transmisión cultural.* Santiago: CIDE.

———. (1996). *A estruturação do discurso pedagógico: classe, códigos e controle.* Petropolis: Vozes.

Carvalho, M. M. C. de. (1989). O novo, o velho, o perigoso: relendo a cultura brasileira. *Cadernos de Pesquisa.* São Paulo, Fundação Carlos Chagas, nov., n° 71.

———. (1997). História da Educação: notas sobre uma questão de fronteiras. *Educação em Revista*, Autêntica/Faculdade de Educação da UFMG, Belo Horizonte, dez., n° 26.

———. (1998). A configuração da historiografia educacional brasileira. In Marcos C. de Freitas (Org.), *Historiografia brasileira em perspectiva.* São Paulo: Contexto.

———. (1999). Pedagogia e usos escolares do impresso: uma incursão nos domínios da história cultural. In M. Narodowski (Org.), *Textos escolares en Latinoamérica. Avatares del pasado y tendencias actuales.* Quilmes, Argentina: Ed. de la Universidad Nacional def Quilmes.

Carvalho, M. M. C. de and Hansen, J. (1996). Modelos culturais e representação: uma leitura de Roger Chartier. *Varia História.* Belo Horizonte, set., n° 16.

Chartier, A.-M. and Hèbrard, J. (1988). L'invention du quotidien une lecture, des usages. *Le Débat.* Paris, Mars-Avril, n. 49.

Chartier, R. (1989). Le monde comme représentation. *Annales Economies Sociétés Civilisations*, nov/dez, n° 6.

———. (1990). *A História cultural: entre práticas e representações.* Lisboa and Rio de Janeiro: Difel; Rio de Janeiro: Bertrand Brasil.

———. (1994). Historia y prácticas culturales. Entrevista a Roger Chartier por Noemi

Goldman y Leonor Arfuch. *Entrepasados*. Revista de Historia, Buenos Aires, ano IV, n.7.

———. (1987). La nebuleuse: enquête sur l'histoire culturelle. In Rioux, Jean Pierre (dir.) *L'Histoire Culturelle de la France Contémporaine (Bilans et perspectives de la recherche)*. Paris: Ministère de la Culture et de la communication/CNRS.

Chauí, M. (1978). Apontamentos para uma crítica da Aço Integralista Brasileira. In M. Chauí and M. S. de C. Franco (Eds.), *Ideologia e mobilização popular*. Rio de Janeiro: Paz e Terra Centro de Estudos de Cultura Contemporânea.

Compère, M.-M. (1995). *L'Histoire de l'éducation en Europe: essai comparatif sur la façon dont elle s'écrit*. Paris: Institut National de Recherche Pédagogique.

———. (1997). *Histoire du temps scolaire en Europe*. Paris: Institut National de Recherche Pédagogique.

Dadoy, M. (1984). Qualification et strutures sociales. *CADRES*, Juin, n° 313.

———. (1987). La notion de qualification chez Georges Friedmann. *Sociologie du Travail*, n° 1.

De Certeau, M. (1994). *A Invenção do cotidiano: 1. Artes de fazer*. Petrópolis: Vozes.

Forquin, J.-C. (1993). *Escola e cultura: as bases sociais e epistemológicas do conhecimento escolar*. Porto Alegre: Artes Médicas.

Foucault, M. (1971). *L'ordre du discours*. Paris: Gallimard.

Gourevitch, A. Y. (1975). O tempo como problema de história cultural. In P. Ricoeur (Ed.). *As culturas e o tempo*. Pretrópolis: Vozes.

Heller, A. (1972). *O quotidiano e a História*. Rio de Janeiro: Paz e Terra.

———. (1977). *Sociologia da vida cotidiana*. Madri: Pensínsula.

Lefebvre, H. (1972). *La vida cotidiana en el Mundo Moderno*. Madri: Alianza Editorial.

Lèvi-Strauss, C. (1962). Histoire y Dialectique. *Pensée Sauvage*. Paris: Plon.

Lima, L. C. (1989). *O controle do imaginário: razão e imaginação nos tempos modernos*. Rio de Janeiro: Forense Universitária.

Lukàcs, G. (1979). *Ontologia do ser social: os princípios ontológicos fundamentais de Marx*. São Paulo: Ciências Humanas.

Munakata, K. (1984). Compromisso do Estado. *Revista de História*, São Paulo, ANPUH/Maro Zero, n° 7.

Narodowski, M. (1997). Hacia una Historia de la Educación sin grandes desafíos. In M. Téllez (Ed.). *Educación, cultura y política*. Caracas: Universidad Central de Venezuela.

Nóvoa, A. and Ossenbach, G. (1997). Por una Historia Comparada de la Educación en España, Portugal y América Latina. In A. Escolano and R. Fernandes (Eds.), *Los caminos hacia la modernidad educativa en España y Portugal (1800–1975)*. Zamora: Fundación Rei Afonso Henriques.

Nunes, C. (1992). Novas Abordagens de velhos objetos. *Teoria e Educação*. Porto Alegre, Pannonica, n° 6.

Nunes, C. and Carvalho, M. M. C. de. (1993). Historiografia da Educação e Fontes. *Cadernos Anped*, Porto Alegre, ANPEd, set., n° 5.

Pècaut, D. (1990). *Os intelectuais e a política no Brasil: entre o povo e a nação*. São Paulo: Ática.

Romano, R. (1997). *Conservadorismo romântico: origem do totalitarismo*. São Paulo: Fundação Editora da UNESP.

Tanguy, L. (1997). Formação: uma atividade em vias de definição? *Veritas*. Porto Alegre, v. 42, jun., n° 2.

Vieira, C. E. (1994). *O historicismo gramsciano e a pesquisa em educação*. Master's dissertation. São Paulo: Pontifícia Universidade Católica de São Paulo.

Vicent, Guy. (1980). L'ecole primaire francaise: e'tude sociologuiquie. Lyon: University de Lyon Presses.

Warde, M. J. (1990a). A favor da Educação, contra a positivização da Filosofia. *Em Aberto*. Brasília, INEP, 9(45):27–33, jan/mar.

———. (1990b). Contribuições de História para a Educação. *Em Aberto*. Brasília, INEP, ano 9, jul/set, n° 47.

———. (1990c). O papel da pesquisa na pós-graduação em educação. *Cadernos de Pesquisa*, São Paulo, Fundação Carlos Chagas, n° 73.

———. (1992). Pesquisa em educação: entre o Estado e a ciência. *Universidade e Educação*. Campinas: Papirus.

———. (1993). A produção discente dos programas de pós-graduação em educação no Brasil (1982–1991): avaliação e perspectivas. *Avaliação e perspectivas na área de educação (1982–91)*. Porto Alegre: Anped.

———. (1998a). Questões teóricas e de método: a História da Educação nos marcos de uma História das Disciplinas. In D. Saviani, et al. (Orgs.). *História e História da Educação*. Campinas: Autores Associados.

———. (1998b). *História da Educação Brasileira: constituição do campo, fronteiras, intelectuais, instituições*. Caxambu: Reunião Anual da ANPEd.

Zarifian, P. (1997). *A competência e os modelos produtivos*. São Paulo, ago./set. (Palestra proferida no XXI Congreso de la Asociación Latinoamericana de Sociologia).

part 3

Constructing
a Cultural History

5

Genealogy of Education

Some Models of Analysis

Julia Varela

Although at present the Nietzschian concept of genealogy is predominantly used to refer to the methodology used by Michel Foucault in his later works, in reality the term can also be used to characterize the outlook of other researchers in the social sciences. Among these are a number of classic scholars such as Marx, Weber, and Durkheim. These seminal figures in the social sciences put into place models for analysis that like those of Foucault and Elias, possess a set of unifying traits. These traits include: a specific use of history with the goal of understanding the present; an emphasis on systematization and conceptualization that assumes continuous interaction between the elaboration of theories and hypotheses (on the assumption that the facts do not speak for themselves); and, in empirical work, the central importance given to power relations in analyzing social processes and change, and the search for means of distancing. This last factor refers not only to the interdependencies established between the functioning of specific powers and the social conditions governing the production of theories and methods of analysis, but also to the social and intellectual position of the researcher.

My reflections about genealogy will be presented in two sections. In the first section, I attempt to characterize the defining traits of the genealogical method; in the second section, I provide an illustration of the use of this method in concrete research related to formal and informal education. In other words, the goal of this work within the field of education is to highlight the complexity of the relationships that are interwoven among various ways of exercising power, the formation of knowledge, and specific forms of subjectification.

From the Classical Sociologists to the Work of Michel Foucault and Norbert Elias

Marx, first, and later Weber and Durkheim carried out important processes of intellectual decentering in respect to the theories and methods of historical analysis in their times. In *The Archaeology of Knowledge*, Michel Foucault carefully describes the decentering accomplished by Marx. Furthermore, although Foucault referred specifically to Marx, the same concept of decentering can be easily extended to Weber and Durkheim. In the face of the global history that held sway in his time, Marx initiated a new type of history, the general history, which did not attempt to restore either the historical and material principals that govern a society, or the immanent law that explains society's harmonious cohesion. Marx broke away from this harmonious vision, as well as from its concomitant history, in order to analyze the salient questions of his period. He asserted the necessity of establishing distinct levels of analysis, as well as studying the interdependencies of these, to search for adequate strategies for understanding the logic behind processes, and to delimit the criteria that would make it possible to select the historical materials to work with. In this way, instead of a chronology that corresponds to teleological reasoning, and instead of a model of consciousness that is constantly unfolding and progressing, Marx argued for the need to develop a kind of history built up by articulating differentiated instances that no longer respond to a law governing a single line of development, but that, instead, possess relative autonomy and unique characteristics. Furthermore, he argued, among these historical instances there exists an interplay of power relations, misadjustments, and specific correlations. In this way, the notions of change, discontinuity, and dispersion can be taken into account within the framework of the general history. This is what is meant by decentering.

The epistemological and methodological questions that were addressed by these classical sociologists made it possible for the nascent social sciences to free themselves from a historicist philosophy of history (in which history is identified with an excessively abstract and teleological rationality). It then became possible to question the presuppositions behind the global history whose analysis was based on a discourse of continuity and of the conscious subject. This questioning focused on the origin of social processes. All three of these classical thinkers were opposed to the concept and use of global history in their research on capitalist relations of production, on specific forms of rationalization, and on the study of the genesis of institutions. In their attempt to explain social processes, they were able to situate their analysis on a different level and to break, not only with the sovereignty of an essentialized subject, but also with the nascent but growing conception of a psychological subject.

For example, Marx and Engels criticized Stirner, accusing him of reducing social relations to representations from which subjects could be constructed. In the same way, Durkheim affirmed that social life must be explained, not by conceptualizing the subjects that participate in it, but instead by looking for deeper causes that are often not consciously accessible. Durkheim also criticized Spencer for asserting that social facts were nothing more than simple developments of psychological facts. Weber was also critical of psychological explanations and was critical of the opinion, current in his time, that psychology would be able to play a role with respect to the "spiritual sciences" similar to the role played by mathematics in relation to the "natural sciences."

Does this mean that subjects do not create history and are destined only to endure it? Nothing could be further from the positions of the classical sociologists. These thinkers, accounting for power relations that cut across the social field and the conflicts that exist between social classes and groups, were opposed to the conception of society as being formed of isolated individuals. They pointed out that human beings make history by acting freely; but at the same time, these free actions take place in a context that is not of their own choosing, but that instead has been imposed on them. Their analysis is concerned precisely with the elucidation of these impositions in order to avoid a subjection that is derived from a consciousness based on an ignorance of these impositions.

Marx, Weber, and Durkheim were all working from the epistemological premise that the social world should be made foreign to us, that an "object" that possesses a social reality does not necessarily constitute a sociological "object." In the process they broke away from a naive realism and advocated the need for systematic conceptualization and reflection, which requires that one situate processes historically if one wishes to understand the logic behind their internal development. In order to carry out this contrastive work, it is important to engage in epistemological vigilance concerning common notions, language, models of formalization, and the techniques that are used. It is important to be conscious of the meaning of the concepts that one uses, so that researchers do not confer this meaning once and for all, but remain conscious that they are conditioned by the theoretical systems of which they form a part, and by the type of episteme in which they are inscribed. These epistemes are in turn linked to specific sociohistorical conditions and power relations. In this way we can understand the limitations and advantages of the categories of knowledge within which we work, and avoid a way of thinking that continues to be excessively dichotomized and oversimplified.

From the beginning, the social sciences were institutionalized as a type of knowledge that attempted to avoid both philosophically essentialist, and positivistic psychological foci. The classical sociologists criticized positivism insofar as positivists considered facts to be data whose meaning is immediately visible through the use of simple techniques. Such attempts to obtain from the facts themselves the problematic and the concepts that make it possible to analyze them generally lead to formalistic, artificial, and tautological theories. This type of theory is not useful for in-depth explorations either of institutions or of social life. Ignoring the necessity of analyzing facts within the context (at least provisionally) of an explicit theoretical framework leads, not to a process of distancing, but instead to the maintenance of uncontrolled factors that are incompatible, and that introduce significant biases, both into the research process and into the results. It is not possible, therefore, to carry out a reflective sociological practice without this interaction between theory and practice.

These dimensions, which can be used to characterize the analytical models of Marx, Weber, and Durkheim (without canceling out the specific qualities of each of these scholars), constitute the framework that articulates the work of Foucault and Elias. Both of these latter figures are situated in the phylum of the general history, the use of which makes it possible to break away from preestablished schemas in order to bring into the foreground the memory of conflicts, to understand how the conditions making up the present were gestated, and to elaborate new forms of knowledge that make it possible to understand the present in a reflexive manner.[1]

In this sense, Foucault pointed out that genealogy was an attempt to liberate historical knowledge from subjection, that is to say, to make it capable of fighting against the coercion of a universal, formal, and scientific theoretical discourse. In other words, genealogy was a means of rejecting the effects of power derived from theories defined as "scientific," in order to eliminate the tyranny of global and globalized discourses that were established with their particular privileges and institutional hierarchies.

It is not, then, surprising that both Foucault and Elias have been particularly concerned with the search for a more reflexive knowledge in order to reexamine the categories of knowledge that have traditionally operated within the milieu of the social and human sciences. Foucault in *The Order of Things* and *The Archaeology of Knowledge* (1972), as well as Elias in *Time: An Essay* (1992) and in *The Symbol Theory* show that the categories of knowledge are of a historical nature, and emerge and function in conjunction with historical changes that have taken place in various fields, among others, the field of knowledge. Both of these scholars emphasize the need to elaborate theories that take into account the conditions in which systems of representation and symbolization are formed, in order to avoid two reductionist tendencies that are, unfortunately, all too common in the social sciences: the historical/transcendental, and the empirical/psychological. Their criticisms are not directed merely towards the various forms of idealism or positivism. They also make extensive criticisms of currents that have dominated the social sciences in recent times, such as structural functionalism and neo-Marxism, because they consider these systems of thought to be excessively linked to partisan interests. Elias also warns against that which he calls contaminated knowledge, that is to say against all of those theories that keep humans from becoming conscious of the fact that success in the struggle for a better world will only be possible through collectively planned social processes, and not through uncontrollable exterior forces, divine or otherwise. All of this, then, necessitates participation in collective decision making, as well as the existence of a shared fund of reflexive knowledge.[2]

In summary, if we wish to characterize, rapidly, and therefore schematically, the genealogical method, as it has been put into use by the classical sociologists as well as by Foucault and Elias, we could point out the following characteristics:

(a) The genealogical method is a method focused on process in two senses of that term. On the one hand, it examines processes of social change in and of themselves; in doing so, it focuses on processes of long duration with the goal of understanding the rules by which a field is formed, including that which it inherits from the past, as well as its innovations. On the other hand, it attempts to decipher the internal logic by which each field functions to understand its own dynamics. It is from this that genealogy draws its particular interest in the interdependencies that are established between the various levels of analysis. Again following the reasoning of the classical theorists, these levels of analysis must be specified. It is necessary for microphysical, local relations to interact with other relations of a more general nature. For this reason, it is important to give the process of mediation a particular importance. This is because it is precisely these mediating processes, together with the need to develop special concepts to take these interactions into account, that make theoretical innovation necessary. The works of Foucault and Elias show the authenticity of this need, which, like the classical sociologists, has caused them to elaborate a whole series of new concepts, such as: configuration, interdependency, changing balance of power, involvement and detachment, affective economy, and identity of me and identity of us, in the case of Elias; and disciplines, biopower, techniques and technologies of governing, political anatomy of the body, forms of subjectivization, *dispositif* of sexuality, regimes of truth, politics of truth, and governmentalization, in the case of Foucault.

The attention given to mediations permit Foucault and Elias to avoid two illusions: the illusion of formalization and the illusion of doxa. The first of these attempts to explain sciences and types of knowledge through recourse to a formal logic, as if knowledge has a sort of social extraterritoriality. The second converts forms of knowledge into mere reflections of determining factors that are extrinsic to these knowledges or into superstructural simulacra which hide the real source of truth, which is always exterior and always inaccessible. More than the total autonomy of thought, or its total dependency that goes beyond logical neopositivism, or the "hermeneutics of suspicion," genealogy advocates the reconstruction within a historical framework of the interplay of material and symbolic processes that cut across the formation of the various knowledges, as well as their institutionalization and development, and the bringing to light of their social functions, that is to say, the investigation of the social conditions under which they were formed.[3]

(b) For the genealogist there is no such thing as either pure knowledge, or knowledge that is absolutely contaminated by determining factors external to it. From these points comes the need to reconstruct the play of interactions that exists between power and knowledge in a specific field and a specific historical moment.

In their approach to the analysis of power, genealogists have broken away in recent decades from a number of common philosophical, juridical, and state conceptions that reify power and convert it into a static entity, in order to understand it as one of the basic aspects of social relations, which is not possessed, but rather exercised, distinguishing between relations of power and relations of domination (see Elias 1994; Foucault 1995a). In this way they have distanced themselves from exclusively negative visions of power that identify power with repression in order to give more attention to the productive aspects of the exercise of power. They have advocated the necessity of basing theories on a minute analysis of power relations within a concrete field in order to determine the mechanisms that are invested, colonized, and transformed to produce strategies that are ever broader and more general, and that can crystallize, although increasingly rarely in Western societies, in strategies of domination.

Genealogists do not, therefore, advocate studying the functioning of various levels of power in a way that is based on preestablished schemas, such as bourgeois domination; neither do they use concepts that depend on an excessively simplistic binary logic involving dominators and dominated. What they attempt is precisely the opposite—to accomplish an ascending analysis of power relations in order to explain how disequilibriums of power, or, in certain cases, domination, were established. In this framework, it is necessary to reimagine conceptions of power and of freedom because in this way of thinking they are no longer opposites. There is no such thing as an absolute absence of power or of freedom, but rather specific distributions of power and freedom, which must be seen in terms of shades and nuances. In general, modern Western society does not produce either absolute autonomy or absolute determinism.

The way in which the functioning of specific powers and knowledges is articulated brings both Foucault and Elias to question, although naturally each in his own way, the emergence of specific forms of "rationalization." Both of these scholars distance themselves from the search for a general Western type of rationality. Foucault emphasizes that his work does not consist of an attempt to establish a discussion with the type of rationality that seems to be particular to Western civilization. The basis of this type of work was already undertaken by members of the Frankfurt School.

"My objective," Foucault said referring to the Frankfurt School, "does not consist of establishing a conversation with [their] works, so important and worthwhile on another level, but instead to propose another model of analysis of the relations between rationalization and power. . . . Not to focus globally on the rationalization of society or culture, but instead, to analyze the process in the different domains, each one of which leads back to a fundamental experience: madness, disease, death, crime, sexuality, etc. What it is necessary to do is to analyze specific rationalities, but not to invoke unceasingly, processes of rationalization in general" (1995b).

In his own work, Foucault gives special attention to the study of the procedures, or rules, according to which our society separates truth from falsehood, rules that tie the production of the truth to particular systems of power, inscribing it within a particular regime of truth. These regimes do not belong to the ideological, or superstructural sphere, given that the meaning of truth is always relative in character, and that its decodification implies the need to take into account the rules that govern the symbolic field in a particular historical moment. These rules take us back to the way in which relationships between meanings (and not just communication) are governed, and are established among groups and between human beings.

Elias also seems to dislike the concept of rationalization when taken from a generalizad perspective. He posits the need to analyze specific rationalities as they pertain to particular knowledges and powers. In this way, he sees courtly rationality as a form of rationalization in which spending, and social prestige, more than economic opportunity, became converted into calculable instruments of power. This type of "rationality," which can initially appear to be irrational from the point of view of the bourgeois-economic rationality, can only be understood within the framework of a specific social configuration—that of the courtly-aristocratic society, which continued its development, partly as an inheritance and partly as a counterimage, into the bourgeois-professional era.

(c) Finally, Foucault and Elias have been interested in understanding the existing imbrications between given forms of the exercise of power, the formation of different types of knowledge, and processes of subjectivization. Both thinkers have attempted, in consequence, to decipher the functions that are accomplished from the moment of their formation by concepts of the individual and of society, and, as a consequence, to break away from the false dichotomy that has been set up between the individual and society. This separation has its roots both in what have been called processes without a subject, and in the ahistorical and asocial conception of the subjectivity, the conception of which is the base of the psychological subject.

Norbert Elias has pointed out what happens when one asks how and why the structure of the social fabric and the structure of the individual change at the same time, in a particular way. One sees, for example, during the transformation from a courtly society to a bourgeois society that there was also transformation of personal desires, instincts, thoughts, and individuality. This amplification from a static to a dynamic vision makes the image of an impermeable wall between one human being and all others, between an interior and an exterior world, disappear. In place of these walls, we have the image of a constant and ever-changing interdependency between human beings. Foucault, on his part, explicitly affirms that his works respond to the desire to understand the relations that are established between forms of subjectivization, games of truth, and practices of power. In concrete terms, in the first volume of *The History of Sexuality* (1979) he shows how, through the dispositif of sexuality, both sexuality and the sexed body are invested with given properties, and inserted into specific regimes of truth through the combination of specific techniques and technologies of governing. For Foucault, there is no single global strategy that governs sexual identities in a uniform manner. There are only specific strategies that must be researched.

Triple Illustration

From the 1970s until his death, Foucault worked on a model of analysis that had undergone, like all intellectual work in progress, numerous modifications. This model, although not applied in a systematic way by Foucault himself to education, has served as a point of reference for numerous researchers in the field of sociology of education (see, e.g., Ball 1990; da Silva 1994; Larrosa 1995).

In his book *Discipline and Punish* (1997), in which he explicitly refers to educational institutions in relation to the functioning of a particular type of power that he calls disciplines, Foucault carries out a developmental analysis of power relations. Starting his analysis on the level of microphysical processes, he pays special attention to mediations, as do other sociologists of education such as Basil Bernstein and Pierre Bourdieu, in order to arrive at a general level of interpretation. Through the elaboration of a whole series of concepts, he explains the transformations that were produced in the area of the exercise of power beginning in the eighteenth century, in connection with the formation of disciplinary knowledges, the establishment of the bourgeois order, and the beginnings of new forms of subjectivization linked to the formation of the individual. The concept of disciplines permits him to analyze changes in the forms and actions of power, and the emergence of a new economy of power, that makes it seem more profitable to supervise and normalize than to repress and punish.

The disciplines imply the establishment of specific technologies and procedures as well as different levels and goals for their application. However, in addition, this concept makes it possible to articulate those changes that are produced at the microphysical level, i.e., the technologies and procedures intended for the control of bodies, gestures, mentality, and the behavior of subjects, with the modifications that take place in the administration of space, time, and activities. The effects of this exercise of disciplinary power, destined to form subjects that are more useful when they are more docile, form the basis of a functional perception of the body (a body-segment, which is articulable with others to form larger groups) that is based on the formation of a space and a time that are serial and analytical (the progressive conception of time, which in turn goes back to an evolutionary sense of history and a linear progress that were so salient in the nineteenth century). It is also based on the new art of governing that organized and distributed subjects, combining their efforts to obtain the maximum possible return on them, individualizing them, hierarchizing them, and dividing them in a way that prevents undesirable and potentially dangerous alliances. In the dawn of the industrial revolution, the accumulation of people became necessary in order to produce an accumulation of wealth. In the same way, the formation of individual personalities, and individual subjects, became necessary so that the profitable fiction that society was composed of isolated individuals could be imposed, precisely at the moment that the legitimacy of power was being based on the "general will."

In his analysis of the function of disciplinary power, Foucault takes a special interest in Jesuit teaching, which formed one of the institutions from which the apparatuses and technologies that make use of this type of power were gestated, as well as one of the spaces in which its effects were best demonstrated. Foucault relates the logic of the functioning of disciplinary power in the social body, and in various institutions (Jesuit colleges, military barracks, hospitals, factories, etc., without canceling out the particular qualities of each one of these) with the process that he names the governmentalization of the state.

The logic of this governmentalization can be traced back to the principles and functions of pastoral power and to its principal technology: the confession. It is in the examination, the central technology of disciplinary power, in which hierarchical surveillance and normalizing sanctions are articulated. This makes it possible not only to compare, control, hierarchize, divide, and normalize subjects, but also to extract knowledges from them (the formation of human and social sciences in intimate interdependency with technologies of observation and examination, but also, more concretely, pedagogy) and confer upon them "an individualized nature," giving them a specific personal identity resulting from the way in which they have passed through different examinations, tests, ranks, and levels throughout the course of their training. Foucault, using the concept of disciplines, puts the transformations that are produced at the microphysical level in relation with more general processes, such as political processes (changes in the forms of the legitimacy of power) and economic, juridical, and demographic processes. Certain readers of *Discipline and Punish* (1997) insist that the subjects to which Foucault refers submit passively to the exercise of disciplinary power; however, Foucault points out that while this is the image that disciplinary power gives itself, most powerfully represented in Jeremy Bentham's panopticon, in fact, subjects resist the exercise of powers, including disciplinary power. Moreover, power relations, although they might be opposed to the desires and needs of subjects, demand their active participation.

Power can thus be studied as something that circulates, that functions, that is exercised through networks in which individuals are never inert blank spaces or accomplices of power, but are instead the elements used for its recomposition. This does not, nevertheless, mean that power is uniformly divided among individuals; on the contrary, it is necessary to depart from an analysis of the effects of power on a local level to understand the way in which the mechanisms are invested, transformed, and used by broader technologies that are able to condense it, and give way, in certain instances, to specific forms of domination. It is not, then, a simple matter of asking who holds power, but instead of asking how things function on the level of those continual and uninterrupted processes that subject the body, govern gestures, control behavior, or, in other words, indicate how actual subjects have been materially constituted from the multiplicity of possible bodies, of strengths, of energies, of materials, of desires, and of thoughts (see Foucault 1992).

The Foucauldian model of analysis, when contrasted with other models of analysis, puts particular emphasis on the "productive functions of the school" rather than that institution's reproductive mechanisms, and breaks away from any type of determinism when explaining the functions of educational institutions, whether these determinisms are economic or any other type. The school is thus a space where new procedures and technologies for exercising power can be tried out. It makes possible the emergence of a new political anatomy of the body, in that, by training subjects it gives them capacities, aptitudes, and so forth. It is also a new physics of power, in that it permits the articulation of power in the search to maximize its strengths—creating, in summation, a new economy of pleasure.

In any case, disciplinary power is, for Foucault, merely a type of power that is located historically, and that uses specific techniques for governing subjects, whose exercise, and whose effects, have not been realized without resistance. In fact, one of Foucault's important interventions referred precisely to the growing resistance to government through individualization. Here he refers to the fight against particular techniques and technologies of power that are incarnated in daily life, that classify subjects while presuming to give them a certain type of innate nature. These resistances simultaneously represent oppositions to certain effects of the privileges of knowledge, to the mystification that certain specialists attempt to impose on the public as the means of communication between the representatives of the world and ourselves. They are finally, resistances against the different forms of subjectivization and submission existing today.[4]

In summary, it is important to point out that, despite the exercise of disciplinary power, and despite this power's totalitarian hunger for intervention, there continue to be subjects and knowledges that are not completely controlled by it. Because of this it is better not to identify the subject with the individual, or "educated culture" with the dominant culture, or to contemplate pedagogical relationships, in the sense of a relationship of teaching, of transmission, on the part of one who knows more to others who know less, uniquely as a relationship of domination. It is better to continue investigating the functions of educational institutions .

For the second illustration, our first reference point is *The Civilizing Process* (1978) not only because it is one of Norbert Elias's first works, but also because it serves as a framework for much of his later research (a constantly evolving framework that leads him to talk in his later works about the process of civilization and decivilization, to separate him more clearly from those who wish to situate him, without having read his work, in an evolutionary phylum). In this work, Elias focused on things usually viewed as insignificant, such as the rules of urbanity, good manners, or, if we prefer, informal education, and clearly traced the transformations that shaped the affective economy in its ways of thinking, seeing, and feeling a person's way of relating to him/ herself and to others. Elias elaborated a sociogenesis of modern forms of interaction that, at the same time as it questions its nature, permits us to understand its meaning, by putting into relief the way in which our habitual behaviors as well as our habitual thought patterns carry with them the mark of certain past social interactions, in the specific form that they adopted in Western societies. These influences include conflicts over power and distinction, and between different social groups, especially those that took place between the courtly nobility and the nascent bourgeoisie.

Elias offers us, through his analysis of the rules of urbanity, an interpretive model that is the result of the application of a rigorous methodology, which makes it possible to delimit the interdependencies that existed between the formation of the modern state and the processes of privacy and individualization. Norbert Elias has been more capable, perhaps, than any other contemporary sociologist of demonstrating the interrelationships that exist between local change processes and instances of a more general character, establishing clear mediations between the two. Furthermore, in this work he has traced out the structure that has made it possible to tie together two aspects: (l) the transformations that affected people's everyday life, and that led particularly the courtly nobility, but also the wealthy bourgeoisie, to submit their impulses, sentiments, and behavior to a discipline and control that were ever more intense; and (2) the characteristics of the modern state and its project of pacification was the result of various struggles, situated on distinct levels, that converged in the monopolization by the Monarchs of new opportunities for power, based on the legitimate use of physical force and of taxes. This project of pacification caused tensions to be displaced slowly from the "public" space, which was occupied increasingly by the state, to a "private" space, which was progressively invaded and emptied of meaning. The formation of these spaces was constituted by the norms of good manners, in this way transferring problems, and thus solutions, to the interior of the subjects themselves.

The transition from a medieval society, dominated by violent warriors, feudal lords dedicated unceasingly to fighting and preparing themselves for war, to absolute statism, would imply strong commotions in social configurations and dynamics, but also in the individual. Taking as a reference the emergence of three terms—courtesy, civility, and civilization—that he has found useful for situating the changes taking place in three precise historical moments, Elias begins his work in the Middle Ages. He pays particular attention to the advent of the absolute state and in the processes that allowed the court to transform itself into a fundamental institution, from the point of view not only of material but also of symbolic power, eventually becoming the center from which good manners radiated. Good manners not only formed part of the code of legitimate comportment, etiquette, and ceremony necessary to live court, but were also instruments that contributed to a distinguished social identity conferred on those residents of the court who, because of their monopoly on good manners, devalued the lifestyles and cultures of other groups, who were, in turn, labeled vulgar, provincial, and ill-mannered.

In addition, another function of the rules of urbanity consisted of the fact that as these roles were learned, and as they imposed a progressive and systematic regulation on numerous aspects of "private" and social life, they also contributed to the emergence of modesty and intimacy. These rules, prohibitions, and taboos, when interiorized and intensified, were, over the course of time, translated into aspects of self-control that acted in a nonconscious and automatic fashion, and gave subjects a new identity. Thus the singular, isolated, and autonomous individual emerged. Lack of understanding of the processes that lead to the predominance of the "identity of myself" over the "identity of us" constitutes an obstacle that makes the comprehension of the long-term modifications that have affected human relations difficult. It also makes it difficult to become conscious of the radical importance held by relations between human beings and their fellow humans, including the way in which humans depend on each other in all circumstances, both in thought and feelings, in love as in hatred, in action and inaction.

Norbert Elias thus advanced the hypothesis that the civilizing process has involved progressive pressure and coactions, since the sixteenth century, on the lives of Western people. The norms of good manners, which regulate the most varied aspects of table manners, gaming, salons, personal grooming, and personal and private behavior, initially affected primarily the upper classes, but later became intensified, transformed, and generalized (although these transformations were neither linear nor identical among the various Western countries), beginning at the end of the eighteenth century when the "bourgeoisie" came into power.

Making use of historical materials, Elias also confronts the task of explaining sociologically the formation of the superego. Emotional control, mastery over feelings, the discipline of the "natural functions," transferred into the interior of subjects the struggles and conflicts that, in other historical eras were played out in the social arena. Tensions were displaced ever more from the social arena, which was ever more dominated by the state, into an intimate space, which was increasingly emptied of meaning. Relationships exist within the interior of each human being, and with them, the structure of his or her impulse control, of his ego and his superego, evolved together with the civilizing process, following the specific transformations of human and social relationships.

In another of his classic works, *The Court Society*, Elias also elaborated in a systematic way the connections between the actions and the merits of various historical actors, as well as the dynamic of the social associations and configurations within which meaning is constructed. In this work he attempted to answer a fundamental question: How was it historically possible that, in the face of a great majority, great opportunities for power were concentrated in the hands of a limited elite? In addition, in order to avoid determinism, the study of social configurations and the positions that various subjects occupied within them was useful for understanding the development of the social personality. This does not eliminate the importance of the personality of a particular subject, but instead it places this personality in relationship to the position occupied, with greater or fewer opportunities for power and action, which this subject has according to his or her position in a specific social dynamic.

Lastly, all of those interested in questions related to education can make use of one of his unfinished works: *Mozart: On the Sociology of a Genius*. This work sets forth the idea that sociology can help us better understand the incomprehensible in our social life as it traces with great detail the complex relationships between individual destiny and social existence. This small work focuses on the familial and musical education of Mozart, in the framework of the relations existing between the courtly nobility of his time and the bourgeoisie in their service, of which Mozart formed a part. To make Mozart comprehensible, both as a human being and as a musician, Elias shows not only how Mozart's rebellion against courtly society, at a time when it was not yet possible to exist as a "free artist," put his life in danger, but also how the excision of his social existence, in the manner in which he occupied two worlds—the aristocratic and the bourgeois—had an impact on the very structure of his personality. The fact that this impact did not prevent Mozart from continuing his struggle for artistic integrity, nor detract from the value of his musical aptitudes, reveals to us the force of his personality and at the same time his musical strengths.[5]

For the third illustration, some of my own works are also situated in a similar perspective. In *Modos de educación en la España de la Contrarreforma* (Modes of education in the Spain of the Counter-Reformation 1983), I have attempted to analyze, in a relational and comparative way, making use of the new concept of modes of education, the manner in which different ways of governing children of a tender age (in the sixteenth century, childhood was still not a well-defined category) were put into place. Distinct ways of governing young children, which could be defined only in relationship to each other, were interconnected with a whole series of transformations linked fundamentally to the formation of the modern state, as well as to struggles to obtain social harmony, and to the imposition of religious orthodoxy as part of efforts to establish religious hegemony. These means of governing "children" were important technologies that intervened, together with other factors, in the formation of social and individual identities at a precise historical moment when the passage from arms to letters, or the process of pacification to which Norbert Elias refers, made it possible, when learning one's letters, to become, at least theoretically, an adherent of the great government of the monarchy.

In order to understand the social function of the modes of education, it is important to stop looking at educational theories and practices as if they were superstructures that depended on, and were derived from, the productive system. This means granting education a relative autonomy, or, in other words, analyzing the social dynamic as it actually functioned. Social classes, and social groups, did not exist prior to modes of education, but were instead their motor and at the same time their effect. In the face of technologies of education as instruments of repression, or a mechanism of mechanic reproduction, it is important to research the productive effects of education, keeping in mind the relations of power that traverse its discourses, and the various practices and institutions competing in this arena.

In this way, it is possible to demonstrate the way in which the modes of education became diversified, and how they responded to the distinct natures that humanists, moralists, and members of the government in the sixteenth and seventeenth centuries attributed to the various types of "childhood" in their fields of study. There were natures of gold, naturally genteel and generous, of brilliant intuition, corresponding to the offspring of the nobility, natures of iron, belonging to the sons of the dregs of the republic, and finally natures of silver, corresponding to the sons of the nascent and growing middle estate, destined to form the fulcrum of the scale, to be situated between the peak and the base of the new configuration of social stratification whose construction was crucial to the formation of moderns modes of education.

These differentiated and differentiating modes of education that paid attention to the care of the soul, to the cultivation of the intellect, and to the dexterity of the body, promoted specific funtion of subjectivization. Little ladies and gentlemen were given qualities of distinction that manifested their knowledge of the norms of protocol, shown when they knew how to eat and drink with refinement and beauty, to move with grace and perfection, to speak different languages with elegance and to dress lavishly. These were the particular qualities of educated subjects who, in addition to being valorous, strong and elegant, (and for those with access to masters of arms, skilled in riding, contests of arms, hunting, etc.) were also to be characterized by the liberal attitudes acquired through education of the liberal faculties (for those who had access to masters of letters.)

It is not for nothing that this mode of education was oriented towards the education of the children of princes and nobles who were born to govern. To children from the middle estates, those who made the perfect Jesuit students, were attributed qualities of a discreet moderation: they had to be modest, well-spoken, polite, devout, quiet, obedient, charitable, studious, and honest. Their physical education did not include, as was true of noble children, elaborate instruction in the use of arms, in riding horseback in different saddles, in the playing of musical instruments, as the Jesuits were not masters of courtly qualities but instead of virtue and of letters. The perfect student was not solely defined in relation to the noble, but was also compared to the vulgar masses. He was expected to differentiate and distance himself from both groups. Finally, the educational program destined for the children of the popular classes was reduced in many cases to learning the catechism and the inculcation of elemental norms of submission and obedience, as was appropriate to the production of subjects who were educated to be dependent and to maintain a state of social and mental inferiority. It is not by chance that the Spanish monarchs in the seventeenth century promoted practices that eliminated the teaching of Latin grammar in the institutions that had been established during the Renaissance, and were intended for the control, care, and discipline of the children of the poor.

The modern modes of education were important instruments for the institution of a new social order and also for the conferring specific identities on subjects, on the sexes, and social groups. A perpective of a "longue durée" analysis shows that it wasn't the mode of education of the nobility—then the dominant estate—that won the battle, but the mode of education instiued by the Jesuits specially destined for the children of the emergent urban middle "classes," who, lacking a specific role, whether as soldiers or in any other craft, were attempting to open up other vocational areas for themselves. It was the increasing attraction of this (Jesuit) model that caused reforms in the universities, and that eventually ended up being slowly imposed as a more general educational model. (Some of the nobles accepted having their children educated in the schools for nobility opened by the Jesuits beginning in the eighteenth century. This is a significant marker for the decline of the nobility). Within this model, the university students lost a whole series of powers ranging from the right to elect their own academic authorities to the right to posses arms. The objective of this dispossession of student power was that students would transform themselves (although they did not submit to these changes without resistance) into disciplined students, or into students who enjoyed a minority status. The success of this specific mode of education was due not only to economic factors, but primarily to political factors, that is, the search for equilibrium between the various social forces, including the religious (the establishment of monogamy and the establishment of new types of relationships between parents and children) and the social (access to positions within the state government requiring a particular type of training).

The system of education imposed by the Jesuits implied a deep rupture with other modes of education current at the time. This process was described by Durkheim in *L'Evolution pedagogique en France* and contributed to the devaluation of modes of education destined for the popular classes, which, from then on, were increasingly identified as classes without education. This system was also the birthplace of subsequent educational institutions. It was within this system that the pieces that would eventually constitute the framework of contemporary educational institutions were refined and assembled. The construction, genesis, and transformation of these educational pieces is the focus of one of my recent studies: *Arqueología de la escuela* (The archaeology of the school).

Arqueología de la escuela analyzes the processes that made possible the formation and articulation of the basic elements that make up the logic of the functioning of modern educational institutions. These include: the definition of a state of childhood, the emergence of an enclosed space in which to educate children, the formation of a body of specialists, the pedagogization of knowledge, and the destruction of other forms of education. These processes put into play certain given categories of space, time, and identity. From that point, in order to understand the functions carried out by the various modes of education, it is not only necessary to keep in mind the configuration adopted by the social dynamic in a given historical moment, but also, and especially, the way in which power relations impact on the organization and definition of legitimate knowledges, and the way in which technologies of governing, including the choice of the type or types of use power, or, in the end, what pedagogies are to be applied to mold subjectivities. This book examines those models to which these educational "pieces" were submitted since the sixteenth century, pointing out the innovations and the readaptations that they underwent up until the institutionalization of compulsory schooling and its effects, ending with the implantation in the state schools of a model of psychological pedagogy.

It is possible to end by saying that these works, in which the genealogical model is put to the test, show that there still exist at present distinct modes of education that can be traced back to a specific social dynamic: to the coexistence of different childhoods, of different forms of perceiving, and of living in the world. It can further be said that these types of childhood are shot through with power relations and conflicts. *Modos de educación en la España de la Contrarreforma* (1983) served, among other things, to point out that the Jesuit system of education, and that of other religious orders that followed a similar model, was of particular importance in causing the so-called bourgeoisie to acquire a specific social identity, as well as for its members to have an individual identity: that of the *honnétte homme*, and for them to gain access to power. This access implied not only that an important part of the members of this social class would gain riches, but also that they would acquire a certain type of knowledge, without which they would never have been able to govern. In the same way, my later works show that educational institutions were, and still are, enormously productive social spaces (not only from an economic point of view), forming laboratories in which specific technologies for governing childhood are gestated that are later extended and amplified to wider populations.

As an example of this we can look to special educational institutions destined for children who have been labeled "delinquent and abnormal" that emerged in the shadow of the enforcement of compulsory schooling on the children of the popular classes in the nineteenth century. In these schools corrective pedagogies were applied to children, putting into practice new technologies of governing that included the use of a type of power which was less coactive and visible than that which characterized traditional pedagogies. Psychopower, a new form of the exercise of power, implied not only changes in spatiotemporal categories and in identity, including the search for the "natural child," but also in the state of knowledge, in the functions attributed to the teacher, and, finally, in the whole conception of pedagogical theory and practice, as well as the functioning of the social world. The extension of this model to other areas of schooling, as well as to the social world in general, leads us to ask what types of social identities and individuals are put into play underneath the surface of the psychological pedagogies, and, in general, what types of mediations exist between these new technologies of government and the new relations of domination and inequality that are developing and are attempting to legitimate themselves in our "advanced capitalist" societies.[6]

Notes

1. I will not enter into the polemic that remains open about whether or not there is a difference between historical sociology and social history, except to say that both Elias and Foucault, in the face of a number of other classical and modern authors—among the latter, well-known figures such as Pierre Bourdieu and Anthony Giddens—defended a differential specificity for historical sociology. For more on this topic see the following classical texts: Elias (1983: introduction) and Foucault (1977). In order to understand the relationship between genealogy and social history it is important to see Castel (1994).

2. As an example of contaminated knowledge, Elias cites Stephen Hawking who, when asked why his theory of the big bang gave so much importance to the "origin" of the universe, answered that apart from his calculations pointing in that direction, he believed that people would feel more content if they believed that the universe had a definite beginning.

3. Foucault and Elias gave a special importance to the analysis of conditions concerning the formation of knowledge in the context of representation, and of the symbolic, but they broke away from the inflation of meaning, from the delirium of interpretation, and distanced themselves from hermeneutics and semiology. In this way, genealogical analysis is not confused with discourse analysis, nor with semiology, because instead of limiting itself to the text, or to to the system of signs, it attempts to look for meaning through the interplay of interrelationships existing between discursive practices and historically contextualized nondiscursive practices.

4. Foucault considered struggles against the submission of subjectivity the defining struggles of our present times. He argued that these struggles could not be studied without taking into account existing mechanisms of exploitation and domination, but also that they could not be reduced to a simple reflex, because they are involved in complex and indirect relations with certain mechanisms that must be analyzed. See Foucault (1970, 1972, 1979, 1991, 1995b, 1997).

5. In this sense *The Civilizing Process* draws a sketch of a complementary piece of research, *L'enfant et la vie familiale sous l'Ancien Regime* (*Centuries of Childhood*) by Philippe Aries. This latter work, however, does not make any reference to Elias. See Elias (1978, 1982, 1983, 1991).

6. See Varela (1983), and Varela and Alvarez-Uria (1991).

References

Ball, S. J. (Ed.). (1990). *Foucault and education: Disciplines and knowledge*. New York: Routledge.

Castel, R. (1994). 'Problematization' as a mode of reading history. In J. Goldstein (Ed.), *Foucault and the writing of history* (237–52). Cambridge: Basil Blackwell.

da Silva, T. T. (Ed.). (1995). *0 Sujeito da Educaìao*. Vozes, Brazil: Estudos Foucaultianos.

Elias, N. (1978). *The civilizing process, vol. I: The history of manners*. New York: Urizen.

———. (1982). *The civilizing process, vol. II: State formation and civilization*. Oxford: Basil Blackwell.

———. (1983). *The court society*. Oxford: Basil Blackwell.

———. (1983). *Introduction to The Court Society*. Oxford: Basil Blackwell.

———. (1991). *Mozart: Zur Soziologie eines Genies [Mozart: On the sociology of a genius]*. Michael Schruter (Ed.). Frankfurt: Suhrkamp.

———. (1992). *Time: An essay*. Cambridge, MA: Blackwell.

———. (1994). *Conocimiento y poder in Conocimiento y poder*. Madrid: La Piqueta.

Foucault, M. (1970). *The order of things: an archaeology of the human sciences*. London: Tavistock.

———. (1972). *The archaeology of knowledge*. London: Tavistock.

———. (1977). (Ed. by D. F. Bouchard). Nietzsche, genealogy, history. In *Language, counter-memory, practice: Selected essays and interviews* (138–64). Ithaca, NY: Cornell University Press.

———. (1979). *The history of sexuality, vol. I*. London: Penguin.

———. (1991). Governmentality. In G. Burchell, C. Gordon, and P. Miller (Eds.), *The Foucault effect: Studies in governmentality* (87–104). Hemel Hempstead, England: Harvester Wheatsheaf.

———. (1992). *Genealogía del Racismo*. Madrid: La Piqueta.

———. (1995a). *La Ética del cuidado de uno mismo como práctica de la libertad in Hermenéutica del sujeto*. Madrid: La Piqueta.

———. (1995b). Por que estudiar el poder: la cuestiùn del sujeto? *VVAA Materiales de sociologia crítica*. Madrid: La Piqueta.

———. (1997). *Discipline and punish: The birth of the prison*. London: Penguin.

Larrosa, J. (Ed) (1995). *Escuela, poder y subjetivación*. Madrid: La Piqueta.

Varela, J. (1983). *Modos de educación en la España de la Contrarreforma*. Madrid: La Piqueta.

Varela, J. and Alvarez-Uria, F. (1991). *Arqueología de la escuela*. Madrid: La Piqueta.

6

History of Education and Cultural History

Possibilities, Problems, Questions[1]

Antonio Viñao

Cultural history rides again, but in order to distinguish itself from the past, from traditional cultural history, it resurfaces, now rejuvenated, under the label of "new cultural history" (Hunt 1989). Rarely a month goes by in which some new book or article does not appear under this rubric, or some new seminar, conference, or symposium is not convened. At this moment, for example, I have within arm's reach yet another announcement, a summer course offered at the Complutense University of Madrid: "'New' cultural history: The Influence of Poststructuralism and the Rise of Interdisciplinarity."

Two features stand out in the above-mentioned title: the quotes around the adjective *new*, and the connection made between this new cultural history and poststructuralism (why not add postmodernism?) and interdisciplinarity.

The new cultural history is, after all, interdisciplinary, at least according to the writings of those who are considered its most significant representatives in the varied fields of knowledge traversed by those who are convened to treat its most characteristic themes (Barnes and Stearns 1989; Hunt 1989; Karsten and Modell 1992). It emerges as well in a moment of epistemological crisis, of doubt and uncertainty about how history operates, about the task of doing history. Doubts and uncertainties reach as far into the possibility of arriving at some knowledge of the past as they do into historical discourse as a form of articulating said knowledge linguistically (regarding the consequences of postmodernism and of the "linguistic turn" for intellectual history—one of the modalities of the cultural history—and for historical operation, in general, the literature is ever more abundant). The new cultural history shows great diversity in theme and focus. For some, it simply represents yet another name for the exhausted and not always well-defined history of ideas. Yet for others, this new cultural history would embrace the history of material culture, together with the world of the passions, feelings, and the imaginary, as well as that of representation and mental imagery. It would encompass the history of the elite or of the great thinkers (intellectual history in its strictest sense), popular culture, the human mind as a sociohistorical product (in the Vygotskian sense), and shared symbolic systems (in the Geertzian sense), cultural objects, products of this same mind, and the language and discursive structures generating subjects and social realities. Moreover, it would accomplish this encompassment from a perspective that is not fragmented but rather cohesive and integrated.

The concept of culture, on the other hand, has been and still is interpreted in vastly different ways. The very polysemy of the term explains its success (Burke 1991a, 1992). All of the problems proposed by Peter Burke relative to the New History, including definition, sources, explanation, and synthesis (Burke 1991b), can also be found in the new cultural history. In this context of imprecise and shifting frontiers, characteristic of life itself, and of fragmenting academic disciplines—economic history, social history, cultural history, psychohistory, and intellectual history—this text attempts to explore some of the possibilities of cultural history as it relates to (or from the perspective of) the history of education, yet another fragment of this splintered history. I cannot say whether these are the most important aspects, but they are those that have appealed to me the most, and with which I have been working over the past few years: the history of the processes involved in the professionalization of teaching and in the development of such academic disciplines as intellectual history, the history of school culture and organization, and the study of the human mind as a sociohistorical product. I approach this from a position that rejects any conceptualization of culture as a unified and uniform system in which conformity predominates, and that is split off from social and cultural history. Suffice it to say, paraphrasing Richard L. Schoenwald, that social history is always cultural, cultural history always social, and that both are finally only history (Schoenwald 1992).

The Professionalization of Teaching, Academic Disciplines, and Intellectual History

There are two weak links in the traditional history of ideas: the first considers ideas to be "uncaused causes," without incoherences or fissures, as though they were "individual agents" that determine thought and action; the second is "methodological individualism":

> the insistence that a belief system must be a sum of discrete and explicit propositions, and that each of these propositions can be traced through its various antecedents to a single original source. (Ringer 1990: 277)

Faced with this traditional history of ideas, the social history of ideas tended at first to accentuate the contexts in which ideas germinated and grew. Occasionally these contexts were conceived of as systems that necessarily determined other systems of ideas no less closed or coherent, which then left off being causal agents and were transformed into caused products.

It is evident that ideas and thoughts cannot be totally separated "from their grounding in institutions, practices, and social relations" (Ringer 1990: 277). But these "institutions, practices and social relations" can be seen and analyzed from different points of view and with different methods that themselves render different results. One of these perspectives is that which, growing out of the concepts of "intellectual field" and "habitus" elaborated by Pierre Bourdieu, tries to discover, in Fritz Ringer's formulation, the "theoretical positions" and the "implicit assumptions ... transmitted by institutions, practices, and social relations" (Ringer 1990: 274), that is:

> the major currents of thought and feeling in a certain intellectual environment ... the forms as well as the contents of arguments, ... [the] recurrent patterns or figures of thought, and ... [the] underlying assumptions that were widely shared but not often explicitly discussed. (Ringer 1990: 276)

A focus of this sort, in its broadest sense, would embrace what is explicit and implicit, as well as ideas and beliefs, values and attitudes, modes of thought and of life, and academic-intellectual as well as social roles. And it would relate all of this as much to a determined field or social formation as it would to some concrete theme or problem. In the first case, the result would be a history of intellectuals, of the cultural and academic elite as a group, of its training, its means of selection and admittance into the group, its professional course and status, its tokens of introduction, identification, and distinction before other social groups, its relations to the varying modes of power, its rituals, its collective, corporate, and individual strategies and patron-client relations, its modes of life and conduct, its mental formations, academic and intellectual contexts, discursive practices, lexica, and so forth. In the second instance, the aforementioned analysis would offer those ideas, explicit and implicit, that are presupposed by a determined intellectual group in so far as these relate to any concrete problem, as well as, if the time period under consideration is sufficiently long, any changes, emergences, and residues in conjunction with them. Let's look at two examples that illustrate both points.

Studies of the academic and intellectual development of significant persons continue to be, and always will be, a topic of interest. What is novel, however, is the attention being paid to the education, the modes of selection, and/or the entrance examinations of certain groups of professionals. And within these groups, to which professors can be found at varying ranks in education, or which intellectuals, writers, and researchers in general end up in a specific area or field. Examples of this research have multiplied in the last few years. For instance, a bibliography was elaborated by Marie-Dominique Couzet in 1991 as a component of a research project entitled *Sélection scolaire et societé dans l'Europe Moderne, XVIe-XIXe siècles* that was coordinated by Dominique Julia at the Department of History and Civilisations of the European University

Institut of Florencia, and which collected and annotated a list (not exhaustive) of 125 titles. Among them were books and articles in German, Spanish, French, English, and Italian, dealing with a total of eleven professional groups and with the elite, in general, of various European countries during the centuries indicated. Almost all of these, moreover, were published in the 1980s. A reading of the titles, and of the prologue and conclusions drawn by the project's director, collected in a special issue of the journal *Paedagogica Historica*, speaks for itself: the prosopographic method and the longitudinal analysis of the processes involved in constructing professional careers (that is, those of a given profession), and the analysis of the entrance and selection procedures of the same, are revealed herein to be extraordinarily useful and powerful lenses for viewing the internal configuration of the various professional and intellectual fields, among them, the academic and scholarly professions (Julia 1994a).

For example, the meticulous study of procedures for selecting the different groupings of professors (requirements, tests, education, degrees and curriculum of candidates, programs or theses presented, exams or exercises completed, evaluators, explicit or implicit criteria of selection, intervention on the part of administrative, ecclesiastical, or political authorities, decisions taken, etc.) is one of the features essential to understanding the process of professionalization in education, and definitively, for constructing a history of teaching as a profession (Julia 1981, 1994b; Nóvoa 1987; Viñao 1994a).

The processes and procedures mentioned above are closely allied, in turn, to the history of scholarly disciplines. I prefer this expression taken from André Chervel (1988) to that of "history of curriculum" because it is a broader term that encompasses the history of academic disciplines and subjects. Furthermore, one history is the complement of the other. Academic disciplines are not abstract entities, nor do they possess universal or static essences. They are born and evolve, emerge and vanish, splinter off and join together, reject and absorb each other. They change in content and denomination. They are spaces of power, of contested power, spaces that cluster actors and interests, actions and strategies. They are social spaces that have configured themselves within the cavities of educational systems and academic institutions, bearing more or less exclusive properties, closed with regard to the practitioners and clientele of other disciplines, and at the same time more or less hegemonic in their dealings with other disciplines and fields. For which reason they become, over time, the exclusive preserve of certain professionals who are accredited and legitimized by their corresponding modes of education, entitlement, and selection, and who by this means go on to control the training and induction of those who hope to join their ranks. The disciplines, then, are a source of power and exclusion that is not only professional but also social. Their inclusion or omission in the curricula of one or another profession constitutes a weapon deployed for assigning determined tasks to one professional group or another. The history of the disciplines, their genesis and configuration as such, autonomous in character, cannot be written without analyzing the education, credentials, and recruitment of those who have dedicated themselves to it or who have attempted to do so. Similarly, the analysis of the process of professionalization, of the candidates and members of a given profession, is one of the most significant features of the complementary process of creation and configuration among these disciplines. One aspect gives rise to the other; they are inseparable.

A discipline is, in this sense, the result of boundaries being set around an intellectual field by professionals, by an academic or scientific community or group who present themselves before society and other groups as experts in the field by virtue of a determined mode of selection and education, and by virtue of their degrees. It follows that an analysis of the education, careers, and degrees of the candidates, graduates, and of the judges charged with selecting them will constitute elements for knowing the level of their professionalization and that of the discipline in question; that is, their consolidation as such and their acceptance by other experts. This is why, in the first phases of a study I undertook a few years ago of the origins of the corps of state professors in Spain from 1770 to 1808, I noticed that I needed to distinguish two interrelated parts: the first, now completed, on the process of selection in the terms already indicated (Viñao 1994a), the other, now in progress, on the education, degrees, academic careers, and merits adduced by the candidates or taken into account by the judges and authorities implicated in the process of selection. A preview of this second part, as it relates to the disciplines of natural law, experimental physics, and mathematics, has recently been published (Viñao 1998b).

The possibilities of this type of study are enormous. They can apply, obviously, to the academic profession, or to any other, or to given social groups. Among the latter, the study of the intellectual formation of the elite, especially the cultural, literary, and scientific elite, seems to be in vogue.[2] Doing such research implies, undoubtedly, having recourse to sources heretofore analyzed, in general, only in terms of individual and personal perspectives, and only rarely in a global or contextual way. Among these are found autobiographies and diaries, personal administrative reports, accounts of professional courses of study and honor rolls, records of entrance examinations and competitions—exercises, programs, memoirs, appraisals, or critiques—and the reports relative to the configuration of programs of study and to the creation, modification or suppression of disciplines, including manuals and textbooks. Also of use, for example, are eulogies and the apologetic writings of different professions. In other cases, however, it will be necessary to reread well-known texts from a perspective that permits one to grasp the explicit and implicit strategies for incorporating, differentiating, and excluding given people, groups, or institutions.

However, it would be wrong to limit the study of intellectual fields, of intellectual history, to that of the training and credentials of these various groups of professionals or, in a strictly historical-educational environment, to the process of educational professionalization and to the parallel configuration of the academic disciplines. This is only one possibility among others. Among these, as I have already said, is the analysis of the explicit or implicit ideas and proposals of a determined intellectual group in relation to a concrete question over a course of time sufficiently long to grasp, within those ideas and proposals, its points of inflection, its ruptures and continuities.

Undoubtedly, an analysis of this sort should attend to the most widely distributed and influential texts and authors, to the most significant of these (for whatever reason), or to those that have introduced ideas, perspectives, and criteria that have been disseminated. But this attention to significance will only make sense in a context, namely that defined by the various theoretical positions and prospects maintained in relation to the topic in question. In a recent study of the weekly and daily distribution of time and work in primary education in Spain from 1838 to 1936—about which I'll speak after other methodological considerations—I have analyzed, for example, the theoretical foundations and specific proposals effected in a total of thirty-eight texts (nineteen from 1838–1899 and another nineteen from 1900–1936) written by professors of pedagogy in normal schools, by inspectors of primary education and by teachers, all in relation to the topic mentioned. Some of these texts were written for the training or professional use of teachers within their own schools (Viñao 1997 1998a). Only a reading of those pages or chapters dedicated to the distribution of time and work in these schools, owing to their number and the span of time involved, will allow one to obtain a global idea of the explicit and implicit assumptions, whether widely held or not, of this given group of authors, as well as their influences and rejections, their ruptures and persistences.

Only this global sort of reading and reflection will allow one to grasp, for example, how an initial concept of the distribution of time and work as a means of discipline turns into others in which the didactic or organizational nature of time and work, or their consideration as a means of external control, come to predominate. Or also, by way of example, how the diffusion of the idea of *surmenage* or mental fatigue, or, in a general sense, of ideas of hygiene, came to coincide over time with the professional aspirations of teachers in relation to expanding vacation periods or introducing recreation and recesses. I repeat, only a global consideration of a wide range of texts and authors that treat, over an extended time, a concrete topic, can facilitate a history of the theoretical concepts, beliefs, and ideas that determine an intellectual field, as well as the different positions and strategies of its constituents within the field and in relation to the topic. From this perspective, the important thing is not what one or another concrete text or particular author may have to say, except in significant cases, but rather the position of these texts and authors as a whole within a field of ideas about a relevant question.

Culture, Organization, and School:
Academic Time and Space

To claim that school—taking this term in its widest sense—is an institution goes without saying; an academic culture exists. It is precisely because school is an institution that we can speak of academic culture, and vice versa. The difficulty arises in coming to some consensus about what is implied in the idea that school is an institution and about what academic culture is. Or indeed, if it wouldn't be preferable to speak of academic cultures in the plural.

What this all implies, at least, is that school should be considered simultaneously by a sociology of institutions and an anthropology of ordinary life. The problem lies in the fact that academic culture, inasmuch as it is a whole comprised of institutionalized aspects that characterize school as an organization, possesses various forms or levels. We can, for example, make reference to the specific culture of a given teaching establishment, of a complex or type of center in contrast with others—for example, of rural schools or law schools— or indeed of a given regional territory or of the academic world in general as it compares with other sectors of society. We can also offer individual, group, organizational, and institutional perspectives on some aspect of that culture. Finally, the already mentioned "whole comprised of institutionalized aspects" includes practices and behaviors, lifestyles, habits and rituals (the everyday history of academic activity), material objects (function, use, distribution in space, outward physical appearance, systems of symbols, inception, transformation, disappearance), and modes of thought, as well as shared meanings and ideas. One might say, everything. Academic culture is surely academic life: facts and ideas, minds and bodies, objects and behaviors, modes of thought, speech and action. Within this aggregate some aspects are more relevant than others, in the sense that they are the organizing elements that shape and define the culture. From among these I will select two that I have devoted some attention to in recent years: academic space and time. Others no less important, such as discursive and linguistic practices, or the technologies and modes of communication employed, will be left to one side for now. These three dimensions or aspects—space, time, and language or modes of communication—affect human beings directly, in their own interior consciousness, in all of their thoughts and activities, individually and in groups, and as a species in relation to nature of which it is a part. They shape minds and actions. They form and are formed by educational institutions. Thus, their importance.

Physical space is, for human beings, appropriated space or territory, and it is disposed, inhabited space (place). In this sense, space is a social construct and academic space one of the forms of its conversion into territory or place. It follows that space is never neutral, but rather a sign, symbol, and trace of the condition and relations of those who occupy it. Space says and communicates;

therefore it educates. It shows, to those who can read it, the use to which it is put by human beings. A use that varies from culture to culture, that is a specific cultural product involving not only the social "I," interpersonal relations (distances, personal space, communication, contacts, conflicts) but also a social liturgy and rites, the symbolism of the disposition of bodies (location, postures) and of objects, their hierarchy and relations.

The spatial dimension of educational activity is neither tangential nor accidental to it. Equal to temporal or communicative-linguistic dimensions, this dimension is, as I have said, a characteristic that constitutes part of its very nature. It is not that space conditions or is conditioned by said activity; rather, space is an integral part of it—it is education. Academic space is neither a "container" nor a "setting," but rather "a kind of discourse which institutes in its materiality a system of values ... various frames for sensory and motor learning and a full semiology which covers different aesthetic, cultural and even ideological symbols" (Escolano 1993–94: 99–100). It is, in short, like academic culture, of which it forms a part, "a silent form of teaching" (Mesmin 1967). Any change in its arrangement as place or territory modifies its cultural and educational nature.

How does one, from this perspective, approach the historical dimension of academic space, its evolution and forms? At least two foci, complementary to each other, seem possible (Viñao 1993–94). The first of these would treat the nature of school as a place. An analysis of this type would detect two basic tendencies: one that moves from nomadism, from itinerancy, to settlement and stability, and another, related to the former, that proceeds from the absence of specialization to its independent establishment and delimitation vis-à-vis other institutions and practices. The primary objective would be to establish a typology of the existing forms in a region and a historical period, forms that would oscillate between itinerancy in its diverse forms, on the one hand, and antiacademic proposals, that is, the negation of the school as a place, on the other. Among one or another there would remain that tendency, historically appreciable, toward specialization and independence, toward an affirmation of the necessity of having its own space, constructed as a place with such an end and bounded as a territory independent of any other ecclesiastical, state, or municipal place. In this sense, academic space would be a place that tends to be bounded as such and to become internally fragmented into a variety of uses and functions of a sort that are at once productive, symbolic, and disciplinary.[3] It would be a space whose internal unfolding, concealment, and closure struggle against transparency and opening.

The second focus, which could be termed *stratigraphic* if this term were not understood in an exclusive or compartmentalized sense, complements the previous one. It constitutes a procedure for analyzing that reality, at once material and mental, which is space as territory. It is a procedure of analysis, of stripping away, that calls to mind one of those Russian dolls that hides in its interior, theoretically into infinity, other, yet smaller dolls. It would begin from the outside, with the site, a location that conditions and explains the connections it has with its surroundings, with other spaces and places distinct from the one set off as school, as well as its arena of attraction and influence. The next step, moving from outside to inside, would be to consider relations among the constructed and unconstructed zones of the school's precincts, of its buildings and campuses, of its distribution and uses. There would be at least two basic points to consider here: (1) the importance conceded to, and the use assigned to, the unconstructed zones, their reassessment or neglect (Lahoz 1991); and (2) the location, disposition, and external presentation of the existing building or buildings, the identifying signs of the establishment in question, which reflect, in a more or less explicit way, the concept or idea that is held of the academic institution in general and, more specifically, of the end to which it is destined.

The internal disposition of the constructed zones, together with the distribution or uses assigned to their various branches or offices, would constitute the next aspect to be analyzed. Their existence or nonexistence, their disposition and relations, reflect the importance, nature, and characteristics of their corresponding function or activity, whether these be headmasters' offices, residence or reception halls, chapels, gymnasiums, or restrooms. An analysis of this type would demonstrate, besides, the predominance or lack, in said disposition, of any criteria of visibility and control, or the weight of the tendency toward fragmentation and differentiation of meeting places and shared spaces.

The last redoubt to consider would be that of personal spaces: the desk, the locker, the closet, or the file. But, before arriving at these, it is still possible to analyze the physical configuration and the internal disposition of persons and objects in particular offices. Among them, the classroom: that place specifically designated for teaching. The historical analysis of the forms of organization and layout of persons and objects in the classroom demonstrates their relation to the prevailing pedagogical system or method. Among those mentioned, this aspect has been granted the most attention among historians of education in the last few years. To observe this, it suffices to review some of the works published, for example, on the organization of space in the classrooms of Jesuit colleges during the modern age, with students divided into *decurias*, and their arrangement oriented toward promoting emulation and competence (Laspalas 1993), on the monitorial system (Hopman 1990; Lessage 1981), on the French method of *salles d'asile* (Dajez 1984 1994) or, from a more general perspective, on the genesis of the idea of class, of simultaneous instruction (Hamilton 1989), or of graduate school (Laska and Juárez 1992; Viñao 1990).

A general overview of this group of texts will demonstrate in this case—that of the relations among the uses of academic space, the organization of teaching centers, and the methods of teaching employed—the play or debate between two opposite tendencies. One of these, the mechanistic tendency, leans toward the configuration of a system or method whose virtues and effects depend more on the exhaustive, nonintegrated, and "rational" arrangement of academic space and time, as well as curriculum, than they do on the person or persons charged with putting them into practice. And the other, the organic tendency, promotes more the attention paid to individuals and their adaptation to circumstances than it does the managerial mechanisms of educational processes. What is behind this dilemma is the attempt—logical but impossible—to instruct and educate a large number of persons by approximating, to the greatest extent possible, the type of relations and methods followed in individual or small group instruction, a question that reflects another, more general one: the negentropic nature of education.

In a brief text published in 1978 that treated the art and means of cataloging books, Georges Perec alluded to something already known: any library that is not put in order will be a mess. He added that this was the example given to him as an explanation of entropy (Perec 1978). The setting apart of specific spaces—constructed places—for the activities of teaching and learning and their distribution and internal organization are nothing more than one more facet of this negative entropy (negentropy) that is education. Whatever needs to be transmitted, taught, or learned should be more or less delimited, bounded, but also ordered and sequenced. The same applies to the context conceived and constructed for teaching and learning. Its arrangement, functions, and uses are not left to chance. This would imply reinforcing the general and growing tendency toward maximum entropy, and with it the horror of emptiness, insecurity, and uncertainty. The unforeseeable, the aleatory, the unstable, would displace the probable, the certain, the foreseeable. It is for this reason that human beings prepare and dispose, order and arrange. The problem occurs when this precision and regularity, normalization and rationalization, are carried out by way of mechanical contrivances and gears or by a mechanistic organization of living beings, when people forget that they are working not with inorganic materials but rather with human beings. Then, curiously, the high efficiency of the designed mechanism is revealed to be highly inefficient. The constructed place becomes a closed system, inflexible and nonadaptive, in which the necessities of territorial appropriation in human beings, as well as the configuration of space, whether personal and external, or shared and common, become nonviable. By structuring or modifying the relation between the internal and the external in the scholarly medium—the borders, what remains inside and outside—between the diverse constructed and nonconstructed zones, among the interior spaces—by opening or closing, by deploying in one way or another boundaries and limits, transitions and communications, people and objects—we are modifying the nature of the place. We are changing not only the boundaries, the persons, or the objects, but also the very place itself. For this reason, it is necessary to open up academic space and construct it as place, and in such a way that it does not restrict diversity of use or adaptation to changing circumstances. This means making an architect of the teacher or professor, that is, an educator, and turning education into a process of the configuration of spaces, of personal and social spaces, and of places. Ultimately, space, like energy, is neither created nor destroyed, but only transformed. The final question is whether it is transformed into a cold, mechanical space or into a warm, living one. Into a space dominated by the need for implacable order and a fixed point of view, or into one that, taking into account the aleatory and a mobile point of view, presents more possibility than limitation. Into a space, finally, for education, a realm that does not belong to the world of mechanism, but rather to that of biology, of living beings.

Social and human, multiple and plural time, is more a social construct than an aspect of reality (Luhmann 1976). This construct is a consequence of, and implies, the establishment of determined relations among the before, the after, and the now—the past, the future, and the present—of a determined temporalization of experience in relation to a present that is also concrete. In this sense, time is a relation, not a stream, a specific human faculty or "act of representation" that brings into view, in a united and connected way, what happens sooner or later, before or after (Elias 1989). A faculty of synthesis and relationship that, together with memory, creates and connects the space of experience with the horizon of expectations (Koselleck 1993: 333).

Temporal experience and temporal consciousness differ greatly, as much in their social configuration as in their individual perception. They are both influenced by aspects like language—the "grammatical variety" of words and of the synthesis of time (Ricoeur 1979)—the modes and techniques of measuring it, controlling it and perceiving it, the various forms and temporal levels existing in a given society (Lewis and Weigert 1981), and the cultural memory of that society (Connerton 1989; Viñao 1996).

One of these temporal forms is academic time, a time that is also diverse and plural, individual and institutional, conditioning and conditioned by other social times. It is a learned time that shapes training in time, a cultural and pedagogical construct, a "cultural fact." Academic time, like academic space and discourse, is not, therefore, "a simple formal scheme or neutral structure" into which education "empties" itself, but rather a sequence, course, or continuous succession of moments in which educational processes, acts, indeed, the academic project, are distributed. It is a time that reflects determined psychopedagogical assumptions, values, and forms of gestation, a time to internalize and learn (Escolano 1992).

Academic time, then, is at once personal time and institutional, organizing time. On the one hand, it has become, from this dual perspective, one of our most powerful instruments for making generalizations, for presenting as natural and unique in our societies a conception and experience of time as something measurable, fragmented, sequenced, linear, and objective, which carries implications of goals and a future. That is to say it provides, at least in theory, a vision of learning and history not as processes of selection and options, of wins and losses, but rather of advancement and progress certified by examinations and by the passage from one course or level to the next.

On the other hand, from an institutional point of view, academic time shows itself, at least formally, to be prescribed and uniform time. Nevertheless, from an individual perspective, it is plural and diverse time. There is no one single time, but a variety of times. That of the professor and that of the student, for starters. But also that of administration and inspection, regulated time. In so far as it is also cultural time, academic time is a historically changing social construct, a cultural product that implies a certain lived experience of time. A time that is socially and culturally organized and constructed as that specific time, but which, simultaneously, is lived not only by teachers and students but also by families and the community taken together, by way of their insertion into and relations with the remaining social rhythms and times.

Institutional academic time offers, in turn, diverse configurations or levels. It constitutes a whole temporal architecture. In this sense we should not speak of academic time in the singular, but rather of academic times. A primary net of temporal relations, of long duration, has its origin in the very structure of the educational system with its cycles, levels, courses, and rites of passage or examinations. Today, in many countries, it ranges from the first years of life until who knows when. Another temporal configuration is that established by academic calendars, academic courses or years, with their beginning, their end, and their interruptions by holiday or vacation. The third form shows the microhistory and the intrahistory of the academic institution. Herein are defined the division of disciplines and activities throughout the established temporal units (academic year, semester, quarter, trimester, month, week, day, morning, afternoon) or even, broken down into its smallest units, each class or activity. It finds material and written expression in class schedules and those of the temporal distribution of tasks and programs.

The end result, that which should be interiorized, is one of those "civilizing coactions," to use Norbert Elias's expression, which, even if they are not constitutive of human nature, in their concrete materialization, come to constitute a "second nature." This coaction is produced and produces an "imperative" sense of time, a need to know at every moment what time it is—and in the most exact way possible—to do things in their time, in that time which is provided for them to take place, to "always arrive on time" and "not to waste time" (Elias 1989: 150–55). This "omnipresent consciousness of time," of a time always regulated and occupied, is one of the characteristics of the academic institution. And it is not an auxiliary or outside characteristic, but rather consubstantial with it. School is not a place one can go to when one wishes to effect a determined educational activity. Its days and hours of operation are already established and distributed according to a schedule—hourly, weekly, and daily—for every academic course, and for the activities and tasks that can take place within it. This is its basic temporal characteristic.

Nor is this, furthermore, a coaction of time in the abstract, but rather a determined time: linear, rectilinear, ascending, and segmented into steps or phases to be surmounted. A time very different from that lived by the illiterate culture that Harrison and Callari Galli explored at the end of the 1960s in some of the towns of Sicily. The inhabitants of this culture, illiterate, possessed a global and spherical, not a segmented or linear, concept of space-time. The individual-group, or group-individual, lived in the present, a continuous present. Their two verb tenses were the present and a remote past and their history "a conglomerate of many presents": The dimension of the group is the present; belonging to an old social role is the non-present, the no-longer-present, something finished forever, which in no way acts upon the present.

To this system of relations there correspond two fundamental verb tenses in the language of the illiterates: the present and the remote past. The future, as a verb tense, does not exist in the language, just as, in social relations, the possibility of imagining oneself outside of the group does not exist; projecting oneself into a tomorrow describes the action of someone who is preparing for duties and functions by imagining them, of someone who formulates his life in terms of a career, a promotion, a goal, of someone who anticipates through thought his passage into another group, another role.

In illiterate culture there exists no "cursus honorum" in which every step follows the preceding and presupposes the next; and the passage from one role into another always occurs because the members of the groups call you, accept you. The present is neither a stage nor a means of arriving at the future in order to obtain some future recompense. The present is in itself, is a good in itself (Harrison and Callari Galli 1972: 144–45).

The journey from illiteracy to academic literacy implies not only learning letters and words or deciphering a written code; it implies, above all, the substitution of a determined conceptualization of space-time—one of linear written culture and of equally linear academic culture—for another. This substitution constitutes the central nucleus of the dual process of schooling and teaching literacy. To consider someone literate in the academic sense, is to suppose, from this perspective, his or her having internalized this imperative or linear sense of time.

Thus understood, the history of academic culture, the history of school as an organization and an institution, is a history of ideas and facts, of objects and practices, of ways of saying, doing, and thinking, that should have recourse, like every history, to the perspective of the moving eye. If the reality under consideration is always complex and if the historian has already renounced the pretense of producing the story, description, and analysis of the whole and definitive truth—not the pretense of veracity, from which no relativism can ever separate itself (Farge 1991)—the position in which it situates itself, and from which it looks out, occupies a central place in the historical operation (Certeau 1975). This position depends, among other things, on the sources and object of analysis; it is, in any case, a personal option among various possible and more or less fruitful alternatives. But it should never be fixed or immobile: "Attending to what changes, seeing the change and seeing while we ourselves move is the beginning of seeing the truth; of the seeing which is life," claims María Zambrano (1989: 25). The historian should learn this lesson and situate herself before her sources, before her theme, in different positions, not exclusive but rather related, or complementary, positions. Even as Clifford Geertz said of cultural and ethnographic analysis, then her analysis will be "intrinsically incomplete" (Geertz 1993: 29). It is incomplete, but not monocausal, fixed, or false. For this reason the historian, like those novelists or cinematographers who resort to the strategy of telling the same story according to the version or point of view of several of its protagonists, should approach the complexity of what is real from differing perspectives.[4] This is especially important in studies of this type, where the social, the institutional, and the individual merge, and should be considered in this way, together with ideas and facts, objects and practices. A single example, relating to the study already mentioned of the weekly and daily distribution of time and work in primary education in Spain during the nineteenth and twentieth centuries (Viñao 1998a), will suffice to demonstrate the possibilities of this sort of multiple focus, which on the other hand is not so unusual if one attends to its unsystematic and unconscious use among historians.

In this study it seemed necessary from the beginning to confront three points of view: the theoretical (the proposals of pedagogues, inspectors and teachers), the legal (the norms that regulated the question), and the academic (what happened in the schools). Theory, legality, and academic reality did not always coincide. Nor were they airtight compartments, totally different. The surprising thing was to discover along the way how they interacted with each other over a period of almost two centuries. How in each of the three aspects there could be seen traces of the other two. How a historical source—a pedagogical or organizational manual, a legal disposition, a diary or scholarly memoir, an autobiography or personal diary, an oral account—made us refer, by way of similarity or contrast, to others; and how, likewise, even though said source belonged to one of the three spheres indicated, within it could be found traces of or allusions to the other two. How the three foci were at the same time valid, since what the goal amounted to, at base, was to analyze not only their evolution and changes, but also their reciprocal influences. Only in this way was it possible to grasp the discontinuities and ruptures, the inertias and persistences, the diversity of practices, the determining elements of said diversity, and in the last analysis, the triple nature of the distribution of academic work as a disciplinary means, a mechanism of curricular organization and rationale, and an instrument of external control; that is, as a basic element that conditions and is conditioned by academic culture.

Cultural History, Intellectual History, and the History of the Mind

Strictly speaking, intellectual history is usually identified with the history of ideas or with the thought of great writers or, as is commonly claimed, with intellectuals. In a wider sense, intellectual history would be the history of ideas or of thought, period; that is, of that which is produced by mind when it thinks. Yet there exists, nonetheless, the possibility of another even wider sense, one that causes intellectual history and the history of the intellect to coincide; in other words, mind's operating mode, mind in itself. What happens is that, just as with the term *culture*, the word *mind* is charged with resonances that are sometimes immaterial, at other times subjectivist, and at yet others, ultimately mechanistic. Mind, however, is "an organized system of dispositions which finds its manifestation in some actions and some things" (Geertz 1993: 58). Its a biological, corporeal support of the brain, a determinate sensory architecture of neuronal nets and links. It is a highly plastic object, capable of infinite possibilities in which habit and repetition, just as intense concentration, give rise to the consolidation—that is, the learning—of determined modes of operation, or rather, of determined capabilities and abilities, dispositions and aptitudes.

In this sense, the mind is a sociohistorical product and the cognitive processes, or what happens on the inside, are processes that can be studied from a historical perspective (Luria 1980), by way of its products (that which is thought) and of the means used to produce them (the many languages, modes of communication, and ways of thinking):

> The problem of the evolution of mind is, therefore, neither a false issue generated by a misconceived metaphysics, nor one of discovering at which point in the history of life an invisible anima was superadded to organic material. It is a matter of tracing the development of certain sorts of abilities, capacities, tendencies, and propensities in organisms and delineating the factors or types of factors upon which the existence of such characteristics depends. (Geertz 1993: 82)

One of these "types of factors" involves "the cultural resources," the "ingredient" elements "not accessory, to human thought." Consequently, as Geertz himself adds, if the analysis "of the human mind demands a joint attack from virtually all of the behavioral sciences, in which the findings of each will force continual theoretical reassessments upon all of the others" (1993: 83), then the historian, especially the historian of education and culture, cannot remain outside this vast program of research. What would his role be? What resources could he count on? What viewpoints would he contribute?

The scientific weakness—which is to say, analytical and heuristic weakness—of the historical focus of the human mind, of an empirically unverifiable and in the best of cases only likely or probable nature, of its interpretations and affir-mations, has been and continues to be maintained, for example, in relation to the historical-cultural study of the consequences of literacy in the human mind and of the cognitive processes of the same (Akinnaso 1981).

Against opinions of this type, sometimes explicit and other times implicit, we need only remember what Vygotsky said concerning psychology and the mode of thought of many psychologists:

> The concept of a historically based psychology is misunderstood by most researchers who study child development. For them, to study something histori-cally means, by definition, to study some past event. Hence they naively imagine an insurmountable barrier between historic study and study of present-day behavioral forms. *To study something historically means to study it in the process of change*; that is the dialectical method's basic demand. To encompass in research the process of a given thing's development in all its phases and changes—from birth to death—fundamentally means to discover its nature, its essence, for "it is only in movement that a body shows what it is." Thus, the his-torical study of behavior is not an auxiliary aspect of theoretical study, but rather forms its very base. (Vygotsky 1978: 64–65)

This paragraph clarifies several questions. Between the historical study of the past and the immediate present there are, of course, differences, but less of an opposition or difference and more of an "insurmountable barrier" is estab-lished. To suppose that they do exist impoverishes both: "if we don't know what a thing is, we cannot know how it evolves and, reciprocally, as Darwin would say, if we don't know how a thing came to be, we do not know it" (Bunge 1989: 142). Without the contribution of history, without the perspec-tive of reality as a process, without that expansion of the space of experience that is presupposed by the historical look, and without that temporal articula-tion that permits the genealogical consideration of what is analyzed, it is not possible to know its nature. It is for this reason that a concept of this type so strongly resists any theory of education that remains a search for a systematic whole of principles and rules of an immutable type—that is, supratemporal and universal, ahistorical and normative—in which the task of the history of educa-tion would be that of demonstrating how these immutable principles and rules have been embodied across history (Depaepe 1983), as is the case with those who crumble history into a series of events, personages, and relations of a par-ticular nature, allowing neither theoretical reflections nor more or less provi-sional generalizations of the sort that correspond to any scientific investigation.

The foundation of the contribution made by history to the study of the mind resides precisely in the nature of this study as a sociohistorical product, in the neuronal plasticity of the brain, or in other words, in the historicity of its struc-ture, disposition, and function, and in the role played in this sociohistorical structure by the predominance and use of the various technologies—tools, instruments, modes of operation—of the intellect, or by the various media, material and immaterial, of communication and information exchange in a given society. These modes correspond to what Kieran Egan has termed *bonnes à penser* (good to think) by analogy with Lévi-Strauss's expression *bonnes à manger* (good to eat), that is, things, instruments, or means with which to think, which determine, at least in part, the modes of thinking, thought, and in the final analysis, mental dispositions (Egan 1988). These transformations and variations depend, not in an exclusive way, but indeed in a primordial way, on changes in the use of the modes and means of communication. Any change in said means and modes of capturing reality, of conserving, recovering, trans-mitting, or receiving it, any change in the technologies of conversation and communication–giving a fuller sense to the term "technology," one that inte-grates the material and the immaterial, and that extends from oral to visual or computerized communication—consolidates or reinforces, in its use or repeated practice, various determined mental structures, dispositions and oper-ations, and not others. The message is not reducible to the medium or vice versa (Ong 1971). Nor can all the means of producing, storing, transmitting, or receiving information be explained simply on the basis of the media employed and their supporting technologies. But it is true that these media do condition their content, or that which is said, to as great an extent as they do their production, preservation, transmission, and reception, that is, the ways of interpreting reality, of perceiving it, ordering it, and expressing it. These means promote or impede, facilitate or hinder, one or another mode of per-ception, thought, or discourse. They structure the mind in one sense or another, and they either make possible or negate the various strategies and dis-positions involving, for example, reading, writing, or speech, among other technologies or uses of the word. It follows that the analysis of the changes that befall the processes of communication and language and the use of the means and modes of "reading" reality (seeing it, arranging it, showing it) will facilitate the comprehension of such structures and dispositions, just as it will any modifications produced by the processes and changes in their modes of operation. Furthermore, such analysis makes a history of these structures and changes in the human mind possible, or rather, a history of a given mentality or cultural mode of seeing reality, of seeing oneself and others, a history of men-tality shaped or educated by means of communication and thought.

Without a doubt, the possibility of doing such a history of the transforma-tions, continuities, and discontinuities in communicative practices owes much to the work of those communication theorists and researchers (Innis, McLuhan, Frye, Havelock, among others) who came together in the 1940s and 1950s at the University of Toronto (Carey 1991). But credit is also due to anthropologists like Jack Goody, psychologists like Luria, Vygotsky, Scribner, and Cole, among others, and to a thinker as unclassifiable as Walter Ong, who has been defined as "the intellectual equivalent of a long-distance runner with peripheral vision (Carey 1991: ix).

The expression *technologies* as it relates to the word or to communication includes, then, the means and material support (including physiological support: the body in general and, more specifically, the eyes, the tongue, the lips, the hands) (Perec 1971), but also above all, the immaterial (the different languages, the rhetorical and discursive forms). Their historical consideration would embrace, as a minimum, the following aspects:

(a) The consequences and changes (continuities and transformations, reinforcements and oppositions, similarities and contrasts, wins and losses) in the interaction between the oral, the written and the visual—orality, writing, and image. An analysis of this type should in principle attend to the interactions among the oral modes of conservation and transmission of knowledge and to those originating in the diffusion and uses of writing, the alphabet, the printing press, and the whole electronic and audiovisual panoply up to, at the moment, computers and video writing (Amat 1994; Nunberg 1996; Olson 1996; Viñao 1994b, 1995, forthcoming).

If the predominance, displacement, or devaluation of one or another medium, one or another use, shapes the whole of images and representations of a given society and, therefore, of the minds of those who comprise it, a history of culture and education cannot ignore these questions. And upon taking interest in them, it will have to pay special attention to:

(b) the modifications that take place in determined modes of thought and expression when these are used by or from a technology different from that which generates them—for instance, the transformation of the concept and uses of the story, the proverb, and the romance when it passes from the oral to the written (Chevalier 1993), as well as the interactions among these based on the analysis of concrete cases—for example, the works included in Baumann (1990), Enos (1990), and Boyarin (1992); and

(c) any changes in the social practices of reading, writing, and arithmetic: systems, modes, representations, supports, contexts, appropriations, and so forth (Cavallo and Chartier 1997; Chartier 1987, 1993a, 1993b, 1995; Petrucci 1986, 1987; Petrucci and Gimeno 1995).[5] The objective pursued would not be so much to become aware of the diversity of these practices, as it would be to promote comparative analyses that would integrate these general perspectives concerning oral-written-visual interaction and its processes of mediation and reception (Boyarin 1992; Resnick and Resnick 1989; Viñao, forthcoming), including:

- the strategies and modes of storage (rhetoric and memory), conservation, access and diffusion of the oral, the written and the visual. The rhetorical uses (the modes of organizing discourse) shape the mind, and vice versa; and memory (the modes of recovering knowledge) together with forgetting, constitute the central nucleus of mental representations and images (Carruthers 1990; Connerton 1989; Flor 1996; Machet 1987; Rossi 1983; Yates 1966); and

- the processes involved in the generation of mental images, that is, of the visual part of thought, or, if you prefer, of the control of imagination and, by definition, of the mind and thought.[6]

The genesis and diffusion of written culture and of the literate mind, or rather, of the long-term process by which the written has gone on to extend itself and impregnate—in interaction with the oral and the visual—the world of law, economics, religion, administration, education, and everyday life (Chartier 1987, 1993a, 1993b; Fabre 1983; Goody 1986; Marchesini 1992; Petrucci 1986, 1987). Its consideration in the educational sphere would presuppose not only an historical analysis of displacement and superposition among the various modes of oral, written, and visual communication in the academic medium, or in that of training in elementary knowledge, but also, above all else, an analysis of the transformations performed within said medium as a consequence of the role played therein by one or another mode of storage, conservation, recovery, access, transmission, reception, and evaluation of information and knowledge.

A concrete example of this type of analysis (see, for example, Chartier, this volume), as yet insufficiently studied by historians of education, will help clarify its possibilities. I am referring to the process by which written methods have replaced oral ones; that is, of the emergence of the text-based education.

The predominance of oral methods in medieval education is well known. The *lectio*, debates and disputations, *quaestiones*, or resorting to the *sic et non*—all of these means of teaching, expression, and thought belonged to the world of orality, even when they made reference to some text or texts. At times, even the responsibility of writing a text did not fall to its author, but rather to an amanuensis or scribe to whom he dictated. Teaching took place in predominantly oral contexts. Underlying it was the idea that the search for truth necessarily involved in a face-to-face debate between two or more human beings, in this instance, men. This emphasis on dialectical and rhetorical methods was progressively displaced, especially after the expansion of the printing press, by the general acceptance of textbooks and printed texts in which one could search for knowledge and information without having to ask anyone, as well as the introduction of written exams. This is another question to be traced and examined throughout all levels of education, and within the university itself, through each college. Included here are the ways in which the curriculum is configured in the form of yearly courses with their corresponding texts and lectures (Hamilton 1989), and the progressive disappearance, also to be traced throughout each educational level and type of institution, of oral exams and public lectures and demonstrations (Viñao 1990).

With regard to the Spanish university, for example, Mariano Peset and José Luis Peset have shown how the diffusion of the printing press put an end to the dictation and exposition of subject matter among teachers, and how these practices were replaced by more flexible explanations and questions in class. In principle, this would seem to contradict the above description of a evolutionary process from the oral to the written. But it would be wrong to interpret such data in this way. What really matters is what happens in the global context producing these events, especially as they relate to exams. In both cases, as these authors indicate in their study of Mayans's 1767 university reform plan, the two typical forms of teaching in the "traditional university" were "the lesson and academic disputation." The formal means of "instructional control" were reduced to "degree examinations." Annual exams "appear sporadically" toward the end of the eighteenth century (in the University of Valencia, for example, in 1786) and these "do not come into general use until the nineteenth century." Students prepared for such exams by participating in the debates and disputations that took place in academies or by engaging themselves in other university activities and institutions. The disputations, in the authors' words, served

> for attaining academic rank, for competing to become chair or for conferring honors upon them, and in general, for learning to defend the fundamental truths with firmness and subtlety. They constitute a scholastic teaching method which the University would conserve until the beginning of the nineteenth century. (Peset and Peset 1975: 68–71)

One writes in order to be read. But to be read aloud or in silence? Let's shift this question to the domain of teaching. When did each of the various levels of education quit emphasizing reading aloud in order to foreground silent or mental reading? Why, for example, as late as the nineteenth century did a manual of poetry and rhetoric, like that of Gómez Hermosilla (published in 1826 and republished at least fifteen times during that century, including editions corrected and edited by Vicente Salvá), a bedside book commonly used by Spanish writers, politicians, and orators especially address itself to the world of orality by way of its title: "Art of speaking in prose and verse" (*Arte de hablar en prosa y en verso*)? And why was it still common, during the nineteenth century and first third of the twentieth, to include a chapter in manuals of rhetoric and poetics on the art of declamation, oratory, and reading aloud?

In Spain, the translation and reception of Legouvé's treatise on the art of reading, only one year after it first appeared in France (Legouvé, 1878), taken together with the work of Faguet (n.d.) bore witness to a general interest in reading aloud, in, as it was said, *bella lectura* (beautiful reading). Reading aloud was held to be the archetypal, the most elevated form of reading. Its importance is confirmed by the wealth of manuals concerning the theory and poetics of reading aloud that were published during the last decades of the nineteenth and first decades of the twentieth centuries (Anchorena, 1891; Blanco y Sánchez, 1894; Escribano Hernández 1916; Regúlez y Bravo, 1884; Vallés y Rebullida, 1883, among others). When did reading aloud cease to be reading's ideal state, and become simply an initial or transitory step in education, one to be overcome in order to arrive at studying's own form or reading, silent and mental? How did it pass from an archetype to being an identifying sign of learning to read? Why did it happen, moreover, that in the final years of the nineteenth and the first of the twentieth centuries, the discipline of rhetoric and poetry was replaced, at the secondary level, by that of literary precepts? What did this change in nomenclature imply? This entire range of questions, and others like them, remains to be investigated. Such research will allow us to deepen and clarify some of the fundamental ideas underlying the historical perspective on education and its recent evolution.

In summary, it is within this double sphere that the history of the mind takes on meaning: that of the history of interactions among the oral, written, and visual, in their different forms and bases, and that of written culture and literate mentality. A sphere in which cultural history and the history of education can be founded. It is possible that this does not pose any problem for the former, in so far as research is concerned. How could one fail to understand that one of the fields of the history of education is the history of the processes of shaping the human mind, that very mind that is itself a sociohistorical product? A field, of course, that is not exclusively its own (is there any aspect or question exclusive of someone?), but that is fundamentally within the intellectual and academic sphere. The problem arises when such questions and approaches (like other new and no less relevant ones—the history of childhood, of the curriculum, of the family and forms of socialization, for example) attempt to incorporate themselves into the teaching of the history of education as a discipline. This is when the difficulties emerge: when one comes to appreciate that the traditional approaches to the teaching of this discipline (and even the innovative ones) do not easily permit such investigations to be incorporated, when teaching and research part ways. From this follow the attempts, generally forced, if not fruitless, to reconcile the incompatible or even to openly configure new programs for teaching the history of education based on social, historical, and cultural approaches similar to those indicated here (Salimova and Johanningmeier 1993).

By Way of Conclusion: Regarding the Possibilities of a History of Academic Culture

In its current configuration, cultural history presents a wide variety of themes and focuses. One of its objects is academic culture, or educational activity as viewed from a cultural perspective, that is: (1) as an institutionalized activity that generates its own culture, with certain specific features; and (2) as an activity of cultural mediation and transference. In this work I have attempted, perhaps in summary fashion, to account for those aspects of academic culture that have concerned me and that I have researched in recent years. Their selection has not been arbitrary. I consider three aspects to be fundamental to this study: the actors involved in the academic culture, the distribution and use made of space and time therein, and the type of language and discourse employed by human beings to shape minds and communicate with each other.

With regard to the actors, no single culture exists, after all. While teachers and professors are in some respects simply one more subculture together with alumni, families, administrators, and regents, they generally have a great influence over the real configuration of curricula and academic disciplines. Only by analyzing their culture—ideas, mentality, habits, practices—can one understand the evolution of the others (and vice versa) or understand the persistence over time of given academic practices inside and outside the classroom.

On the other hand, the distribution and uses of space and time are neither neutral aspects of academic culture nor marginal to it. Rather, in every instance they constitute key elements for understanding its concrete configuration and for clarifying the ultimate nature of educational activity.

Finally, the investigation of the mind as a sociohistorical product leads us to the study of the means of communication utilized in education, including language and discourse. Such analysis touches academic culture in a double sense. In the first place, it reveals which modes and means of communication are predominant for every society and culture—and within these, for every social group. It shows how these interact, which of them at any given moment exercises the strongest sway in shaping the minds that belong to them. That is, it selects for some mental predispositions, whether linguistic, discursive, or of thought, and not others. On the other hand, such analysis permits us to recognize which of academic culture's means and modes of communication come into use among various actors in everyday situations, to see how these forms of communication interact with each other inside and outside the classroom, and to understand thereby which kinds of structures and mental dispositions they favor and promote, and which they mask and banish.

Notes

1. Text translated by Professor Daniel Hunt, College of Arts and Sciences, Idaho State University.
2. A recent example of this interest would be the colloquium on "La cultura de las élites españolas en la Edad Moderna: Poder, Letras, Ciencias" organized, in May of 1995(and whose papers were published in *Bulletin Hispanique*, 97–1 [1995]), by François Lopez from the Institut d'Études Ibériques et IbéroAméricain of the University Michel de Montaigne of Bourdeaux as part of the wider research project entitled "Para una historia de la educación y de las lecturas de los españoles en la Edad Moderna."

3. These three functions, assigned by Foucault (1979: 23) to work, are completely applicable to school as a place.
4. Kurosawa's film *Rashomon* is undoubtedly the most frequently cited example. But it is not the only one, although it stands as one of the best representations of the tendency, habitual moreover, to reflect—and analyze—the different points of view of those who observed or took part in events. Among literary examples there is, for example, *Exercices de style* (1947) in which the same fact is narrated by means of different techniques and styles; its author, Raymond Queneau, is one of the more outstanding members of the OULIPO Group—an influential literary workshop—whose members—Georges Perec and Italo Calvino, among others—frequently resort to narrative strategies of this type, as well as others in which a great variety of forms, authors, texts, and readers remain implied. Regarding the possibilities, in general, of having recourse to some of the techniques of modern narrative in order to make the past intelligible and illuminate it more adequately, see as well Peter Burke's reflections (1991b: 237–46, and 1992: 126–29).
5. The question of arithmetic has been less studied; however, in the last few years there has been a growing interest in its analysis as a social and cultural practice.
6. On the production and control of mental images, I refer the reader to what Italo Calvino has said about "visibility" (1989: 97–113). His writing is full of suggestions for the historian of education. Regarding the role of the imagination in education and cognitive processes, see Gabriel Janer (1989) and Kieran Egan and Dan Nadaner (1988) among others in an increasingly abundant literature.

References

Akinnaso, F. N. (1981). The consequences of literacy in pragmatic and theoretical perspectives. *Anthropology & Education Quarterly* XII(3): 163–200.

Amat, N. (1994). *El libro mudo: Las aventuras del escritor entre el ordenador y la pluma*. Madrid: Anaya & Mario Muchnick.

Anchorena, J. (1891). *Principios generales sobre el arte de la lectura*. Madrid: Imprenta y estereotipia de El Liberal.

Barnes, A. E. and Stearns, P. N. (Eds.). (1989). *Social history and issues in human consciousness: Some interdisciplinary connections*. New York: New York University Press.

Baumann, G. (Ed.). (1990). *The written word: Literacy in transition*. Oxford: Clarendon Press.

Blanco y Sánchez, R. (1894). *Arte de la lectura*. Madrid: Imp. de la Revista de Archivos.

Boyarin, J. (Ed.). (1992). *The ethnography of reading*. Berkeley: University of California Press.

Bunge, M. (1989). *Mente y sociedad: Ensayos irritantes*. Madrid: Alianza.

Burke, P. (1991a). *La cultura popular en la Europa Moderna*. Madrid: Alianza.

———. (1991b). Overture: The new history, its past, and its future. In P. Burke (Ed.), *New perspectives in historical writing*. Cambridge: Polity Press.

———. (1992). *History and social theory*. Cambridge: Polity Press.

Calvino, I. (1989). *Seis propuestas para el próximo milenio*. Madrid: Siruela.

Carey, J. W. (1991). Foreword. In B. E. Gronbeck, T. J. Farrell, and P. A. Soukup (Eds.), *Media, consciousness, and culture: Explorations of Walter Ong's thought* (pp. VII-X). Newbury Park, CA: Sage Publications.

Carruthers, M. (1990). *The book of memory: A study of memory in medieval culture*. Cambridge: Cambridge University Press.

Cavallo, G. and Chartier, R. (Dir.). (1997). *Histoire de la lecture dans le monde occidental*. Paris: Seuil.

148   Antonio Viñao

Certeau, M. de (1975). *L'écriture de l'histoire*. Paris: Gallimard.
Chartier, R. (1987). Las prácticas de lo escrito. In P. Ariès and G. Duby (Eds.), *Historia de la vida privada. 5. El proceso de cambio en la sociedad del siglo XVI a la sociedad del siglo XVIII* (113–62). Madrid: Taurus.
———. (Ed.). (1993a). *Pratiques de la lecture*. Paris: Payot and Rivages.
———. (1993b). *Libros, lecturas y lectores en la Edad Moderna*. Madrid: Alianza.
———. (Ed.) (1995). *Histoires de la lecture. Un bilan de recherches*. Paris: IMEC Éditions.
Chervel, A. (1988). Histoire des disciplines scolaires: Réflexions sur un domaine de recherche. *Histoire de l'Éducation* 38, 59–119.
Chevalier, M. (1993). Conte, proverbe, romance: trois formes traditionnelles en question au siècle d'or. *Bulletin Hispanique* 95 (1): 237–64.
Connerton, P. (1989). *How societies remember*. Cambridge: Cambridge University Press.
Dajez, F. (1984). Une technologie de la petite enfance: le méthode des salles d'asile (1827–1860). *Historiae Infantiae* 1: 35–44.
———. (1994). *Les origines de l'école maternelle*. Paris: PUF.
Depaepe, M. (1983). *On the relationship of theory and history in pedagogy*. Leuven: Leuven University Press.
Egan, K. (1988). *Primary understanding education in early childhood*. New York: Routledge, Chapman and Hall.
Egan, K. and Nadaner, D. (Eds.). (1988). *Imagination and education*. New York: Teachers College Press.
Elias, N. (1989). *Sobre el tiempo*. México: Fondo de Cultura Económica.
Enos, R. L. (Ed.). (1990). *Oral and written communication: Historical approaches*. Newbury Park, CA: Sage Productions.
Escolano, A. (1992). Tiempo y educación: Notas para una genealogía del almanaque escolar. *Revista de Educación*, 298, 55–79.
———. (1993–94).La arquitectura como programa: Espacio-escuela y curriculum. *Historia de la Educación* 12–13: 97–120.
Escribano Hernández, G. (1916). *Teoría y mecanismo de la lectura*. Madrid: Imprenta de La Enseñanza.
Fabre, D. (Ed.). (1993). *Écritures ordinaires*. Paris: Centre Georges Pompidou, BPI.
Faguet, E. (n.d.). *El arte de leer*. Madrid: Editorial Española-Americana.
Farge, A. (1991). *La atracción del archivo*. Valencia: Edicions Alfons el Magnànim.
Flor, F. R. de la (1996). *Teatro de la memoria. Siete ensayos sobre mnemotecnia española de los siglos XVII y XVIII*. Salamanca: Junta de Castilla y León. Consejería de Educación y Cultura.
Foucault, M. (1979). El ojo del poder. In J. Bentham (Ed.), *El panóptico* (9–26). Madrid: La Piqueta.
Geertz, C. (1993). *The interpretation of cultures*. London: Fontana Press.
Goody, J. (1986). *The logic of writing and the organization of society*. Cambridge: Cambridge University Press.
Hamilton, D. (1989). *Towards a theory of schooling*. London: Falmer Press.
Harrison, G. and Callari Galli, M. (1972). *La cultura analfabeta*. Barcelona: Dopesa.
Hopman, S. (1990). The monitorial movement and the rise of curriculum administration: A comparative view. In H. Haft and S. Hopman (Eds.), *Case studies in curriculum administration history* (13–30). London: Falmer Press.
Hunt, L. (Ed.). (1989). *The new cultural history*. Berkeley: University of California Press.
Janer, G. (1989). *La pedagogía de la imaginación poética*. Barcelona: Aliorna.
Julia, D. (1981). La naissance du corps professoral. *Actes de la Recherche en Sciences Sociales* 39: 71–86.

———. (Ed.). (1994a). Aux sources de la compétence professionelle: Critères scolaires et classements sociaux dans les carrières intellectuelles en Europe, XVIIe-XIXe siècles. *Paedagogica Historica: International Journal of History of Education* XXX(1).

———. (1994b). Le choix des professeurs en France: Vocation ou concours? 1700–1850. *Paedagogica Historica: International Journal of History of Education* XXX(1): 175–205.

Karsten, P. and Modell, J. (Eds.). (1992). *Theory, method, and practice in social and cultural history*. New York: New York University Press.

Koselleck, R. (1993). *Futuro pasado: Para una semántica de los tiempos históricos.* Barcelona: Paidós.

Lahoz, P. (1991). El modelo froebeliano de espacio-escuela: Su introducción en España. *Historia de la Educación* 10, 107–33.

Laska, J. A. and Juarez, T. (Eds.). (1992). *Grading and marking in american schools: Two centuries of debate*. Springfield, IL: Charles C. Thomas Publishers.

Laspalas, F. J. (1993). *La reinvención de la escuela: Cinco estudios sobre la enseñanza elemental durante la Edad Moderna.* Pamplona: EUNSA.

Legouvé, E. (1878). *El arte de la lectura.* Madrid: Imprenta de El Imparcial.

Lessage, G. (1981). L'enseignement mutuel. In G. Mialaret and J. Vial (Eds.). *Histoire mondiale de l'éducation. 3. De 1815 á 1945* (241–50). Paris: PUF.

Lewis, J. D. and Weigert, A. J. (1981). The structure and meaning of social time. *Social Forces* 60(2): 423–62.

Luhmann, N. (1976). The future cannot begin: Temporal structures in modern society. *Social Research* 43: 130–52.

Luria, A. R. (1980). *Los procesos cognitivos: Análisis socio-histórico.* Barcelona: Fontanella.

Machet, A. (1987). *Si la memoire m'était comptée: simbolique des nombres et mémoires artificielles de l'Antiquité à nos jours.* Lyon: Presses Universitaires de Lyon.

Marchesini, D. (1992). *Il bisogno di scrivere. Usi della scrittura nell'Italia moderna.* Roma: Laterza.

Mesmin, G. (1967). La arquitectura escolar, forma silenciosa de enseñanza. *Janus* 10: 62–66.

Nóvoa, A. (1987). *Le temps des professeurs: Analyse socio-historique de la profession enseignante au Portugal (XVIIIe–XXe siècle).* Lisboa: Instituto Nacional de Investigaçao Científica.

Nunberg, G. (Ed.). (1996). *The future of the book*. Belgium: Brepols.

Olson, D. R. (1996). *The world on paper: The conceptual and cognitive implications of writing and reading.* Cambridge: Cambridge University Press.

Ong, W. J. (1971). *Rhetoric, romance, and technology: Studies in the interaction of expression and culture.* New York: Ithaca.

Perec, G. (1971). Lire: Esquisse sociophysiologique. *Esprit* 453, 9–20.

———. (1978). Notes brèves sur l'art et la manière de ranger ses livres. *L'Humidité* 25: 35–38.

Peset, M. and Peset, J. L. (1975). *Gregorio Mayans y la reforma universitaria.* Valencia: Publicaciones del Ayuntamiento de Oliva.

Petrucci, A. (1986). *La scrittura: Ideologia e rappresentazione.* Torino: Einaudi.

———. (1987). *Scrivere e no: Politiche della scrittura e analfabetismo nel mondo d'oggi.* Roma: Editori Reuniti.

Petrucci, A. and Gimeno, F. (Eds.). (1995). *Escribir y leer en Occidente: Naturaleza, funciones, conflictos.* Valencia: Departamento de Historia de la Antigüedad y de la Cultura Escrita, Universidad de Valencia.

Regúlez y Bravo, V. (1884). *Teoría de la lectura.* Madrid: Imprenta de la viuda de J.M. Pérez.

Resnick, D. P. and Resnick, L. B. (1989). Varieties of literacy. In A. E. Barnes and P. S. Stearns (Eds.), *Social history and issues in human consciousness* (171–96). New York: New York University Press.

Ricoeur, P. (1979). Introducción. *Las culturas y el tiempo* (37–66). Salamanca and Paris: Sígueme/UNESCO.

Ringer, F. (1990). The intellectual field, intellectual history, and the sociology of knowledge. *Theory and History* 19(3): 269–94.

Rossi, P. (1983). *Clavis Universalis: Arti della memoria e logica combinatoria da Lulio a Leibniz.* Bologna: Società editrice il Mulino.

Salimova, K. and Johanningmeier, E. V. (Eds.). (1993). *Why should we teach history of education?* Moscow: The Library of the International Academy of Self Improvement.

Schoenwald, R. L. (1992). Social history is always intellectual history or intellectual history is always social history or finally, there is only history. In P. Karsten and J. Modell (Eds.), *Theory, method, and practice in social and cultural history* (125–33). New York: New York University Press.

Vallés y Rebullida, M. (1883). *Lectura y escritura teóricas.* Terual: Imprenta de Beficencia.

Viñao, A. (1990). *Innovación pedagógica y racionalidad científica: La escuela graduada pública en España (1898–1936).* Madrid: Akal.

———. (1993–94). Del espacio escolar y la escuela como lugar: propuestas y cuestiones. *Historia de la Educación* 12–13: 17–74.

———. (1994a). Les origines du corps professoral en Espagne: Les Reales Estudios de San Isidro, 1770–1808. *Paedagogica Historica: International Journal of History of Education* XXX(1): 119–74.

———. (1994b). Cultura tipográfica y cultura televisiva. *I Congreso Nacional del Libro Infantil y Juvenil: El libro y la lectura* (123–45). Madrid: Asociación Española del Libro Infantil y Juvenil.

———. (1995). A propósito del neoanalfabetismo: observaciones sobre las prácticas y usos de lo escrito en la España contemporánea. In A. Petrucci and F. Gimeno (Eds.), *Escribir y leer en Occidente: Naturaleza, funciones, conflictos* (183–211). Valencia: Departamento de Historia de la Antigüedad y de la Cultura Escrita, Universidad de Valencia.

———. (1996). *Espacio y tiempo. Educación e historia.* Morelia: Instituto Michoacano de Ciencias de la Educación.

———. (1997). La distribution hebdomaire et quotidienne du temps et du travail dans l'enseignement primaire en Espagne (1838–1936). Théorie, réglementation et pratiques. In M.-M. Compère (Dir.), *Histoire du temps scolaire en Europe* (67–108). Paris: Institut Nationale de Recherche Pédagogogique/Éditions Économica.

———. (1998a). *Tiempos escolares, tiempos sociales. La distribución del tiempo y del trabajo en al enseñanza primaria en España (1838–1936).* Barcelona: Ariel.

———. (1998b). Disciplinas académicas y profesionalización docente: los Reales Estudios de San Isidro (1770–1808). In J.-L. Guereña and E. M. Fell (Eds.), *L'Université en Espagne et en Amérique Latine du Moyen Âge à nos jours. II. Enjeux, contenus, images* (303–23). Tours: Centre Interuniversitaire sur l'Éducation dans le Monde Ibérique et Ibéro-Américaine (CIREMIA). Universite de Tours.

———. (forthcoming). *Leer y escribir. Historia de dos prácticas culturales.* México: Educación, valores y vuelos.

Vygotsky, L. S. (1978). *Mind in society: The development of higher psychological processes.* London: Harvard University Press.

Yates, F. A. (1966). *The art of memory.* London: Routledge & Kegan Paul.

Zambrano, M. (1989). *Delirio y destino (Los veinte años de una española).* Madrid: Mondadori.

7

The Production of Reason and Power

Curriculum History and Intellectual Traditions

Thomas S. Popkewitz

My argument in this paper can be stated in the following way: Curricula are historically formed within systems of ideas that inscribe styles of reasoning, standards, and conceptual distinctions in school practices and its subjects. Further, the systems of reasoning embodied in schooling are the effects of power. That power is in the manner in which the categories and distinctions of curriculum shape and fashion interpretation and action. In this sense, curriculum is a practice of governing and the effect of power. The question of what is curriculum history is also a question about the politics of the knowledge embodied in disciplinary work. Two enduring assumptions of the Enlightenment inscribed in contemporary educational history and research are explored. One identifies social progress as tied to an evolutionary conception of change. The second relates to the epistemological assumption that inquiry must identify the actors as causal agents who bring or suppress social change. Both of these assumptions are, I argue, grounded in a particular doctrine of modernity and the effects of power. I argue for an alternative conception of intellectual work and its relation to social change through viewing intellectual work as a strategy for destabilizing or "troubling" the conventions of "reason" that intern and enclose the present and its consideration of innovation.[1]

I will begin in an unorthodox way by talking about how I became involved in the problem of history and then talk about the particular kind of history in which I am interested. (My tribal card is not that of an historian.) Let me be biographical for a moment and say that I majored as an undergraduate in history, but my doctorate related curriculum issues to a sociology of knowledge in the political sciences. It may be in that intersection that I recognized the importance of a social science of schooling that is historical in quality. You might say my interest is historical sociology or social history. I think neither of these labels, however, does justice to what I'm interested in. I say this because the Anglo-American traditions by which we define either social history or intellectual history tend to be organized according to chronological sequences and implicit teleologies that, at points, are only partially adequate for understanding the issues of change and power that operate through schooling.

My concern with history is to understand how the current problems of schooling, defined as school reform, become constituted as they are: How is it that we think about reform as we do? How is it that we pose problems of school knowledge, children, teaching, and evaluation as we do? These questions take the sociology of curriculum knowledge as a central problematic in the study of schooling. I take the categories, distinctions, and differentiations of schooling as historical and social monuments that can be interrogated as governing practices related to issues of power.

Now I recognize that these two paragraphs provide both a thumbnail sketch of a broad argument and intellectual mouthfuls, so I will back up a little. First, I seek an understanding of history as an activity that does not merely construct interpretations from the data examined. I argue that history is a theoretical activity that fabricates its object of research through its distinctions and categories of historical phenomena. I use the verb to *fabricate* with two meanings: to fictionalize and to "make." If this sounds like a relativist argument, it is not, as I am interested in patterns of relations that do not impose dichotomies of value/fact, nature/individual, subject/object, which are inscribed in demarcations of arguments about relativism (see Latour 1999).[2]

Our "scientific" training often fails to include discussions of how the reasoning of science consists of historically constructed principles of classification and ordering. I then proceed to discuss the study of curriculum. I view curriculum as a particular, historically formed knowledge that inscribes rules and standards by which we "reason" about the world and our "self" as a productive member of that world. The rules for "telling the truth" in curriculum, however, are not only about the construction of objects for our scrutiny and observation. Curriculum is a disciplining technology that directs how the individual is to act, feel, talk, and "see" the world and "self." As such, curriculum is a governing practice.

I explore the effects of curriculum through what I call a social epistemology of schooling (Popkewitz 1991, 1997, 1998). I use *epistemology* to refer to how the systems of ideas in schooling organize perceptions, ways of responding to the world, and conceptions of "self." The *social* in social epistemology emphasizes the relational and social embeddedness of knowledge, in contrast to an American philosophical concern with epistemology as a search for universal knowledge claims about the nature, origins, and limits of knowledge (see Toulmin 1972 and 1988 for a discussion of science that relates to my usage of epistemology). Making the construction of knowledge central to historical study raises questions about the relation of methodology, intellectuals as a social group, and social change.[3] Issues of the intellectual and of power are considered in the final sections.

Making the Object: Historical Studies as Discursive Practices

In the best of our intellectual traditions, we realize that there is not one tribal view of history, but that history is composed of different traditions of interpretation and, implicitly, purpose (Toews 1987; Novick 1988; Lloyd 1991). But to enter into a discussion of a historical tradition is to do more than consider different interpretations of similar data. History, in its modern senses, involves procedures that construct objects through conceptual lenses. By construction, I mean how the categories and distinctions of historical reasoning have the effect of making phenomena into a field of social events and thus data. This does not mean that "things" in the world do not happen. I place restriction on the use of "social construction" by attending to practices through which historians give expression to what is conceived as "data" and as fact in research.[4] The rules of disciplinary study re-make the "things" of the world into "data" that are to be interpreted and explained—while people may vote in elections, there is no voting "behavior" or, for that matter, "school achievement," until one asks questions that assume that these are "things" of the world.[5] Further, the way in which we order and place things together as "reason" is never a "pure" philosophical question but part of cultural fields (Henriques et al. 1984; Shapiro 1992).

I use two brief illustrative examples to pose the question about "reason" as a field of cultural practice in fabricating historical "data." The first example is that of the pyramids in Egypt. It was not until the late eighteenth century that the pyramids were made into objects of inquiry. To ask about the "history" or the human placement of large stone structures that rise in the middle of a desert required a particular self-reflectivity by which people could ask about how knowledge and institutions are socially constructed. Prior to this time, the pyramids were blocks of stone standing virtually unnoticed at least by Western eyes (Bloch 1963). People in the early eighteenth century wrote graffiti as they rode past the pyramids. The pyramids did not become "facts" of a disciplined history until Europeans began to ask questions of them as exemplars of a civilization and as artifacts of the graves of those who could afford to have such burials.[6]

The interpretations of the Egyptian tombs were made possible through a progressive, evolutionary, or "modern" form of reason. This "modern" reason refers to a particular structuring of knowledge associated with social transformations of the past few hundred years in Europe.[7] Modern reason made possible the visioning of the artifacts of Egypt as part of particular abstract systems of relations from which the particular artifacts, images, and narratives could be placed as a memory of a civilization.

The categories of historical interpretation that placed events in a secular chronology were inventions made possible by the multiple trajectories of the nineteenth century (Williams 1981). The structuring of historical reason "made" the tombs appear part of the universal flow of social and human development rather than as stones and places for graffiti. The histories could position the pyramids into a narrative of a global history in which the particularities of Egyptian time and space were placed into a more general, evolutionary notion of development about, for example, Western societies. Egypt became part of a cosmology of a "Western Civilization" whose particular "reflectivity" established a continuum of a past in relation to a present and a future that had a progressive chronology and hierarchical structure of social development.

Embedded in the possibility of an Egyptian history was the invention of "fact." It was assumed that if one went to an archive of some sort and "found" a document, the document provided a source that was of a nonhistorical nature and thus beyond revision. Positivistically speaking, documents and social objects were viewed as containing information that could serve as the basis for observations similar to the "facts" that occur in natural sciences. The more numerous the observations or the more precise the "triangulation," the more reliable the research. It is interesting to note that the historical "fact" as a foundation for history does not appear until the nineteenth century, when positivism was introduced into the study of the past (Topolski 1976: 113; see also Stoianovich 1976).

As we historicize the placement of the Egyptian pyramids into narratives about human development, the historical interpretations are not just about positivistically conceived "data." The making of the tombs as historical "data" embodied profound and complex sets of relations, not the least of which is how reason (and its opposite, nonreason) was constructed. Historical reason embodied a new epistemological space that visioned the world as organized structures and events that have an extrahistoricity that provide the links and functions in an emergence of successions to produce history.

To put this construction of historical "reason" in some perspective, we can compare three views: Herodotus's notion of history as a chronicle to describe the cycles of truth that appear in the past; the Church's practices in the medieval annals that chronicled divine intervention and providence; and contemporary ways of ordering of time and space as sequentially describing relationships among people and events. In the contemporary reasoning, history is no longer a compilation of factual successions or sequences but a mode of reasoning that requires empirical evidence and reflectivity about the order of things. The changes in the meaning of history, I will argue further, are not a progression to human understanding but changes in principles of classification and reasoning that have no single origin but are the effect of multiple trajectories.

The second illustrative example of the "making" of historical data is the commonplace of schooling that names the child as a "learner."[8] The child as learner has become so natural in the late twentieth century that it is difficult to think of children as anything else but learners; yet in a historical sense, the making of the child-as-learner involved particular transformations in the social reasoning that we now associate with modernity. The category "learner" emerged in the past century as part of a system of ideas whose consequence was to revise the rules of reason through which individuality was ordered. The current categories of "student" and "pupil," for example, did not exist in the early nineteenth century when talking about schooling. The child was called a scholar. The late-nineteenth-century invention of the pedagogical category of the "student" and, later, "learner" reconstructed the child as an object of the teacher's scrutiny. The early-nineteenth-century teacher saw the child in relation to the prophetic task of "professing" Christian faith; that vision has been replaced with an object of teaching that is calculable and rational. To make children "learners" is to introduce a modern conception of childhood.[9]

Childhood is an effect of transformations in institutional relations, technologies, and systems of ideas that was to change how identity is to be "seen," understood, and acted upon. As Giddens (1987) argues more generally, the modern "self" lives within a social field where the immediate practices are continually repositioned within abstract systems of ideas. The systems of generalized and abstract ideas enable individuals to interpret and define their relationships. The new, abstract, and generalized systems were meant to guide individuals as they organized everyday practices. The "modern" child is an example of this transformation; the child has become someone no longer related to conceptions of time and space bounded in one's community. A child can now be seen as cosmopolitan in accordance with universal traits irrespective of the child's geographical place. The categories of learning make the modern child into someone who gives attention to the study of things in the world rather than one who relies on transcendental faith. The attentiveness given by the teacher is thought to be measurable in secular, scientific ways. The modern child is also seen by others and understands him or herself as a rational, "problem-solving," and "developing" person.

One can read much of modern curriculum theory as constructions and reconstructions of the capacities of children through shifts in the systems of reason through which the child is classified, ordered, and divided (Baker 1998; in press). The universal stages of development, psychological categories of the "self," and rational measures of achievement make the classifications seem timeless and universal, with no apparent basis in any particular locality or concrete relation of time and space. But the fabrications of the child are also systems that "make," through which the child is supervised and subjectivities constructed. There is a recursive quality as the systems of reason are brought back into face-to-face interactions to determine individual competence and achievement.

My brief discussion of the construction of an "Egyptian" past and the production of the "learning" child addresses the case that narratives of the past are more than merely interpretations of data. Our principles for classifying and "reasoning" about school knowledge construct how the objects of study are constituted in time and space. This construction embodies accepted strategies for organizing questions, and the concepts (implicit or explicit) that shape and fashion how empirical data are managed and ordered as objects of inquiry. Research embodies dispositions towards what is to be looked at and how that looking is to conceive of the "things" of the world.

Historical Traditions: The Philosophy of Consciousness and the Linguistic Turns

From the two examples above, we can begin to explore two different problematics in the forming of historical knowledge.[10] I recognize that, in some sense, all histories can be considered historicist. Some are historical narratives that consider how people and events change over time. Much American intellectual history is constructed in this manner. The biographies of John Dewey and Edward Thorndike provide two examples in which ideas are described to explain changes in how actors perceived events or how events shaped what actors perceived (Karier 1986; Joncich 1968). A different form of historicist reasoning, and one that I focus on here, is a conceptual mapping that tracks how the categories, distinctions, and differentiations of schooling change over time. This focus on knowledge as a field of cultural practice is related to this book's theme of a cultural history. For the sake of the argument of this essay, we can associate the former narrative of historical events and people as a historicist tradition tied to the philosophy of consciousness. The latter tradition of historicism I call a social epistemology; it is associated with the intersection of "linguistic traditions" or what are sometimes called the "linguistic turns" in literature with cultural and political theories in postmodern and postcolonial literatures.[11] While multiple in emphasis, there is a focus on language as a constitutive element in the construction of social life and "identity."

The historicist tradition has dominated the construction of social science and history for at least the past hundred years.[12] We can think of this historicism as a privileging of the philosophy of consciousness and theories of action. In this tradition of thought, social theory privileges the actors whose intents and purposes are enacted in the ongoing events that the researcher discovers through, for example, archival documents. People are seen as purposeful actors who produce change through their actions—sometimes willfully, sometimes with unintended consequences. To position historical actors in the construction of knowledge about the past, it is believed, enables the actor in the present to become a purposeful agent of change. The philosophy of consciousness gives sovereignty to actors and agency to humans in explanations of change in those structures.

Progress (or its denial) that places the actor as the a priori causal agent in change is a central motif in the epistemology: History written according to the philosophy of consciousness tells of the past so that the present can be understood and the future reordered and controlled. Progress is conceived as the rational outcome of human thought and reason as applied to social conditions (Kantian and Lockean), or as the identification of contradictions from which a new synthesis can be organized (Hegelian and Marxist). The historical identification of actors and the chronological ordering of events from positive data are viewed as the precursor of any meaningful change.

The concern with actors as purposeful agents was a radical invention of the Enlightenment. Historical practices no longer relegated social organization and change to transcendental forces, such as God. But with the philosophy of consciousness, a particular doctrine of modernity emerges to form rules for the Enlightenment project (Foucault 1984).

The philosophy of consciousness also adheres to critical studies of schooling, but that progress is tied to Hegelian assumptions of uncovering contradictions. The Hegelian notion of contradictions seeks to produce a new synthesis. That synthesis is related to a millennial vision in which there is an eventual replacement of previous and present historical configurations. In current reform efforts, words like "empowerment," "agency," and "resistance" signify a historical view that invests power in the actions of people as they struggle to change their world for the better. As with reformist traditions, a *foundational assumption is that progressive change cannot occur without knowledge that first identifies the actors who will bring about or prevent that change.*

To consider historicist tradition and its commitment to the philosophy of consciousness, we need to historicize the philosophical assumption that posits actors as an a priori assumption about change.[13] The focus on actors is, in part, related to the emergence of positivism within nineteenth-century German historicism. German idealist conceptions of history were being challenged by the emergence of the social sciences. To regain legitimacy for historical studies, a scientific outlook was established. Historiography gave positive attention to the "facts" of the past. These "facts" were to be located in specific documents that gave historical narratives a specific, concrete location in a regular time and space.

The exploration of the evolution of human purpose and intent involved a systematic scrutiny that illuminated all of life's concrete forms. The methodological strategies of historicism privileged the physical place in which an action occurred. Time and space were perceived as containing a particular concreteness through a rational ordering of events and people's thoughts. Each event belonged to a precise and unique social context. Social realities were determined by putting the single events together into an unfolding pattern. The use of extensive identification of sources of "data" through footnotes in historical texts stand as testimonials to the "reality" being portrayed and the scientific discipline in which knowledge is excavated from the "data."

While the concern with actors as purposeful agents was a radical invention of the Enlightenment (part of the effort to no longer relegate the social order and change to transcendental forces), the philosophy of consciousness embodies a particular doctrine of modernity (Foucault 1984). The main goal of historicism was to objectify all social life; reality was explained "as it really happened" through an ordering of singular events or the thoughts of individuals. Events and actors were placed together through a chronological ordering of concrete practices in time. With facts as the guiding force, the historian was to interfere as little as possible in writing the "facts" of history.[14]

In contrast to the historicist tradition, this essay focuses on a social epistemology.[15] My concern is with how the systems of ideas construct, shape, and coordinate action through the relations and ordering principles they establish. In this sense, knowledge is a field of cultural practices that has social consequences. The ordering, disciplining, and regulating through discursive rules becomes centrally important as schooling embodies an authorized knowledge of the world and the child's "self." My earlier discussion of the historical shifts from the teacher who "sees" teaching as internalizing Christian sincerity, to the teacher who views the child as a "learner" is an example of such an epistemological focus. The different systems of ideas place the child into calculable epistemological spaces through which competence, achievement, and salvation are understood and acted upon. But the viewing of language as constitutive of the world is not only to understand "texts," but to view the rules of "reasoning" as located in an amalgamation of social conditions in which the classifications are constituted (Crary 1990). It is for this reason, again, that I talk about a *social* epistemology.

At this point, I return briefly to the argument about the philosophy of consciousness as the bedrock of historicism. The cornerstone of the argument is that the actor makes history, and when the actor is absent a determinist world is introduced that has no possibility of change. My argument challenges that view of theory and change by considering the reasoning and principles that fabricate the actors who are the agents of change. This challenge to the historicism of the "actor" involves a paradox. The actor is paradoxically reintroduced, but not by looking for the agent in the narrative of inquiry. The agent is introduced through a destabilization of the conditions that confine and intern consciousness and its principles of order. Making the rules for "telling the truth" contingent, historical, and susceptible to critique creates a greater range of possibility for action through dislodging the ordering principles that define our subjectivities. I will return to these issues after a discussion of curriculum and power.

Curriculum as a Governing Practice

A social epistemology poses certain questions about the social construction of knowledge, although my use of the social construction of knowledge is very different from that of educational constructivist psychologies that have little to do with historicizing ideas (see my chapter on Vygotsky and Dewey in this book). What is learned in school is not only about what to do and what to know. Learning about spelling, science, mathematics, or geography is also learning dispositions, awarenesses, and sensibilities about the world. My emphasis on curriculum in this essay is to make the problem of knowledge and reasoning in schools—the forms by which we "tell the truth" about ourselves and others—an issue of governing.

The idea of knowledge as governing may produce a strong reaction as it affects a sensitive nerve of the predisposition (derived from the Enlightenment) that places a high value on individual initiative and human purpose in giving direction to social affairs. My concern with governing, however, should not be read as disregarding Enlightenment sensitivities to reason and rationality. But we cannot assume reason and rationality are a unified and universal system by which we can talk about what is true and false. My concern in this essay is to consider how particular doctrines of reason are the effects of power, to explore the particular systems of ideas and rules of reasoning that are embedded in the practices of schools.[16]

In light of these concerns, I ask how we might approach a history of curriculum that focuses on knowledge as a governing practice. At the same time, my strategy has two other foci: to construct a historical inquiry of curriculum that makes problematic the assumptions of positivism and the philosophy of consciousness; and to engage in a self-reflective stance towards the relation of intellectual work to social movements.

Curriculum as Systems of Governing and Discipline

Curriculum (or the broader concept of pedagogy) exists within an institution called schooling that is a relatively recent invention of Western society, one that quickly became part of the world system (Meyer 1987). I say "Western society" because there are examples of learning and curriculum in the Islamic midrash and the Jewish yeshiva that suggest other forms of social relationships around which to organize institutionally transmitted knowledge for the young than those found in the construct of schooling (Gerholm 1987; also the chapters in this book by Hamilton and by Chartier and Hébrard). Curriculum, then, can be viewed as an invention of modernity that, I will argue, involves forms of knowledge whose functions are to regulate and discipline the individual.

The idea of curriculum has been one of a particular organization of knowledge by which individuals regulate and discipline themselves as members of a community/society (Kliebard 1986; Lundgren 1983; Hamilton 1989; Englund 1991).[17] Since at least the Protestant Reformation, schools have been institutions that relate the state, civil (and religious) authority, and moral discipline.[18] The reforms introduced by Martin Luther made education a "disciplining" mechanism important to the Reformation (Luke 1989). The German reforms of the sixteenth century did more than simply educate the masses along the lines of humanistic principles. Curriculum inscribed certain rules through which the individual should reason about the "self" and discipline the actions to be taken. The inscriptions were not enacted through brute force, but through the principles that ordered the symbolic systems by which one was to interpret, organize, and act in the world.

Childhood and literacy became institutionalized as strategies to confront social disorder through privileging standards of religious, social, and moral values. The Jesuits of the sixteenth century recognized the disciplining qualities of pedagogy as part of the Counter-Reformation (Durkheim 1977). They developed classroom practices that reinterpreted the humanist and secular literature of the Counter-Reformation to assert the values of the Catholic church. Their strategy was to read texts without historical contexts so as to insert Catholic moral precepts into pagan literature. The schools were expected to promote true faith, service to the state, and the proper functioning of the family.

We can think of mass public schooling of the late nineteenth and early twentieth centuries as a continuation of the disciplining and governing project of the Reformation. But mass schooling was also a break in the systems of knowledge by which individuals would become productive members of society. U.S. modern mass schooling, for example, was the product of multiple trajectories. It encapsulated moral tenets that joined the emerging tasks associated with the modern welfare state and a universalized, civil religion associated with Protestantism.[19] Industrialization, urbanization, immigration, the new political organizations associated with democracies, as well as intellectual thought that combined utilitarian and pragmatic themes–all were part of the transformations inscribed in schooling.[20] The curriculum of the late nineteenth century American school was an outcome of a transformation that linked the governing patterns of society and the inner governing "mentalities" of the individual (see, Hunter 1994). The school was an institutional form located within the changing patterns of governing.

Michel Foucault's (1979) notion of "governmentality" is helpful here. It focuses on the new principles of governing embodied in pedagogy. In the nineteenth century, Foucault argues, there occurred a new relation between state governing practices and individual behaviors and dispositions.[21] The administrative patterns of the society were constituted by the link between the states responsibility for the welfare of its citizens and the capabilities of individuals to govern themselves. In multiple social arenas, the art of governing occurs as new institutions of health, labor, education, and mental structures appear alongside the emergence of the new social welfare goals of the state.[22]

In certain ways, the production of new governing patterns was made possible through the concept of "childhood." The spread of mass schooling embodied "salvation stories" that connected the individual to a larger collective sense of mission and progress through the practices of schooling, among other modern institutions (Thomas et al. 1987). In the United States, these salvation stories were tied to the transformations of the governing principles of a liberal democracy by which individuals were expected to participate in society. The new salvation story was told in the name of the new, secular citizen who in the early nineteenth century was to shed the previous beliefs and dispositions of religion and an inherited social order and replace them with a subjectivity that embodied the obligations, responsibilities, and personal discipline embodied in liberal democratic ideals. Christopher Lasch (1977) has argued, for example, that "new" ideas of childhood helped to precipitate the new idea of the family as interwoven problems of the social administration of the state, public health, and moralists.

Pedagogy was a central strategy in the social administration of the child. The new psychologies of problem-solving, measurement, and child development that emerged embodied distinctions and differentiations that were to regulate not only how information was formed about schooling and how problems were described but also the discursive systems that embodied categories of personal competence and achievement. The language of the child as "learner" placed faith in the rational individual as the locus of change (Meyer 1987).

And embedded in the new pedagogies that begin to appear were discourses of science (Bledstein 1976; Wallenstein 1984, 1990; Popkewitz 1991). Science was seen as part of the Enlightenment heritage by which society could progress. As did the physical sciences for the natural world, the social sciences were to describe, explain, and give direction for solving "the social problem." But the systems of ideas in the social sciences were not "merely" ideas to think about and to use to interpret social life; the concepts were recursively brought into social practices.

The new pedagogical theories and sciences of education were governing practices as moral and political concepts were brought into the social sciences and reclassified as those of schooling. Baker (1998) has argued, for example, that late-nineteenth-century American discourses of childhood embodied a notion of the child as "rescued" from the effects of a modern society. But that notion of "childhood-as-rescue" inscribe certain binaries (two "things" that stand in opposition to each other)—"whiteness/blackness" and "male/female." The binaries were not explicit but rather implicit in the ways that the texts told what was to be known and acted upon as "childhood."

Pedagogy was also a strategy that related political rationalities with individual consciousness. At one level, we can think of the child study research at the turn of the century as ordering principles that became part of a common sense for locating individuals in a new sense of reason and normalcy. That normalcy included binaries that placed certain individuals (black, female) as "noneducable" as they existed outside of "reason" and salvation.

At a different level, the child study movement was formed within a larger domain of knowledge that included the invention of statistics (a French term for state arithmetic). The reason of statistics was mutually constituted by social and cultural governing. Applying a calculus of probability, the state reforms and the policing of health and wealth constructed social groupings and interests by reference to statistical aggregates of populations. Population reasoning divided people into specific units that could be calculated, organized, and reflected on through the administration of the state, such as controlling epidemics and crime (Hacking 1991).[23]

But population reasoning was to produce new cultural forms for constructing individuality. Its "reasoning" is one in which the person is defined normatively in relation to statistical aggregates that ascribe a "growth" or "development" of a person that can be monitored and supervised. Such reasoning, however, is not only of state science and administration.

When we approach curriculum history as a problem of governing, the issues about "child development" and educational research are not only about what knowledge is to be taught. The modern school and its curriculum were related to diverse trajectories about the social and culture forms through which individuals were to "understand" and "participate intelligently" within new sets of relations and institutions that included the state, bureaucracies, commerce, and work. The modern school was a break in the systems of knowledge through which individuals were to regulate and discipline "selves." Whereas the previous world sought its truth in divine providence, the "modern" pedagogical knowledge took certain religious views about salvation and combined them with a scientific disposition towards the search for truth and self-governing. What is constituted as teaching, learning, and school assessment, therefore, is not merely "there" or negotiated by those who work in schools. The different curriculum foci inscribe ways of thinking and reasoning about community and self that cannot be assumed but must be historicized.

Knowledge as Disciplining Technologies

The notion of governing is not meant to ascribe good/bad or moral/evil distinctions when talking about schooling. It recognizes the sociological premise that all social situations have historically embedded restraints and constraints. Even to say that one is going "to act alone" is a statement that occurs within structuring principles. While a strong faith in individuality exists in American folklore, to speak of the individual is also to invoke a theory of society that defines individuality (Popkewitz 1983). At this point, then, I proceed to explore further the notion of governing embodied in curriculum.

We can think about curriculum as a governing strategy at two different layers. First, schooling defines the boundaries of what is to be known. This is the Spencerian question that has dominated U.S. curriculum theory: "What knowledge is of most worth?" Information is selected from a great array of possibilities. The selection of curriculum shapes and fashions how social and personal events are organized for reflection and practice. The selection processes operate as "lenses" that define problems through the classifications that are sanctioned.

A different layer of governing, and for me one that is constitutive for understanding schools, is that the selection of knowledge is politically sanctioned ways for individuals to organize their views of "self." That is, schooling is the primary institution of the state concerned with upbringing and labor training (Meyer, 1987). The implications of this sanctioning can be understood through feminist scholarship over the past decade that has located how discursive practices are not only representative of things in the world but are important elements of power relations (Lather 1986; Nicholson 1986, Weedon 1987; Fraser 1992).

Schooling, then, is a set of strategies to direct how students reason about the world-at-large and the self in that world. The methods to effect school knowledge establish the parameters for how people are to inquire, organize, and understand their world and "self." Curriculum is an ensemble of methods and strategies that inscribe principles for action. Models of literacy in schooling display "particular postures (correct way of maintaining one's body when reading), silences, gestures and signs of 'being in' the lesson that encode particular ways of acting like a student." (Walkerdine 1988, 1990). Studies of the cognitive development of children, for example, have enabled a focus on what seemed noncontroversial—the teaching of mathematics—as embodying norms that relate teaching to issues of gender and social class differentiation. The discourses of pedagogy, following Luke's (1990) studies of classrooms, "operate not as an abstract set of ideas to be transposed into, inside of, or within mind/consciousness," but as a material series of processes that inscribe attributes of subjectivity into the social body.

Curriculum as a governing through reason circulates through cultural and social practices. Much of the sociology of the turn of the century gave attention to concepts of social control that explicitly recognized the relation of institutional patterns and individual development (Franklin 1986; Ross 1991). Psychology was introduced into mass schooling as a technology for the restructuring of how individuals were to be seen, defined, and evaluated (O'Donnell 1985). The psychologies were made into technologies to organize classroom didactics, instructional materials, and the time-slotting of school subjects around which children were to "learn" (Goodson 1987; Popkewitz 1987). The organization of teaching through lesson planning, the establishing of a hierarchy of objectives in a basal reading series, and the administration of achievement tests to assess school success/failure established social forms that intersected with the field of cultural production in which knowledge works.

My focus on curriculum as systems of reason, then, is to consider different practices through which individuality is fabricated, in its two senses discussed earlier. It is also to consider how curriculum is inscribed in a field of cultural practice through the rules and standards by which reason and individuality are constructed. The rules and standards produce governing practices, but that governing as I have argued, is not only what is cognitively understood. It is a governing related to Foucault's governmentality, the sensibilities, dispositions, and awarenesses by which individuals act and participate in the world.

History and Social Epistemologies

In light of this book and its emphasis on cultural history, I have thought that it might be appropriate to think of a curriculum history as a cultural rather than as a social epistemology.[24] I decided, however, to keep the phrasing of social epistemology but in doing so, to emphasize the significance of the relation of the social (the organization, the operational systems of rules and relations among actors and actions) to the cultural that is encapsulated in the notion of epistemology. With knowledge as the center of inquiry, the assumptions of the subject and actor in the philosophy of consciousness are also radically altered. Historical change is viewed as one of the breaks in the structuring of knowledge rather than as an evolutionary process of universal progress.

To think of historical change as rupture has an important consequence beyond that of how historical narratives are constructed. In the final sections of this essay, I explore the politics of knowledge and intellectual work. Too often the literature on intellectual work makes a quick leap from what is studied to what people need to do to produce change. (For discussion of this issue, see Callewaert, 1999; Muller, 2000.) This is a consequence, I argue, of the a priori philosophical assumption of progress in the formulations of theoretical knowledge. Intellectuals are placed in a position of being both prophets and oracles. In contrast, a potential implication of the reconstruction of history as breaks in knowledge systems is to remove progress as an a priori philosophical formulation, but, in doing so, without necessarily losing site of commitments to social change. To foreshadow my argument, the strategy for historical study in this essay is not to do away with the subject or with purposeful action, but to change the manner in which the subject is brought into history to produce change.[25]

A "Linguistic" Turn, Reason, and the Decentering of the Subject

The "linguistic turn" in social science and history can be viewed as a recasting of modernist doctrines associated with the Enlightenment project. It "decentered" the actor and agency from the center stage of interpretation. The focus becomes how discursive "spaces" are constructed to organize and produce subordination; for example, on the construction of "blackness" rather than blacks, "gender" rather than women, "childhood" rather than the child, and the construction of "teacher" rather than teachers. Further, I consider not only discourse but overlapping discourses that fabricate the "self" in fields of cultural practices. Historical attention is given to how the categories, distinctions, and differentiations of systems of ideas change over time to construct the "subjects" of our practices.

The shift in focus to reason occurs, I argue, without giving up the Enlightenment recognition of a world that is socially constructed, or eliminating agents or actors in change, but rather relocates the terrains in which such change is produced.[26] Let me explore this further as one of the major debates has been centered on change as it is posited in the philosophy of consciousness and theories of action.

Making knowledge a central problem of historical studies has been provocatively labeled "the decentering of the subject," to mark the departure from the actor-centerd subject of the philosophy of consciousness. The (re)moving of the subject is directed at understanding how, at different historical times, people are made into subjects through a weaving of different social practices and institutional patterns. For example, Riley (1988) explored how the concept of "woman" has moved over the past few hundred years from its placement in religious spaces as a "soul" dominated by the church to social spaces that revisioned women through their bodies and sexuality. The concept of "woman" is historicized to take what is seen as unproblematic—woman as the subject to be observed, scrutinized, and practiced—and to make the constitution of that subject a center of analysis; that is, to understand how particular forms of knowledge are privileged in particular social relations and historically defined power relations.

To make the subject into a historical construction that is interrogated is central to Foucault's (1980) argument about history as genealogy: "One has to dispense with the constituent subject, to get rid of the subject itself . . . to arrive at an analysis which can account for the constitution of the subject within a historical framework. And this is what I would call genealogy . . . a form of history which can account for the constitution of knowledges, discourses, domains of objects, etc. without having to make reference to a subject which is either transcendental in relation to the field of events or runs its empty sameness throughout the course of history."

This notion of genealogy is related to my use of social epistemology. My concern, however, shifts the focus to knowledge as a field of cultural practice and cultural reproduction. In this sense of a social epistemology, I focus on "systems of reason" to understand how different discourses about the child, teaching, learning, school administration, and sociopolitical discourses overlap to become the common sense of schooling and its practices. While I sometimes use the concept of "discourse," this is done more as a literary device, although discourse theories tend to deemphasize the historicity of language systems.

This approach to history has been popularized in the work of Kuhn (1970), although I use Kuhn advisedly here because of his idealistic conception of change. Kuhn studied in what can be called an epistemological tradition that is tied to French and German history and the philosophy of science (Canguilhem 1978, 1988; Bachelard 1984; Koselleck 1991; see also Tally 1990) and was brought to the study of social sciences through the work of Michel Foucault.[27] Kuhn, the European philosophers of science like Bachelard and Canguilhem, as well as Foucault *entail a shift in focus from the intentions of people to the structures of knowledge itself.*

One part of the "linguistic turn" is to recognize that when we "use" language, it may not be "us" speaking. Our speech is language historically formed and then brought into the present. It is, to borrow from Bakhtin (1981), over-populated with the intentions of others. For example, a contemporary commitment in some educational research is to talk about the "voice" of teachers and students. The "wisdom" of teachers' practices become authorial and "authentic." Yet when we interrogate the acts of teachers' writing and speaking historically, we find nothing "natural" in talking about school as "management," or teachers' "voices" and "wisdom." The discourses in which "voices" and the "wisdom" of teachers' are inscribed embody patterns of "reasoning" constructed prior to teachers' entrance to the scene of schooling. The different discursive strategies occur within an ensemble of symbolic and non-symbolic practices, technologies, and institutions that emerge over time and that are the effects of power.

Recent studies of rhetoric and science enable us to consider how even the seemingly "objective" academic languages that we speak may not be our own. The principles of scientific discourses are active elements in the constructions of the world, not "merely" descriptive of action and purpose. For example, writing in seemingly academic style is often associated with placing a string of references at the end of a sentence, such as prescribed in the style manual of the American Psychological Association (APA). Referencing in this manner is to adopt a strategy about knowledge developed in behavioral psychology during the 1920s. That strategy was part of the legitimating practices of behaviorism through the inscribing in science the assumption that scientific knowledge was cumulative and sequential (Brazerman 1987).

We can pursue the pedagogical discourses of teachers as not one single practice but as the mobilization of multiple discourses that come together to express particular historical relations about schooling through the systems of reasoning applied. Teachers in a study of urban and rural schools, for example, gave intent and purposes to the practices of teaching through an overlapping of different discourses about the "needy" child that embodied a particular population reasoning to classify children of color and poverty (Popkewitz 1998). The children were defined as having particular attributes in need of remediation—the child's whose "learning style" is "field-dependent," who learns only "by doing," who lacks a "healthy self-concept," and whose parents are on welfare or whose mother is an "unwed mother." The population reasoning inscribed in this speech is not "natural" to the teacher; rather it is an historically formed reasoning related to the problem of "governmentality" and the discipline of the "self" discussed earlier. The practices of population reasoning in teacher discourses positioned the children of color and poverty as the anthropological "others" who were normatively different.

The analysis of systems of reason of teaching and teacher education enables an understanding of how discourses change over time to inscribe intent, purpose, and direction in the practices of schooling. Fendler's (1998) study of the changing meaning of "the educated subject," for example, provides a way to understand how our reasoning about "teacher thinking" and the "wisdom of practice," two contemporary slogans about school reform, are the effect of power; they are not emancipatory. Fendler argues that the concept of an "educated subject" is not a constant entity nor one that can be studied solely as a "philosophical" idea that is stable over time. It is a concept that has changed as the systems that regulate the person have shifted within changing social circumstances. Exploring conceptions of the "educated subject" in ancient Greece, in medieval and modern times, and in the contemporary discourses of American educational reform, she identifies discursive breaks in the substance of what makes an educated person, the obligations and justifications of the person who is "educated," and the means and goals of that education. Further, she maps the changing relations of concepts of the "educated subject" to social and political conditions in which that "educated person" is constructed.

The analysis calls attention to radical shifts in the forms of disciplining and governing the "child" in contemporary school reform discourses. When examining contemporary school didactics and teacher education reforms in the light of Fendler's analysis, we are able to identify new relations of knowledge and power. The new "educated subject" embodies new "technologies of the self"; that is, drawing on Foucault and feminist theories, a revisioning of the teacher and the child as objects that are systematically classified, legislated, standardized, and normalized. Fendler argues that the new technologies of pedagogy move institutional norms directly into the subjective space of the individual as the reforms seek to change the capabilities and dispositions of children. What is rhetorically signaled as "teachers' wisdom" in contemporary research, we can reason from Fendler's genealogy, is an effect of political rationalities brought into the pedagogy through which children and teachers are to think and act in the world. The desires, dispositions, and capabilities of the child in school, Fendler argues, is "mutually constitutive with society" rather than different.

Why move to a social epistemological approach to the study of history rather than maintain the assumptions of the philosophy of consciousness? It has been argued that focusing on the intent and purposes of social actors provides an important social as well as scientific commitment. It places people and their social worlds in history. To remove people from history is to make the world seem deterministic and outside the possibility of intervention.

These arguments about the removal of the actor are articulated within the philosophy of consciousness.[28] Not to have a visible actor—groupings of people and individuals—in narratives of social affairs is made to seem antihumanistic (and even antidemocratic). It is not uncommon to hear people react to stories about schools by asking, "Where are the people in the story?" The assumption is of a world in which salvation can be found only by identifying a priori who will do the good works. One might even say, "Yes, we can understand that discourses do construct what it is possible to say and think, but it is people who do that construction."

My argument is not to deny that people act and that there are different rules of reason that compete with each other at different times. Rather, while the argument about the centering of human purpose and actors might seem an appropriate analytic argument, the political consequence of this intellectual stance has not always been empowering. Without getting too far ahead of my argument, the practical consequences of an unquestioned centering of a subject entail multiple issues of power that are hidden in the rhetoric. Butler (1992) argues, drawing on feminist and postcolonial literature, that the centering of the subject is a particular invention of Western philosophy. When the subject is taken uncritically as the locus of struggle for knowledge about enfranchisement and democracy, scholarship draws from the very models that have oppressed through the principles that govern the production of subjects. Such a strategy is both a consolidation and concealment of those power relations. For example, feminist scholarship has helped to problematize the concept of "woman" in a manner that allows us to understand that the qualities we associate with gender are historically constructed attributes formed in power relations. Where the agency of individuals or groups are made to seem as natural, there is a tendency to lose sight of how the agendas and categories that define oppositions are historically formed. The systems of relevancies are taken for granted.

Such feminist arguments are important in this analysis. The historical conception of discourses as the amalgamation of multiple transformations is important. It provides a way to locate the inscription of power in schooling and curriculum that is obscured within the traditions that privilege the intent and purpose of actors.

Decentering the subject is not to quiet action or change by removing the actor or to remove commitments formed as part of the Enlightenment project. The strategy of decentering the subject, I believe, is itself a product of the very self-reflectivity produced through the Enlightenment. There is an acceptance of the need to construct knowledge that can enable people to act intentionally, but this insertion occurs in a different location than that argued in the philosophy of consciousness. The possibility of action is found in questioning the givenness of the subject through exploring its historical constructedness. The subject is made into a dimension of the questionable and of "insistent contest and resignification" (Butler 1992), not as a foundation of research that is taken as the unquestionable. Constructing histories about how our subjectivities are formed (making the agendas and categories of the subject problematic) can provide a potential space for alternative acts and alternative intentions that are not articulated through the available common senses.

Decentering Progress: From Evolution to a History of Breaks

My focus on the categories and rules of reason leads to a second structuring principle of a historical social epistemology: change is not in the evolutionary progression of events or in the past efforts of people to influence those events. Change is in disrupting or troubling, as Butler (1992) suggests, the ways in which our forms of reasoning and identities "consolidate and conceal power relations."

The history of science provides one example of a view of change as embedded in the structuring of knowledge. Kuhn (1970), for example, talked about revolutionary and normal sciences as issues of power as well as knowledge (Toulmin 1972 1988). Kuhn considered a historical change that did not involve intent and the practice of individuals, even though individuals and particular practices were part of his narrative about science.[29] "Revolutionary science" involves different sets of rules and standards about truth—what is to be studied, why and how—from those of normal science. New questions (and sets of relations) are generated about phenomena for which older paradigms are inadequate. Further, the distinction between how truth is told in normal and revolutionary science, is not cumulative; rather, it involves ruptures in belief and cognition that occur within particular historical conjunctures. These ruptures did not occur easily as the new structures of knowledge challenged the imputed realities of scientists. "Evidence" from empirical studies was not sufficient to produce paradigmatic shifts.

But we must go further than Kuhn in thinking about conceptual changes. How people tell the truth about the world is part of and expressive of how our relationships with the world and our "selves" are established. It is through locating changes in the rules of reason that we can think about change. Foucault (1975), for example, locates the birth of modern medicine in changes to what was made visible and what was expressed about disease. In the eighteenth century, Foucault (1975) argues, the spatial configurations of disease and the localizing of illness in particular pathologies replaced a classification system that had dominated medicine. The latter (classification system) saw the primary problem of medicine as the "envelopments, subordinations, divisions, resemblances" rather than as disease localized in organs. The new way of "seeing" enabled a clinical gaze that generated particular issues as related to pathologies of individual organs rather than as related to the functioning of the organism as a whole. The new configurations of a medical gaze occurred alongside of and were made possible through the development of the teaching hospital and other institutional places in which medicine was practiced.

The history of medical practices was not a chronological one of a progressive advancement, or of a serial progress; it was of a time that "goes at a thousand different paces, swift and slow, which bear almost no relation to the day-to-day rhythm of a chronicle or of traditional history" (Braudel 1980). We can turn, as well, to the later Wittgenstein (1966) who provided a way of understanding historical change as multiple rates developing across different institutions at different times that come together in what can be called a historical conjunction. Wittgenstein likened historical change to a thread made up of many fibers. The strength of the thread does not reside in the fact that some fibers run its entire length but in the fact that many fibers overlap. To focus on "the day-to-day rhythm of a chronicle or of traditional history" of actors is to lose sight of the long-term transformations and their significance.

My concern with a social epistemology is to give attention to the plural and unstable patterns in which schooling is constructed. As in Hamilton's chapter of this book, the set of relations that become schooling—in its forms of expression and performances—exists across different dimensions of time and space and provides examples for organizing cases and recognizing shifts in what was previously seen as continuous. Mass schooling, for example, was a nineteenth-century invention that emerged from different movements within society that, at a certain level, worked autonomously.[30] Overlapping with changes in classroom teaching were the creations of institutions for teacher education (normal schools), the rise of the modern university, the formation of social sciences, and the emergence of the discipline of psychology. These multiple arenas of social practice occurred in conjunction with the modern American welfare state, which assumed the governing functions in the new institution of mass schooling. Interpretations of mass schooling, therefore, need to account for the multiple intersections of knowledge constructed in these varied arenas. It is in the conjuncture of the nineteenth-century practices that the assumptions of currently favored terms—such as "professionalism," "subject matter teaching," and teacher's "voice"—need to be placed and their implications examined.[31]

To that end we can explore social epistemology in the curriculum histories.[32] Hamilton (1989) seeks to understand how particular words such as "class" and "curriculum" came about and changed over time in relation to the social, economic, and cultural conditions in which those words existed. Hamilton argues, for example, that Calvinist influences in Britain were brought to the United States to emphasize instructional systems with well-ordered forms of social organization that could provide more efficient systems of moral supervision and labor organization. He argues, further, that there is a close relation between changing pedagogical discursive practices, changing conceptions of labor processes, and changing assumptions about the individual and the state. Englund (1991), also pursuing this tradition, distinguishes between consensus historians for whom there is one approach and one answer to a given problem, and an epistemological curriculum history in which there is an "ongoing, never-ending struggle of the social epistemology of school knowledge and a closer analysis of differences in interpretations and how the content changes." This struggle, Englund continues, "takes place at several levels, those of public debate, syllabuses, teaching materials, and concrete teaching."

From these examples of historicizing school knowledge, a social mapping is drawn of the epistemological changes in the practices of schooling. This is to enable an understanding of the prior rules and standards by which, and the conditions in which, truth is told about teaching and children in schooling, and how these rules change over time. The historical concern decenters particular actors in order to interpret how social practices and subjectivities are constituted.

Cultural Practices and Regional Histories

This essay began with the distinctions between the historicism of the philosophy of consciousness and a social epistemology in the study of schooling and curriculum. In drawing this distinction, I suggested that historical change can be understood as the breaks and ruptures through which systems of ideas construct the objects of schooling. In this final section, the notion of a "regionalized" history is introduced.

At first glance, the idea of a regional history may be misread as a study that is specific and located in a particular geographic place, such as the study of schooling in New England or "case" studies of a reform effort. My interest in region, however, is not of that type. A region here is not a geographical place. It is a cultural field that positions how the child and teacher are known and know the world. The child as "an adolescent," "a learner," a "personality" with or without "self-esteem," a member of a social class (an "at-risk" child, a "learning-disabled" child)—all such definitions position the child within a field of cultural practices that constructs the child as an object and subject.[33] The notion of cultural field is introduced to consider how particular discursive practices come together as reason or a common sense that makes possible the scrutiny, observation, and "self-reflection" of the person. To think of a cultural field is to think about the systems of reason that cross the institutions involved, such as schools, medicine, social welfare, law, psychology, and cultural institutions related to family.[34] The classifications produce a "space" to define the competence, achievement and well-being of the child.

But the placing of the "child" into a cultural field embodies an amalgamation of ideas, institutions, and social practices. If we take Hultqvist's (1998) study of the changing patterns of "reasoning" embodied in conceptions of childhood in Sweden, the discursive positioning of the child as a "thinking," rational, and acting subject is, at the same time, the enactment of the political rationalities of the Swedish state inserted into the world as a practice. Focusing on the situation of the preschool child, Hultqvist explores how the school and related social welfare activities contribute to producing children and young people as subjects of particular ways of living. Comparing the concept of "the child" in Swedish welfare models of the 1930s and the 1940s with the educational psychology and didactics of the 1970s, he argues that there appeared a new "decentralized" child who would be self-motivated and self-governing. The discourse of the "decentralized" child is part of contemporary "decentralization" of the social welfare state and a wider reconstitution of governing practices that include pedagogy and social science in the 1990s. Hultqvist's studies locate the reasoning about the child and the teacher within a broad historical cultural field of the governing of the "child."

The significance of the idea of cultural field is that it enables a focus on how different cultural practices weave together to define individuality. The histories that Foucault writes, for example, are not global histories of discipline or power. They are histories of the construction of subjectivities that invade particular institutional patterns but are not reducible to those patterns. His studies of the prison and the criminal, the asylum and the insane, the medical gaze, and bodily desires in the history of sexuality are examples of the constructions of discursive regions through which individuality is defined in multiple institutions of modernity.

The concept of cultural practice provides a way to think of the central actors of the modern school (the teacher, the child, the student, the behaviorally disabled child, and the school curriculum) as "objects" of a cultural field whose construction change over time. These changes are not merely about how one "thinks" the world but also about how the world is to be ordered and acted on.

The field of cultural practices is illustrated in a recent study of educational reform in Iceland (Jóhannesson in this book; also see Ingó fur Ásgeir Johannesson 1991 & 1993). From the 1960s on, Icelandic educational reform has been a key link in the state's project of school modernization. This modernization entails a rationalizing of the organization of schools and the Icelandic College of Education. But that organization involves more than establishing organizational linkages and personnel hierarchies. The modernization embodies a reclassification of the knowledge through which schooling is apprehended. Underlying the curriculum reforms in biology and social studies, for example, are particular sets of beliefs from which the school subjects are formed. Inscribed in the "new" curriculum knowledges are dispositions about historical progress, scientific reasoning, and child development, and democratic concerns about how schooling can produce a more just society. The post–World War II reform movement in Iceland replaced the prereform discourses with professional discourses of reform. Jóhannesson explores how the discursive themes moved among different agencies and institutions: the teacher unions, the Icelandic College of Education, the Icelandic University, the Ministry of Education, the Icelandic Institute for School Development and Evaluation.

We can think of Jóhannesson's mapping of Iceland as a way to locate changing power relations in the field of education through shifts in the field of cultural practices. The mapping of the epistemological practices explores changing boundaries about what is to be authorized as reason/nonreason with respect to the objects of schooling. It also maps certain changes in the governing principles of subjectivity that tie together various institutions.

The study of knowledge as a field of cultural practice is part of a strategy that does not privilege a notion of chronological time and physical place, such as occurs in the strategy of historicism in the philosophy of consciousness. It moves from a positivism to particular rules and standards of truth that cross institutional patterns and are not reducible to those patterns. The historical concern with knowledge as a field of cultural practice is that it provides a way to make the "actor" an object of scrutiny, and how those rules change over time.

Conclusions

My argument in this essay has moved through different layers of the problem of constructing a historical narrative. My initial move was to focus on curriculum as a problem of power produced through the production of rules and standards of truth. To do curriculum history as a "social epistemology" is to ask about what counts as evidence, the rules by which truth is established, and the effects of having some things count as evidence and truth while other things are deauthorized and made false (e.g., Wickham 1990). But, as I argued, such a history is "more" than studying the rules of "telling the truth." Curriculum deploys power through the manner in which and the condition on which knowledge is selected, organized, and evaluated in schools. To do history is to "see" shifting true/false divisions in a society as related to power relations rather than as a direct result of the existence of a given reality.

The historical studies enable us to understand how a certain normativity and selectivity is introduced into problem-solving about schooling in the present. The reasoning about "childhood," "curriculum," and "the educated subject" in contemporary reforms are not part of some prior grand design or structure but emerge from different social trajectories that come together in the modern school. Further, a social epistemology enables us to consider how the distinctions and differentiations of schooling construct a normativity whose effects are governing systems that include and exclude, an important contribution as we seek to construct more democratic societies and schools. Finally, the histories are of the present, enabling us to understand how the rules of contemporary pedagogy and teacher education reform emerge and link political rationalities with the "reasoning" that constructs the objects of schooling and its reform—what is defined as the child to be taught.

I can, at this moment, consider certain criticisms of a social epistemology that have appeared in social theory and history. One is, to decenter the subject and to remove a notion of "progress" within a philosophy of science is a nihilistic relativism incapable of furnishing norms, one that eradicates political activism through its denial of the subject. My response, which draws on Butler (1992), recognizes a certain Western ethnocentrism in the argument assuming the centered subject as an unquestionable universal category. The strategy that claims that all inquiry must focus on the subject as the only legitimate theoretical and political strategy for change is itself a political act of disquieting. It asserts that there can be no political opposition to specifying the subject prior to the act of inquiry or informed critique. This stance of an a priori subject in theorizing, Butler (1992) argues, "becomes an authoritarian ruse by which political conflict over the status of the subject is summarily silenced."

In response to such criticism, I suggest that social epistemology is a political as well as a conceptual practice. Embedded in the philosophy of consciousness is a particular social position of the researcher. This position is one of an oracle who would bring change and progress to the world. This role of prophecy is not necessarily one of personal intent but of the epistemologies that order and characterize the discourses about disciplined knowledge (I discuss this more fully in Popkewitz 1991). The social reformist traditions in social science and history, for example, practice this tradition of "prophecy" in the identification of universal developmental patterns in schooling—learning from history so that future planning can gain from the hindsight of the past. The promise is that efficiency and rationality will produce social progress. In critical sciences with Hegelian assumptions, the rule of prophecy and redemption is also present, but its purpose is to identify the repressive functioning of the present in order to move social practices toward some universal synthesis that produces the good. What is labeled the good is also called the progressive.

In both instances of the philosophy of consciousness, but in different ways, intellectuals position themselves as capable of identifying the future significance of present interpretations. This intellectual strategy establishes social scientists and historians as the legitimate and authoritative figures for the design of social affairs. I consider this assumption about progress in the sciences and histories of education to be dangerous in a democracy. Historical examples of intellectuals as experts in the service of the democratic ideal are filled with their own contradictions.[35]

One can consider the intellectual tradition in which I place a social epistemology as an attempt to alter the relation of disciplinary knowledge, the researcher, and the public spheres in which people struggle to make their world better. To understand change as ruptures and breaks is to question any inherent teleology in the knowledge production of intellectuals. Since there are no patterns of progress to discover, there is no privileged role of the intellectual in bringing about that progressive world.

But to consider historical change as epistemological breaks does not mean that political action is preempted. Political action occurs through making problematic "the subject" that has been so central to modern scholarship and its regulatory effects. This does not negate or dispense with such a notion. The strategy of historicizing the subject ("decentering") is one that reinserts humanity into social projects through making the governing systems of order, appropriation, and exclusion visible and confrontable. It is to ask about the processes of construction, political meaning, and the consequences of talking about the subject as a requirement or presupposition of theory (Butler 1992). The paradoxical task of placing ourselves into history is that we may, collectively through our actions in the present, poke holes in the causality that organizes the constructions of our "selves." And, in that process, there is the possibility of opening new systems for our collective and individual lives.

The stance towards a social epistemology recognizes the politics of knowledge as part of the reflective conditions of the production of knowledge. A historical sensitivity to how we construct our subjectivity is part of the epistemological vigilance that Bourdieu et al. (1991) speak about when they urge the need for reflexivity in the methods of study. Focusing on a social epistemology is a theoretical strategy that "sees" power as pervading the conceptual frameworks that construct the objects of inquiry, including the subject position of the critic, the theoretical moves that establish its foundational assumptions, and the assumptions that are excluded or foreclosed. The study of history is the study of the objectification of those elements that historians consider to be objectively given.[36]

Finally, my interest has been to link questions of sociology, psychology, and history to the study of schooling. The study of the subject and subjectivites of schooling requires that we take seriously what social linguistic theories have been telling us for at least the last seventy years. The discourses constructed about education in policy-making, reform reports, and documents from other institutionally legitimate positions of authority are not "merely" languages about education; they are part of the productive processes of society by which problems are classified and practices mobilized. There is no distinction, as many would like to believe, between theory and practice, or between the "real world of schooling" and university practices about schooling; what we have are systems of relations in which power is deployed. Nor should we be unreflective about the subject position of the critic and the epistemologies of progress that inhere in the educational community.

Notes

This discussion is derived from my attempt to develop an understanding of the reform movement of the last decade in the United States, a work in which I sought to make the current categories and distinctions of school and curriculum change sensitive to both historical and sociological questions (Popkewitz 1991). I wish to thank Barry Franklin, Tomas Englund, Christina Florin, Jodi Hall, Ulla Jóhannesson, António Nóvoa, Miguel Pereyra, Lynda Stone, and the Wednesday Group at the University of

Wisconsin-Madison and the Pedagogical Seminar at Umeå University in Sweden for their conversations with me about the ideas in this essay.

1. I borrow "trouble" from the work of Judith Butler (e.g., 1992), and also from a range of other considerations about change, politics and the position of intellectuals and intellectual work in change (e.g., Dean, 1994; Canning, 1994, among others).

2. Typically, arguments about relativism remove phenomena and facts from an historical discussion and from any further revision. These claims about the "other" person's relativism assert the moral and political superiority of those who make the argument of relativism.

3. I use the notion of intellectual as a social grouping that has increasingly been associated with issues of power, the state and governing in modernity. See Bauman (1987), Foucault (1988a, 1988b), Giddens (1990), Ross (1991).

4. I recognize that there are accepted historical techniques for interrogating the tracks of the past. My discussion here recognizes the importance of discipline in systematic inquiry, but also emphasizes that this discipline involves communal rules that are socially constructed and influenced by how the objects of inquiry are theoretically constructed. See my example about the Egyptian tombs later in this section.

5. People vote and children do things in school but these acts become interpretable and, thus, data only when questions are asked about their functions and implications.

6. My intent here is not to colonialize historiography as a European invention but to focus on a particular form of Eurocentric narrative that inscribed Egyptian artifacts within a larger cosmology of development.

7. The notions of "modern" and "modernity" refer to a particular constellation of technologies, institutions, and systems of ideas that are different from previous constellations. The notion of modern, however, is viewed as a sociological concept rather than an evolutionary notion (see endnote 9).

8. I borrow the notion of *commonplace* from a famous essay in education by Joseph Schwab (1969), but intend to make the commonplaces problematic, rather than natural and essential, to schooling.

9. My use of *modern* and *modernization* here is related to social histories that have located a change in the ways in which people thought about phenomena after the seventeenth century. It is not meant to imply a notion of progress but to suggest that a certain type of self-reflectivity on the human condition that is different from previous schemes that maintained a transcendental view of the human condition. This modernization also encompasses a change in how individuals are located in time and space, producing different everyday patterns of communication than those found in traditional communities, as I will discuss below. This discussion is drawn, in part, from the theoretical discussion of Giddens (1990).

10. The distinctions that I make are for comparative purposes and each of the problematics involves multiple nuances and at some points, overlapping historical practices that are beyond the scope of this paper. I also recognize the limitations of setting what might seem as dichotomies to make comparisons, but do so because the limitations of space that otherwise require certain juxtapositions of arguments about historical narratives. My purpose is to consider substantive intellectual issues about disciplinary knowledge rather than to examine the particular differences within "paradigms." My citations throughout the text provide the reader with sources to explore further the arguments made.

11. While the "linguistic turn" is sometimes used to recognize multiple arguments and movements within literary studies, feminisms, philosophy, and history, Lynda Stone has reminded me of the plurality of strands that exist within the

social sciences and humanities. See Butler (1992), Shapiro (1992), Dean (1994), and Chartier (1988). My interest here is with knowledge and reason and how "linguistic turns" relate to history and social/cultural theory.

12. For a more general discussion of different historical traditions, see Popkewitz (1986).

13. *To historicize,* as I use the term, is to place knowledge and social practices in the context of struggles—that classifies, orders, and defines the objects of the world. In contrast, *historicism,* a view of history that dominates American historical studies and is assumed in ethnographic studies, focuses on the actor and events of the world as the ultimate cause of social change.

14. It is interesting to note that positivism became a directing force in historical studies prior to the development of the social sciences as we now think of them. It is also ironic that much critical science, while rejecting the disinterest of science, maintains the historicist traditions of facts and texts.

15. One could ask, Why use social epistemology rather than the other terms to describe the historicist tradition being discussed? My reason is relatively simple: it is the relation of the knowledge as a cultural field of practices that interrelate with social phenomena in producing principles of action and practice.

16. My concern with governing is not to impute evil or suggest some transcendent good through overcoming control, but rather to recognize that working through an intellectual tradition that I have called a "social epistemology" does not absolve a self-reflexivity toward knowledge and power. Knowledge continually embodies a double relation of recognition and disciplining and thus while all knowledge is not bad, it is always potentially dangerous.

17. I use the words "community" and "society" as distinctions that are of historical significance. Community involves time/space relations that are local. Society involves more abstract conceptions of self as a citizen of a nation, as a worker, or as a member of an ethnic group within some larger sets of relations. As abstract notions of society are made part of one's definition of "self," the meaning and relationships in which communities are defined is changed.

18. While discussions of learning and socialization in the United States tend to structure out these considerations of deeper issues of upbringing, philosophically, at least, Marxist pedagogical discussions understood this relation of cognition and affect with political moral responsibility (Mikhailov 1976; Ilyenkov 1977).

19. For a discussion of the secularization of religion into civics, see Bellah (1968).

20. It is important to note that most of the discourses about schooling and curriculum were pragmatic, although there was a difference between the instrumental pragmatism of behaviorist psychology and the writings of Dewey.

21. The word "police" (and I assume later, "policy') was used to ensure a downward continuity between the ruler of the state and its populations. In the Middle Ages, governing was an extrinsic activity: the power of the prince was to protect his geographic principality, with the question of regulation of souls left to the church in preparing for an afterlife. By the nineteenth century, the meaning of governing involved a state as regulating and coordinating practices of individual behaviors and dispositions. The ensemble of institutions, procedures, analyses, reflections, calculations, and tactics that define people as populations becomes paramount to the art of governing. The idea of social contract is made into a way of defining the mutual pledge of rulers and subjects.

22. These appearances of institutions, rather than emerging from a grand design, are a historical conjuncture. It is the coming together of the multiple developments in multiple arenas of social life that forms what I will later call a break or rupture.

23. There was debate in the early social sciences about how to reason about the

world, of which statistical reasoning was only one part. Also, early statistical reasoning about social problems involved ethnographic discussions as well as groupings of people according to population thinking. What is important for me is that population thinking is very much a part of current definitions of social problems. In my current research on urban and rural teacher education, teachers continually classify the problems of schools and teaching through population reasoning.

24. I should note that Foucault rejects the use of the term "epistemology" in his work, but his reference is to a philosophical tradition that treats epistemology as a search for the essential rules of knowledge. My use of epistemology as a socially constructed practice is related to Foucault's notion of "regimes of truth." I place greater emphasis on the relation of epistemology to other social practices.

25. Nor am I denying the political implications of intellectual knowledge production, but recognize that its politics is in knowledge production. I explore this issue more fully in Popkewitz (1984, 1991).

26. Reason, however, is itself revised. It is seen as a pragmatic intervention in the world rather than as a search for universal principles about the world (Rorty 1989; Cherryholmes 1993).

27. One might argue here that my movement from epistemology to the work of people reinscribes a philosophy of consciousness. The movement to a subject may also be noted earlier in my use of "I." These uses of a subject, however, do not reintroduce a subject as in the philosophy of consciousness. Rather, as Butler (1992: 9) argues, it is "to position the subject with the grammar that authorizes it. The writing is mine, or an author's, through its replaying and resignifying theoretical positions that constitute us and by which we work through the possibilities of its convergence and the accounting for the possibilities of those that are systematically excluded. The inclusion of 'I,' therefore, is to recognize 'the transfer point of that replay' in which I am constituted through material practices and discourses that produce me as a subject."

28. One needs to read current literary theory and feminist scholarship, as well as critiques of postmodernism in education to realize how political a question privileging the subject is.

29. While reference to Kuhn appears in discussions of constructivist science education, it is a very selective reading that ignores the epistemological social and political questions that Kuhn raises. Kuhn appears only as an "icon" to legitimate a psychology of mental structuring.

30. I explore this history in Popkewitz (1991).

31. I discuss professionalism and the concern with research on "subject matter teaching" in Popkewitz (1993).

32. Hamilton avoids discussion of theory although it is clear from his references and method that theory, as an epistemological orienting and framing of questions, is integral to the problem of the study itself. Englund much more readily acknowledges the intellectual debts inscribed in his work. Others who contribute to this discussion are Barry Franklin (1994) on special education, and Ivor Goodson (1987) in his pioneering scholarship on school subjects.

33. There are many references in the work of Michel Foucault and Pierre Bourdieu to the notion of region as a site of symbolic power.

34. I am using the notion of region and field interchangeably here. They provide metaphors that signal complex sets of relations through which the objects of the world are known. The notions of region and field also provide a way to consider the location of various discursive systems that interact and change over time. This overlapping of discourses in different social locations and institutions is

explored in relation to the intersection of family, community, the child in Popke-witz and Bloch (in press).

35. For a discussion of the relation of reformist traditions and critical traditions as part of particular European conceptions of "sameness" and "Otherness," see Young (1990, 1995). He argues that the universal projects of these traditions need to be understood in relation to nineteenth-century colonialism.

36. The radical potential of this tradition is in its combination with the neoprag-matic traditions appearing in recent scholarship. Neopragmatism provides a strategy to help us rethink the contingent qualities of knowledge and social prac-tices as we engage in public struggles to construct new possibilities. But the social epistemology that I speak about in this essay and the neopragmatism of recent scholarship should not be collapsed into one. They represent different moves about social change and interpretation: a destabilizing move and a move to develop a progressive program of action. (I want to thank Fazel Rizvi for a conversation that helped me understand this relation.) Each move, though, requires the other. The construction of historical knowledge as breaks and rup-tures helps to destabilize existing discursive fields and their power relations, and, at the same time, removes the intellectual as the oracle of social progress. With a destabilizing strategy, neopragmatism provides a defensible position from which to consider the practices of public debate (for the latter in education, see Cherry-holmes 1988, 1992). Intellectuals participate in these public debates through the production of knowledge as part of their politics, but at the same time, the con-tingent and nonprogressive qualities of their knowledge provide them with no privileged location.

References

Bachelard, G. (1984). *The new scientific spirit* (trans. by A. Goldhammer). Boston: Beacon Press.

Baker, B. (1998). "Childhood" in the emergence and spread of U.S. public schools. In T. Popkewitz and M. Brennan (Eds.), *Foucault's challenge: Discourse, knowledge and power in education.* (117–43). New York: Teachers College Press.

Baker, B. (2000). *In perpetual motion; theories of power, educational history, and the child.* New York: Peter Lang.

Bakhtin, M. (1981). *The dialogic imagination: four essays.* Austin: University of Texas Press.

Bauman, Z. (1987). *Legislators and interpreters: On modernity, postmodernity and intellectuals.* Ithaca, NY: Cornell University Press.

Bellah, R. (1968). Civil religion in America. In W. G. McLoughlin and R. Bellah (Eds.), *Religion in America* (3–23). Boston: Houghton Mifflin.

Bledstein, B. (1976). *The culture of professionalism: the middle class and the develop-ment of higher education in America.* New York: Norton.

Bloch, M. (1963). *The historian's craft.* New York: Knopf.

Bourdieu, P., Chamboroden, J., and Passeron, J. (1991). *The craft of sociology: Epis-temological preliminaries* (trans. by R. Nice). New York: Walter de Gruyter.

Braudel, F. (1980). *On history* (trans. by S. Matthews). Chicago: University of Chicago Press.

Brazerman, C. (1987). Codifying the scientific style. In J. Nelson, A. Mogill, and D. McCloskey (Eds.), *The rhetoric of the human sciences* (125–44). Madison: Uni-versity of Wisconsin Press.

Butler, J. (1992). Contingent foundations: feminism and the question of "postmodernism." In J. Butler and J. Scott (Eds.), *Feminists theorize the political* (3–21). New York: Routledge.

Callewaert, S. (1999). Philosophy of education, Frankfurt critical theory and the sociology of Pierre Boudieu. (117–44). In T. Popkewitz and L. Fendler (Eds.). *Critical theories in education: Changing terrains of knowledge and politics.* New York: Routledge.

Canguilhem, G. (1978). *On the normal and the pathological* (trans. by C. Fawcett). Boston: D. Reidel.

———. (1988). *Ideology and rationality in the history of the life sciences* (trans. by A. Goldhammer). Cambridge, MA: MIT Press.

Canning, C. (1994). Feminist history after the linguistic turn: historicizing discourse and experience. *Signs: Journal of Women in Culture and Society* 19(3): 68–404.

Chartier, R. (1988). *Cultural history: Between practices and representations.* Ithaca, NY: Cornell University Press.

Cherryholmes, C. (1988). *Power and criticism: Poststructural investigations in education.* New York: Teachers College Press.

———. (1992). Notes on pragmatism and scientific realism. *Educational Researcher* 21(1): 13–17.

———. (1993). Reading research. *Journal of Curriculum Studies* 25(1): 1–32.

Crary, J. (1990). *Techniques of the observer: On vision and modernity in the nineteenth century.* Cambridge, MA: MIT Press.

Dean, M. (1994). *Critical and effective histories: Foucault's methods and historical sociology.* New York: Routledge.

Durkheim, E. (1977). *The evolution of educational thought: Lectures on the formation and development of secondary education in France* (trans. by P. Collins). London: Routledge and Kegan Paul.

Englund, T. (1986). *Curriculum as a political problem: Changing educational conceptions with special reference to citizenship education.* Uppsala, Sweden: Student Literature, Chartwell-Bratt.

———. (1991). *The public and the text.* Journal of Curriculum Studies. 28(1): 1–35.

Fendler, L. (1998). What is it impossible to think? A genealogy of the educated subject. In T. Popkewitz and M. Brennan (Eds.), *Foucault's challenge: Discourse, knowledge, and power in education* (39–63). New York: Teachers College Press.

Foucault, M. (1975). *The birth of the clinic: An archaeology of medical perception* (trans. by A. Smith). New York: Pantheon.

———. (1979). Governmentality. *Ideology and Consciousness* 6: 5–22.

———. (1980). *Power/Knowledge: Selected interviews and other writings* (trans. and ed. by C. Gordon). New York: Pantheon.

———. (1984). What is enlightenment? In P. Rabinow (Ed.), *The Foucault reader* (32–50). New York: Pantheon.

———. (1988a). The political technology of individuals. In L. Martin, H. Gutman, and P. Huttan (Eds.), *Technologies of the self* (145–62). Amherst: University of Massachusetts Press.

———. (1988b). *Politics, philosophy, culture: Interviews and other writings 1977-1984.* New York: Routledge.

Franklin, B. (1986). *Building the American community: The school curriculum and the search for social control.* London: Falmer.

———. (1994). *From "backwardness" to "at-risk": Childhood learning difficulties and the contradictions of school reform.* Albany: State University of New York Press.

Fraser, N. (1992). Sex, lies, and the public sphere: Some reflections on the confirmation of Clarence Thomas. *Critical Inquiry* 18(3), 295–312.

Gerhohm, T. (1987). The ethos of higher education systems: a view from anthropology. *Disciplinary Perspectives on Higher Education and Research, Report 37* (63–78). Stockholm: Group for the Study of Higher Education and Research Policy, University of Stockholm.

Giddens, A. (1987). *Social theory and modern sociology*. Stanford, CA: Stanford University Press.

———. (1990). *The consequences of modernity*. Stanford, CA: Stanford University Press.

Goodson, I. (1987). *School subjects and curriculum change*. London: Falmer.

Hacking, I. (1991). How should we do the history of statistics? In G. Burchell, C. Gordon, and P. Miller (Eds.), *The Foucault effect: Studies in governmentality* (181–96). Chicago: University of Chicago Press.

Hamilton, D. (1989). *Towards a theory of schooling*. London: Falmer.

Hay, C. (1990). What is sociological history? In S. Kendrick, P. Straw, and D. McCrone (Eds.), *Interpreting the past, understanding the present* (24–37). New York: St. Martin's Press.

Henriques, J., Hollway, W., Urwim, C., Venn, C., and Walkerdine, V. (1984). *Changing the subject: Psychology, social regulation and subjectivity*. London: Methuen.

Hultqvist, K. (1998). A history of the present on children's welfare in Sweden: From Fröbel to present-day decentralization projects (91–116). In T. Popkewitz and M. Brennan (Eds.), *Foucault's challenge: Discourse, knowledge and power in education*. New York: Teachers College Press.

Hunter, I. (1994). *Rethinking the school: Subjectivity, bureaucracy, criticism*. New York: St. Martin's Press.

Ilyenkov, E. (1977). *Dialectical logic: Essays on its history and theory* (trans. by H. Creghton). Moscow: Progress Press.

Ingófur Asgeir Jóhannesson. (1991). *The formation of educational reform as a social field in Iceland and the social strategies of educationalist 1966–1991*. Unpublished doctoral dissertation, University of Wisconsin-Madison.

———. (1993). Principles of legitimation in educational discourses in Iceland and the production of progress. *Journal of Educational Policy* 8(3): 39–51.

Joncich, G. (1968). *The sane positivist: A bibliography of Edward Thorndike*. Middleton, CT: Wesleyan University Press.

Kaestle, C. (1985). The history of literacy and the history of readers. In E. Gordon (Ed.), *Review of research in education* (11–54). Washington: AERA.

Karier, C. (1986). *Scientists of the mind: Intellectual founders of modern psychology*. Urbana: University of Illinois Press.

Kliebard, H. (1987). *Struggle for the American curriculum*. London: Routledge and Kegan Paul.

Koselleck, R. (1991). *Futures past: On the semantics of historical time* (trans. by K. Tribe). Cambridge, MA: MIT Press.

Kuhn, T. (1970). *The structure of scientific revolutions* (2nd ed.). Chicago: University of Chicago Press.

Lasch, C. (1977). Haven in a heartless world: The family besieged. New York: Basic Books.

Lather, P. (1986). Research as praxis. *Harvard Educational Review* 56(2), 57–75.

Latour, B. (1999). *Pandora's hope: Essays on the reality of science studies*. Cambridge, MA: Harvard University Press.

Lloyd, C. (1991). The methodologies of social history: a critical survey and defense of structurism. *History and Theory: Studies in the Philosophy of History* 30(2): 180–219.

Luke, A. (1990). *The body literate: Discursive inscription in early literacy training*. Paper given at the 12th World Congress of Sociology, Madrid, Spain (Faculty of Education, James Cook University, Townsville, Australia).

Luke, C. (1989). *Pedagogy, printing, and Protestantism: The discourse as childhood*. Albany: State University of New York Press.

Lundgren, U. P. (1983). *Between hope and happening: Text and contexts in curriculum*. Geelong, Australia: Deakin University Press.

Manuel, F., and Manuel, F. (1979). *Utopian thought in the Western world*. Cambridge, MA: Harvard University Press.

Maravall, J. (1986). *Culture of the Baroque: Analysis of historical structure* (trans. by T. Cochran). Minneapolis: University of Minnesota Press.

Meyer, J. (1987) Self and the life course: institutionalization and its effects. In G. Thomas, J. Meyer, F. Ramirez, and J. Boli (Eds.), *Institutional structure: Constituting state, society, and the individual* (242–60). Newbury Park, CA: Sage Publications.

Mikhailov, F. (1976). *The riddle of the self* (trans. by R. Daglish). Moscow: Progress Press.

Muller, J. (2000). Critics reconstruction: On the emergence of progressive educational expertise in South Africa. In T. Popkewitz (Ed.), *Educational knowledge: Changing relations between the state, civil society, and the educational community* (265–84). Albany: State University of New York Press.

Nicholson, L. (1986). *Gender and history: The limits of social theory in the age of the family*. New York: Columbia University Press.

Novick, P. (1988). *That noble dream: The 'objectivity question': and the American historical profession*. New York: Cambridge University Press.

O'Donnell, J. (1985). *The origins of behaviorism: American psychology, 1876–1920*. New York: New York University Press.

Omi, M., and Winant, H. (1986). *Racial formation in the United States from the 1960s to the 1980s*. Boston: Routledge and Kegan Paul.

Popkewitz, T. (Ed.). (1983). *Change and stability in schooling: The dual quality of educational reform*. Geelong, Australia: Deakin University Press.

———. (1984). *Paradigm and ideology in educational research: Social functions of the intellectual*. London: Falmer.

———. (1986). History in education science: educational science as history. In A. Pitman (Ed.), *Educational inquiry*. Geelong, Australia: Deakin University.

———. (1987). *The formation of school subjects: The struggle for creating an American institution*. London: Falmer.

———. (1991). *A political sociology of educational reform: Power/Knowledge in teaching, teacher education, and research*. New York: Teachers College Press.

———. (1993). Professionalization in teaching and teacher education: some notes on its history, ideology and potential. *Teaching and Teacher Education* 10(1), 1–14.

———. (1997). A changing terrain of knowledge and power: A social epistemology of educational research. *Educational Researcher* 26(9), 1–12.

———. (1998). *Struggling for the soul: The politics of education and the construction of the teacher*. New York: Teachers College Press.

Popkewitz, T., and Bloch, M. (in press). Bringing the parent and community back: A history of the present social administration of the parent to rescue the child for society. In K. Hultqvist and G. Dahlberg (Eds.), *The changing child in a changing world*. New York: Routledge.

Rajchman, J. (1985). *Michel Foucault: The freedom of philosophy*. New York: Columbia University Press.

Riley, D. (1988). *Am I that name? Feminism and the category of "women" in history*. Minneapolis: University of Minnesota Press.

Rorty, R. (1989). *Contingency, irony, and solidarity*. New York: Cambridge University Press.

Ross, D. (1991). *The origins of American social science*. New York: Cambridge University Press.

Sampson, E. (1993). Identity politics: challenges to psychology's understanding. *American Psychologist*, 48(12): 19–30.

Schwab, J. (1969). The practical: A language for curriculum. *School Review* 79: 1–24.

Shapiro, M. (1992). *Reading the postmodern polity: Political theory as textual practice*. Minneapolis: University of Minnesota Press.

Silva, E. and Slaughter, S. (1984). *Serving power: The making of the academic social science expert*. Westport, CT: Greenwood Press.

Simola, H. (1993). Educational science, the state, and teachers: forming the corporate regulation of teacher education in Finland. In T. Popkewitz (Ed.), *Changing patterns of power: Social regulation and teacher education reform* (161–210). Albany: State University of New York Press.

Simola, H., Heikkinen, S., and Silvonen, J. (1998). A catalogue of possibilities: outlining a perspective of history of truth for educational research. In T. Popkewitz and M. Brennan (Eds.), *Foucault's challenge: Discourse, knowledge and power in education* (64–90). New York: Teachers College Press.

Stoianovich, T. (1976). *French historical method: The Annales paradigm*. Ithaca, NY: Cornell University Press.

Tally, C. (1990). Future history. In S. Kendrick, P. Straw, and D. McCrone (Eds.), *Interpreting the past, understanding the present* (9–19). New York: St. Martin's Press.

Thomas, G., Meyer, J., Ramirez, F., and Boli, J. (1987). *Institutional structure: Constituting state, society, and the individual*. Newbury Park, CA: Sage Publications.

Toews, J. (1987). Intellectual history after the linguistic turn: The autonomy of meaning and the irreducibility of experience. *American Historical Review* 92: 879–907.

Topolski, J. (1976). *Methodology of history* (trans. by O. Wojtasiewicz). Boston: Reidel.

Toulmin, S. (1972). *Human understanding: The collective uses and evolution of concepts*. Princeton, NJ: Princeton University Press.

——. (1988). The recovery of practical philosophy. *American Scholar* 57(3): 37–52.

Walkerdine, V. (1988). *The mastery of reason: Cognitive development and the production of rationality*. London: Routledge.

——. (1990). *Schoolgirl fictions*. London: Verso.

Wallenstein, I. (1984). *The politics of the world economy: The states, the movements, and the civilizations*. Cambridge: Cambridge University Press.

——. (1990). *Geopolitics and geoculture: Essays in the changing world-system*. Cambridge: Cambridge University Press.

Weedon, C. (1987). *Feminist practice and poststructural theory*. London: Blackwell.

Wickham, G. (1990). The currency of history for sociology. In S. Kendrick, P. Straw, and D. McCrone (Eds.), *Interpreting the past, understanding the present* (33–58). New York: St. Martin's Press.

Williams, R. (1981). *Culture*. Glasgow: Fontana.

Wittgenstein, L. (1966). *The philosophical investigations: A collection of critical essays* (G. Pilcher, Ed.). Notre Dame, IN: University of Notre Dame Press.

Young, R. (1990). *White mythologies: Writing, history, and the west*. New York: Routledge.

——. (1995). *Colonial desire: Hybridity in theory, culture, and race*. London: Routledge.

part 4

Schooling as Fields
of Cultural Practice

8

Notes from Nowhere

(On the Beginnings of Modern Schooling)

David Hamilton

Charles Hoole's *A New Discovery of the Old Art of Teaching Schoole* was published in 1660. It comprised "four small treatises" (335 pages) which report the "*method* and *order*" that "concernes the profession of a schoolmaster." Charles Hoole (1610–1667) had gathered these ideas as a grammar school pupil in his home town of Wakefield (Yorkshire), as a student of Lincoln College (Oxford), and during thirty years teaching "publick schoole" in Rotherham, London and Essex.

Hoole's "small Manual," however, was more than a compendium of educational procedures. As Hoole proclaimed, it was also a "new discovery" of an "old art." Hoole used classical sources and ideas as his old art; and his new disclosure—a seventeenth-century meaning of "discovery"—was the rendering of the old art in a form that, he felt, could be adopted by his contemporaries.

A new edition of Hoole's manual was also published in 1913. It was edited and introduced by Ernest Trafford Campagnac, classicist and professor of education at Liverpool University from 1908 to 1938. In Campagnac's eyes, Hoole's work had a double significance. First, it "deserves attention" because it is "one of the richest sources in the history of education." And secondly, Campagnac felt that Hoole's work merited republication because it was still "accessible" to "teachers in our own time." It "may still," he suggested, "be found of practical utility" (1913: 11).

Hoole was not alone in his efforts to refocus educational practice. Other seventeenth-century writers made comparable efforts to recapture and rework the cumulative wisdom of earlier centuries. Indeed, the most famous European educational innovator of the period was John Amos Comenius (1592–1670), a Czech who spoke four languages and travelled throughout Europe. Comenius's *A Reformation of Schooles*—a "general reformation of common learning"— had appeared in English in 1642. It expressed Comenius's conviction that the "straggling methods fancied by luxuriant braines" might be "removed out of the way" and that "at last all things might be handled in one order, and method" (1642: 18).

Scholar-innovators, like Hoole and Comenius, represented a reforming, modernist movement in educational thought. They reworked an educational heritage that reached back through the Reformation and the Renaissance to the resurgence of classical ideas in the late Middle Ages. But Comenius and Hoole were not seeking a return to a mythical past. They recognized, instead, that old ideas could be mobilized in the interests of innovation. Their writings, therefore, were contributions to a much wider social transformation—the reconfiguration of politics and the rise of the modern state. Thus, in micro-cosm, the *Scholastick Discipline or the Way of Order in Grammar Schoole* (Hoole's fourth treatise) was a codification or representation of the discipline and order of the modern state. And it is against this political background—the parallel emergence of modern schooling and the modern state—that works like *A Reformation of Schooles* and *A New Discovery of the Old Art of Teaching Schoole* should be evaluated.

Notes from Nowhere

But where did modern schooling come from? And why did it take the revised forms disclosed by Hoole, Comenius, and others? The first of these questions is typically answered in the same form adopted by Hoole; that new (or modern) schooling emerged from ancient schooling. Such assumptions, however, are immediately constraining. They give preferential attention to continuity over change. They highlight the evolution rather than the genesis of social institutions. Moreover, such evolutionary histories—sometimes characterized as "one damn thing after another" histories—are comparatively easy to construct. They recount sequential and consequential changes in an already-existing institution. By slipping comfortably into a "Darwinian" groove (Grafton 1983: 73), their narratives are unjustifiably trammeled. The complexity of the histor-ical record is simplified, not clarified.

This chapter does not appeal to the logic—or shortcomings—of evolution-ary history. It seeks understanding elsewhere—in the realms of cultural history. Its perspective is that historical writings are never abstract, never linear. They not only interpret evidence, they also represent a response to contemporary debates. They constitute a dialogue between the present and the past. Thus, cultural history should highlight this dialectic. Further, it must find ways to acknowledge, even celebrate, the existence of this dialogue, the author's explicit reflexivity and, not least, the enduring historicity of the author's efforts.

This chapter, for instance, recognizes the research potential of Walter Ong's reference to the "crisis," forced by humanism, that "impugned the whole cur-ricular organization and the teaching profession as such" (Ong 1958: 166). It sees opportunities in Terrence Heath's statement that "In spite of general agree-ment on what happened, the history of change within the schools and curriculum is little known" (Heath 1971: 9). It is inspired by the revisionists who are reevaluating those "humanists who revolutionized secondary schools and arts faculties in Renaissance Europe" (Grafton and Jardine 1986: xii). And, above all, it seeks to go beyond the historiographics practices—variously hagiographic, celebratory and predatory—that have debilitated English-language educational studies for more than a century.

Accordingly, this essay starts with an eccentric (off-center) assumption: that modern schooling had no institutional ancestry. While self-consciously challenging and discomforting, this working assumption—that modern schooling came from nowhere—is also liberating. It releases the investigation of modern schooling from the steer of linear, one-thing-before-another theorising. Two recent accounts of pre-seventeenth century educational practices—*The Growth of English Schooling 1340–1548* (Moran 1985) and *Schooling in Renaissance Italy 1300–1600* (Grendler 1989)—illustrate such tracking problems.

Both Moran and Grendler identified and analyzed new sources; but, at the same time, also encountered recurrent interpretation problems. Grendler, for instance, wrestled with the problem that

> the use of *scholas* (schools) in Renaissance academic documents, including Jesuit papers of the late sixteenth century, is a little disconcerting. One might translate *tenet scholas* (holds schools) more literally as "holds classes" or "teaches classes." But "teaches school" is the meaning. (1989: 24n)

Three comments can be made about this revealing footnote. First, Grendler noted the absence of the word "classes." Secondly, he translated a latin plural (*scholas*) into an English singular (school). And thirdly, he noted the persistence of *schola* in later "Jesuit papers."

Fortunately, Grendler's discomfort can be relieved. The word "class" did not reappear in Renaissance documents until the early decades of the sixteenth century (see Hamilton 1989, ch. 2). In the meantime, *schola* could refer to a group of people (cf. a school of thought), with *scholas* referring to groups of people (cf. classes). And finally, the educational innovations associated with the reintroduction of the classical Latin word *classis* seem to have occurred earlier in Northern European Protestant writings than in their Southern European Catholic counterparts (see below).

Moran reports comparable feelings of unease. Her evolutionary account contains a variety of qualifying comments. Many elementary schools, she writes, were "transitory." The reported "status and training of the schoolmaster" was "full of ambiguities." It was "something of a mystery" that she could find "so few" manuscript copies of the "simplest elementary English primer." And she could only find "not very satisfactory" evidence for the "use of English primers in the schools" (Moran 1985: 222, 71, 44, 45).

Moran's commentary suggests that a tension existed between the (dis)organization of teaching and (clearly defined) structures of schooling. Although a "confusion" of teaching duties was "not unusual throughout this period," Moran notes that "separate levels of education and even separate schools" were understood to exist at that time (1985: 56). Overall, it seems that Moran projects her data onto an interpretative backcloth of social order and social stability. Other commentators, however, might feel more comfortable using the same data as indices of social flux and institutional transience.

The problematic yet nascent stability of medieval schools is, however, sensitively acknowledged in *Education and Society in Medieval and Renaissance England* (Orme 1989). Orme was well aware, for instance, that "it is not until after the Norman conquest, in the late eleventh and twelfth centuries, that schools begin to be mentioned as separate institutions in particular places in significant numbers." Yet, as Orme also accepts—and Moran demonstrates—such educational agencies were not distinctively or securely located within their social fabric. "Most medieval thinkers and writers," Orme concluded, "failed to distinguish children as a separate group, or education as a process separate from human life in general" (1989: 3–4, 156).

Moran and Grendler uncovered valuable evidence; but they encountered manifest difficulty in devising and presenting their interpretations. They wrote assuredly about an era when the phenomena of schools and schooling are unevenly etched on the historical record. During that period, for instance, it was only just becoming reasonable to distinguish home teaching from school teaching. References to teachers and teaching, therefore, should not be read as references to schools and schooling. Nor should a diversity of school provision be equated with a centrally-administered system of schooling. In short, medieval educational practice did not enjoy the conceptual infrastructure that supports the framework of modern schooling.

The "touchstone" figure who smuggled such an infrastructure into the (English-language) interpretation of medieval school provision was Arthur Francis Leach. His thirty-year investigation into *The Schools of Medieval England* (Leach 1915) "formed the basis for all subsequent work on medieval and Reformation schooling until the publication of Nicholas Orme's *English Schools in the Middle Ages* in 1973" (Moran 1985: 4). Yet, as Moran notes, Leach encountered the same kind of interpretative difficulties that have bothered generations of his intellectual successors. Leach's claims, she suggests, were "not always sufficiently supported by his sources." He, too, was drawn to anachronistic explanations based on social order and social stability. He was liable, for instance, to argue for the centuries-long existence of a school from "one or two recorded instances;" just as he was "prone" to affirm the "existence of a *grammar* school" when the source documents only referred to "the teaching of young children" (1985: 3, 5, italics added).

The evidence gathered by Leach and his successors illuminates educational practices and educational change during the Middle Ages. But the implication—

carried in their book titles—that such changes also constituted the wholesale institutionalization and systematization of educational practice is, I believe, an unjustified foreshortening of the historical record. Teaching had been self-consciously organized and debated since classical times. But the consolidation and perseverance of such activities—"separate from human life *in general*" (italics added)—was a different process. The history of schooling is not the same as the history of education—a point forcefully made by another revisionist analysis— Joan Simon's *The Social Origins of English Education* (1971).

The schools of medieval England should be remembered, perhaps, not as the carefully organized seedbed of modern schooling but rather, in evolutionary terms, as undomesticated so-called "sports" (accidental or abnormal variations). They were the ill-nurtured precursors rather than hardy harbingers of modern schooling. They did not survive intact. Instead, they were significantly effaced by other developments—the subject of the remainder of this chapter.

This essay, then, seeks to avoid the constrained conservatism of conventional accounts. It examines secondary sources that cover the period from the discovery of a complete version of Quintilian's *Institutio oratoria* in the early fifteenth century, to the appearance of Hoole's *A New Discovery of the Old Art of Teaching Schoole* in the middle of the seventeenth century. In the process, it pays particular attention to the web of educational saliences—like textbook, curriculum, catechesis, discipline, and didactics—that gave cultural identity to both modern schooling and modern European society.

The Changing Status of Knowledge

One major reshaping process was the Renaissance reconfiguration of the educational knowledge base of the academy. Classical sources (e.g., Aristotle, Cicero) were resuscitated, revised and, above all, reworked. Ostensibly, this renewal had a conservative purpose—the faithful recovery of texts corrupted by repeated medieval copying and/or mistranslation. Medieval translators had worked according to the principle of *verbum e verbo* (word from word). Their conventions, however, were challenged by Greeks who settled in Italy (e.g., Manuel Chrysoloras, c. 1350–1414), by native Italians who had studied in Greece (e.g., Guarino of Verona, 1374–1460), and by associates of incoming Greek translators (e.g., Leonardo Bruni, c. 1369–1444). Bruni, for instance, sought to represent whole Greek phrases in the form of acceptable Latin constructions, and he rejected the transliteration of Greek technical terms into medieval neologisms or barbarized Latin.

Furthermore, closer attention to sources also led to a sharper awareness of the circumstances surrounding their original creation. Honoring the elegance and rhetoric of an author's voice was, so Renaissance translators believed, integral to the preservation of an author's meaning. Classical Greek, they felt, merited translation into classical rather than medieval Latin. And this self-consciousness was clearly articulated in the commentaries, annotations, and even "polemics" that accompanied their humanist efforts (Schmitt 1983: 64).

The influence of these new translations and associated practices was multiplied by the advent of moveable-type printing (see, for instance, Eisenstein 1979). By the end of the fifteenth century, nearly the whole corpus of Aristotle had, according to Schmitt, been "freshly rendered into Latin" and, in the following century, "more new translations of many works and revisions of existing translations were made ... than during all the previous centuries combined" (1983: 68, 70).

But the combination of new printing technologies and new translation practices also had a qualitative consequence. Renaissance translation rationales also shaded into practices of intentional adaptation and amendment. Texts began to appear not so much in different translations as in different versions. They were produced, for instance, as parallel editions, expositions, paraphrases, catechisms, and compendia. Indeed, many of these versions were also produced "for classroom use" (Schmitt 1988: 792), presumably by translators who also practiced as teachers.

The educational importance of this last development is paramount. According to Schmitt, classroom variants (e.g., structured summaries) became "increasingly popular during the late sixteenth century and dominated for the next hundred years." Moreover, Schmitt's comments also imply that these new variants also began to impinge upon the language of educational practice. Their introduction corresponded to a redefinition of the word *cursus* (course) which, he suggests, was "used in this sense first at the end of the sixteenth century" (1988: 792). It may be no accident, therefore, that the word *cursus* took such a form at the same time as the word "curriculum" also seems to have entered the educational lexicon (see Hamilton 1989: chapter 2).

Pedagogics and Didactics

As indicated, sixteenth century texts came to be organized for a variety of educational purposes. Such texts can be ranged along a continuum. At one end are educational texts designed for parents; while, at the other end, are texts reworked for schoolteachers. The former serve pedagogic (i.e., upbringing) purposes; whereas the latter can be characterized as didactic devices (i.e., for instruction). By the same token, too, materials designed for self-instruction can be designated as autodidactic texts. In effect, sixteenth century educational innovation made possible a distinction between pedagogics and didactics.

Hoole's *A New Discovery of the Old Art of Teaching Schoole* unequivocally falls within the didactic genre. But many of its forerunners are less easily categorized. Pedagogic and didactic practices overlapped and were easily conflated in the educational writings of the sixteenth century. This nonseparation of educational concepts, already discussed with respect to the early Renaissance use of *schola* and *classis*, is illustrated in a seminal account of sixteenth century educational practices—T.W. Baldwin's *William Shakspere's Small Latine and Lesse Greeke* (1944). Baldwin's title comes from Ben Jonson (1572–1637), who claimed that Shakespeare had received only a perfunctory classical education (viz. "small Latine and lesse Greek"). Jonson believed, therefore, that Shakespeare lacked the erudition expected of someone who had completed a school course (see Baldwin 1944, vol. 1: 2, 9).

Baldwin's two-volume, 1,525-page work reevaluates Jonson's ascription against the background of sixteenth-century educational practices and influences:

> Whether or not Shakspere ever spent a single day in petty or grammar school, nonetheless petty and grammar school were a powerful shaping influence upon him, as they were, and were planned to be, upon the whole society of his day. Directly and through others these instruments would help to mould Shakspere. (1944, vol. 1: vii)

Baldwin concludes that it is of "no importance at all whether Shakspere did or did not complete grammar school." Whether absorbed "from the air" or acquired from "formal drill" or the "accrued background" of the Renaissance and Reformation, such ideas suffused not only school practices but also the "less formal" cultural settings of the same period (1944, vol. 2: 663–64).

Further evidence for the intermingling of pedagogics and didactics can be found in other sixteenth-century publications. The problematic differentiation of upbringing from schooling is evident, for instance, in the titles and contents of works such as Thomas Elyot's *Boke Named the Gouvernour* (1531) and *The Education or Bringing Up of Children* (c. 1533), Roger Ascham's *Scholemaster* (1570), and Richard Mulcaster's *The First Part of the Elementarie* (1582).

The books of Elyot and Ascham were "intended as guides to the proper education of the sons of nobility and gentlemen" (Pepper 1966: vii–viii). They brought a normative (or reformative) dimension into discussions of upbringing. Despite Ascham's title, such arguments were distant from the organization of schools. Neither Elyot nor Ascham had ever been "master of a grammar school." Indeed, according to Pepper, the "first" work to discuss the English common-school curriculum in a "systematic piece of detailed exposition" (1966: vii) appeared a little later—as William Kempe's *The Education of Children in Learning* (1588).

Mulcaster, by contrast, appears to have straddled both pedagogic and didactic practices. He followed the same prescriptive style—guides to "proper" education—as Elyot and Ascham. Yet, despite serving as a schoolmaster in London for fifty years, "nowhere" did Mulcaster "describe . . . the actual curriculum of the schools in which he taught" (Pepper 1966: viii).

Difficulty interpreting sixteenth-century usage of "scholemaster" also surrounds the Greek word *pedagogus*. Should it be translated, for instance, as "servant," "mentor," "tutor," or "teacher"? Does it denote a household servant who attended to the nurturance of a young person? Did such servants have mentoring (i.e., advisory) responsibilities? Or could they be charged with the active, didactic instruction of their charges? In practice, these roles probably overlapped—as when, for instance, servants not only accompanied young persons to distant colleges but also participated—as chaperones, mentors, tutors, and instructors—in the advancement of their college studies (see, for instance, Grafton and Jardine 1986, 149–57).

These translation difficulties, however, need not be regarded as a consequence of conceptual confusion. Rather, they are a function of the fluid—or unbalanced—educational circumstances of the sixteenth century. Longstanding childrearing (i.e., pedagogic) practices became increasingly subject to interference from didactic suppositions that, in their turn, emerged alongside the reworking of classical ideas and their incorporation into the texts and practices of sixteenth-century colleges and schools. Gradually, pedagogic practices (i.e., teaching-as-upbringing) became synonymous with, and steered by, the newer didactic practices of schoolteaching (i.e., teaching-as-instruction). Indeed, as discussed below, there may be a significant difference between the autodidactic underpinnings of the Jesuit *Ratio Studiorum* (1599) and the didacticism of Comenius's *Great Didactic* (1632). As McClintock wryly observed, "Comenius cared nought for study, teaching and learning were his thing" (1972: 178).

Method and Discipline

The reorganization of texts, together with the prioritization of didactics, can also be appreciated against the contemporaneous importance of two other notions—method and discipline. The reorganization of texts, whether for pedagogic or didactic purposes, meant that learning and/or teaching became "methodized" (Hoole, 1630: v). Methodization offered a shortcut to learning. Equally, to follow a methodized sequence was to follow a *cursus* or curriculum. Thus, the defining feature of a sixteenth-century *cursus* or curriculum was not its content (derived from texts) but its methodization—the editing and ordering that has gone into its reworking.

For this reason there was a close association between methodization and discipline. Originating in a Latin root concerned with "getting" learning "into" the child, discipline denoted, according to Hoskin (1990: 30), the "dual process" of "presenting a certain knowledge to the learner, and . . . of keeping the learner present before such knowledge."

By the sixteenth and seventeenth centuries, this duality seems to have become more explicit. At the risk of oversimplification, the Renaissance contributed the idea that discipline relates to the presentation of knowledge—its reworking according to method and order; while the Reformation offered a variety of reasons for keeping learners before such knowledge. Needless to say, these different meanings survived into the twentieth century—to the degree that a discipline denotes both a body of knowledge and a mode of restraint.

In the sixteenth century, therefore, discipline and didactics had a joint concern for the establishment of order and the promotion of method. They could refer to the promotion of a mental discipline or they could refer to the inculcation of bodily discipline. Together, these elements foreshadowed the molding of docile (i.e., teachable) bodies (Foucault 1979: 135ff.). By the seventeenth century, too, conceptions of discipline were extended from the body corporal to the body politic. Discipline was as relevant to the emergence of modern schooling as it was to the emergence of the "secular sovereign state as the dominant structure in society" (Collins 1989: 7).

The rise of Protestantism offers illustration of the dual processes of mental and bodily discipline. The "dominant strain" in Martin Luther's intellectual heritage, "overshadowing all other post-Biblical influences" (Dickens 1976: 83) was the theology of Augustine of Hippo (354–430). The inherited understanding of Augustine, was that the Fall of Adam had rendered humankind powerless to save itself. Humanity suffered, therefore, from a "hereditary moral disease" (Cross 1957: 107) that rendered it "hopelessly corrupt [and] morally helpless" (Dickens 1976: 84).

Luther (1483–1546) came to share Augustine's view that humanity lacked the resources to overcome such moral and spiritual corruption. This deficit was rectified, in Lutheran terms, by God's gift of righteousness or faith. Further, Lutherans came to believe that the instantaneous acquisition of faith—or justification by faith—also needed to be complemented by a secondary and enduring cleansing process—sanctification. In a formulation popularized by Phillip Melanchthon (1497–1560), justification is the process of being declared righteous, and sanctification is the process of being made righteous (McGrath 1994: 387).

These ideas about justification and sanctification were extended in the writings of Jean Calvin (1509–1564) on "double grace":

> First the believer's union with Christ leads directly to his or her *justification* . . .
> Second, on account of the believer's union with Christ—and *not* on account of
> his or her justification—the believer begins the process of being made like Christ
> through regeneration. Calvin asserts that both justification and regeneration are
> the results of the believer's union with Christ through faith. (McGrath 1994: 388)

Thus, among Protestants, there was a close theological and historical association surrounding notions of sanctification, regeneration, and reform. The reform of social life—with respect to the scriptures (the word of God), religious observance (faith) and the promulgation of righteousness (sanctification)—was also the reform (or regeneration) of social institutions. It is not surprising, therefore, that Lutheran reformers worked towards the "inculcation of practical disciplines" which would sanctify the "useful member of church and society" (Strauss 1976: 77).

The integrated organization of personal life, family life, and public life to meet the overlapping disciplinary purposes of mental, bodily, and social order is an enduring feature of Europe in the sixteenth and seventeenth centuries. Lutherans, Calvinists and, Catholics reworked their Christian heritage, derived from Augustine, Aquinas, and others. They created and followed a broad intellectual highway, paved with church orders, school orders, and political orders. This highway linked the Calvinist foundation of the Academy of Geneva in 1559; the publication of the Catholic Jesuit scheme of studies (*Ratio Studiorum*) in 1599; the Catholic Jansenist (c.f. Augustinian) discipline of the seventeenth-century Petites Écoles of Port Royal, Paris (see Barnard 1913); the appearance, in English, of Comenius's *A Reformation of Schooles* (1642); and, in the same year, the declaration by the political philosopher, Thomas Hobbes (1588–1679), that the aim of "civil science" was to investigate the "rights of states and the duties of subjects" (quoted in Skinner 1978, vol 2: 349).

Teaching and Preaching as Delivery

But if a discipline was to be inculcated, how might it be structured? What, in sixteenth or seventeenth-century terms, constituted the method and order of a discipline? In fact, the model was provided by the classical discipline of rhetoric. Curricula and disciplines were to be delivered, that is, in much the same way as a speech or a sermon (see, for instance, Howell 1956, *passsim*).

Indeed, the concurrence of this usage is evident in Mulcaster's *Elementarie*. His "promise" was "to help parents in their virtuous performance and to assist teachers in their learned direction, that both delivery in one may proceed with order, and receipt in the other, may profit with delight." Further, Mulcaster also prioritized the audiences of his work, in favor of teachers over parents: "I proffered my service in general to them all, but first of them all to the elementary teacher" (1582: 5, English modernized).

It is for this reason—a connection between teaching, preaching, and oratory—that the *Institutio oratorio* of Quintilian (c. 35–c. 100) received detailed attention in the fifteenth and sixteenth centuries. Quintilian's *Institutio* was an elaboration of the educational ideals and practical models advocated by Cicero (106–43 B.C.). His key assumption was that the creation of orators should be built around a methodized and disciplined education in argument and eloquence. By the Renaissance, it was also accepted that such practical arts were equally well suited to the advancement of "powerful and lucrative professions" (Grafton and Jardine 1986: xiii).

But the insertion of Ciceronian models was not merely a matter of injecting fresh ideas into the educational thinking of the Renaissance. It was a more disruptive process. It represented a reordering of the trivium—the preparatory stage of the liberal arts (viz. grammar, logic, and rhetoric). During the Middle Ages, grammar and logic (then also known as dialectic) had received particular attention. But Ciceronian arguments led to the displacement of logic by rhetoric. The logic of argument, that is, was deemed to be more useful that the logic of proof. As McConica notes:

> throughout northern Europe the arts faculties shifted away from speculative, dialectical disciplines towards the oral and rhetorical conceptions of language; logic everywhere survived, but it was the logic of the assembly and the debating hall, rather than the logic of the philosopher of language. (1983: 42–43; see also McConica 1979: 294)

Inspired by Ciceronian precepts, scholars and students withdrew from the medieval activity of disputation and, instead, prepared, rehearsed, and delivered declamations. And the compilation of such declamations was a focus of their methodizing and ordering education. Inspired, perhaps, by Cicero's aphorism—"the pen, best and chief teacher of oratory" (see Kennedy 1962: 117)—such efforts were also precursors of the seminar papers, student essays and debating societies that occupied subsequent generations of students (Costello 1958: 31–34).

But what was the relationship between rhetoric and oratory? Written in Cicero's old age, *De oratore* (55 B.C.) is much more than a manual of rhetoric. Rhetorical skills were not to be learned in a vacuum but, rather, were to be the culmination of a much broader education—the *puerilis institutio* (training of the young) conventionally enjoyed by privileged young Romans (see Gwynn 1964). To prepare a worthwhile oration, an orator needed to know the whole field of knowledge, not merely the rules of elegant and persuasive delivery.

Quintilian's *Institutio oratoria* was published 140 years after *De oratore*. It was based on Quintilian's experiences of holding a "public chair" (*publicam scholam*) in Latin rhetoric (Gwynn 1964: 182). The form of this position is not clear. Smail describes Quintilian's position as "Professor of Rhetoric," a position that was the "first official recognition of the state's responsibility in the matter of public instruction" (1938: vi). Quintilian held this position from A.D. 70 to A.D. 90, during which he not only acted as a teacher but also as a "pleader" in legal cases, experiences that became "rich stores of practical knowledge and experience" (Smail 1938: vii).

The title of *Institutio oratore*, which can be translated as *The Education of an Orator*, marks it off from narrower manuals focusing on the rhetorical arts. For Quintilian and Cicero, an orator was not merely someone versed in the narrow art of rhetoric but, in Quintilian's (translated) words, a man with sufficient instruments to lead an upright and honorable life ... [an] ideal citizen, fitted to take his share in the management of public and private affairs, able to govern cities by his wise counsel, to establish them upon a sure foundation of good laws and to improve them by the administration of impartial justice. (Quoted in Smail 1938: 5)

Such ideals—in their originals, in translation, or in reworked variants—appealed to Renaissance humanists who, in turn, carried them into the preaching and teaching practices of the fifteenth and sixteenth centuries. One of the earliest English treatises devoted "exclusively" to the art of preaching was originally written in 1555 by an "influential" protestant theologian (André Gerhard). Originally appearing in Latin, an English version appeared in 1577 under the title *The Practice of Preaching, Otherwise called the Pathway to the Pulpit: containing an Excellent Method How to Frame Divine Sermons*. As Howell notes, Gerhard's work was based on the "rhetoric of Cicero" but reworked in such a way as to demonstrate an "awareness of the difference between the orator and the pulpit speaker" (1956: 110–12).

Another link between oratory and teaching is suggested by an incomplete set of outline declamations, usually attributed to Quintilian, known as the *Declamationes minores*. Whatever their authorship, more than half of the synoptic declamations in the *Declamationes minores* are accompanied by a *sermo* (plural, *sermones*). These, among other things, comprized practical suggestions for the development and presentation of an argument. For example:

If I sometimes repeat the same thing several times over in my analyses of these *controversiae*, remember that I do so partly for the sake of the new-comers, partly because the analysis involves repetition. For those who were not at the earlier classes must be taught the general principles which are applicable to all *controversiae*, and analysis (*divisio*) is especially important in the kind of *controversia* that we are now doing. (Quoted in Gwynn 1964: 217)

It is not unreasonable to assume that such classical advice about method and order also appealed to Renaissance teachers and Reformation preachers concerned with the delivery—or didactics—of sermons and curricula.

Rhetoric and Doctrine

But attention to classical ideas also created theological disputes and political divisions. If classical ideas were pre-Christian (i.e., pagan), how could they stand alongside authoritative Christian sources? One reconciliation initiative stemmed from the thirteenth-century recovery of the logical works of Aristotle. Albertus Magnus (c. 1200–1280) and one of his students, Thomas Aquinas (1225–1274), inserted Aristotelian logical principles into the fabric of medieval Christian theology. They accepted that the doctrines of Christian faith could not, ultimately, be established by reason. Yet, at the same time, they felt that Aristotelian practices could confirm Christian theology as a logically coherent canon of ideas.

Scholasticism is the name given to the medieval movement, flourishing between 1200 and 1500, that emphasized the rational validation of religious beliefs. Nevertheless, the rapprochement of Christian and pagan ideas was never complete. Notions of a "double logic" or "double truth" survived, acknowledging the "subordination of the relative truth of philosophy to the absolute truth of theology" (Dickens 1976: 80; and Kraye 1993: 17).

Disputes about hierarchy and subordination lay behind another important chapter in the partitioning of theological doctrine—the so-called "Great Schism." The death of Pope Gregory XI in 1378 led to rival succession claims. An Italian faction supported Urban VI, while Clement VII received French support. Parallel popes coexisted until 1417; for a short period around 1409, the papacy attracted three claimants. The dispute was eventually resolved by the accession of Pope Martin V, a consequence of the Council of Constance (1414–17). The Great Schism, however, did not eliminate theological rivalry. Conflicting interpretations remained. Was church power in the hands of church councils or the pope?

Further theological rivalries arose from reworkings of the Vulgate Bible—the authorized Latin translation prepared during the fifth century. One of the foremost humanists, Desiderius Erasmus of Rotterdam (c. 1466–1530), discovered notes on the Greek text of the New Testament that had been prepared by Lorenzo Valla (1407–1457). Assisted by these notes, Erasmus published the first printed Greek New Testament in 1516. For the first time, theologians and others shared the opportunity to compare an early Greek text with the Vulgate version.

Erasmus's version not only questioned the accuracy of the Vulgate Bible, it also cast doubt on practices claimed to be positively sanctioned by the Latin scriptures. For example, the Vulgate Bible spoke of marriage as a *sacramentum*—a ceremony that enjoyed the imprimatur of Jesus. Following Valla, Erasmus pointed out that the original Greek word had weaker connotations, merely meaning "mystery." Another example related to Mary, the mother of Jesus. The Vulgate Bible deemed Mary to be "full of grace" which meant that she, too, was a significant carrier of God's powers. Again, Erasmus followed Valla and pointed out that the Greek original could just as easily mean "one who had found favor" (see McGrath 1988: 39–40).

Overall, humanist translators self-consciously injected fresh uncertainties into Christian doctrine. In addition, the invention of printing led to the circulation of texts that drew attention to these uncertainties—as in the case of Erasmus's "wildy successful, constantly reissued, revised and re-edited textbooks, translations, and editions" (Jardine 1993: 5). The reworking of texts to strengthen the discipline of public speaking had all kinds of contrary political consequences. Eloquence was a practical art that could also serve practical politics. As McGrath put it, "for the humanists, rhetoric promoted eloquence; for the Reformers it promoted the Reformation" (1988: 48).

The efforts of the humanists, therefore, were transposed into a variety of parallel subdisciplines. These arose from religious and geographic differences but, together, they constituted the broad highway of modern schooling. Indeed, modern schooling arose from a partial fusion of these differences. And the process that enhanced this educational fusion was the gradual separation of theological and political assumptions.

Church and Government

The label "Protestant" relates to the six German princes and fourteen city governments who objected to the ending of Lutheran toleration as decreed by the Diet of Speyer (1529). As this example illustrates, disputes of Reformation history were linked with geographical and political units that came into conflict with Vatican authority. In turn, breakaway groups began to give their attention to the art of self-government and to the maintenance of their own worldly authority.

But what should be the basis of such authority? Lutheran debates of the 1520s and 1530s illustrate this problem. Insofar as the faithful based their practices on scriptural authority, what role was to be played by the visible institutions of the church? And what was the theological basis for the insertion of such institutions between the union of the individual believer and God? Such questioning led Luther to a new perspective on the church. It was to be a fellowship or congregation—a so-called "priesthood of all believers"—with no real existence except in the hearts of the faithful.

This new interpretation allowed Lutherans to reject the forms of authority that, previously, had been invested in the structures of the Church. The Church could not rule its members because it had no separate authority. Responsibility for the maintenance of social order, via schemes of sanctification, was increasing adopted by public institutions, leaving the church with the evangelical responsibility of preaching the gospel.

After 1530, however, a complete "volte face" (Skinner 1978, vol. 2: 74) seems to have taken place. Struggles within the Lutheran church disrupted the coexistence of Church and civic authorities. The supervisory responsibilities of rulers and magistrates could no longer be guaranteed. Theology and politics became disjoined. The political authority of local councils, like the authority of the church councils of Rome, could be legitimately challenged by appeal to other authorities (e.g., new translations of the Bible).

The consequences of this reaction to political authority were twofold. First, splits in the fabric of "mainstream" or "magisterial" Reformation theology provided an opening for "radical" Lutherans, some of whom went on to establish the Reformed or Calvinist Church (McGrath 1988: 6). And secondly, Luther gave his support to the shift of educational responsibility from private to public institutions. In effect, the families or congregations of the faithful were to be organized in ways that would assure their faith. It may not be insignificant, for instance, that Luther published his *Little Catechism* and *Greater Catechism* (for adults as well as children) in 1529 and, in the same year, wrote to the Margrave George of Brandenburg suggesting that "one or two universities" as well as "good primary schools" be established in "all towns and villages" (quoted in Eby 1971: 98–99).

In effect, the Lutheran Church turned its attention from domestic pedagogics to public didactics. Such a reorientation became a powerful feature in the Lutheran polity, bringing together ideas about preaching, teaching, and political oversight. "Only public education," Strauss suggests,

> could introduce these traits uniformly and equitably. The fate of the entire commonwealth was therefore thought to hinge on effective public teaching of doctrine and discipline. (1978: 152)

Protestant realignment of political and theological practice also had parallels in Catholic educational practice. But Catholic and Protestant educational reforms differed in an important respect. Luther was influenced by Augustine, whereas the Catholic reformation was inspired by Thomism. Indeed, the sixteenth-century was marked by a strengthening of Thomist influence: Pope Pius V declared Thomas Aquinas "Doctor of the Church" in 1567, encouraging Thomist thinking to gain a "firm hold" upon the practices of the post-Reformation Catholic colleges and seminaries (Dickens 1976: 80).

Such differences can be discerned in the foundation and development of the Society of Jesus (also known as the Jesuits). After injury terminated his career as a professional soldier, Ignatius of Loyola (1491–1556) took up a spiritual career that led him though pilgrimages, the life of a hermit, and the universities of Alcala and Salamanca. Loyola eventually took up studies in 1528 at the University of Paris. The Society of Jesus dates from 1534. Loyola and six companions pledged themselves to a life of poverty, chastity, crusading missionary work, and absolute obedience to the pope. And the Jesuit's petition to the pope, approved in 1540, envisaged a society of clerics propagating the faith by spiritual exercises, sermons, works of charity, and the instruction of children and others in Christian principles.

The Jesuit "spur to militant missionary effort" (Dickens 1968: 80) was the *Spiritual Exercises*—a manual of orderly, yet transformative, meditations around the life and death of Christ. The Jesuits believed that faith was not so much achieved by instantaneous infusion of supernatural grace as by repeated exercise of the human intellect. Both the *Spiritual Exercises* (prepared before 1535) and the Jesuit's school manual, the *Ratio Studiorum* (1599), reflect this programmatic sense of discipline (viz. a pathway to knowledge).

Thus, it may be an oversimplification to characterize the *Ratio Studiorum* as a didactic source. Certainly, it was strongly influenced by Ciceronian consider-ations about method and order. But in historical terms it is probably more rea-sonable to regard the *Spiritual Exercises*, the *Ratio Studiorum*, Comenius's *Reformation of Schooles*, and Hoole's *A New Discovery of the Old Art of Teaching Schoole* as a continuum exemplifying the gradual substitution of didactics for pedagogics. In fact, the didacticism stereotypically associated with Jesuit practice may have come later—through tensions that arose between the missionary work of the Jesuits and the political priorities of their secular patrons and sponsors.

From Faith to Citizenship

In the event, however, differences between Protestant and Catholic theology were less than permanent. Considerable cross-fertilization took place as the-ologians, teachers, parents, and pedagogues repeatedly shifted their religious affiliations. One renowned crossover theorist was Justus Lipsius (1547–1606) who was Lutheran in Jena (1572–74), Calvinist in Leiden (1579–90), and Catholic in Louvain (1592–1606). Indeed, Lipsius changed his faith so often that he became stigmatized in print as *Lipsius Proteus*—a man who, "with so much abandon," reframed his ideas to his changing circumstances (Grafton 1983: 65). Despite—or because of—his theological pragmatism, Lipsius fos-tered a significant contribution to sixteenth- and seventeenth-century thought: the extension of the notion of discipline into the political domain.

Lipsius also drew on classical sources, notably Cicero and Seneca. From Cicero he took the importance of rhetoric as the construction of rational argu-mentation; from the Stoic Seneca (who also impressed John Calvin), Lipsius took the assumption that mastery over the emotions could be achieved through the application of reason. Through links with "several hundred [European] correspondents," Lipsus became pivotal in a "neo-stoic," post-Reformation political network that operated "alongside Calvinism and Jesuitism" (Oestre-ich 1982: 60, 8).

The practicalities of the neo-Stoic project were assisted by Lipsius's *Politics* (1589) and through the production of two associated handbooks in 1604: the *Manductio* and the *Physiologica*. The latter were systematic presentations of Lipsius's Stoicism that were used in support of self-study or instruction (Mor-ford 1991: 168–71). Among other things, the Neo-Stoic intervention trans-posed the discipline of personal diligence into the virtue of public duty. A rational call to duty was deemed to efface or neutralize the suffering (or burden) that might arise from religious, social, or political activities. In short, neo-Stoicism translated the duties of the individual into the responsibilities of citizenship. According to Oestreich:

> The ideal citizen in the political world, as portrayed by Lipsius ... is the citizen who acts according to reason, is answerable to himself, controls his emotions, and is ready to fight. (1982: 30)

Such responsibilities gradually informed new theories of the modern state—conceptualizations of the relationships that might be forged among different segments of a social group. Political absolutism, for instance, which grew out of neo-Stoicism, held that only a strong monarchy could maintain political unity and military peace.

One of the most influential absolutist theorists was Jean Bodin (1530–1596), who had narrowly escaped with his life in the St. Bartholomew's Day Massacre (Paris, 1572). Bodin's critique of earlier political theories—commenced in *Six Books of a Commonweal* (1576)— addressed the frailty of the existing order. Absolutism, therefore, gained wider political credibility because it elevated political sovereignty above Reformation sectarianism. It prioritized, that is, state power over church power. Further, the fundamental aim of an absolutist government was to "secure 'order' rather than liberty" (Skinner 1978, vol. 2: 287).

The pursuit of neo-Stoicism and its derivatives was marked by three ideological corollaries. First, the state was to become a locus of centralized authority, public discipline, and personal duty. Secondly, the maintenance of such political power was to be achieved through a variety of formal institutions (e.g., diplomatic corps and standing armies). Finally, the political aspirations of the modern state were to be fostered through a state-sponsored institutional matrix—modern schooling (see also Melton 1988: chapter 1).

Conclusion

These, then, were some of the political and ideological tributaries that rendered Charles Hoole's *A New Discovery of the Old Art of Teaching Schoole* as a new paradigm of educational practice. Hoole's aim was "to discover the old Art of teaching Schoole, and how it may be improved in every part suitable to the years and capacities of such children as are now commonly taught." Further, Hoole's efforts to inject method and order into teaching and learning were intended to appeal not only to parents but also to his schoolteacher contemporaries. For the latter, he suggested, (neo-Stoic) school teaching was "a most necessary calling"—a profession, "commanded by God," whose "great discouragements ... with Fortitude [could] be conquered." Yet, Hoole recognized that such moral arguments were insufficient to offset the "burden of schoolteaching." Rather, the "irksome" provocations of school teaching—indeed, its "daily torture"—might best be addressed by a technical procedure—the adoption of method and order.

But, ultimately, Hoole's appeal was directed elsewhere, to the "benefitting of Church and Commonwealth." Suitably organized, school teaching could achieve the "training up" of children into "serviceable instruments of much good in [Church and Commonwealth]." And without the political sustenance provided by the institutions of schooling, the "State" would wither away, like "the body," because "no member would discharge its proper function" (1660: 1, viii–xiv).

But Hoole was not solely responsible for reporting these ideas. The emergence of schooling was not a linear, evolutionary process, As this chapter suggests, disorderly ideas came together, drawn from different complex systems. The juxtaposition and interaction of these ideas generated new assumptions and practices. And the significance of this new constellation of ideas and practices—the primal soup of modern schooling—was contemporaneously recognized and publicized by European and North American innovators, including Hoole and Comenius. Their efforts embraced both the aggregation of ideas (re)drawn from the past and, as a result, the creation of a launching pad for the new world order they projected into the future.

References

Baldwin, T. W. (1944). *William Shakspere's small latine and lesse Greeke* (2. vols.). Urbana: University of Illinois Press.

Barnard, H. C. (1913). *The little schools of Port Royal.* Cambridge: Cambridge University Press.

Collins, S. L. (1989). *From divine cosmos to sovereign state: An intellectual history of consciousness and the idea of order in Renaissance England.* Oxford: Oxford University Press.

Comenius, J. A. (1642). *A reformation of schooles.* London: Michael Sparke (facsimile reprint [1969] Menston, England: Scholar Press.

Costello, W. T. (1958). *The scholastic curriculum at early seventeenth-century Cambridge.* Cambridge, MA: Harvard University Press.

Cross, F. L. (Ed.). (1957). *The Oxford Dictionary of the Christian Church.* London: Oxford University Press.

Dickens, A. G. (1968). *The counter reformation.* London: Thames and Hudson.

———. (1976). *The German nation and Martin Luther.* Glasgow: Fontana.

Eby, F. (1971). *Early Protestant educators.* New York: AMS Press (original work published in 1931).

Eisenstein, E. L. (1979). *The printing press as an agent of change* (2 vols.). Cambridge: Cambridge University Press.

Foucault, M. (1979). *Discipline and punish* (trans. A. Sheridan). Harmondsworth: Penguin.

Grafton, A. (1983). From Ramus to Ruddiman: The *studia humanitas* in a scientific age. In N. T. Phillipson (Ed.), *Universities, society, and the ruture* (62–81). Edinburgh: Edinburgh University Press.

Grafton, A. and Jardine, L. (1986). *From humanism to the humanities: Education and the liberal arts in fifteenth and sixteenth-century Europe.* London: Duckworth.

Grendler, P. F. (1989). *Schooling in Renaissance Italy: Literacy and learning, 1300–1600*. Baltimore: Johns Hopkins University Press.

Gwynn, A. (1964). *Roman education from Cicero to Quintilian*. New York: Russell and Russell (original work published in 1926).

Hamilton, D. (1989). *Towards a theory of schooling*. London: Falmer.

Heath, T. (1971). Logical grammar, grammatical logic, and humanism in three German Universities. *Studies in the Renaissance* 18: 9–64.

Hoole, C. (1660). *A new discovery of the old art of teaching schoole*. London: Andrew Crook. (Version with an introduction by E.T. Campagnac. [1913]. Liverpool: Liverpool University Press).

Hoskin, K. (1990). Foucault under examination: The crypto-educationalist unmasked. In S. Ball (Ed.), *Foucault and education: Disciplines and knowledge* (29–53). London: Routledge.

Howell, W. S. (1956). *Logic and rhetoric in England, 1500–1700*. Princeton, NJ: Princeton University Press.

Jardine, L. (1993). *Erasmus, man of letters: The construction of charisma in print*. Princeton, NJ: Princeton University Press.

Kennedy, B. H. (1962). *The revised Latin primer*. London: Longmans.

Kraye, J. (1993). The philosophy of the Italian Renaissance. In G.H.R. Parkinson (Ed.), *The Renaissance and seventeenth century rationalism* (*Routledge History of Philosophy*, vol. 4 (16–69). London: Routledge.

Leach, A. F. (1915). *The schools of Medieval England*. London: Methuen.

McConica, J. (1979). Humanism and Aristotle in Tudor Oxford. *English Historical Review*, 94: 291–317.

———. (1983). The fate of Erasmian Humanism. In N. T. Phillipson (Ed.), *Universities, society, and the future* (37–61). Edinburgh: Edinburgh University Press.

McGrath, A. E. (1988). *Reformation thought: An introduction*. Oxford: Blackwell.

———. (1994). *Christian theology: An introduction*. Oxford: Blackwell.

McClintock, P. (1972). Towards a place for study in a world of instruction. *Teachers College Record* 73: 161–205.

Melton, J. V. H. (1988). *Absolutism and the eighteenth century origins of compulsory schooling in Prussia and Austria*. Cambridge: Cambridge University Press.

Moran, J. A. H. (1985). *The growth of English schooling, 1340–1548*. Princeton, NJ: Princeton University Press.

Morford, M. (1991). *Stoics and neostoics*. Princeton, NJ: Princeton University Press.

Mulcaster, R. (1582). *The first part of the elementarie*. London: Vautrollier. (Facsimile reprint [1970]. Menston, England: Scholar Press).

Oestreich, G. (1982). *Neostocism and the early modern state* (trans. D. McLintock). Cambridge: Cambridge University Press.

Ong, W. J. (1958). *Ramus, method, and the decay of dialogue*. Cambridge, MA: Harvard University Press.

Orme, N. (1973). *English schools in the middle ages*. London: Methuen.

———. (1989). *Education and society in medieval and renaissance England*. London: Hambledon Press.

Pepper, R. D. (Ed.). (1966). *Four tudor books on education*. Gainesville, FL: Scholars' Facsimiles and Reprints.

Schmitt, C. B. (1983). *Aristotle and the renaissance*. London: Harvard University Press.

———. (1988). The rise of the philosophical textbook. In C.B. Schmitt, Q. Skinner, E. Kessler, and J. Kraye (Eds.), *The Cambridge history of renaissance philosophy* (792–804). Cambridge: Cambridge University Press.

Simon, J. (1971). *The social origins of English education*. London: Routledge.

Smail, W. M. (1938). *Quintilian on education*. Oxford: Clarendon Press.

Skinner, Q. (1978). *The foundations of modern political thought* (2 vols.). Cambridge: Cambridge University Press.

Strauss, G. (1976). The state of pedagogical theory c1530: What Protestant reformers knew about education. In L. Stone (Ed.), *Schooling and society: Studies in the history of education* (69–94). Baltimore: Johns Hopkins University Press.

———. (1978). *Luther's house of learning: Indoctrination of the young in the German reformation*. Baltimore: Johns Hopkins University Press.

9

School Uniforms and the Disciplining of Appearances

Towards a History of the Regulation of Bodies in Modern Educational Systems

Inés Dussel

At the beginning of his wonderful history of clothing in the nineteenth century, Philippe Perrot asserts that "nothing appears less serious than a pair of underpants or more laughable than a necktie or a sock" (Perrot 1994:1). There is an irony in the fact that clothes seem the most inconsequential and trivial of things and yet we devote so much time to them in our daily lives. I myself have been confronted with similar arguments about the triviality of this subject when presenting my work on school uniforms. Don't we have more pressing things to be concerned about? Isn't it frivolous to talk about clothes when schools are faced with enormous challenges?

However, the life of schools is made of many of these "inconsequential things" that have far more influence on the ways teachers and students perceive themselves and relate to others than might be presumed from the space given to them by educational research. A recent study on educational "marginalia" points out to what extent sports, vestibules, gatherings, and uniforms constitute the bedrock features of the institutional culture of schools (Symes and Meadmore 1999). In particular, school uniforms are seen as sets of habiliments in the moral economy of schools that manifest the kinds of subjectivities valued by educational institutions (Synott and Symes 1995: 140). School uniforms are signs and signifying practices that carry along meanings about identity and difference, and that enact the disciplining of the body by a power that subjects and subjectifies (produces subjectivities). As such, uniforms are not external "screens" on which meanings are reflected but are part of technologies of power that "govern and regulate both the outward and inward disposition of the pupil" (Synott and Symes, op.cit.).

It can be said, then, that uniforms and dress codes are an important part of the cultural history of schooling and of school bodies. The practice of school uniformation in public schools has been ongoing for centuries in the majority of modern educational systems. In several U.S. cities, however, uniforms have been adopted only recently, in a movement that goes against the grain of an international trend of "flexibilization" of dress codes. It is remarkable that the

debates surrounding the implementation of school uniform policies have centered on the opposition of individualism versus conformity, of freedom versus
discipline. Uniforms appear as an attack on the quintessential character of
American life, individual freedom, or as the solution to the multifaceted problems confronted by contemporary schools: violence, crisis of authority, and
loss of focus on educational tasks.

My aim in this chapter is to interrupt these debates with a history of the present of school uniforms, that is, a historical problematization of the very terms
in which we have come to think of schooling, its problems, and its solutions
(see this book's introductory chapter). My project, then, is not intended merely
to add new domains to cultural history, as if to produce a complete, exhaustive
map of the life of the school through recording its minutiae, but to historicize
the ways in which we think about schools, teachers and students, and their
bodies. I will argue that uniforms are not all-solving policies nor the deadliest
of our foes, but instead have to be considered as longstanding technologies of
power that, together with other institutional procedures, have produced both
conformity and individuality in schools and in the larger society. In order to
understand how the present school uniformation policies have been configured, it needs to be reinscribed within a cultural history of the regulation of
school bodies that traces the discursive formations and technologies that
shaped their trajectory and that enables us to distinguish the scaffolding of
meanings that have become attached to them.[1]

Using a Foucauldian framework, particularly from Discipline and Punish
(1977) and his later work (1991 1994), I explore the emergence of school uniforms in the context of mass schooling. In my approach, the body is not a
"natural" element in society but is part of a web of categories dominated by
moral expectations (Vigarello 1989) and political strategies and tactics (Popkewitz 1998).[2] I will look at dress codes and school uniformation policies in
the Western geopolitical space from the seventeenth to the nineteenth century.
I build upon Ian Hunter's (1994) analysis of the modern school as a combination of pastoral techniques and bureaucratic needs to analyze the links between
contemporary uniforms and the dress codes that were prevalent at charity
schools and Lasallean (Christian) Brothers' orphanages in the 17th and 18th
centuries. These earlier forms of corporeal regulation set some patterns that
were later adopted by their modern counterparts. The emergence of disciplinary technologies transformed the military and the political field, and together
with the bourgeois revolutions they gave new vigor to the idea of uniforms,
which were perceived as symbols of docility, homogeneity and equity. The popularity of school uniforms was also a product of other historical events that
influenced schooling. Among them, I refer to changes in the ways bodies were
conceived and how they were to be "corrected" and cared for (Vigarello 1978
1988), the emergence of a new sartorial régime that valued austerity and deco-

rum (Roche 1994; Perrot 1987), and last but not least, the irruption of medical and philosophical discourses that prescribe a "return" to simplicity and nature.

In the course of this essay, I will engage in a theoretical and political discussion of "discipline" as a privileged category for the cultural history of education and educational reform. For many critics, "discipline" is equivalent to a "sterilization of life," a machine-like model that sees only domination and replication everywhere (Vigarello 1995). On the contrary, I argue that "discipline" as a positive economy is based on the activity, not the passivity, of the body. As it is seen in the history of school uniforms, the introduction of disciplines implied that children were asked to perform new activities, to learn new behaviors and ways of relating to themselves and to others. Children and their docile bodies "not only acquire more strength through controlled exercises but they also find, at the end and within a society in which oppression is no longer a question of torture and blood, a new game in autonomy" (Vigarello 1995: 161). "Discipline," with its coupling of individualizing techniques and collective docility, challenges contemporary discourses on school reform that are based solely on an affirmation of individual freedom and autonomy, as if they were separate and easily distinguishable from social constraints. Instead, it compels us to look for new spaces of freedom that both acknowledge our social bonds and struggle to expand the scope of our experiences.

The Cultural History of Bodies

> Foucault has made a formidable contribution to
> cultural history when proving that
> writing the history of the body is a political act.
>
> (Willem Frijhoff 1999: 97)

> The body is the first place where the adult hand marks the infant, the first space where psychological and social boundaries are set to his/her behavior. It is the emblem upon which culture writes its signs as if they were heraldry.
>
> (Georges Vigarello 1978: 9)

Bodies are fashionable topics in contemporary social theory (McWilliam 1996), and have recently been reappraised as a preeminent material upon which inscriptions of culture and its discourses become embedded (Shapiro 1994). For example, identity, a central issue to today's politics and theories, has been conceptualized as a material practice that is located primarily in the body (Butler 1993). It has been said that the identity scripts for African Americans, Latinos, women, and homosexuals imply significant differences in the bodily conducts that are set as "normal" for each of these groups (Donald and Rattansi 1992). Bodies then are seen as privileged sites for the construction of society, and great attention has been paid to the bodily practices that function as regulatory ideas of the self.

These theoretical and political shifts owe a great deal to Michel Foucault's work on bodies and power. For the French philosopher, subjectivation takes place basically through the body and the material practices that shape our behavior. Thus, the regulation of social life is first and foremost the regulation of bodies: "Now the phenomenon of the social body is the effect not of a consensus but of the materiality of power operating on the very bodies of the individuals" (Foucault 1980a: 55). Inverting the traditional dualism of mind/body, Foucault once said that "the soul is the prison of the body," implying that the way we feel and act is already regulated by the disciplinarian techniques that have constituted our "soul" (Rose 1990; Popkewitz 1998).

The centrality of the history of the body for his historicopolitical project cannot be overlooked. Foucault said that the history of modernity should not be read as the "enlightenment of the masses" but as a ritualized body-inscription that was no less painful or more "humane" than previous experiences. Instead of thinking of history as a progressive and totalizing teleology, the genealogy of modernity[3] should recognize that the normalization of bodies is never accomplished once and forever, but is the object of a permanent struggle. Arguing against the Marxist notion of class conflict, he made it explicit that "the coherence of such a [genealogical] history does not derive from the revelation of a project but from a logic of opposing strategies" (Foucault 1980a: 61). This struggle is indefinite, because for each move of the adversary there is an answer by the other. In relation to the history of the body, Foucault argued that from the eighteenth to the twentieth century, the control over the body was heavy, ponderous, meticulous, and constant, and thus formidable disciplinary regimes emerged, such as the school, hospitals, barracks, factories, cities, families. The "sexual revolution" in the 1960s made it evident that a more flexible form of control over the body would be more effective than coercion. But that did not mean that the age of "sexual liberation" implied less constraints or regulations than did Victorian morality. Foucault, who was suspicious of this revolution, warned us about the fact that power can retreat here, but only to "reorganize its forces, invest itself elsewhere . . . and so the battle continues" (Foucault 1980a: 56).[4]

Other examples from the sociology and history of the body and of bodily practices show that the regulation of bodies is the outcome of many strategies and techniques that followed no predetermined route. One well-known example is the "civilizing process" studied by Norbert Elias, who analyzed the transition from feudal to modern times. The process of individuation has proceeded through the regulating of how to speak and how to behave socially, and the setting of standards of good manners, decency, and decorum (Elias 1982). Elias was mostly concerned with how the ways in which power is exercised articulate each other, and how society is shaped through an interweaving of the social and the psychological registers. Though his inquiry was oriented within a Weberian framework, he shared with Foucault a preoccupation with how specific forms of power–generally the more microscopic ones—generate the social (Revel 1997).

Elizabeth Grosz has called this approach "inscriptive" as it conceptualizes the body as a surface on which social law, morality, and values ("civilization" for Elias) are inscribed (Grosz 1995: 33ff.). This does not mean that bodies are restricted to, or contained exclusively by, this social inscription; there seems to be something that always escapes fixation in the body, although it is never clear where it comes from. This ambivalence is evident in the following remark by Foucault: "[t]he body is the inscribed surface of events . . . the locus of a disso-ciated self . . . and a volume in perpetual disintegration. [The task of geneal-ogy, thus,] is to expose a body totally imprinted by history and the process of history's destruction of the body" (Foucault 1984: 83). The body is what is destructed by history, and in that respect it may seem prior to history itself; but it is also its product. Bodies and histories are thus elements in tension in Fou-cault's theory. Although this ambivalence is present in his writings, in his his-torical studies it is never clear where this resistance and ungraspability comes from, or what produces it.

Michel de Certeau explored this ambivalence much more thoroughly than Foucault did. The French Jesuit, one of the most significant intellectuals in the field of culture, attempted to consider simultaneously both the scriptural econ-omy of society and the "ungovernability" (slippages) of the bodies. The body is, in de Certeau's words, defined, delimited, and articulated by what writes it; the body is repaired, educated, fabricated by mechanisms of social articulation that want to produce the text of a law. Bodies become the engravings and maps of the social conquests, of the "docilization" of transgression, of the perfora-tion of autonomy. But bodies are also the site of poaching, of popular ruses within the city, of laughter and pain that can not be recuperated by the institu-tion. In that, they are the place *par excéllence* of ambiguity, and of the unsayable—namely, death (de Certeau 1984).

The French historian Georges Vigarello, influenced by Foucault and Michel de Certeau, has taken this ambivalence to the historical terrain. A representative illustration is his thoughtful and rigorous history of the frontier between the healthy and the unhealthy since the Middle Ages. For Vigarello, this border is flexible and movable, and it changes over time. If the amber apples that were carried around in the seventeenth century to clean the air seemed ridiculous a century later, the same happened to eighteenth-century notions that perfume and good odor were signs of good health. Vigarello shows that this history of the body is not centered on an increasing and progressive mastery of evil and dis-ease. "It is the territory of risk that extends itself, at the same time that knowl-edge increases. Science and technique conduct us to master danger as well as to renew it. They overcome ancient threats while deploying new ones" (Vigarello

1993a: 325–26; see also Vigarello 1993b). The history of the body and bodily practices is for Vigarello the history of what is fixated and what escapes fixation as well, of that which is mastered and that which remains ungovernable.

Despite their differences, histories such as the ones written by Foucault, de Certeau, Elias, and Vigarello remind us that "the body does not cease to be (re)fabricated over time" (Bernuzzi de Sant'Anna 1995: 12). The body is, according to this Brazilian historian, a mutant memory of the laws and codes of any culture, and a privileged record of the scientific and technological limits and solutions of any historical period. One cannot take it for granted, limiting its history to the study of how representations change or are distorted over time, as if there were a zero degree of culture where one could find a body uncontaminated by culture. As Vigarello and Bernuzzi Sant'Anna cleverly argue, if bodies are caught up in a system of moral and political classifications and categories, it is important to identify the problematizations that made it possible for a series of bodily practices and representations to emerge and to be systematized and set to work in social life.

The history of bodies and bodily practices then becomes the genealogy of bodily problematizations and of the technologies that organize them. As for the first term, Foucault said in *The Use of Pleasure* that problematization is a kind of history that intends "to define the conditions in which human beings "problematize" what they are, what they do, and the world in which they live" (Foucault 1990: 10). It "develops the conditions in which possible responses can be given; it defines the elements that will constitute what the different solutions attempt to respond to" (Foucault, quoted in Campbell 1998). Problematization questions thoughts, gestures, and attitudes that seem natural, and tries to rewrite them as part of the transformations of a practice that faces difficulties and obstacles and for which diverse practical solutions appear as reasonable and feasible.[5] It is not a rhetorical trope or a topic, but a way of conceiving a subject, of looking at a problem, and of defining codes and discourses that are appropriate to deal with it.

As described by Peter Miller and Nikolas Rose, the history of technologies pays special attention to "the analysis of the activity of ruling, [. . .] the actual mechanisms through which authorities of various sorts have sought to shape, normalize and instrumentalise the conduct, thought, decisions and aspirations of others in order to achieve the objectives they consider desirable . . . the humble and mundane mechanisms which appear to make it possible to govern" (quoted in McWilliam 1996: 15). Technology is an assemblage of heterogeneous elements: knowledges, types of authority, vocabularies, practices of calculation, architectural forms, human capacities (Rose 1999: 52). The schoolroom can be looked at as a technology that combined different techniques (timetables, registers of students and teachers, moralizing aspirations, professional ethos, drills and exercises, architectural dispositions, among others) in order to shape the conduct of children in precise ways.

Given this framework, my writing of the history of school uniforms will focus on the ways in which they emerged as a problem, the discourses used to support them, and the institutional practices and technologies that turned them into an efficient and desirable dress code. Before proceeding with the historical arguments, I will start by analyzing clothing and uniforms and the specific ways in which they regulate the body. This theoretical framework allows me to consider the history of dress codes in a different way, understanding uniforms as signs within the particular language of clothing. This social readability of clothes will illuminate my exploration on the history of school uniforms from the seventeenth to the nineteenth centuries and how they shaped the "schooled body."

Dressing Bodies at School: The Trajectory of an Incision

> Every power, including the power of law,
> is written first of all on the backs of its subjects.
> (Michel de Certeau)

"Clothes don't make the person," the saying goes. Or "appearances are deceiving." However true this sounds as commonsense knowledge, its opposite also holds true. "You are not what you wear" may be a good slogan for compelling anticonsumerist ads paid for by advocates of school uniforms in contemporary America, but it does not acknowledge that clothes give plenty of information about the person who wears them, i.e., her or his aesthetic dispositions, resources, and social functions. Even those who claim that they don't care what they wear are also conveying meanings through their garments, although these meanings are not to be read through verbal language but through another language that has its own code (Harvey 1995).

The "language of clothing," as Alison Lurie (1981) called it, has been studied as the semiotics of clothing and fashion. Roland Barthes, Umberto Eco, and others have sought to find the distinctive syntaxis of fashion and of the ways people dress themselves (see for example, Barthes 1983). While I will be using some conceptual tools from the semiology of clothing (which bears important nexus to the analysis of school uniforms as part of governmentality, as Symes and Meadore [1996] argue), in this chapter, I will emphasize a different approach informed, as I have said, by Foucault's work.

Clothing is a very powerful way in which social regulation is enacted: it turns bodies into "readable" signs, making the observer recognize patterns of docility and transgression, and social positioning. Elizabeth Grosz remarks that clothes mark the subject's body as deeply as a surgical incision, binding individuals to systems of significance in which they become signs to be read, both by others and by themselves (Grosz 1995). Arguing along the same line, Michel de Certeau argues that clothing is one of two ways through which the body is inscribed in the text of law. The first one wants to eliminate that which is excessive, diseased, or unaesthetic from the body; the second one proceeds through adding to the body what it lacks. Cutting, tearing up, extracting, removing, or inserting, covering up, assembling, articulating, are the main operations that take place on the body. They are carried out by reference to a code, keeping bodies within the limits of a norm. "[C]lothes themselves can be regarded as instruments through which a social law maintains its hold on bodies and its members, regulates them and exercises them . . ." (de Certeau 1984: 147). They have the effect of making the body tell the code—they realize a social language, they recount a law that has been "historied and historicized" (*histoirée* and *historicisée*) and thus made more effective.

Given the fact that clothing functions as a distinctive marker between populational groups and can enact disciplinary power, dress codes have been important in the formation of public schooling. Both the teachers' dress and the students' attire have been subjected to formal rules so as to ensure "decency" and "decorum" (Middleton 1997: 14–15), in a movement that could be read as an extension of Elias's thesis on the civilizing process. With the relaxing of the formal rules in many countries, there has been a shift to informal regulation that nonetheless continues to inscribe particular "scripts of identity" on students and teachers. Part of this informality has been the displacement of the authority to regulate dress codes from the national state to the school and even to the students themselves, a policy that has been called "devolution"—as in the devolution of decision-making to local communities (cf. Meadmore and Symes 1997) . The notion that "the development of sensible attitudes towards matters of dressing" is part of the self-management that the school wants to promote (as claims a New Zealand regulation quoted in Middleton 1997: 54) is in line with the flexible forms of regulation that Nikolas Rose has described as prevalent in contemporary societies (Rose 1999). This flexibilization and reshaping of dress codes is also visible in Japan, which has a rigid tradition of uniformizing students at different levels of their education, where top designers from the world of fashion have been called to make special garments for schools in order to make the wearing of uniforms more attractive to young people (McVeigh 1997: 190).

How can uniforms be read as a sign within the spectrum of dress codes? The topic has not received a great deal of attention in the sociology of clothing, which has mainly focused on the structure and dynamics of fashion and the distinctiveness of individual appearance. Contrasted to them, uniforms appear as a secondary and almost boring topic. Uniforms have been defined by prestigious scholars in the field as the "extreme form of conventional dress," "the costume totally determined by others." Again, the contrast disfavors uniforms due to their rejection of the liberal ideal of fashion, which is to express oneself freely. According to Alison Lurie, to wear uniforms is "to give up one's right to act as an individual—in terms of speech, to be partially or wholly censored. What one does, as well as what one wears, will be determined by external authorities . . ." The uniform acts as a sign that the wearer should not be treated as a human being, but as part of a bureaucratic structure. "It is no accident that people in uniform, rather than speaking to us honestly and straightforwardly, often repeat mechanical lies. 'It was a pleasure having you on board,' they say; 'I can not give you that information'; or 'The doctor will see you shortly.'" (Lurie 1981: 17–18)

Following this conceptualizing of uniforms, based on the idea of a liberal individual who can freely choose her/his options, uniforms provide oneself with a "false" identity because they do not allow one's true self to express itself. The approach I will take in this chapter is quite the contrary: as the opening quote of this section says, bodies are already inscribed by law as soon as we are part of a society, no matter what we wear. To use blue denims, wear casual, or walk the streets clothed and not naked, are part of social rules and laws, and there is no "natural" way of dressing ourselves that can express our "true" identities without already being related and indebted to these laws and rules. Clothing is, as Roland Barthes defined it, a standardized image of expected social behaviors, and thus it only makes sense in relation to a set of collective norms (Barthes 1957: 434, 440). As social selves, we are always defined in and by vestimentary codes.

Notwithstanding what I see as its shortcomings, Lurie's approach (which I will call "mainstream sociology of clothing," keeping in mind, as Spivak persuasively argues, that "the mainstream has never run clean, perhaps never can" [Spivak 1999: 2]) can still provide some clues about the specificity of the uniform as a sign within the language of clothing. In the example of the stewardess or the doctor's secretary or nurse, it becomes clear that uniforms have a performative function, that is, they carry along a distinctive pattern of behaviors with them. "Constant wearing of official costume can so transform someone that it becomes difficult or impossible for him or her to react normally" (Lurie 1981: 19). "Normality" here should be read inversely from what Lurie suggests: uniforms as regulatory practices that are exerted on bodies do inscribe standard attitudes and behaviors and prescribe what is considered to be "normal" and "abnormal." Far from compelling us to act "abnormally," they mark the bench for the standard of normality for a particular populational group. This performative quality is enhanced by the fact that, unlike other clothing, uniforms are often consciously and deliberately symbolic. They identify their wearers as members of a group and locate them within a hierarchy; sometimes, as in the case of the military or sport fraternities, they also give information about singular achievements (Joseph 1986).

Uniforms, albeit seen by some scholars as dull and insipid garments, are as dense and complex cultural artifacts as any other clothing item. The use of colors, fabrics, badges; the distinctions and honors they provide; the enforcement and level of regulation of the dress codes, and their cultural significance, provide distinct information about the social hierarchies and cultural values that are prevalent in a given power/knowledge regime. For example, the preponderance of some colors to which are ascribed "neutrality" over others that seem to "excite" the senses does not affect every student equally. Gray and blue, identified with conformist, conservative office dress, were traditionally associated with middle-class, educated individuals. White, with its "cultured significance" as marker of life, purity, and power, carried along racial hierarchies as well (Kidwell and Steele 1989: 75). Through these traits, uniforms authorize particular kinds of subjectivities that are held to be important in the educational endeavor, and exclude others (Synott and Symes 1995). They provide "scripts of identity" (a compendium of dispositions and conducts regulated for specific social positions) and draw boundaries for detecting and policing their limits.

This social "readability" has a long history in Western societies, and particularly in the history of education. Since the Middle Ages, university students wore special gowns and coats for the ceremonies of graduation. Their relevance increased when the universities turned into more elitist enclosures, as they became secular settings paid by the students and adopted some patterns of the medieval guilds such as hereditary membership and strict rules of admission. Clothing became part of their rituals, and was used as a symbol of distinction, both due to their cost and their exclusiveness (Le Goff 1981).

In fact, clothing was regulated with considerable detail for each social group in the early modern period. Philippe Ariès spoke of "uniforms" when he referred to the garments children wore from the sixteenth to the eighteenth century (Ariès 1962, ch. 3). Cassocks, ribbons, robes, were part of sartorial indications that distinguished among classes, ages, and sexes. Boys were the first specialized group of children: getting older implied changing costumes and adopting progressively the clothes of adult men. Following Ariès, such distinction and progression did not take place in the case of girls' clothing.

Dress was a very important part of social life because it denoted social hierarchy. In his manual on manners written in 1530, Erasmus of Rotterdam spoke of clothing as "the body's body" and said that from it "one may infer the state of a man's character" (quoted in Roche 1994: 6). Given the high cost of clothes, they constituted a great portion of the expenditure of a household (Roche 1994). Not surprisingly, the regulation of dress took two distinctive forms: first, placing a curb on luxury clothes and imposing expenditure limits; and second, assuring that certain types of cloth or styles were reserved for specific social categories. For example, peasants were required to wear a single color (black or grey) at the beginning of the last millennium, while it was established that ermine was only to be worn by nobles (Hunt 1996: 26–27). A French decree from 1514 prohibited "absolutely categorically all persons, commoners, non-nobles . . . from assuming the title of nobility either in their style or in their clothes" (quoted in Roche 1994: 49). Clothes had to remain a distinct symbol of social rank and order. These functions were strengthened by the religious turmoil that followed the Reformation and the confessionaliza-tion of Europe (Hsia 1989).[6]

With the decline of feudalism, and against the grain of common assump-tions, dress codes became more important and there was more, rather than less, preoccupation with the preservation of hierarchy (Hunt 1996: 28ff). In societies with increased mobility (urbanization, religious wars, capitalist accu-mulation) and with emergent national boundaries, distinctions had to be con-tinuously reassured. A Nuremberg ordinance from 1657 made this concern explicit: "It is unfortunately an established fact that both men and women-folk have, in utterly irresponsible manner, driven extravagance in dress and new styles to such shameful and wanton extremes that the different classes are barely to be known apart" (quoted in Hunt 1996: 1). As several historians argue, these difficulties in recognizing social distinctions were aggravated by theft and second-hand shopping that circulated clothes from one rank to the other (Lemire 1990–91; Roche 1994). Thus, the emphasis on dress regulation has to be read as the confluence of different governmental projects that included moral and economic regulation (Hunt 1996: 40–41).

Educating the Poor: Pastoral Power and the Emergence of Disciplines

It is in this setting that the Christian Brothers and other charity schools started to prescribe uniforms for their students. In France, Jean-Baptiste de La Salle (1651–1719) founded the Brothers of the Christian Schools in 1680 to estab-lish schools and orphanages for poor children, which were supported by both private and public donations often in concert with town councils. The com-munity of Christian Brothers joined a network of institutions that were con-cerned with providing shelter, food, and suitable employment for the aged, the crippled, and the orphaned ("the internment of the pauper"), and that dedi-cated themselves to the education of the poor (Hufton 1974).

Lasallean schools are probably the first model of elementary schooling in modern times (Hamilton 1990), and are, according to Foucault one of the most conspicuous exemplars of disciplinary power. Discipline, as the "art of correct training," "makes" individuals: "it is the specific technique of power that regards individuals both as objects and as instruments of its exercise. [. . .] [I]t is a modest, suspicious power, which functions as a calculated, but perma-nent economy" (Foucault 1977: 170). La Salle thought of a method that included both socialization and individualization. "In every class, there will be places assigned for all the pupils of all the lessons, so that all those attending the same lesson will always occupy the same place." There was a serial orga-nization of space that granted supervision of each individual and of the collec-tive group at the same time.

His "pedagogy of the detail" regulated with great precision the daily life of schools, including ways of entering and leaving the classroom, spatial arrangements, positions of the body when reading, writing, or praying, and signs and gestures directed by the teacher to the students. Silence became a privileged mode of communication, and the primary evidence of order. Disciplinary power pervaded the classroom through the works of microtechniques that intended to tame the body and conquer the soul, and that classified children according to their progress, worth, character, cleanliness, application, and parents' fortune (Foucault 1977; Narodowski 1995).

This disciplinary system was also organized as a pastoral power (see Popkewitz 1998; Dussel and Caruso, forthcoming). Pastoral power is exercised as the rule of the shepherd over his flock. The shepherd guides the flock to salvation, which requires sacrifices at times, and has to watch over it all the time, looking after each individual to guarantee that it does not follow the wrong track. In order to do so, it has to know "the inside of people's minds, . . . explor[e] their souls, . . . mak[e] them reveal their innermost secrets" (Foucault 1982: 214). Foucault saw this type of power working in modern states, and believed it constituted the matrix for individualization. One can take as an example La Salle's propositions about punishment in schools in his *Conduct of Christian Schools*: "By the word punishment, one must understand everything that is capable of making children feel the offence they have committed, everything that is capable of humiliating them, of conducing them: . . . a certain coldness, a certain indifference, a question, a humiliation, a removal from office" (quoted in Foucault 1977: 178). The teacher guided the child not so much through coercion as through molding his/her soul so that he/she felt humiliated and despised by the teacher and the group.

One of the first principles that La Salle stated for the community's schools was that of uniformity. "It has been necessary to prepare this guide for Christian Schools so that all may be done uniformly in all schools and in all places where there are Brothers of this Institute, and that the practices there will always be the same. . . . [All in the Order should learn this guide] and will proceed in such a way that teachers observe exactly all the practices that are prescribed for them, even the least in order to procure by this means great order in the schools, a well regulated and uniform conduct on the part of the teachers who will be in charge of them, and a very considerable benefit for the children who will be taught there" (1703/1833: 45–46). In this precept, as in many others, La Salle set the basis for a reordering of space in terms of a homogeneous, continuous series, that at the same time allowed room for differentiation. One instance of this simultaneous workings of homogenization and individualization was the organization of breakfast and lunch. According to the *Conduct*, each student should bring his/her own meal to eat; but those who could not afford it received the remainings of their classmates' food, which was deposited in a lunch basket in the middle of the room. Solidarity and distinction were constructed at the same time. All children were encouraged to eat at school so that they would learn how to do so with propriety and decorum.

The body was a privileged site of regulation for La Salle. In a section of the *Conduct* called "The Correct Position of the Body," he stressed that students should "hold their bodies as erect as possible, only slightly inclined but without touching the table, so that with the elbow placed on the table, the chin can be rested upon the hand." If this sounds overzealous, there is even more: "The body must be somewhat turned and free on the same side. The teacher . . . will take care above all that they do not hold their right arm from their bodies and that they do not press their stomachs against the table; for, besides being very ungraceful, this posture might cause them great inconvenience." It should be noted that the "sin" performed by bad posture is breaking a code of elegance, rather than healthy or hygienic precepts—as will become common in the eighteenth and nineteenth centuries (Vigarello 1989). Also, the actions to remedy bad posture differ from what we would think of today: "In order to make [the pupil] hold his body correctly, the teacher will himself place the pupil in the posture which he should maintain, with each limb where it should be. Whenever he sees a pupil change this position, he will take care to put him back into it" (1720/1996: 93). The body seems to be part of a picture or drawing that has to stay as still as possible. The teacher acts as a stake guiding the young tree, although the metaphor is not totally apt because there is almost no sense of growth or change conveyed in this image of the body.

Within these politics of the body, clothes received attention as part of this code of elegance and the value of external appearances. While there is not an explicit reference to the donning of uniforms by students in the *Conduct of Christian Schools*, there are several indications that there was a concern with what was worn. Teachers, like the other brothers of the community, wore a *capote*, an ample mantle with loose sleeves, used by peasants; for indoor garb, they had a cassock of black cloth, fastened in front with hooks and eyes, with a white neckband and a three-corned hat (1720/1996: Introduction). They were to deport themselves with great seriousness and have a modest demeanor. In the *Rules for Propriety*, written in 1703, La Salle condemned "singularity in dress" as a proof of madness or ridiculous stubbornness: "the fashion of the country where one lives is the rule that has to be followed when choosing the form of clothes" (1703/1833: 40). Singularity versus common fashion—the path toward uniformation was starting to be paved.

In the case of England, uniforms seem to have been part of mass schooling since the sixteenth century (Davidson 1990). The Society for Promoting Christian Knowledge, which led the movement for educating the poor, was established in 1698 "[f]or the Education of Poor Children in the Knowledge and Practice of the Christian Religion, as profess'd and Taught in the Church of England; and for Teaching them such other things as are most suitable to their condition" (Account of Charity Schools, 1704–1732, quoted in Sylvester 1970: 171). The society established charity schools that were supposed to be in session every day from April to September, except on Sundays, from seven to twelve in the morning and from one to five in the afternoon. Children were separated in lower and upper classes according to their progress in learning. Clothes were given to each child; for example, in Leeds Charity School, a complete sartorial outfit (consisting of a coat, breeches, stockings, two new shirts, a band, two check stocks) was distributed every Christmas day, and a pair of shoes twice a year. Part of the outfit could have been spun by the children themselves as part of chores done in the school. Even though charity schools do not seem to have reached the level of detailed organization suggested by the Lasallean method, they were also part of an emerging disciplinarian power that promoted a detailed account of the movement of students and teachers, their characteristics and wrongdoings, as well as a system of rewards and penalties based on a close supervision of increasingly autonomous subjects.

Charity schools started the use of uniforms in order to keep the students clean and distinguish them from other children. Their prototype was the religious cassock, generally blue as that was the color worn by the servile classes. Interestingly, blue was also associated with sadness and sorrow.[7] Christ's Hospital in England, founded in 1553 and later a renowned public school, housed poor children supported by benefactors; here a yellow petticoat was worn below the cassock, yellow being supposed to discourage vermin (while white was supposed to promote their breeding). The reference to a color (yellow or white) as an efficient way of warding off vermin or lice was symptomatic of a change in how the body and its diseases were thought of. Georges Vigarello says that until the seventeenth century pests were conceived as the expression of a bodily condition, of corrupt humors which could be controlled basically by changing the diet, and not as the product of the lack of cleanliness (1988: 42ff.). Symptoms of a new discursive formation, they outlived it largely: these yellow petticoats were only retired in 1865 (Davidson 1990: 11). As for other articles of clothing, it seems likely that breeches started to be used in the eighteenth century. In France, the cassock was also regularly used in schools and orphanages. The robe was the descendant of the longcoat of the Middle Ages (Ariès 1962: 55), which later become shorter for most parts of society but stayed long for priests, judges, and children. One can see a complex scaffolding of moral regulations, social hierarchies, and hygienic principles supporting its use.

This uniform was to be worn by the child both on the school premises and anywhere else a school-sponsored activity was engaged in. It had to be cleaned and watched after by the child's family. Reportedly children looked like little monks and were supposed to behave accordingly (Davidson 1990: 1). Thomas Secker, the archbishop of Canterbury, remarked that children's "moral behavior, a point of vastly more consequence than their learning, should be diligently watched, both in the school, and as possible out of it too; for which purpose they are distinguished by a peculiar dress" (sermon preached to the gathering of the London charity school children, 1743, quoted in Sylvester 1970: 182).

The uniforms thus made children's bodies docile, clearly visible, and subject to surveillance.

Clothing still worked, as in late medieval times, as a marker for a particular social rank. Dress codes at schools can be seen as variations of sumptuary laws, in that they prescribe which clothes are to be worn by whom. Archbishop Secker said in his sermon that the clothes of the students "should be no better, or so good, as they may hope to wear all the rest of their lives; no gaiety of color, no trifling ornaments permitted; nor any distinction between them and other children, in which they can possibly be tempted to take pleasure" (Sylvester 1970: 185). Dress was a cartographic sign to read the map of social distinctions in early modern England.

However, schools disrupted this order in more respects than they imagined. The position of Bernard de Mandeville, who was a sharp critic of these schools because they promoted "idleness among the pauper," gives some clues about the changes in the production and circulation of clothes and thus of social symbols brought about by uniforms. "How perverse must be the judgement of those, who would not rather see children decently dressed, with clean linen at least once a week, that in orderly manner follow their master to church, than in every open place meet with a company of black-guards without shirts or anything whole about them . . . !" (Mandeville, 1724, quoted in Sylvester 1970: 176). Up to that moment, linen had been reserved for the noble and upper classes (Vigarello 1988) and only reached the lower classes through theft or gifts. Mandeville makes it clear that charity schools were slowly distributing it to other social strata in a sanctioned, official way, and that there was a general consensus that wearing linen was better than going around "without shirts." It should be noted that linen was particularly apt for introducing larger changes. Because it was a fragile piece of cloth and great care had to be taken in order to wash it, and also because its whiteness denounced untidiness much more openly than other garments, it contributed to spreading new habits of hygiene and cleanliness. Besides, linen was thought of as an underwear or "second skin," and its diffusion across society helped to shape new conceptions about the private and public domains, setting new boundaries between the intimate and the outer appearance (Roche 1994).

Uniforms as Part of a New Sartorial Regime

Beyond their distinctiveness, the uniforms of charity schools and the regulations on dress instituted by the Christian Brothers shared some general characteristics that made them part of the same sartorial regime.

First, they had to express humility and make appearances look modest. In this respect, uniforms expressed a generalized concern with the body in the seventeenth and eighteenth centuries that can be found in treatises of civility and manners. The end of all conduct was self-control and the achievement modesty, bringing one closer to God (LaSalle 1703/1833). "Physical uprightness and control have moral connotations. Through a bearing that must always be 'honest' and unchanging, one is able to disguise the emotions" (Vigarello 1989: 177).

Concerning modesty, Gracián, writing a manual of manners in the seventeenth century, said that "nothing must show on the outside." This involved the deployment of practices that led to the mastery of the self, to the control of passions, in other words, what Foucault (1988) calls techniques of the self. La Salle is illustrative in this respect. In his *Rules for Propriety*, he devoted several pages to clothes and how and where to wear them. Neither too long nor too short nor too big, clothes had to respect a sense of proportion and decorum, which implied the moral and spiritual development of its wearer. "Negligence in dress is a sign of neglect of God's presence, or of insufficient respect for Him; it also reveals a lack of respect for one's own body, which should be honored as the animate temple of the Holy Spirit, and the tabernacle where Jesus Christ is good enough often to repose" (quoted in Roche 1994: 10). Elsewhere, La Salle stated that "exterior disorder is usually a consequence of the disorder that reigns in the soul." Beware of the lazy, and always exhibit your clothes with attention and preparation—clothes were signs of a moral order that had to be imposed and respected daily.

The rule of modesty led to bans on exaggeratedly luxurious garments and those that nurtured a "despicable vanity." In schools, such bans were applied more on the female population than on the male students. Girls had to use caps to conceal their hair and have their necks covered with white tippets (Cunnington and Lucas 1978: 20). Following the rule, most uniforms and garments were plain and sober, and of just one color.

Second, uniforms embodied a distinctive notion of tradition. The uniforms that identified schools and school children generally persisted across time; as Cunnington and Lucas describe, it is only by the end of the nineteenth century that changes in colors and fabrics were introduced. They became symbols of tradition on another level as well. Uniforms were directly involved with the perpetuation of memory. Frequently they were designed as commemorative symbols that were part of the recognition of a debt. Many donors and their trustees in the seventeenth and eighteenth centuries stipulated that children at charity school had to acknowledge their debt to the giver. School children had to wear particular colors, badges, or family heraldry and acted as "walking reminders" of the donor's memory (Cunnington and Lucas 1978: 32ff). This bodily practice of "wearing a debt" can be read as the construction of an educated subject who had a sense of his/her duties and obligations to society. Uniforms were thus part of the transmission of memory, inscribed in a series of legacies and debts that left traces in the bodies and souls of the new generations.

Third, given the fact that most children were poor, most of the clothes belonged to the school—which created another kind of debt. "Clothes were a constant reminder [. . .] to the children themselves and to the rest of society that they were indeed 'charity-children,' provided for by others" (Sylvester 1970: 170). Wearing the school's uniform implied a whole array of learnings that had to do with economic and moral regulations of social life: private property, care of goods, maintenance of their value. At Leeds Charity School, the parent had to sign a form that detailed the clothes that were given to him/her and their children and that established the obligations of the family. The form said that "I [the parent] do hereby promise and undertake to keep all the said Garments in sufficient repair and in case the Committee of the said school, shall for any misbehavior of the said [child] expel him [. . .], [a]ll the said Garments shall upon demand to me, my Executors or Administrators be delivered up whole in decent repair unto the Master of the said Charity School or pay money for the value of the cloaths upon Demand." (Leeds Charity School form, 1735, quoted in Sylvester 1970: 188). A similar measure was taken at St. Leonard's School in Shoreditch, where it was decreed that "children whose clothes were stolen by their parents would be ignominiously expelled from school, on grounds that charity clothes were school property" (quoted in Davidson 1990: 20). As has been said, theft of clothes was a common practice in the France during the ancien regime and in early modern England (Roche 1994). Christian and charity schools sought to intervene and change these extended social practices through the children's bodies, combining moral obligations with a new sense of private and social properties.

This sartorial regime was part of a disciplinary regime that connected the government of people with the techniques of producing able, obedient, and disciplined bodies. Discipline is what linked the rationale of political rule to the arts of self-government, thus producing an individual who would conform to the needs of the state (Rose 1990: 222). The adoption of uniforms fostered both social obedience and self-scrutiny and regulation, providing an economic way of monitoring adherence to norms and a new practice for caring for oneself, involving hygienic habits, "decent" attire, and the private property of clothes.

To summarize this section, I have argued that these earlier forms of corporeal regulation set some patterns that were to be adopted by their modern counterparts. They ordered the school space into a uniform set of bodies that was homogeneous and whose obedience to the pastor/teacher was easier to control than in highly diversified groups, prevalent up to that moment. They also established a classifying device that distinguished schooled children from the rest of the population, and they promoted a disciplined relationship to oneself, as it is evident in the prescriptions about cleanliness and tidiness of children's clothes and the prohibition against lending them to others or wearing them in non-school-associated milieus. In these practices, one can see how Christian pedagogy contributed to the development of mass school systems in critical ways (Hunter 1994). The organizing routines, pedagogical practices, personal disciplines, and interpersonal relationships that are common in today's school still carry some of its traces. The classroom became "a space of ethical formation in which students are placed under the continuous ethical supervision and problematization of a teacher who embodies both moral authority and pastoral care" (Hunter 1994: 83). School uniforms also played a part in the orchestration of a pastoral power that reshaped the ways in which people were to think of themselves, perceive their bodies, and relate to others.

The Disciplining of Bodies in the Eighteenth Century: The Military and the Revolutionary

The century of the double revolution (as Eric Hobsbawm has called the political and economical transformations of the eighteenth century) witnessed some changes in the politics of the body that would gave new impulses to uniforms as privileged dress codes. By the mid-eighteenth century, and due to many factors (the advancement of capitalism, the demographic revolution, the emergence of new doctrines of liberty and rights), there was an extension of the techniques and discourses of disciplinary power that pervaded different social arenas. It is important to underline that Foucault sees disciplines not as "sudden discoveries" but as sometimes old techniques that emerged at scattered locations and that circulated in some cases slowly and discreetly (such as the militarization of the workshops), in other cases, very rapidly and efficiently (the militarization of schools). Discipline as a "political anatomy of detail" defined a detailed political investment of the body, a new "microphysics" of power, that rearranged existing mechanisms and inscribed them within a new power-knowledge regime (Foucault 1977: 138–139). Disciplinary power worked through serial and analytical inclusion of elements. While these technologies were also present in the Christian and charity schools, in the next century there would be an acceleration and refinement of their techniques and tactics. Registers of students, for example, would know a much more detailed existence; the development of criminology, statistics, and other sciences helped develop a tighter control of the population and led to the appearance of new conflicts and problematizations. Uniforms were another case in which old technologies were relocated within new discourses and strategies.

The extension of disciplinary power ran parallel to the political shift from an absolutist state to a modern democracy, one of whose conditions was the existence of modern political subjects. These subjects did not require a continual external policing because they had internalized the ethics of discipline and were prepared to assume responsibility for their actions (Rose 1990: 223). These subjects had to think of society as a collective construction made out of a common contract that obliged everyone to follow the rules and that would benefit each accordingly. If the power came from the people and not the king, there had to be a new game of loyalties between the state and the people: the state served its citizens while the latter served the state. This mutual relationship of service is one of the characteristics of modern political relationships (Ehrenberg 1983: 42ff).

These transformations in the political regime had immediate effects on bodies. An image provided by Foucault in *Discipline and Punish* can illustrate these shifts. In the Classical Age, the body of the condemned man was "the king's property, on which the sovereign left his mark and brought down the effects of his power"; however, in the eighteenth century the prisoner's body was "the property of society, the object of a collective and useful appropriation" (Foucault 1977: 109). The right to punish had shifted from the vengeance of the sovereign to the defence of society. The person who broke the rules was therefore equated to an enemy or a traitor, who had to be punished by those who did abide by the law and who remained sensible, rational beings. Foucault said compellingly: "It is an unequal struggle: on the one side are all the forces, all the power, all the rights" (1977: 90). But, as I will show later in this section, the introduction of the language of rights did change the ways in which people perceived their bodies and managed them.

There were also changes in the discourses that were used to talk about and correct the body. Georges Vigarello provides a wonderful account of this shift in his book on the history of the posture of the body. In early modern times, the body was conceived of as a fixed entity, a state of being, as is clear from the Lasallean prescriptions on the uprightness of the body. Exercise was secondary, and had to do with a code of hygiene that took into account fluids and humors (Vigarello 1989). While childhood was thought of as a period of enormous malleability, the primary agents for correction were the surgeon and the nurse, and much attention was given to the practical advice provided by manuals on manners and etiquette. In the seventeenth century, a cautious renewal emerged, of which La Salle was but one symptom. Bodies had to conform to a code of elegance, to a courtly spectacle; they did so through the learning of performance skills: dance, theater, elocution. Theater was a privileged pedagogical device to teach young people how to perform in court society, as can be seen in the Jesuit schools (Varela 1983; Hsia 1989).

In the eighteenth and nineteenth centuries, however, these politics of the body changed dramatically. The body started to be seen as an organic machine, whose organic devices could be decoded. "The privileged image becomes the force whose perfectibility is increasingly and insistently underlined" (Vigarello 1978: 93). A new culture of the body emerged whose pivotal texts were not treatises on manners but textbooks on hygiene and pedagogy. The new assumption was that it was necessary to perform some work in order to gain strength, physical exertion that could be conducted according to scientific knowledge on how the body functioned. Thus emerged the arts of training the body. While decency and decorum did not disappear completely (and are still present today, as seen previously in Middleton's quote), the new catchwords for the body were potency, strength, force, vigor. Pedagogy was thought of as an *orthos-paidos,* and the correction and normalization of children's bodies through scientifically prescribed exercises became the principal concern of schools.

Vigarello stresses that "for the strength of the child to grow, both the child's power and the constraint exerted on him had to increase" (1978: 161). The objects of control were no longer passions but basically muscles and blood masses. Drills and repetitive exercises were to make the body more efficient and also more autonomous. There was a basic confidence in the resources and perfectibility of bodies. This optimism about nature's potentialities coexisted somewhat paradoxically with an increasingly rationalized perspective on how to control and improve its developments. Vigarello suggests that the price paid for this autonomy and confidence in nature was way too high when he lists the overwhelming array of disciplinarian practices, each more meticulous and repetitive than the next, deployed upon children's bodies in the form of gymnastic exercises, health controls, and regulations of posture and movements.

The Military: Uniforms as the Production of Modern Bodies

One of the major sites where this transformation in the politics of the body can be followed is the military, which itself has had an enormous impact on the spread of uniforming in schools. The influence of the military model in the history of education has usually been neglected. Accounts of how public schools emerged generally take into account the role of the religious orders and of the political dreams and designs of the Enlightenment. However, the military life also provided both signs and tactics that were to be adopted by civilians. As Michel Foucault eloquently puts it, "[h]istorians of ideas usually attribute the dream of a perfect society to the philosophers and jurists of the eighteenth century; but there was also a military dream of society" (Foucault 1977: 169). This dream, as I have argued, contained the image of an automatic body, of a perfectible social self, of a machinelike social life that could be trained through drills and exercises, and uniforms had a relevant role to play in attaining such a body.

During the first half of the eighteenth century, the increasingly sophistication of artillery as well as the lightening and increased speed of the musket and the invention of the rifle changed both tactics and the military organization. For example, the role and importance of the cavalry was displaced by the infantry, and gunmen were to march first, not the mounted officers as had been common; armies had to be reorganized in order to maximize the effectiveness of troops ready to penetrate deep into the enemy's field. A new tactic of maneuvers was developed, characterized by army corps capable of the shifting from marching to attacking in a quick and orderly manner. The soldier had to learn a new sense of docility and flexibility through long hours of repetitive training with his battalion. It was not mastery of combat that was expected from him, but that he would docilely go on marching under open fire (Ehrenberg 1983).

These transformations can also be read as political reflections on how to govern society. War provided a model for the education of citizens, and was itself a school for the people. The reformers of the French army in the 1760s and 1770s, many of them later officers of the revolution, thought that a new authority had to be established. As stated, a mutual relationship of service between the state and the people was established. Every citizen was potentially a combatant in that the state had to be defended (Ehrenberg 1983: 42ff). This political relationship disciplined the bodies of citizens by calling upon their bodily forces, and mobilized populations, reaffirming the bonds that tied them together. "Citizen" and "soldiers" were almost equivalent terms, an association that became much tighter with the revolutionary wars and the notion of the "nation in arms."

The reform of the military also involved the donning of uniforms. According to Daniel Roche, the purpose behind the standardization of military dress was less the tactical aim of making troops recognizable in action than the formation and training of bodies for combat (Roche 1994: 229). The uniform "imposes control, a source of efficiency and means to social power." But it was not only a means of coercion or repression; it educated, recognizing the significance of the citizen-soldier and affirming a political project.

The introduction of modern uniforms in the French army was part of a scaffolding of discourses that combined medical and health precepts, tactical rationales, and newly available materials and technologies. Before, costumes were used in parades or to distinguish its wearer in any social milieu; they were related to the code of elegance and bodily performances that I have described above. But by the mid-eighteenth century, uniforms were created to fulfill different demands. J. H. de Guibert, a leading reformer, complained bitterly about the excessive time and money devoted to military garments, but underscored that: "[i]t is to the excesses of uniform which I attack and not the uniform itself. Up to a point, it is necessary. It contributes to the soldier's health. It raises him above ordinary people. It puts him into the class of well off and happy citizens" (Guibert, 1772, quoted in Roche 1994: 230). The new decrees and orders of 1776–1788 established that uniforms had to be more flexible, more rational, and heed the laws of autonomy. They had to be easy to look after, simple to repair, light in weight, and convenient to put on and take off. They had to be functional and adaptable to different climates and geographies. The resulting shift in how bodies and uniforms were problematized is significant.

Daniel Roche argues that uniforms led to changes in manners, in a similar way that linen did. In campaigns that were long and distant from home, soldiers had to know how to take care of the uniform, and learned sewing and washing methods.[8] Uniforms, in this way, became vehicles for collective hygiene, inculcating habits of cleanliness to a large population. In a time when water and soap were scarce, and when, at any rate, water was thought more as a means of transmitting disease than as a cleaning or purifying medium, soldiers took pains to keep their uniforms tidy. Due to the fabric with which they were made, many uniforms had to be washed dry, with stones for scraping stains and bran to clean white cloths. Cleanliness became a sign that distinguished "decent people." Men got used to regular inspections and examinations; along with collective discipline, there was an increased sense of individuality that was to be measured in relation to a norm (Ewald 1990).

The Revolutionary: Uniforms as the Production of Equity

With the French Revolution, military uniforms took on other meanings. As a symbol of monarchic power, they were often contested, rejected, or even travestied in popular festivals that followed the fall of the Bastille. But the revolutionary wars quickly reinstalled a sense of uniformity, now transformed into a metaphor for equity. Rousseau's words were influential: "Fancy dictates [clothing], pride rules; it serves to distinguish wealth and rank. It is an abuse which cries out for reform; it would accord with the spirit of the regeneration of France to return costume to its original purpose and to egalitarian ways" (Considération sur les avantages de changer la costume français par la société populaire et républicaine des Arts, quoted in Roche 1994: 151). He went on to say that "wouldn't it be better to substitute for this vicious way of clothing a national costume, dictated by reason and approved by good taste? With a clothing more knowing than ours, men would become healthier, stronger, more agile, readier to defend their freedom; women would give to the State children who are well-nurtured" [les femmes donneraient à l'Etat des enfans mieux constitués] (quoted in Perrot 1984: 104). It is important to point out that, before and after Rousseau, similar proposals for a national costume were made; the historian of fashion Philippe Perrot mentions that between 1740 and 1803 at least five works were written by physicians recommending a uniform garment for all nationals (Perrot 1994: 203). This continuity of technologies and problematizations was in fact Foucault's point when he scarcely distinguished a pre- and postrevolutionary time in *Discipline and Punish*.[9]

However, the plebeian impulse catalyzed by the revolution refigured uniforms in such a way that they came to be distinguished as the most egalitarian garment, and this is probably the equivalence that made them so popular in the liberal republics of the late nineteenth century. The uniform became more ubiquitous as part of a double movement of becoming more plebeian and more impersonal, with a discipline enforced equally on officers and soldiers and with a systematic training for the roles with which the uniform was associated (Binaghi Olivari 1991). At the turn of the eighteenth century, uniforms were adopted by voluntary troops and by many other groupings such as musical bands or town servicemen. These civilian uniforms were known as "civic habits," a term that made reference to the religious origins of coats and cas-socks but that was also used as a contrast to monarchic power.

For many, this was a sign of secularization. Yet, even though notions of indi-vidual merit and achievement, obedience to a civic authority, and respect for a legalistic order introduced ruptures with the religious model, it should be noted that many of these assumptions were part of the same ethical system that they supposedly opposed. This emerging secular power, with plebeian tendencies, appealed to signs and ways of structuring authority and obedience that were not totally different from those of the kind of pastoral power that was exer-cised before. In fact, pastoral power was central for the liberal republics of the nineteenth and twentieth centuries (Foucault 1982). Uniforms were a signifi-cant device in the construction of this new type of national citizenship that combined conformity and individuality. As Daniel Roche puts it, "[u]niform is central to a utopian and voluntary vision of the social which reconciles the conflict between automatic docility and the concrete economy of the individual liberty in which the autonomy of each constitutes the measure of his obedi-ence" (Roche 1994: 229).[10] A new game of autonomy was at stake: the lan-guage of rights, liberties and the rule of law (unheard of in the experience of the Christian Brothers and charity schools) became integrated into a web of disciplinarian techniques hitherto devised for passive, servant subjects.

The utopia of egalitarian uniformation extended itself to schools, conferring new meanings to the tradition of homogeneous dress codes that was already present. A landmark in this process are the revolutionary plans of the National Convention, and particularly Michel de Lepelletier's plan (1793) proposing the adoption of children by the state in a national, compulsory educational system.[11] Robespierre, who was a member of the Committee for Public Instruc-tion, read Lepelletier's plan. Robespierre demanded ". . . that you [the Com-mittee for Public Instruction] decree that from 5 to 12 years of age in the case of boys, and to 11 years of age in that of girls, all children without any distinc-tion and exception will be raised in common at the expense of the Republic, and that *all, under the saint law of equity, will receive the same garment, same nurturing, same instruction, same care*" (Robespierre, reporting to the Com-mittee for Public Instruction the proposal written by Michel Lepelletier de Saint-Fargeau, July 17, 1793, quoted in Pellegrin 1989: 184; see also Chevallier and Gosperrin 1971, italics added). The "saint law of equity": what a good summary of the Jacobins' program.[12] Schools would be known as "maisons d'egalité" (houses of equity). The uniform was part of a program that was based on political, medical, and economic discourses, as it is seen in the goals Lepelletier imagined for national education: "To develop in children a good habit of life; to increase their powers; to encourage their growth; to foster them strength, dexterity and activity; to render them insensitive to fatigue, the rigors of the weather and temporary deprivation of the necessities of life" (quoted in Barnard 1969: 121). The body that was the object of such training practices and uniformation appeared as a bundle of muscles and blood, as an entity that had a power to develop, as the site of a labor that would extend the body's potentialities. Clearly, there was a sense of "empowering" children's bodies through a totalizing control of their movements and activities.[13]

The Medico-Sartorial Utopia and the Appeal to Nature

There was another plan that went beyond Lepelletier's proposal. Dr. Bernhard-Christophe Faust, a doctor from Westphalia, presented a project to the National Convention that provided "scientific grounds" for uniformising children. In his "[I]deas on a uniform and reasonable garment for the use of children" (Strassbourg, 1791), he complained that "our clothes are made of iron. They are the invention of barbarian and gothic centuries. To be free and happy, [one has to] break these irons." Clearly influenced by Rousseau, Faust argued that contemporary clothing was pernicious for children. They were clothed as adults, a fact that could only excite their senses and incite masturbation. One might be stunned by the appearance of this term in eighteenth-century literature, but according to Foucault it was precisely at that time that its use became popular to denote "abnormal" individuals and explain the cause of their pathology.[14] Dr. Faust's critique had clear social connotations that did not spare any social class: "the untidy and chaotic clothing with which peasants dress their children weakens their health; the visible inequity of fortunes gives some children magnificent garments while [it] provides others with rags that degrade themselves in their own eyes; finally, the closed habits produce material and psychological hindrances to them" (Pellegrin 1989: 185). The revolution had to be one of appearances too.

Following his Rousseauian inspiration, Dr. Faust proposed a deep reform in the clothing of children. He suggested that children wear a coat made of cloth, in a light-blue color, or even striped in white and light blue; the garment would be completed with a white shirt beneath, blue or white socks, and shoes. In winter a wool overcoat would be worn, identical to the lighter coat. The design of the coat or smock was similar to the Roman tunic.[15] It had to be very simple: opened in the front, without buttons, and with ample sleeves that let the air circulate, fortifying the limbs. The length of this tunic was not to exceed the knee by two inches. This garment was the same for both sexes, and children would use it from two years of age to fourteen in the case of boys and twelve in the case of girls. No indication was given on which garments they would wear after these ages.

Dr. Faust suggested that corsets, baleines, waistbelts, stockings, necks, ties, and culottes (underwear) were to be forbidden for children (Pellegrin 1989: 185). The reason was a theory that the body's humors had to circulate freely and without impediments. In a way, as Vigarello remarks, this was outdated medical knowledge, but one has to keep in mind that the notion of circulation was a privileged image in the eighteenth century, "the great metonymy for water" from physics to economy and medicine (Roche 1994: 464). All these constraints over the body would deprive children of their inalienable rights to indulge in innocent games appropriate to their tender age, would make them weak and frail, and later would make them heavy, clumsy, insensitive men "who are narrow-minded and are only good for servitude" (quoted in Garnier 1995: 105). An emphasis on the autonomy of the child emerged, which was to be further developed by Pestalozzi and other Rousseau-inspired pedagogists in the nineteenth and twentieth centuries.

Besides his medical knowledge, Dr. Faust knew and practiced the language of rights: "The child and the body have rights that should be sacred." The rights of the children were to be protected in order that they could become accomplished citizens; the right of the body was to reach its perfect achievement so that it could be mastered. The legal discourses of the revolution became mingled with the new politics of the body with the aim of turning it into a perfectible machine with an endless potentiality; this mingling produced a rhetoric of the "rights of the body" phrased in quite different terms than the ones we hear today. Dr. Faust ended his work with a quasi-religious invocation to the Frenchmen: "Your constitution, your freedom and your happiness rest on equity. Only when your children, reintegrated in the sacred rights of nature and in the happy state of childhood are dressed without any distinction with an ideal garment, uniform, open and free, embellished with the saint colors of the Nation and the Homeland, . . . a true and natural equity will be born among you, it is then that generous Nature will open its treasures and spread happiness and prosperity over France and her fortunate citizens" (quoted in Pellegrin 1989: 185).

Dr. Faust joined a large group of physicians who wrote about clothing and health in the second half of the eighteenth century. According to Daniel Roche, "clothing became an important way of expressing the new, less traditional, medical vision of the body" (1994: 463). Its legislation encompassed moral reform and social utopianism as well: clothing should restore freedom to the body and regenerate humanity. It was the time of the emergence of a new politics of health (Foucault 1980b), an increased medicalization that led doctors to intervene in more areas of social life. This was often done in the name of "nature," as can be seen in Faust's proposal. Drawing from Rousseau, most physicians thought that clothing could, as society, cause sickness, and that it was necessary to reestablish the body's natural freedom (Roche 1994: 465). Their medico-sartorial utopia consisted in a return to "nature," constructed through medical knowledge and moral regulations, which transformed into political moralities that supported the development of disciplinary power.

As a recapitulation of this section, I would say that the military reforms and the bourgeois revolution gave new impulse to the uniformation of society, particularly of children and the school population. The body became the site of a work to be done, of a potentiality to be exploited and developed; autonomy of the body and authority over the body were increased in parallel by the emergence of new disciplinary knowledge and technologies. Uniforms were adopted by the military as a way of training the body and turning it into a homogeneous and docile entity, but they also contributed to transformations in habits of cleanliness, social manners, conceptions of frontiers of private/public life, and gender roles, which produced new subjectivities. Uniforms were a significant device in the construction of a new national citizenship that combined conformity and individuality. In the French Revolution, they became strongly associated with notions of egalitarianism and social leveling. Children's bodies in particular became a matter of concern and increased regulation, and several plans for uniformizing children's clothing were proposed that combined a "return to nature" with medical knowledge and moral regulations.

This rhetoric of uniformation should not mislead us to think that social differences disappeared and the mass became homogeneous. The historian Keith Baker coined a neologism, dedifferentiation, to speak about the simultaneous individualization of human subjects and the universalization of their relations that took place during the French Revolution and afterwards (Baker 1994: 190). Dedifferentiation was a technology of power that proceeded through abolishing established differences and creating new legal apparatuses and politicizations. It appeared as the realization of a universal communion, but was at the same time the enactment of new differences. In this increased uniformation and undifferentiation, under a generalized leveling of all citizens, a subtle system of differences, no less profound, emerged, where detail and nuances were the critical point. Philippe Perrot speaks of a new sartorial regime centered on austerity and decorum (Perrot 1987); based apparently on a puritanical ethics that was opposed to luxury and ostentation, this regime in fact reshaped the map of social distinctions that was typical of early modern societies and established new hierarchies. Tocqueville observed that "the barrier has changed its shape rather its position" (*Democracy in America*, quoted by Perrot, 1994: 189). The detail "revealed" everything, and the skills and patterns of social observation and mapping became more refined. Personality and conformity were the new poles around which technologies of the self were defined (Perrot 1984: 107).

Concluding Remarks: Why Have Uniforms Persisted across Time?

I have argued in this chapter that school uniforms emerged and were transformed as part of disciplinary techniques "designed to hierarchize and normalize populations" through the regulation of bodies (Meadmore and Symes 1997: 182). These disciplinarian techniques, intended both to individualize and control people, can be broadly dated—not without risk of leaving outside important phenomena correlated to them—in the centuries that stretch from the decline of feudalism to the consolidation of modern nation states. While he refused to stipulate periodizations and successive stages for the different forms of power, Foucault acknowledged that the triumph of "population" as the basis of the government of society introduced deep changes in the ways society was managed and thought of, and that it brought about new techniques and devices, more centered on collective solidarities than in individual subjects with rights and duties (Foucault 1991; Rose 1990).

Yet uniforms were not abandoned, as happened with other contemporaneous disciplinary techniques such as corporal punishments or means for correcting the body's posture. Quite the contrary, they were a considerable success, a success that challenges us to rethink theoretically the way societies and schools change and the relationship between different regimes of power. By the end of the nineteenth century, school uniforms were adopted in several educational systems that were being nationally organized. To name but a few examples: in Queensland in 1875, the regulations of the Department of Public Instruction stated that "children must come to school respectably clothed and clean"; secondary schools prescribed uniforms beginning in 1912 (Meadmore and Symes 1997: 175). In Japan, uniforms were introduced in the Tokyo Imperial University in 1885, and then or soon after in elementary and secondary schools (McVeigh 1997). In France, students wore a dark cassock or blouse in schools at the beginning of this century; student teachers had a more elaborate uniform that consisted of a black frock-coat with gold palms, later replaced with a less pretentious outfit in plain cloth (Ozouf 1967: 91). In Argentina, elementary and secondary school students donned a white smock, the same as the Uruguayans, who also wore a distinctive blue ribbon, from the beginnings of this century onwards.

The reasons for this popularity are manifold and each case deserves an in-depth analysis that falls far beyond the scope of this chapter. I can however make some broader observations. Uniforms, particularly the aprons that became common in France, New Zealand, and South America, were the object of social hygiene discourses, replicating the medical model and its "war on microbes" declared by Pasteur and his acolytes (Latour 1988). There were, in the nineteenth and early twentieth centuries, changes in the ways the body was conceived and "corrected" or "reeducated" (Vigarello 1978); also, the austere sartorial regime grew firmer roots (Perrot 1987), and last but not least, new disciplinary discourses that prescribed how to think and act towards the infantile body emerged. All of these discursive changes were incorporated to school uniformation policies and gave them renewed support.

Despite these changes, there are remarkable continuities with the discourses that shaped the emergence of uniforms in the seventeenth and eighteenth centuries that I have described earlier in this chapter. For example, a connection can be easily established between the disciplinary techniques of the seventeenth and eighteenth centuries and the extremely zealous regulation of schools in the late nineteenth century, both of them distinguishable as two distinctive forms of modern power (Hunt 1996: 11; Foucault 1991). It might be the case that, while La Salle and the Christian Brothers would preside over a history of detail in the eighteenth century, as Foucault suggested, their dreams of a minutely regulated school life would only be realizable with the emergence of new techniques and knowledges. The normal school teacher, the national supervisors, the medical inspector, the textbooks produced en masse, and most of all the expansion of the juridical and military capacity of the state to enforce its rule made it possible to achieve a surveillance of small movements and small bodies, a surveillance that was based on a political awareness of these small things and gestures for the control of people (Foucault 1977: 141). On the other hand, someone could argue that the irruption of progressivism and its emphasis on self-regulation was a break with existing patterns. But it should be said that the medico-sartorial utopias of Rousseau and Dr. Faust are close relatives to the advocates of children's freedom and natural development, and that continuities might prove to be even greater than in the case of adult-centered pedagogies.

Alan Hunt advances an explanation for the changes and continuities of sumptuary laws that I find useful for dealing with uniforms as well. For him, it is rare that social change is effected by the displacement of one discursive formation by another one; instead, there are always processes of recombination, of coupling and uncoupling, that explain the dynamics of change. In the case of sumptuary laws, "the different discursive elements were present from the beginning; what changes is their respective 'weight' and the combinatory repertoires" (Hunt 1996: 41). In regard to school dress codes, it can be said that medical discourses, moral and economic regulations, political discourses of autonomy and obedience, reemerge in somewhat different contexts and with diverse arrangements, in a movement that both allows for transformation but maintains links with previous formations. For example, the notion of the body as a social property and of the outcast as a traitor or unfaithful citizen that emerged by mid-eighteenth century can find some parallels in contemporary practices on the enforcement of uniforms, which construct similar associations. Phillip Corrigan's memories of being the only child in a school of six hundred to wear a gray blazer instead of the required blue or black jacket, informs us of analogous effects: the breaking of a dress code put one on the position of outcast, immediately recognizable, humiliated, and separated (Corrigan 1988). Also, Guacira Lopes Louro's comments on her experience as a school girl in Brazil point to the collective appropriation of the body: dressed in school uniforms, the girls were made responsible for "representing the school" to the whole society. The uniform imposed the duty on its wearer of behaving well, appropriate and respectfully, at any place and at any time (Lopes Louro 1998: 19). The construction of the body as a social property, and of transgression as betrayal, has shaped the ways in which uniforms and dress codes were and still are enforced in schools.

The parallelism should not be pushed too far, though. These practices and semantic associations are inscribed within systems with a different definition of what "social" means, and what kind of loyalty is expected. In the twentieth century, the public welfare regime implied the substitution of a social being whose powers and obligations were thought of as social responsibilities and collective solidarities for a legal subject with rights and duties. New technologies (social security, child welfare) and new regimes of knowledge (experts, counselors, health visitors) gave way to different patterns of subjectification, of reward and punishment, of social recognition. There was a shift in moral regulation that rearranged the whole set of such patterns. Uniforms became signs to be read on a different social map, with new signs and topographies.

In this respect, credit should be given to the versatility of school dress, a fluent and economic way for embodying different patterns of social regulation and governing (Meadmore and Symes 1997). Uniformizations were and continue to be efficient disciplinary techniques because they are able to accommodate different discourses and power relations. The surface of uniforms has been written upon with multiple meanings: the need for docile bodies, the promise of social inclusiveness and equity, the care of the self. Uniforms have been talked about in the language of obedience to God, service to the State, the rights of the citizen, and the freedom of the child. Certainly, there are some features of this technique that allow room for accommodation and adaptation.

Between autonomy and docility, between freedom and normativity, uniforms have been part of the consolidation of modern forms of power that enhance autonomy while intensifying techniques of ruling and control. And that is still the case today: a new pattern of authority is being constructed, made of a combination of health discourses, bodily practices, marketing strategies, and cultural assumptions about the body (Courtine 1995). I hope it is by now clear why I think that contemporary debates on school uniformation policies that stay focused on an antagonistic and irreducible opposition between individualism and conformity are misleading and unproductive. As the Brazilian historian Denise Bernuzzi says, it is important to think beyond the opposition that distinguishes freedom and repression, natural body and artificial body, society and individual, not to deny their existence, but to analyze them where they have always been: inscribed in history, thus datable, provisional, plural, and most of all, closely intertwined. The liberties of the body always imply new responsibilities and coercions. The control of bodies, created with scientific and technical supports, occurred parallel to the discovering of new coercions to be outsmarted, new zones where to lose control, new mysteries and risks. To recognize the existence of these doublets does not imply that we give up the dreams of justice and liberty, but urges us to struggle for new spaces of freedom that both acknowledge our social constraints and strive in which we can expand the scope of our experiences.

Notes

I want to thank Tom Popkewitz, Marcelo Caruso, Gustavo Fischman, Miguel Pereyra, Pablo Pineau, Estanislao Antelo, Tomaz Tadeu da Silva, and Guacira Lopes Louro for giving me insightful comments on earlier drafts and for suggesting wonderful books for me to read They helped me in more ways than I can acknowledge. Also, special thanks go to my friend and colleague Valeria Cohen who assisted me in collecting information in Buenos Aires, and to the librarians from the National Teachers Library (Argentina) and Milbank Library, Teachers College, Columbia University.

1. I take the notion of scaffolding from Tom Popkewitz. He uses it to argue that teaching was shaped through a variety of discourses that contributed with heterogeneous statements to its definition as a pastoral work involving the salvation of the soul through scientific and professional knowledge (Popkewitz, 1998).

2. This does not mean that the body does not have a materiality itself, but that this materiality is only graspable through discourse and meaning (cf Butler, 1997).

3. "Genealogy," as a political project of writing history, was a gray, meticulous task that demanded relentless erudition in order to find the "myriad of events through which—thanks to which, against which—they were formed" (Foucault, 1984, 81). This approach would reestablish the singularity of the event, its disruptive power, and cut across our knowledge, interrupting the continuity of the administration of our future in order to shake it and destabilize it.

4. There are, and probably will be even more in the future, many critical accounts of Foucault's view of history, whose arguments range from the absence of agency to his use of incorrect historical information (Noiriel, 1994; Castel, 1994; Frijhoff, 1999, among the most insightful for me). Most of these critiques reduce his thought to one dimension—the dimension that most troubles the critic at that time (Connolly 1991: 208), ignoring a work that is complex and that has changed over time. While I do not want to reintroduce the notion of agency in order to open up a space for conflicts and transformations (see Rose, 1999 for a compelling argument on this), I agree with Frijhoff's affirmation that some of Foucault's works are based on a somewhat simplistic historical narrative (*Discipline and Punish* among them). But as this historian remarks, Foucault provides a good counterbalance to the tendency of historians to be epistemologically naive or eclectic in their way of constructing historical narratives. As I hope will be clear in this chapter, concurring with some critiques is not an obstacle for making use of Foucault's theories and observations.

5. This notion was used by Foucault in his study of ancient sexuality, in relation to which he pointed out four forms of problematization: fear, an ideal of conduct, an image, and a model of abstention

6. Because of space constraints, I will not deal with the impact of the Reformation and Counter-Reformation on dress codes, although their effects would be felt in the moral regulations that emerged in the seventeenth century I refer to Hsia (1989), Schmidt (1989), and Greven (1978) for accounts of how they shaped a "moral police" and particularly clothing behavior.

7. For example, in Venice, after the plague of 1347–1348, the Senate issued sumptuary laws that forbade the wearing of dark-blue garments to encourage general happiness (Hunt 1996: 36).

8. Roche says that it led to the permutation of gender roles, even though this only happened "for a while and to a degree." Soldiers had to cook, sew, mend, clean clothes. The essential objects a soldier took with him were needles, soap, leather paste, thread, spirits (Roche 1994: 33).

9. As Keith Baker (1994) has pointed out, the French Revolution poses several questions to a Foucauldian approach. In *The Archeology of Knowledge*, Fou-

cault said that "the French Revolution . . . does not play the role of an event exterior to discourse, whose divisive effect one is under some kind of obligation to discover in all discourses: it functions as a complex, articulated, describable group of transformations that left a number of positivities intact, fixed a number of others rules that are still with us, and also established positivities that have recently disappeared or are still disappearing before our eyes" (quoted in Baker 1994: 189). But in *Discipline and Punish*, Foucault emphasized the role of contingencies, eventualities, "the possibility that it could have been otherwise," although he refused to give the revolution a founding character. I agree with Keith Baker's remarks on what was missed in Foucault's account of this period: a more precise analysis of the technologies of power it created or reutilized, a more careful study of the conflicting discourses and technologies at play, an appraisal of its effects in the discursive formations and institutional apparatuses that were constituted confronting it or reclaiming it. That is why I will try to introduce some kind of "eventalisation" in my own account of the history of uniforms, signaling breaks and new discursive equivalencies that, albeit not entirely new (but what is entirely new in history?), were opened up by the event of the French Revolution.

10. There were also at that time other utopias about the sartorial regime Daniel Roche refers to a revolutionary measure taken in Year II that established freedom in garment: "No-one may constrain any citizen or citizenness to dress in a particular manner, on pain of being regarded as suspect and so treated, and prosecuted as a disturber of the public peace; everyone is free to wear whatever garment or whatever outfit of their sex they please" (Roche 1994: 58). Interestingly, "freedom" did not include cross-dressing or transvestism.

11. Michel de Lepelletier was a radicalized aristocrat who was assassinated by a royalist the day after the decree to execute the King was voted on (Lepelletier, despite having been elected as a noble, supported the execution). He became a martyr of the Revolution, and among his late papers, a plan for general instruction was found. The idea of adoption of the children by the state was not entirely new, nor was it a product merely of the revolution. Foucault quotes Joseph Servan who, in 1780, suggested that in order to become good soldiers children should be adopted "by the nation, and brought up in special schools" (Foucault 1977: 158). Servan, one of the reformers of the army who later served as minister of war during the first years of the revolution, was following Jean-Jacques Rousseau's project of confining Emile to a secluded and protected area that in this case was to be regulated by the *philosophe*. Again, the lines that bound utopian dreams with disciplinarian technologies can be traced to prerevolutionary France.

12. This program can be compared to two others The first one was written by Louis Philipon de la Madeleine in 1783. Philipon was a moderate lawyer who first opposed the revolution and had a minor appointment during the Convention. He proposed compulsory, free education for the poor people, which was to be of the "right sort" (limited intellectual teaching, farming, and physical education). The schools would provide food, clothes, and lodging. The food would be frugal (rye bread, water, and fruits), whereas the clothing would be simple but sufficient. Children were to go to school barefoot and bare-headed. Beds would be forbidden, and children would sleep on the floor or on the table, fully dressed and without any coverings or mattresses. Poor children thus would learn what was right and useful for their state (Barnard 1969: 42–43). The second was written during the radicalization of the revolution, by a Parisian "citizen of the Section of the Tuileries" who submitted his proposal to the *sectionnaire* or district popular association. It was similar to Lepelletier's plan in that it argued that

children belonged to the state and not to their parents; it went further in proposing a sort of popular surveillance of the ways in which children were raised. Anyone could report and denounce the parents of a child who was raised improperly. There would be no boarding schools, but children would be given the same clothes and would eat the same plain food. "They would learn to swim, throw the javelin, and spend stormy nights outdoors" (Palmer 1985: 156–157).

13. Uniformation also reached secondary and tertiary schools, particularly during the revolutionary wars and in the Napoleonic era. For example, the students of the lycées wore a military costume, rifle, and sword. One of the chief school punishments was to deprive the students of their right to wear the uniform, and instead oblige them to wear a "cloath of gross fabric" (Barnard 1969: 222). They were taught military maneuvers by army personnel twice a week. In 1815, with the Restoration, students were disarmed and had to use a "civil" costume, i.e., a bourgeois suit with a long hat (Gerbod 1968: 102). The Ecole de Mars, a military school created in 1794, had a special uniform designed by a painter that consisted of a blue tunic with red and white trimmings reaching the knees, which was worn with red trousers and black boots. A black shoulder-vest was used in which the words "Egalité" and "Liberté" were inscribed. Students were given two linen shirts as underwear (Barnard 1969: 142ff.).

14. Infant masturbation was among the "abnormalities" that Foucault sought to study in his lectures at the Collège de France in 1974–1975, and was also one of the planned volumes of the *History of Sexuality* that he never wrote. According to Foucault, the figure of "'the self-stimulating infant' appears at the end of the eighteenth century, within the field of the family and in a small, restricted space: the bed, the room, the body." "It is a universal secret that has to be unveiled, because it is the cause of all evils in the world, particularly of nervous and psychic diseases. It acts as a principle for explaining the pathological singularity" (Foucault 1999: 54–55).

15. The appeal of the Roman republic was quite widespread during the French Revolution (cf Baker 1994).

References

Ariès, P. (1962). *Centuries of childhood: A social history of family life* (trans. by R. Baldick). New York: Vintage Books.

Baker, K. (1994). A Foucauldian French revolution?" In J. Goldstein (Ed.), *Foucault and the writing of history* (187–205). Oxford and Cambridge, MA: Basil Blackwell.

Barnard, H. C. (1969). *Education and the French revolution.* Cambridge: Cambridge University Press.

Barthes, R. (1983). *The fashion system* (trans. by Richard Howard, Farrar, Strauss, and Giroux).

———. (1957). Histoire et sociologie du vêtement. Quelques observations méthodologiques. *Annales Economies—Societés—Civilisations* 12e. année, No. 3, Juillet-Septembre: 430–41.

Bernuzzi de Sant'A. D. (1995). Apresentaçao. In D. Bernuzzi de Sant'Anna (Ed.), *Políticas do Corpo. Elementos para uma história das práticas corporais* (11–20). Sao Paulo: Estaçao Liberdade.

Binaghi O. M. (1991). *L'Abito Civico. I corpi dell'antica provincia di Milano nei figurini dell'Archivio di Stato.* Roma: Edizioni Bolis.

Butler, J. (1993). Bodies that matter. New York: Routledge.

———. (1997). *The psychic life of power: Theories of subjection.* Stanford, CA: Stanford University Press.

Campbell, D. (1998). *National deconstruction: Violence, identity, and justice in Bosnia*. Minneapolis and London: University of Minnesota Press.

Castel, R. (1994). "Problematization" as a mode of reading history (trans. by P. Wissing). In J. Goldstein (Ed.), *Foucault and the writing of history* (237–52). Oxford and Cambridge, MA: Basil Blackwell.

Certeau, M., de. (1984). *The practice of everyday life* (trans. by Steven Rendall). Berkeley and London: University of California Press.

Chevallier, P. and Grosperrin, B. (1971). *L'Enseignement français de la Révolution à nos jours. Vol. II: Documents*. Paris and La Haye: Mouton.

Connolly, W. (1991). *The ethos of pluralization*. Minneapolis and London: University of Minnesota Press.

Corrigan, P. (1988). The making of the boy: Meditations on what grammar school did with, to, and for my body. *Journal of Education* 170(3): 142–61.

Courtine, J. J. (1995). Os Stakhanovistas do Narcisismo: Body-building e puritanismo ostentatorio na cultura americana do corpo. In D. Bernuzzi de Sant'Anna (Ed.), *Políticas do Corpo. Elementos para uma história das práticas corporais* (81–114). Sao Paulo: Estaçao Liberdade.

Cunnington, P. and Lucas, C. (1978). *Charity costumes of children, scholars, almsfolk, pensioners*. New York: Barnes & Noble Books.

Davidson, A. (1990). *Blazers, badgers and boaters: A pictorial history of the school uniform*. Horndean: Scope Books.

Donald, J. and Rattansi, A. (1992). "Race," culture and difference. Newbury Park, CA: Sage Publications/Open University.

Dussel, I. and Caruso, M. (forthcoming). *La invención pedagógica del aula. Una genealogía de las formas de enseñar*. Buenos Aires: Ed. Santillana.

Ehrenberg, A. (1983). *Le corps militaire. Politique et pédagogie en démocratie*. Paris: Ed. Aubier.

Elias, N. (1982). *The civilizing process. Vol. 2: Power and civility* (trans. by Edmund Jephcott). New York: Pantheon Books.

Ewald, F. (1990). Norms, discipline, and the Law. *Representations* 30: 138–61.

Foucault, M. (1977). *Discipline and punish: The birth of the prison* (trans. by Alan Sheridan). New York: Pantheon Books.

———. (1980a). Body/Power (trans. C. Gordon, L. Marshall, J. Mepham, K. Soper). In C. Gordon (Ed.), *Power/ Knowledge: Selected interviews and other writings 1972–1977* (55–62). New York: Pantheon Books.

———. (1980b). The politics of health in the eighteenth century (166–82). In C. Gordon (Ed.), *Power/Knowledge: Selected interviews and other writings 1972–1977* (160–81) (trans. C. Gordon, L. Marshall, J. Mepham, K. Soper). New York: Pantheon Books.

———. (1982). The subject and power. In H. Dreyfus and P. Rabinow (Eds.), *Michel Foucault: Beyond structuralism and hermeneutics* (208–26). Chicago, IL: University of Chicago Press, Chicago.

———. (1984). Nietzsche, genealogy, history (trans. by D. Bouchard and S. Simon). In P. Rabinow (Ed.), *The Foucault reader* (76–100). New York: Pantheon Books.

———. (1988). Technologies of the self. In L. Martin, H. Gutman, and P. Hutton (Eds.), *Technologies of the self: A seminar with Michel Foucault* (16–49). Amherst: The University of Massachusetts Press.

———. (1990). *The use of pleasure. Vol. 2. The history of sexuality* (trans. by R. Hurley). New York: Vintage Books.

———. (1991). Governmentality (trans. by R. Braidotti and C. Gordon). In G. Burchell, C. Gordon and P. Miller (Eds.), *The Foucault effect: Studies in governmentality* (87–104). Chicago: University of Chicago Press.

———. (1994). Hermeneutica del sujecto (edited and translated by Julia Varela). Ediciones de La Piqueta. Madrid, Spain.

————. (1999). *Les Anormaux. Cours au Collège de France 1974–1975*. Paris: Gallimard/Le Seuil.

Frijhoff, W. (1999). Foucault reformed by Certeau: Historical strategies of discipline and everyday tactics of appropriation. In J. Neubauer (Ed.), *Cultural history after Foucault* (83- 97). New York: Aldine de Gruyter.

Garnier, P. (1995). *Ce dont les enfants sont capables. Marcher XVIIIe. siècle, travailler XIXe. siècle, nager XXe. siècle*. Paris: Metailie.

Gerbod, P. (1968). *La vie quotidienne dans les lycées et collèges au XIXe. siècle*. Paris: Hachette.

Greven, P. (1978). *The protestant temperament: Patterns of child-rearing, religious experience, and the self in early America*. Chicago: University of Chicago Press.

Grosz, E. (1995). *Space, time, and perversion: Essays on the politics of bodies*. New York and London: Routledge.

Hamilton, D. (1989). *Towards a theory of schooling*. London, New York, and Philadelphia: Falmer Press.

Harvey, J. (1995). *Men in black*. Chicago: University of Chicago Press.

Hsia, R. P.-C. (1989). *Social discipline in the reformation: Central Europe, 1550–1750*. London and New York: Routledge.

Hufton, O. (1974). *The poor of eighteenth-century France*. London: Oxford at Clarendon Press.

Hunt, A. (1996). *Governance of the consuming passions: A history of sumptuary law*. New York: St. Martin's Press.

Hunter, I. (1994). *Rethinking the school: Subjectivity, bureaucracy, criticism*. New York: St. Martin's Press.

Joseph, N. (1986). *Uniforms and nonuniforms: Communication through clothing*. New York and Westport, CO: Greenwood Press.

Kidwell, C. B., and Steele, V. (1989) (Eds.). Men and women: Dressing the part. Smithsonian Institution Press.

La Salle, J.-B., de (1703/1833). *Les règles de la bienséance et de la civilité chrétienne, divisées en deux parties, à l'usage des écoles chrétiennes*. Lyon: Roussard, Imprimeur des Frères des Ecoles Chrétiennes.

————. (1720/1996). *The conduct of Christian schools* (trans. by F. de LaFontainerie and R.Arnandez). Landover, MD: Lasallian Publications.

Latour, B. (1988). *The pasteurization of France* (trans. by A. Sheridan and J. Law). Cambridge, MA, and London: Harvard University Press.

Le Goff, J. (1981). *Los intelectuales en la edad media*. Barcelona: Gedisa.

Lemire, B. (1990–1991). The theft of clothes and popular consumerism in early modern England. *Journal of Social History* 24(2): 255–76.

Lopes L. G. (1999). Pedagogias da sexualidade. In G. L. Louro (Ed.), *O corpo educado: Pedagogias da sexualidade* (7–34). Autentica: Belo Horizonte.

Lurie, A. (1981). *The language of clothes*. New York: Random House.

McVeigh, B. (1997). Wearing ideology: How uniforms discipline minds and bodies in Japan. *Fashion Theory* 1(2): 189–214.

McWilliam, E. (1996). Pedagogies, technologies, bodies. In E. McWilliam and P. Taylor (Eds.), *Pedagogy, technology, and the body* (1–22). New York: Peter Lang.

Meadmore, D. and Symes, C. (1997). Keeping up appearances: Uniform policy for school diversity? *British Journal of Educational Studies* 45(2), 174–86.

Middleton, S. (1998). *Disciplining sexuality: Foucault, life histories, and education*. New York and London: Teachers College Press.

Narodowski, M. (1995). *Infancia y poder. La conformación de la pedagogía moderna*. Buenos Aires: Aique.

Ozouf, J. (Ed.) (1967). *Nous les maîtres d'école. Autobiographies d'instituteurs e la Belle Epoque présentées par Jacques Ozouf*. Paris: René Juillard.

Palmer, R. (1985). *The improvement of humanity: Education and the French revolution*. Princeton, NJ: Princeton University Press.

Pellegrin, N. (1989). *Les vêtements de la liberté. Abécédaire des pratiques vestimentaires en France de 1780 à 1800*. Aix-en-Provence: Ed. Alinea.

Perrot, P. (1984). *Le travail des apparences, ou les transformations du corps féminin, XVIIIe-XIXe siècle*. Paris: Ed. du Seuil.

———. (1987). La richesse cachée: Pour une généalogie de l'austerité des apparences. *Communications* 46, 157–79.

———. (1994). *Fashioning the Bourgoisie. A history of clothing in the nineteenth century* (trans. by Richard Bienvenu). Princeton, NJ: Princeton University Press.

Popkewitz, T. (1998). *Struggling for the soul: The politics of schooling and the construction of the teacher*. New York: Teachers' College Press.

Revel, J. (1997). Machines, stratégies, conduites: ce qu'entendent les historiens. In D. Franche, S. Prokhoris, Y. Roussel, and R. Rotman (Eds.), *Au Risque de Foucault* (109–28). Paris: Centre Michel Foucault.

Roche, D. (1994). *The culture of clothing: Dress and fashion in the "ancien regime"* (trans. by Jean Birrell). Cambridge and New York: Cambridge University Press.

Rose, N. (1990). *Governing the soul: The shaping of the private self*. London and New York: Routledge.

———. (1999). *Powers of freedom: Reframing political thought*. Cambridge and New York: Cambridge University Press.

Schmidt, L. E. (1989). "A church-going people are a dress-loving people": Clothes, communication, and religious culture in early America. *Church History* 58(1): 36–51.

Shapiro, S. (1994). Re-membering the body in critical pedagogy. *Education and Society* 12(1): 61–79.

Spivak, G. Ch. (1999). *A critique of postcolonial reason: Toward a history of the vanishing present*. Cambridge, MA: Harvard University Press.

Sylvester, D.W. (1970). *Educational documents, 800–1816*. London: Methuen.

Symes, C. and Meadmore, D. (1996). Force of habit: The school uniform as a body of knowledge. In E. McWilliam and P. Taylor (Eds.), *Pedagogy, technology, and the body* (171–91). New York: Peter Lang.

———. (1999). *The extra-ordinary school: Parergonality and pedagogy*. New York: Peter Lang.

Synott, J. and Symes, C. (1995). The genealogy of the school: An iconography of badges and mottoes. *British Journal of Sociology of Education* 16(2): 139–53.

Varela, J. (1983). *Modos de educación en la España de la Contrarreforma*. Madrid: Ed. La Piqueta.

Vigarello, G. (1978). *Le corps redressé. Histoire d'un pouvoir pédagogique*. Paris: Jean Pierre Délarge.

———. (1988). *Concepts of cleanliness: Changing attitudes in France since the middle ages*. Cambridge and Paris: Cambridge University Press/Ed. de la Maison des Sciences de l'Homme.

———. (1989). The upward training of the body from the age of chivalry to courtly civility. In M. Féher, R. Naddaff, and N. Tazi (Eds.), *Fragments for a history of the human body. Part Two* (148–199). New York: Incorporations/Zone Books.

———. (1993a). *Le sain et le malsain. Santé et mieux-être depuis le Moyen Age*. Paris: Ed. du Seuil.

———. (1993b). Modèles anciens et modernes d'entretien de la santé. *Communications* 56: 5–23.

———. (1995). The life of the body in *Discipline and Punish*. *Sociology of Sports Journal* 12: 158–63.

10

Ideas in a Historical Web

A Genealogy of Educational Ideas and Reforms in Iceland

Ingólfur Ásgeir Jóhannesson

Introduction

The subject—the "text"—studied in this essay is the story of a government-sponsored reform in elementary education (covering ages six to sixteen), first proposed in the late 1960s, in Iceland. The reform, put forward by the Department of Educational Research and Development within the Ministry of Culture and Education (hereafter DERD), has been presented as one of the key links in a chain of projects toward modernizing Iceland. Educationists involved in the reform, whom I call reformers, typically argued for the reform on the basis of its power to improve society and move the country into the modern world.

The focus of the essay is on the rupture in the discourse on education that occurred in the 1970s and 1980s in Iceland. The rupture was a conflict between educational ideas and the practices of a rural country with its cultural traditions, on the one hand, and beliefs that educational reform should be based on scientific knowledge and modern curricular thought, on the other. While the essay tells the story of how the ideas that predated reform clashed with the reform ideas, its major purpose is to develop a conceptual framework for studying educational reform as well as the discourse on such reform. I have utilized the conceptual framework of the French sociologist Pierre Bourdieu, which he calls reflexive sociology (e.g., Bourdieu and Wacquant 1992), and the genealogical method of the French historian of systems of thought Michel Foucault.

In utilizing these approaches, I argue that I am indeed embracing "discursive understandings of culture," as called for by Bonnell and Hunt, a focus on educational discourses as cultural practices. They point out that "despite greater engagement of historians with sociology and sociologists with history, the much-discussed convergence of the two disciplines remains elusive" (1999: 5). This is so, they argue, because historians, and to a greater extent, sociologists, insist on their disciplines' foundations. The merging of reflexive sociology with a genealogical approach to history, on the other hand, by-passes such boundaries.

Genealogy

To interpret the story of how the educational reform in Iceland in the 1970s and 1980s conflicted with the pedagogy prior to the reform, I use a genealogical approach similar to that of Foucault (1971, 1972, 1977, 1980; see also Noujain, 1987; Luke, 1989; Popkewitz and Brennan, 1998). A genealogical analysis of history traces how discursive elements—e.g., educational ideas, pedagogical practices, social and religious beliefs—break up and reconnect to form new discursive elements and beliefs. Genealogy searches for continuities and discontinuities, ruptures and breaks in discourses and social practices, and it examines the relationship between these continuities and discontinuities. Such events I call historical conjunctures.[1] In this view, there is no intrinsic nature of an idea or a practice, or a fundamental source they can be traced to; rather, I trace the trajectory of an idea or a practice through earlier conjunctures of discourses. By trajectory I mean that the history of the reform is unique, yet it does have a logic which can only partially be uncovered as it is only partially predictable.

The main strength of the genealogical approach is that it enables us to see how the significance of these elements of discourse, which I call discursive themes, emerged in a particular place and time. How, for example, did the ideas of Martin Luther and the Icelandic storytelling tradition merge into a particular form of pedagogy? This is discussed later in the essay. Genealogical analysis differs from conventional historical approaches that tend to search for causal relationships or record the chronology of events. Therefore, I trace the connections of ideas and search for ruptures in the educational discourse. I focus on the specificities of the historical conjuncture of the reform, as opposed to relating the reform to universal explanations of modernity and evolution of societies. For instance, I do not claim that the connection between Lutheran practices and Icelandic traditions has universal explanations. Yet my goal is not to reject other history; as Foucault puts it, "critical and genealogical descriptions are to alternate, support and complete each other" (1971: 27). My goal is to offer an alternative account of how, rather than why, a particular pedagogy emerged at a certain time and place.

Social Fields and Legitimating Principles

To interpret how certain pedagogical ideas and practices gained value—symbolic capital—in discursive struggles, I have borrowed and adapted the conceptual framework of Bourdieu (e.g., 1984, 1985, 1988, 1990a, 1990b; see also Bourdieu and Wacquant 1992). The concept of capital refers to different forms of legitimacy for ideas and practices. These forms are, "principally, economic capital (in its different kinds), cultural capital and social capital as well as symbolic capital, commonly called prestige, reputation, renown, etc., which is the form in which the different forms [economic, cultural, social] of capital are perceived and recognized as legitimate" (Bourdieu 1985: 724). Examples of each form of capital are: for economic capital, money; for cultural capital, knowledge of art or philosophy; and for social capital, family relationships that can provide access to power. Here I focus on the cultural capital of certain ideas and practices.

Bourdieu focuses on the site of struggle as the key to understanding the structural relations and social strategies which result in producing different versions of capital. The site of struggle is the social field and what is struggled over is the legitimacy of ideas and practices; that is, whether these ideas and practices as discursive themes can become symbolic capital. An example could be the legitimacy of different testing and grading practices in schools. A practice such as the use of objective grades in numbers from one to ten, which is a form of cultural capital, has in discursive struggles gained value as symbolic capital. A social field, in Bourdieu's relational, structural definition, refers to the way of talking about social relationships as if they were taking place in geographical space. In this case, educational reformers and other individuals who fought battles became "players" in a field where they occupied certain positions that contradicted each other, such as arguing over the use of grading systems. It is interesting how this "game" takes place.

The Bourdieuean perspective draws attention to the processes (trajectories) of legitimation that shape the given social field. These processes I call legitimating principles. Legitimating principles are the chief analytical concept in the genealogical analysis in this essay. They consist of discursive themes that fall into patterns around these principles. They function as hierarchies of values in the sense that some discursive themes carry more symbolic capital than other themes. In studying these legitimating patterns by a genealogical investigation, I teased out the significance of the points of intersection by asking specific questions about the structured and structuring processes (that is, the legitimating principles) in the field of reform. How did a particular practice emerge and relate to other practices? How did, for example, written tests in Iceland relate to the storytelling tradition? How did they receive so much symbolic capital? On these trajectories, what can count as symbolic capital becomes restructured, which, in turn, restructures the legitimating principles. In fact, the term legitimating processes might better capture what I mean. Yet these principles are most of the time not particularly steady, hence the term legitimating principle.

The social field of educational reform in Iceland since the late 1960s is a site of struggles, structured around the spectra of legitimating principles that are the available means for individuals to make sense of reform. The discursive themes of the reform derived from developmental psychology, scientific curriculum theories, and progressive pedagogical approaches—the legitimating principle of reform—became the cultural capital of reformers, specific to the place and time. They employed the discursive themes of the reform as social strategies against the prereform pedagogy. The concept of social strategies refers to the way in which reformers became immersed, consciously and unconsciously, in reform work. The reform themes became a part of them because they internalized beliefs in the importance of the reform to improve education and society.

Discourses in Education in Iceland

This section focuses on the collision of discourses about elementary education in Iceland in the 1970s and 1980s. Employing the genealogical approach to understand this historical conjuncture, I observe educational ideas and practices in Iceland in patterns of discursive themes. These ideas and practices, discursive themes, fall into three spectra of historically and socially constructed legitimating principles that operate in the social field of educational reform in Iceland. These spectra are a reform versus prereform spectrum, a spectrum within the reform with technological and progressive poles, and a traditional academic capital versus curriculum theory capital spectrum (see, e.g., Ingólfur Ásgeir Jóhannesson 1991a, 1993b).

The "Stage"

Iceland is a rather rural country. Only 280,000 people live on an island of 39,000 square miles just below the arctic circle. The history of compulsory schooling in Iceland is very brief. The first educational legislation in Iceland to make schooling compulsory took effect in 1908 (the Education of Children Act of 1907). This legislation made four-year schooling compulsory for every child, ten to fourteen years old. Parents and guardians were expected to continue a practice of home education in reading, writing, and arithmethic, required since 1790.

New comprehensive legislation on education in 1946 (the School System and Compulsory Education Act and the Education of Children Act) required compulsory schooling for children from age seven to fourteen. By the 1960s, however, the educational legislation of 1946 had still not been fully implemented. Children in Reykjavík and many large towns went to school nine months a year for eight years. But in villages and rural areas the school year was shorter (seven or eight months), and in some cases children did not begin to go to school until the age of nine or ten. In addition, it was common practice in rural areas for children to spend only two weeks in school and the next two weeks at home. This meant, for example, that when a child turned thirteen, he or she had, perhaps, only a total of nine or ten months of schooling (e.g., Ísaksson, 1975).

The early 1970s was a period of rapid economic development. The inhabitants of the coastal villages were able to buy large trawlers with which they could fish in much worse weather than was possible with smaller boats; farmers equipped themselves with modern machinery; and the nation made a sudden leap into the modern world of consumption. Educational leaders and politicians believed that the education system should play a leading role in this development process.

In the remainder of this section I briefly discuss the ideas that had symbolic capital prior to the reform and how they constitute the preform legitimating principle. Then I discuss the ways in which discursive themes of the reform conflicted with preform themes and practices and argue that the rupture between the reform and preform themes was a discursive break with the tradition.

The Prereform Pedagogy Web

The term preform pedagogy, which I use when I talk about education in Iceland prior to the work of DERD, is a relational term; I focus on the differences between the earlier assumptions, priorities, and distinctions, on the one hand, and the discursive themes of the reform, on the other. In genealogical terms, I locate ruptures and points of intersection in the historical discourse on education in Iceland. Reformers often assessed the wisdom of the reform pedagogy in terms of how bad and elitist they believed the preform pedagogy was. To examine the preform ideas and practices, I have looked at secondary accounts that reformers, education researchers, and other writers have produced. Some of these accounts (e.g., Ólafur J. Proppé 1983) were produced to combat preform practices and therefore, highlight the differences, reformers believing it was necessary to distance their ideas from the preform pedagogy as much as possible. By highlighting the differences, these accounts illustrate how these views as cultural assumptions have a prescriptive quality about what should be taught, how, and why.

I have arranged this investigation around several overarching discursive themes. These themes are: knowledge and intelligence, excellence and achievement; congregational pedagogy and the Icelandic storytelling tradition, nationalism, objectivism, and written tests. Each theme is sketched out to emphasize the differences and continuities between the preform and reform pedagogy and the interplay of these relations. These sketches form patterns of cultural assumptions and educational traditions. Most importantly, cultural assumptions and educational traditions show a legitimating principle that conflicts with that of the reform.[2]

The first pattern I discuss is what I call cultural assumptions about knowledge and intelligence, excellence and achievement. Individuals who have accumulated a huge volume of knowledge—primarily cultural literacy in terms of knowing names, literature, and locations—are celebrated for intelligence in Icelandic society. Reformer Ólafur J. Proppé discusses the kind of knowledge and intelligence that is most valued among Icelanders. He argues that "knowledge which can be defined, documented and treated as law has high social status in Iceland." He also points out that in Icelandic culture intelligence "seems to mean something close to the ability to . . . acquire and recite knowledge", individuals are born with it, and people believe it is "more or less constant during each person's lifetime" (1983: 318, 319). The radical teacher Arthúr Morthens (1987a, 1987b) and U.S. sociologist Richard F. Tomasson (1980) have come to similar conclusions.

As I discuss later, I am particularly interested in the delegitimating effects such assumptions have had on reform themes, such as on inquiry teaching methods and process evaluation. In short, it is difficult to argue for pedagogical ideas or practices that contrast with the cultural assumptions about knowledge and intelligence, excellence and achievement as these cultural assumptions count as symbolic capital.

The second pattern I discuss is that of congregational pedagogy, a term borrowed from a study by researcher Thorsteinn Gunnarsson, which he uses to describe "the older dominant Icelandic pedagogical tradition." The term refers to a group of students in a classroom as if they were a congregation in front of a minister in a Lutheran church service. In the public school, "the teacher became the minister, the textbooks replaced the scriptures and the students represented the [passive] congregation" (1990: 42, 268; see also Gunnarsson and Jóhannesson, 1990). These pedagogical practices acquired symbolic capital that they carried with them into educational discourse. In turn, congregational pedagogy delegitimizes alternative suggestions about classroom practices. I shall, therefore, trace the trajectory of how these practices became conventional in the Icelandic context.

Strong links between state, church, and education in Iceland have a long history. After Martin Luther posted his theses on the portals of the castle church in Wittenberg in 1517, much of Northern Europe quickly converted to Lutheranism. Denmark was converted in the 1530s and Iceland in the 1540s and early 1550s. Today, over 90 percent of the Icelandic population officially belong to Lutheran state church congregations and, out of the remaining 10 percent, almost ten thousand people (more than a third) belong to independent Lutheran churches.

Carmen Luke has examined the conjuncture of pedagogy, printing, and Protestantism in sixteenth-century Germany. She associates a break in pedagogical principles and practices with Luther's work. To promote the new faith, Luther wanted to educate the public in his style, and for that task he needed a pedagogy. Luke points out that Luther "considered universal rudimentary literacy . . . essential in enabling all people to have access to the words of scripture" and that he wanted "a mass readership of the Bible" (1989: 11, 135). She explains how oral transmission and printing of Luther's pedagogical ideas complemented each other. The almost brand-new printing press allowed various religious interpreters (pastors, teachers) and later the general reading public access to Luther's ideas, in relatively "clean," unadulterated form.

These ideas and events are significant for the emergence of public education in Iceland, and, not surprisingly, the first book to be printed in Icelandic was the Bible in the sixteenth century (Sigurdur Bjarnason, 1989). In Luther's "ideal situation," it is important that "family and community members . . . gather together and listen to the reading of the holy word by those who were literate" (Luke 1989: 77). Furthermore, social historian Loftur Guttormsson, who has examined the publication of Luther's work in Iceland, argues that Luther's catechismus has become "by far the longest-living textbook in the history of Icelandic education" (1989: 176). Close ties between the church and the colonial state in Iceland, which in the late nineteenth and early twentieth centuries gradually became independent from Denmark, further paved the way for education to become Lutheran in style as legislation in the eigtheenth and nineteenth centuries gave the ministers responsiblility for children's education.

The Icelandic institution of the *kvöldvaka* (shared family evening) became the main channel for religious and cultural upbringing (Kjær, 1935; Magnús Gíslason, 1977). During the *kvöldvaka*, family members, servants, and others in the household sat together in the living room, working the wool and performing other household chores. It is believed that in every household there was at least one person who could read aloud fluently while others listened, worked, and discussed the stories. Originally this was an oral tradition, but the written word became more and more important and the text took over the role of the narrated story in the oral tradition.

The fusion of a storytelling tradition, Icelandic literature, religious literature, and the learning of reading needs a much closer consideration. But what matters for my purposes here are the myths of the *kvöldvaka* culture and the relationship of its pedagogical practices to public education; that is, how these myths in conjunction with the power of congregational teaching and other perspectives, such as nationalism, may have legitimized a certain form of knowledge and style of presentation. Thorsteinn Gunnarsson has described how the situation was at the beginning of "the reformist 1960s." He argues that the Icelandic school system was "meritocratic, tilted towards classical education, teacher and subject oriented and characterized by transmission of knowledge through lectures and recitations." Further, that the school system was "aiming at national unity" and that "the organizational realities of Icelandic schools such as fragmented lessons and fragmented and double-shift school days are much . . . friendlier to . . . congregational pedagogy than to an inquiry pedagogy" (1990: 49, 268).

Thirdly, I consider the impact of nationalism on educational perspectives in Iceland, in particular on history as a school subject. Gunnar Karlsson, professor of history at the University of Iceland (1982), has analyzed Icelandic history textbooks in the twentieth century. He places them in the context of a European tradition. History in Europe in the nineteenth century became nationalistic; the aim of the new history was to awaken patriotism and cultivate the idea that one was the citizen of a remarkable nation. Another aim was to celebrate the role of the individual and her/his abilities and achievements. To achieve these objectives, teaching methods looked to inspire the pupils with stories about heroes who fought and defeated evil for the good of the nation.

Jónas Jónsson, an educator and influential politician (he was minister of education for several years in the late 1920s and early 1930s), wrote *Íslands saga* (originally titled *Íslandssaga handa börnum* [that is, History of Iceland for Children] when he was supervising teaching practicum students at the Teacher Training College in the 1910s. His books tell the story of a constant struggle between Icelanders and those who suppressed and colonized the nation. (Norwegians and later Danes ruled Iceland from about 1262 to 1918 when Iceland received sovereignty.) Jónas Jónsson celebrates the "great" Icelandic men of history in terms of what they had achieved in the struggle for the independence of Iceland and how they contributed to the cultural identity of the nation.

The impact of this approach is, of course, interrelated to the congregational pedagogy that the books are based on; they tell a story that emphasizes continuity and is grounded in a specific version of truth. In *Íslands saga*, Jónas Jónsson unknowingly organized a knowledge base that still appeals to those of a variety of political stances, not only to the bourgeoisie and farmers but also to socialists, who tend to be nationalistic in Iceland (Thorsteinn Gunnarsson 1990: 47). This is typical of how discursive themes and practices intersect: cultural assumptions and pedagogical practices support each other to strengthen the power and persistence of knowledge that was considered useful in creating a cultural identity in the colonial struggle.

The fourth pattern I discuss here is objectivism, a twentieth-century thread in this web. According to Gunnar Karlsson (1982), objectivist history has no specific pedagogical aims and those who ascribe to the objectivist perspective in education have nothing except the conventional selection of content (facts, events, etc.) to rely on. Because explicit values are omitted, the objectivist approach fragments the knowledge into disconnected pieces, often called facts. A new series of objectivist history textbooks, written by educator and writer Thórleifur Bjarnason, was prepared in the 1960s (see Thórleifur Bjarnason [1966]/1970–1971). The new series paralleled the Jónas Jónsson books— Gunnar Karlsson (1982) has compared these two series and found out that the selection and sequence of material was almost identical.

It seems apparent that the Thórleifur Bjarnason books helped to legitimize the knowledge base that had been structured by nationalistic views, sanctioned by the need to inspire and empower people under colonial rule. As a consequence, a knowledge base sanctioned by nationalistic perspectives continued to determine what was considered important for children to know about the past for a long time after the colonial struggle had ended. Wolfgang Edelstein, a chief figure in the reform, described this very well in a speech to a group of historians in the 1970s:

> When historicism broke the web of meaning, the facts without references remained in the minds of many generations of pupils. At the same time, the older bourgeois contemporary goal was maintained as ideology. The historicism preserved the collection of facts and the honorable status of history. We know similar examples from religious history: The rituals remain when the power of the faith fades. (Edelstein, 1988: 181)

Similar examples of changes in the direction of objectivism are to be found in textbooks in geography, home studies, and civics (Thorsteinn Gunnarsson, 1990: 64–67). Also as part of this tendency, prereform biological sciences (botany, human physiology, and zoology) were taught as classification exercises, the teaching of Icelandic grammar was based on having children try to master rigid structures and rules, and poems were supposed to be learned by heart. The syllabus for elementary education, issued by the Ministry of Culture and Education in 1960, officially sanctioned these kinds of methods (Thorsteinn Gunnarsson 1990: 62). Triggered by the objectivism and congregational pedagogy, these were the chief teaching methods in Icelandic elementary schools, at least until the 1960s and the 1970s.

Finally, written "objective" tests have been and remain very common in Icelandic schools. Written tests were instituted in the 1920s and quickly became the major means of evaluation in Icelandic schools. A study of teaching practices in grades five to seven in 1987 and 1988 showed that 4.5 percent of the time in 667 lessons that the researcher observed was used for testing (Ingvar Sigurgeirsson 1994: 35). And it is safe to assume that the time used for tests may be much greater in grades eight to ten. Tests also seem to be taken for granted among most people in the country, educators and the public alike.

Written tests are particularly well suited to test knowledge that appears objective. They sanction the transmission of a nationalistic and fragmentary knowledge base that, once established, is difficult to change and appears objective because it has been stripped of its explicit values. And they are well suited to the cultural assumptions about knowledge and intelligence, excellence and achievement because they "objectively" report who is knowledgeable and intelligent.

In summary, the drawing of a web of cultural assumptions about knowledge and intelligence, congregational pedagogy, nationalistic views, and prereform scientistic ideas and practices, such as objectivism and written tests, enables us to see how these patterns are interwoven. Memorization of fragmentary, cultural literacy–type knowledge, taught in a congregational manner and tested

252   Ingólfur Ásgeir Jóhannesson

by "objective" tests, generates a historically woven web of ideas and practices. This constitutes an historically and socially constructed legitimating principle that favors certain types of pedagogy and curriculum work over others. This principle is the available means to legitimate current practices or delegitimate new work. (For a further discussion of the prereform pedagogy, see Ingólfur Ásgeir Jóhannesson, 1991a; 1991b: ch. 3.)

The Reform

As already noted, the reform in elementary education that was launched in Iceland in the late 1960s was put forward by a governmental agency, the Department of Educational Research and Development (DERD). DERD organized curriculum revision projects in subjects such as physics and chemistry, biology, mathematics, Christian studies, Icelandic, Danish, English, social studies, arts and crafts, and physical education.

In the reform discourse there is a pattern of scientistic arguments for democratic and child-centered concerns. There is a belief in progressive education; in particular, open schools were celebrated as models of the best reform practices. There is a belief in scientific curriculum models, such as the Bloom taxonomy (Bloom 1956; Krathwohl, Bloom, and Masia 1964) and the Taba curriculum spiral (e.g., Taba 1962; Taba et al. 1971), as well as in developmental psychology *à la* Piaget (1970) and Kohlberg (Kohlberg and Mayer 1972). Other themes include the belief that knowledge is a process, that the learner is active, that evaluation needs to be continuous, and that subject matter needs to be integrated. Common catch terms are, for instance, activity, inquiry, hands-on, integration of subjects, and integration of students.[3]

The reform measures were presented as the most important project of innovation in Icelandic education. Indeed the reform measures appear as a major change. For instance, the organization of many of the new school subjects— that is, the integration of previously separate subject matter such as history and geography into social studies, or zoology and botany into biology—signifies a major point of departure from the prereform curricula that were, by and large, structured around academic disciplines. The introduction of large-scale use of cooperative learning and other interactive teaching methods (Ingólfur Ásgeir Jóhannesson 1991a: Ch. 4.1) is also a departure from the prereform pedagogical tradition. Further, as discussed below, new perspectives on evaluation and testing also played a major role in the reform discourse.

Reformers highlighted their child-centered views as well as the importance of democratic school practice. Antitesting perspectives and the view of evaluation as process were instrumental in establishing a vision of democratic, child-centered reform in education. Antitesting rhetoric was used to challenge the teaching of what were depicted as useless facts, and reformers claimed that they could offer methods more child-centered and democratic than tests to evaluate children's progress. Reformers stressed the creativity of the child and democratic rights to evaluate her/himself by nonquantitative methods.

This reform movement was heavily criticized by conservative forces in the 1980s. Among the most outspoken critics were so-called traditionalists, including journalist-columnist Gudmundur Magnússon of the conservative newspaper *Morgunbladid* and Arnór Hannibalsson, professor of philosophy at the University of Iceland (Thorsteinn Gunnarsson 1990; see also Gunnar Karlsson 1984; Edelstein 1987).[4] In brief, the traditionalists argued that reformers were suggesting that the traditional perspectives of knowledge and intelligence, excellence and achievement were no longer viable in the school. They maintained that the "discovery" orientation of many reform projects could threaten the necessary cultural literacy–type knowledge base of children and adolescents. They thought that inquiry teaching merely suggested mindless busy work. Further, they argued that most contemporary psychology and pedagogy was nonsense, at best, and a leftist subversion aimed at destroying Icelandic nationality, at worst. In this view, everything concerning the methodology of teaching diverts attention away from serious learning; what is needed is simply a sound nationalistic knowledge base.

Testing practices were a much-debated issue in the 1970s and the early 1980s. Child-centered ideas of evaluating a child's progress by comparison to her/himself were manifested in the elementary school legislation of 1974 (the Elementary School Act). This law declared it illegal to use test results or grade point averages to identify the most "intelligent" child in a class. Instead, the reformers emphasized evaluation as a process, identified by the term *námsmat* (evaluation of learning). Simultaneously a "normal" (grading) curve was instituted for the elementary school exit examination in 1977.[5] Both practices were quite radical in their rejection of the use of "absolute" grades.

The normal curve and the nonquantitative stance of evaluation reform were equally disliked by the traditionalists who argued that they were imported ideas, unsuitable to Icelandic culture. The stance against traditional testing was depicted as reformers' celebration of stupidity and laziness, and the normal curve, by eliminating "absolute" grades, was criticized for giving inaccurate information about children's progress. For instance, Gudmundur Magnússon argued that parents have the right "to receive information about where their children stand *in comparison with other children*" (1989, original emphasis).

Given the high status of fragmentary, cultural literacy–type knowledge in Icelandic society, and the strength of the nationalistic knowledge base stripped of explicit values in the elementary school curriculum, it is easy to understand how difficult it was to introduce the idea that acquiring the ability to democratically cooperate and developing the skills to achieve knowledge through inquiry could be more important than memorizing and reciting. The notion of knowledge as encyclopedic fragments conflicts with the view that knowledge is an interactive process of social construction, and the notion of inherited intel-

ligence conflicts with the idea of "every child as an intellectual." The traditional Icelandic view of knowledge, in part revealed in the tendency to admire
intellectuals and celebrate historical figures from the country's past, sees intelligence as a trait. The traditional view is represented in the common cultural
habit of considering some families more intelligent than others—only because
they happen to be the ancestors of someone viewed as intelligent. A dialectical,
interactionist view of knowledge, screened through theorists such as Kohlberg
and Mayer (1972), conflicts with such a perspective. The myth of intelligence
as a biological trait seems indeed to be an important factor in explaining the
difficulty in accepting interactionist views of knowledge in Iceland.

By presenting itself in opposition to the prereform pedagogy, reform has
become a legitimating principle, capable of structuring a social field of educational reform that is based on a sense of logic different from that of the larger
field of education and different from the logic of other intellectual fields. It does
not matter whether the prereform pedagogy was in fact plagued by uncritical
transmission of outdated facts. What matters is the ability of the reformers to
present inquiry learning and hands-on pedagogy as different from and better
(that is, more democratic, more scientific) than the prereform pedagogy. What
matters is the ability to create a vision of a child-centered democratic reform—
the ability to challenge the old hierarchy of values and structure the new arena
that I have named the field of educational reform.

Epistemological or discursive break?

The break between the two legitimating principles—the one of the reform and
the one of the prereform tradition—may stem in part from epistemological differences; that is, transmission of knowledge as fixed versus interactive models
of knowledge acquisition, testing of facts versus evaluation as a process, pre-
scientific knowledge of the child versus scientific knowledge of the "learner,"
and so forth. But epistemological differences never turn automatically into discursive conflicts; epistemological differences become discursive conflicts in a
conjuncture of historical and political conditions. Therefore, if the reform is a
rupture with the prereform tradition, it is much more a political rupture, "produced" by those who believe they can benefit from reversing the hierarchy of
educational values, than it is an epistemological break.

Reformers made a considerable effort to establish the argument that the
reform policies were different from previous school practices and more effective in bringing about progressive social change. Undermining that argument
was that various themes and practices, such as inquiry pedagogy, had been presented earlier in the century without becoming mainstream, and elements of
modernist thought, such as written tests, can be identified in the prereform
principle of legitimation. In an ironic way, the contest with the traditionalists,
in which reformers were defeated politically speaking, may have helped the

reformers to capitalize on the theme that the reform movement was fundamentally different from the allegedly nondemocratic tradition. After all, the reform was directed against an old system that was deemed unsuitable for education in a democratic and scientific modern society. Consequently, the protradition criticisms may, to some extent, have benefited the political process of claiming credibility for the reform as different from traditional school practices. To use the Bourdieuean approach: the social strategies of both parties rested in their beliefs in the ideas and practices—discursive themes—that they argued for. These struggles resulted in the conversion of cultural capital into symbolic capital.

This was in part possible because of the fact that the field of educational reform in Iceland has emerged as an intermediate field, relatively open to unconventional discursive themes and nontraditional people. By an intermediate field, I mean that it is in a "gray" area in the social space, one in which it is not easy to establish what "rules" and capital are most valued, as opposed to more conventionally defined fields such as law, medicine, history, biology, and labor relations (class struggle, in a more traditional Marxist language). The field of educational reform in Iceland, emerging in the last twenty-five to thirty years, is an intermediate field in which what works as capital had not been determined by convention (Ingólfur Ásgeir Jóhannesson 1993a). Therefore, it is reasonable to expect social strategies in this field to be unconventional; that is, it is a space where unusual kinds of capital and strategies may become successful.

I have identified what I call the professionalization of progress and educational expertise (Ingólfur Ásgeir Jóhannesson 1991a, 1991b, 1993a, 1993b). By professionalization of progress and educational expertise I mean that reformers were able to tie the goal of improving education for children to modern science and rationality in a vein similar to the public rhetoric of schooling in the United States that emerged in the late ninteenth century within professional communities (Popkewitz 1991). In other words, scientist arguments for progressive social goals were put forward by experts who sought to "take care of business."

In light of the fact that there is an increasing number of institutions involved in reform work and an increasing number of people participating in debates on educational innovations or attached to the reform through social networks, it is safe to suggest that the reform hierarchy of values is now the primary object of contestation in the field of educational reform. A new principle of legitimation, that of reform, strives to separate itself from as many of the existing practices and principles as possible. Thus reform signifies a political and discursive break in educational politics in Iceland.

Summary and Reflections

Events, such as the reform in elementary education in Iceland in the last twenty-five to thirty years, can be interpreted as a historical conjuncture with a unique trajectory. By employing the notions of genealogy and legitimating principles, it is possible to portray how the reformers carved out a space—a relationally constructed social field—where social strategies converted previously less-valued discursive themes (educational theory, democratic, child-centered goals, etc.) into symbolic capital (educational expertise, teacher professionalism, etc.).

The insertion of a reform discourse and the formation of a field signifies a rupture in the discursive practices in education in Iceland. The rupture is identified by a new type of discourse: academic discussions and debates on education only existed to a limited extent prior to the reform. Although many of the specific reform measures were previously known, never before had such ideas counted as symbolic capital. Never before had the idea of the active child or other reform themes been able to cause a discursive rupture. Never before had there been an emergence of a social field around education reform discussions. Even though the reform proposals may not have been broadly implemented in the schools, the insertion of a discourse on educational reform and the formation of a field of reform, with the professionalization of progress and educational expertise as a major tenet, nevertheless took place (Ingólfur Ásgeir Jóhannesson 1993a). Further, prior to the reform, educational theory was not a separate academic discipline in Iceland (in fact, all social sciences have a short history in Iceland). Now, in the 1990s, educational theory, developmental psychology, and so forth are taken for granted. Therefore, the social strategies employed to make political advances for the emerging field of educational reform were especially unpredictable; educational theories such as developmental psychology and curricular taxonomies were so new in the Icelandic context that there were no "rules of the game."

The research presented in this essay belongs to a growing body of historical and sociological research in education that represents a departure from historicism to a genealogy of the educational ideas or, in the language adopted here, discursive themes (e.g., Luke 1989; Lather 1991; Popkewitz 1991; Labaree 1992; Popkewitz and Brennan 1998). I have traced these themes—not to record when they were "invented"—but to understand how they were introduced into new discursive contexts, to understand how they merged or contrasted with existing themes and practices in a way that created different discursive themes. The concept of legitimating principles "combines" the genealogical method to the analysis of social fields. Legitimating principles are historically and socially constructed in the struggles over what counts as capital in the social field—in this case, the field of reform.

While I tell my story as a story, and believe that doing so is an important part of the interpretation (see also Ingólfur Ásgeir Jóhannesson 1993b: 348–49), the narrative is focused through the lens of a comprehensive conceptual framework; that is, through looking at relations between individuals, discursive themes, and institutions in a social field. The method of telling a story through such a lens also represents a departure from historicism and conventional critical history.

There are many advantages to this type of theorizing. While Foucault, Bourdieu, and their followers (often nicknamed "the posties") have been criticized by neo-Marxists for despair and pessimism, their theories said to be unsuitable for studying change (e.g., Ingólfur Ásgeir Jóhannesson 1993c), one of the greatest assets of the concepts of discursive themes, legitimating principles, capital, and social field is indeed their suitability for studying change. From the Bourdieuean perspective, struggles in the field of educational reform are seen as struggles for the currency of the discursive themes and practices that an individual wants to be counted as capital. This perspective is suited to a search for ruptures that can be exploited; discursive themes are disconnected from each other and then reconnected. In short, I believe that arguing for the potential of a progressive curriculum theory, based on and supported by, for instance, feminist pedagogy, as opposed to scientific curriculum theory, based on, for instance, developmental psychology, would be a utilization of the rift between technological and progressive views that can be found among reform themes.

The preoccupation with producing progress, in research and practice alike, often prevents reformers from taking a reflective stance on the foundations of reform proposals. The belief in historical progress, scientific knowledge, and the power of schooling to change society leads reformers to view progress and change as natural. This tends to make reformers try to find someone or something external to blame when what had once been seen as an excellent solution is later perceived as a failure. The relational, genealogical framework, on the other hand, encourages the researcher to be critical of the assumption that research ought to give a direct and "utilitarian" guidance for intervention.

By being critical of the idea that education should produce progress and that schools can change society, reflexive sociology à la Bourdieu and genealogical analysis à la Foucault offer the possibility of being involved in "progressive" work in education without being "stuck" in it (Ingólfur Ásgeir Jóhannesson 1993b 1998). My awareness of the epistemological and historical bases of, for instance, the social studies project is not a reason to shelve my convictions that subject matter integration, inquiry learning, or process evaluation are useful devices in preparing children for democratic participation in society. But this awareness certainly distances my psychological self because it enables me to think more about how I think. As Patti Lather puts it, we must adopt "a discursively reflexive position which recognizes how our knowledge is mediated by the concepts and categories of our understanding" (1991: 39). Seeing the symbolic character of progressive positions as they serve to create distinctions from other positions and stances in the field of reform helps one to avoid the temptation to think that a proposal is essentially good for children merely because it is based on democratic and child-centered beliefs. Thus the Bourdieuean framework, where positions and stances are objectified as social strategies to gain capital, provides researchers and practioners in the field with the potential of being reflective on their involvement in the symbolic struggles in the field without blaming themselves for failures.

Notes

Brief sections of the essay have previously appeared in the *Journal of Education Policy*, published by Taylor and Frances Ltd. (see Ingólfur Ásegeir Jóhannesson 1993b). Special thanks to David Shutkin, Sigurjón Myrdal, Ólafur J. Proppé, Hannu Simola, Thorsteinn Gunnarsson, Ingvar Sigurgeirsson, and my advisor Thomas S. Popkewitz who have spent uncounted hours discussing various aspects of this research. Grants from the Icelandic Science Council in 1991 and 1994 have also helped to prepare the essay.

1. The concept *conjuncture* is used here in a more narrow sense than the French *Annales* school of history and historian Fernand Braudel (1980) use it. In my usage, conjuncture is more closely equivalent to a "complicated event" or somewhere between event and conjuncture as Braudel uses these terms.

2. The description of the prereform web is based on an extensive analysis of original and secondary sources. The secondary sources include work written in English, Icelandic, Danish, Norwegian, and Swedish (e.g., Arthúr Morthens 1987a 1987b; Edelstein 1987 1988; Fox 1990; Gunnar Karlsson 1980 1982; Kjær 1935; Loftur Guttormsson 1989; Luke 1989; Magnús Gíslason 1977; Ólafur J. Proppé 1983; Sigurdur Bjarnason 1989; Thorsteinn Gunnarsson 1990; Thorsteinn Gunnarsson and Ingólfur Ásgeir Jóhannesson 1990; Tomasson 1980).

3. The identification of the discursive themes of the reform is based on investigations and analyses of various types of sources. They include, but are not limited to, a draft of the *General Syllabus for Elementary Schools* (1983), the elementary school teachers' union *School Policy* (1990), information about what was emphasized in teacher education institutions in Iceland around 1980 (among other sources are classnotes), conference proceedings, debates on crucial issues, interviews with teacher leaders and teacher educators, letters and correspondences, and unpublished materials, as well as secondary sources.

4. Arnór's statement refers to the fact that in a social studies textbook for nine-year-old children, Tanzania is used as an example of how people in warm countries live.

5. Between 1977 and 1984, the grades of the students exiting the Icelandic elementary school were placed on a normal curve in four centralized examinations. Seven percent of the students in each subject matter were given a grade of A, 24 percent received a B, 31 percent received a C, 24 percent received a D, and 7 percent received an E. Ragnhildur Helgadóttir, the conservative minister of culture and education from 1983 to 1985, discontinued the unpopular grading practice before the examinations were held in 1985.

References

Following tradition, Icelandic individuals are referred to by first and last names in citations, for example: (Gunnar Karlsson 1980), and alphabetically ranked by first name.

Andri Ísaksson. (1975). "Education." In *Iceland 874–1974* (310–22). Reykjavík: Central Bank of Iceland.

Arnór Hannibalsson. (1983). Um sögu og menntastefnu. [On history and educational policy]. *Morgunbladid*. December 7.

Arthúr Morthens. (1987a). *Hvordan formålsparagrafens intensjoner realiseres in grunnskolen* [Norwegian]. [How the intentions of the goal article in the Elementary School Act are practiced in elementary schools]. Thesis (hovedoppgave) toward a degree in special education. Oslo: State Special Education Teachers College.

———. (1987b) I hvilken grad realiseres formålsparagrafens intensjoner i den islandske grunnskolen? [To what extent is the goal article in the Elementary School Act practiced in Icelandic elementary schools?]. An occasional paper, a summary of 1987a.

Bloom, B. S. (Ed.). (1956). *Taxonomy of educational objectives: The classification of educational goals. Handbook I: Cognitive domain*. New York: David McKay.

Bonnell, V. E. and Hunt, L. (1999). Introduction. In V. E. Bonnell and L. Hunt (Eds.), *Beyond the cultural turn: New directions in the study of society and culture* (1–32). Berkeley: University of California Press.

Bourdieu, P. (1984). *Distinction: A social critique of the judgment of taste* (trans. by R. Nice). Cambridge, MA: Harvard University Press.

———. (1985). Social space and the genesis of groups (trans. by R. Nice). *Theory and Society* 14: 723–44.

———. (1988). *Homo academicus* (trans. by P. Collier). Stanford: Stanford University Press.

———. (1990a). *The logic of practice* (trans. by R. Nice). Stanford: Stanford University Press.

———. (1990b). *In other words: Essays towards a reflexive sociology* (trans. by M. Adamson). Stanford, CA: Stanford University Press.

Bourdieu, P. and Wacquant, J. D. (1992). *An invitation to reflexive sociology*. Chicago: University of Chicago Press.

Braudel, F. (1980). *On history* (trans. by S. Matthews). Chicago: University of Chicago Press.

Edelstein, W. (1987). The rise and fall of the social science curriculum project in Iceland 1974–1984: Reflections on reason and power in educational progress. *Journal of Curriculum Studies* 19(1): 1–23. [Often referred to as Edelstein 1986, because of a typo on page 1 in the journal.]

———. (1988). *Skóli-nám-samfélag* [School, learning, society]. Reykjavík: Idunn.

Education of Children Act (Lög um frædslu barna). (1907, November 22). No. 59.

Education of Children Act (Lög um frædslu barna). (1946, April 29). No. 34.

Elementary School Act (Lög um grunnskóla). (1974, May 21). No. 63.

Foucault, M. (1971). Orders of discourse (trans. by R. Swyer). *Social Science Information*, (10)2, 7–30.

———. (1972). *The archaeology of knowledge* (trans. by A. M. S. Smith). New York: Harper & Row.

———. (1977). Nietzsche, genealogy, history. In D. F. Bouchard (Ed.), *Language, counter-memory, practice: Selected essays and interviews* (trans. by F. F. Bouchard and S. Simon). Ithaca, NY: Cornell University Press.

———. (1980). In C. Gordon (Ed.), *Power/Knowledge: Selected interviews and other writings 1972–1977*. (trans. by C. Gordon, L. Marshall, J. Mepham, and K. Soper). New York: Pantheon.

Fox, G. T. (1990). *Cocoon or butterfly? A study of schools that have transformed themselves to a university level education*. Reykjavík: Ministry of Culture and Education.

General syllabus for elementary schools. (1983). (*Adalnámskrá grunnskóla. Almennur hluti.- Drög.*) Reykjavík: Ministry of Culture and Education.

Gudmundur Magnússon. (1984). Um skilning og throska barna. [On understanding and development in children]. *Morgunbladid.* February 18.

———. (1989). Betur má ef duga skal. [Not yet good enough]. *Morgunbladid.* April 11.

Gunnar Karlsson. (1980). Icelandic Nationalism and the Inspiration of History. In *The Roots of Nationalism: Studies in Northern Europe* (ed. by Rosalind Mitchison) (77–89). Edinburgh: John Donald.

———. (1982). Markmid sögukennslu. Söguleg athugun og hugleidingar um framtídarstefnu." [The aim for teaching history. Historical investigation and reflection on future policy]. *Saga* 20: 173–222.

———. (1984). Sögukennsluskammdegid 1983/84. [The long winter-nights of history teaching]. *Tímarit Máls og menningar* 45: 405–15.

Ingólfur Ásgeir Jóhannesson. (1989). Wolfgang Edelstein og fagvitund kennara [Edelstein and teachers' occupational consciousness]. *Skírnir* 163: 459–71.

———. (1991a). *The formation of educational reform as a social field in Iceland and the social strategies of educationists 1966–1991.* A thesis submitted in partial fulfillment of the requirements for the degree of Doctor of Philosophy (Curriculum and Instruction). University of Wisconsin-Madison.

———. (1991b). ¿Por qué estudiar las reformas y los reformadores? La formación en la reforma educativa como campo social en Islandia 1966–1991 [Why study reform and reformers? The formation of educational reform as a social field in Iceland 1966–1991]. *Revista de educación* 296: 99–135.

———. (1993a). Professionalization of progress and expertise among teacher educators in Iceland. A Bourdieuean interpretation. *Teaching and Teacher Education* 9: 269–81.

———. (1993b). Principles of legitimation in educational discourses in Iceland and the production of progress. *Journal of Education Policy* 8: 339–51.

———. (1993c). Bourdieu and Neo-Marxist educational theorists in Great Britain and the United States. Presentation at the Annual Convention of the American Educational Research Association, Atlanta, April 12–16.

———. (1998). Genealogy and progressive politics: Reflections on the notion of usefulness. In T. S. Popkewitz and M. Brennan (Eds.), *Foucault's challenge: Discourse, knowledge, and power in education* (297–315). New York: Teachers College Press.

Ingvar Sigurgeirsson. (1994). *Notkun námsefnis í 10–12 ára deildum grunnskóla og vidhorf kennara og nemenda til thess* [The use of curriculum materials in classes with ten to twelve year old children and teachers' and students' perspectives of these materials]. Reykjavík: Research Institute of the Icelandic College of Education.

Jónas Jónsson. (1915–1916/1966). *Íslands saga.* (2 vol.) Reykjavík: State Textbook Publishing House. (Originally entitled *Íslandssaga handa börnum*) [History of Iceland for children.]

Kjær, Holger. (1935). *Kampen om Hjemmet. Nordisk Folkeopdragelse. Fortid og Fremtid* [in Danish] [The struggle about the home. Nordic public upbringing. Past and present]. Copenhagen: Gad.

Kohlberg, L. and Mayer, R. (1972). Development as the aim of education. *Harvard Educational Review* 42: 449–96.

Krathwohl, D. R., Bloom, B. S., and Masia, B. B. (1964). *Taxonomy of educational objectives: The classification of educational goals. Handbook II: Affective domain.* New York: David McKay.

Labaree, D. F. (1992). Power, knowledge, and the rationalization of teaching: A genealogy of the movement to professionalize teaching. *Harvard Educational Review* 62: 123–54.

Lather, P. (1991). *Getting smart: Feminist research and pedagogy with/in the postmodern.* New York: Routledge.

Loftur Guttormsson. (1989). Áhrif sidbreytingarinnar á althydufrædslu [The reformation's impact on public education]. In Gunnar Kristjánsson and Hreinn Hákonarson (Eds.), *Lúther og íslenskt thjódlíf* [Luther and the Icelandic culture and history] (173–91). Reykjavík: Skálholt and The Icelandic Luther Association.

Luke, C. (1989). *Pedagogy, printing, and Protestantism: The discourse on childhood.* Albany: State University of New York Press.

Magnús Gíslason. (1977). *Kvällsvaka: en islandsk kulturtradition belyst genom studier i bondebefolkningens vardagsliv och miljö under hälften av 1800-talen og början av 1900-talen* [in Swedish]. [Kvöldvaka: an Icelandic cultural tradition as observed through studies of farmers' daily life in the latter half of the 1800s and the beginning of the 1900s]. Uppsala: Uppsala University.

Noujain, E. G. (1987). History as genealogy: An exploration of Foucault's approach to history. In A. Phillips Griffith (Ed.), *Contemporary French philosophy* (157–74). New York: Cambridge University Press.

Ólafur J. Proppé. (1983). *A dialectical perspective on evaluation as evolution: A critical view of assessment in Icelandic schools.* Thesis submitted in partial fulfillment of the requirements for the degree of Doctor of Philosophy in Education in the Graduate College of the University of Illinois at Urbana-Champaign.

Piaget, J. (1970). *Genetic epistemology* (trans. by Eleanor Duckworth). New York: Columbia University Press.

Popkewitz, T. (1991). *A political sociology of educational reform: Power/Knowledge in teaching, teacher education, and research.* New York: Teachers College Press.

Popkewitz, T. and Brennan, M. (1998). *Foucault's challenge: Discourse, knowledge, and power in education.* New York: Teachers College Press.

School Policy (1990) (3rd ed.). (Full title is *Skólastefna Kennarasambands Íslands. Mennt er máttur* [The school policy of the Teachers' Union of Iceland: Education is power]). Reykjavík: The Teachers' Union of Iceland.

School System and Compulsory Education Act (Lög um skólakerfi og frædsluskyldu). (1946, April 10). No. 22.

Sigurdur Bjarnason. (1989). Um thydingarstarf Odds Gottskálkssonar [On the translations of Oddur Gottskálksson]. In Gunnar Kristjánsson and Hreinn Hákonarson (eds.), *Lúther og íslenskt thjódlíf* [Luther and the Icelandic culture and history] (67–73). Reykjavík: Skálholt and Icelandic Luther Association.

Taba, H. (1962). *Curriculum development: Theory and practice.* New York: Harcourt, Brace and World.

Taba, H. et al. (1971). *A teacher's handbook to elementary social studies: An inductive approach.* Reading, MA: Addison-Wesley.

Thórleifur Bjarnason. ([1966] / 1970–1971). *Íslandssaga.* (2 vol.) [History of Iceland]. Reykjavík: State Textbook Publishing House.

Thorsteinn Gunnarsson. (1990). *Controlling curriculum knowledge: A documentary study of the Icelandic social science curriculum project (SSCP) 1974–1984.* A dissertation presented to the faculty of the College of Education, Ohio University.

Thorsteinn Gunnarsson and Ingólfur Ásgeir Jóhannesson. (1990). Safnadarkennsla eda uppeldisfrædi til framsóknar. Átök um skólastefnu [Congregational teaching or pedagogy for progress? The struggle over educational politics]. *Ny menntamál* 8(2): 14–22.

Tomasson, R. F. (1980). *Iceland: The first new society.* Minneapolis: University of Minnesota Press.

11
Literacy and Schooling from a Cultural Historian's Point of View

Anne-Marie Chartier and Jean Hébrard

The history of subjects as they are taught in schools is currently a growing field in France. Since the creation of an academic sector for the training of teachers of primary and secondary education, many teachers within the IUFM, Institut Universitaire de Formation des Maitres [university institutes for the training of teachers], have moved from focusing solely on the subjects in which they had been trained—mathematics, arts, music—to addressing the problems raised by the teaching of these subjects. Some have chosen to do so from a pedagogical perspective—examining the methods of teaching mathematics, languages—others have tried to explain current practice through a historical perspective—looking at the history of the teaching of math, of languages. This new field has been explored mainly by experts in their respective subjects, rather than by historians. The new studies have, however, strongly stimulated the interest of historians in the history of taught knowledge, particularly within three areas: the history of science, the history of education, and cultural history.

The history of science traditionally focuses on the way in which scientific knowledge is created and how it subsequently develops (Latour 1987). The history of education has focused in the past mainly on the political aspects of the development of school systems (Bachelard 1938; Canguilhem 1952; Delaporte 1994; Koyré 1957). Recently however, it has turned to studying taught knowledge and the ways in which this knowledge is passed on. Finally, cultural history has also developed an interest in the schooling process, but from a different perspective. In this context, one of society's major problematics is seen as the history of interactions between spoken and written cultures, an issue on which much research was carried out in the 1970s. More recently, the rapid development of research into the history of reading and writing practices (Chartier 1985, 1987, 1996) and into the oral diffusion of written culture (theater, preaching, and so on), has enabled this large field of inquiry to progress even further, focusing on what Lucien Febvre (1942) referred to as the "acquisition of mental tools" in a society at a given time in its history.

Historically, schools were not considered as the sole, or even the predominant places in which a society's intellectual tools were developed and transmitted. They did, however, play an important role (to a greater or lesser extent at different times) in defining those tools, especially by establishing the legitimacy of their use. According to circumstances, they could either emphasize or slow down the diffusion of those tools to social groups that were increasingly distanced from their technical use, learned or literary. Thus, the Council of Trent declared that in order to pass on the "science of salvation" that it was necessary to ensure that all Christians were literate. Following that decision, the Catholic Church promoted the rapid development of parish schools, and the school bodies established by the new teaching congregations; from that point forward a history of written culture cannot be recreated without taking into account the way in which this culture was introduced into the schools.

For the past ten years, a series of surveys has been undertaken by the authors of this article on the diffusion of basic intellectual tools for written culture, which consist of reading, but also writing (and later, composing) or calculating with a quill and paper. Our aim is to try to understand the specific role that the *petites écoles* (little schools) under the ancien régime, and primary schools after the revolution, played in this diffusion. In order to present a synthesis of some of our results, we have focused on three eras that represent three turning points in this history of the transmission of elementary skills.

Regarding French as a taught subject, the first turning point occurred at the end of the seventeenth century with the creation by Jean-Baptiste de la Salle of a new kind of school for the urban working classes, centered around reading and catechism, and, more significantly, around the diffusion of the skills necessary for urban small-scale trading (writing, arithmetic, bookkeeping) (Toscani 1984).

A second turning point—just as crucial—occurred between 1833 and 1882, when schools, by then dominated by the state, looked to improve the standard of mass literacy, and tried to establish a way of teaching writing in primary schools that would go beyond instilling the elementary ability to copy texts in order to reach the stage of "knowing how to compose." At the time when reading enabled the reader to detach himself/herself from skills learned orally (for example, through the catechism, prayers, the ordinary of the mass), thus enabling him/her to have access to unknown texts, writing also had to emancipate the children of the working classes, by allowing them to go beyond the act of merely copying exemplary texts. They had to be able to compose, a skill until then available only to the sons of well-to-do people who went to secondary school.

Finally, the third turning point occurred in the years preceding the Second World War when, an education of at least five years having finally been ensured for all pupils, the foundation of a new school culture with a coherent curriculum was created. Reading and writing were no longer seen as the ultimate goal of schooling, but as a means to acquire other skills and knowledge. History, geography, natural sciences, and secular morality were skills that were taught through books aimed at enabling children to perceive the world around them in a different way. Some of the great texts from national literature could also be used as common references between children from village schools and urban, middle-class children who went on to secondary school.

The Advent of the Reading-Writing-Reckoning Trilogy

The recent innovative research on literacy has been based on one obvious fact: reading, writing, and arithmetic reckoning were skills that were supposed to be clearly identifiable, and to remain constant in the longer term. The proportion of educated children increased with each generation, to a greater or lesser degree, and teaching methods developed, but all this was happening as if "knowing how to read," "knowing how to write," and "knowing how to reckon" designated the same skills, regardless of the century or of the teaching methods used. However, the old learning sequence resulted in skills that had little to do with what we understand today as knowing how to read and knowing how to write (Hébrard 1988). Immediately before the revolution, children were learning to read before learning writing and reckoning, and only a minority continued beyond the reading classes.[1] Between the illiterate—who did not "know A from B" and the "educated"—who could "read, write and reckon"— there were all those who left school "able only to read." It is hard for people from the twentieth century, who learned to read and write at the same time, to imagine the practical repercussions of this distinction. What practical circumstances would require the use of reading without writing? What prevented writing and reckoning from being more widely diffused?

Before becoming basic disciplines in schools, writing techniques—reading aloud or reading to oneself, comparing, copying or interpreting texts, taking notes, composition, drawing up a page, drawing up lists, calculating with quill and paper—were the learned activities of specific professional positions, particularly, since the early Middle Ages, of clerks, who did not all enter the church (Le Goff 1985). Clerks were engaged in reading and writing in Latin (Clanchy 1993; Riché 1979). The language of the church, the learned language, the language of law, medicine, and international correspondence between "well-read" people, was a working language that required a well-developed familiarity with the texts that needed to be memorized. It was therefore compulsory for those whose functions led them to be in daily contact with administrative, legal, or "scholastic" writings, to start learning at an early stage, whether they were destined to become humble clerks or powerful magistrates, simple priests or princes of the church. By establishing schools aimed at training the children of the elite, the teaching orders (Jesuits, Benedictines, Dominicans, and Gratorians) naturally organized the school curriculum around what was their working as well as their cultural language. They shifted the frame of reference, however, by replacing the Latin of scholastic texts, of universities, with the Latin of the humanities that formed the new school culture (Dainville 1978; Giard 1995). Throughout the curriculum, starting with the grammar classes all the way through to the class of rhetoric, pupils used to compose texts in verse and in prose in imitation of the ancient authors, using much Latin prose and translation. The reading of texts was not for them an end in itself, but more an introduction to writing, since everyone used the same frame of references, knew the same "commonplaces," (Blaire 1992; Goyet 1996) and respected the same stylistic rules. As for the basic skills necessary for the schooling process (reading and writing), they were not taught in secondary schools. Pupils who arrived in the first year of secondary school could read and hold a quill, owing to a training that had been taken care of by the family. They were therefore only rarely concerned with the issues in illiteracy that arose in the instruction of working-class children.

There were other professions that required the use of writing. Merchants in large trading companies (from Venice or towns in the Hanseatlc League, for example) had to be able to use a quill in order to keep their accounts up to date and to carry out their correspondence with customers and suppliers. Unlike clerks, they had to write in their own vernacular, and to be able to reckon. For a long time they were trained on the job; each family had a set of archetypical letters and registers, among which each generation could find the examples they needed. At the end of the fifteenth century, however, with the rapid expansion of towns and cities, professionals started offering their services to craftsmen and shopkeepers, either to write letters for them and keep their registers up to date or to teach their children to write and calculate (Petrucci 1978; Bruneton and Moreaux 1997). In 1570, The corporation des Maitres-écrivains arithméciens (a Guild of craftsmen and arithmeticians) in France was given the "right and authority to teach the art of writing and reckoning," in shops that they started opening up in towns. Those who passed on these skills cared little about literary culture or French literature, and were merely concerned with "writing and reckoning." Until the end of the eighteenth century, in spite of the competition from increasingly competent school masters, they succeeded in maintaining a culture and skills that gradually acquired structure and rules of their own (Hébrard 1995).

From the sixteenth century on, a third model of the interaction with writing started to develop, and was put into practice by the petit écoles (Blaire 1990). In a world where the church was divided and religious dogmas were the cause of ruthless wars, it was no longer enough, in order to make Christians, to baptize them after their birth in the religious community they belonged to. They had to be "trained," i.e. to be taught the truths of their religion. The letter of the doctrine therefore had be fixed and memorized perfectly, so that the faithful did not hold heresies or sacrilegious statements as truth. In order to set the "science of salvation" in formulas that everyone would be able to "confess," catechisms were written by the great Protestant reformers, followed by Catholic bishops. These books were initially a guide for the teachers, as the prayers and main doctrinal points were presented as a series of questions and answers. This verbal teaching (listening/memorizing/reciting) was a first initiation into the written culture, since the minister had to make the pupils learn "word for word" a written text, printed and stable.[2]

One century later, the catechism was no longer "the schoolmaster's book," but a book for pupils in seventeenth-century Catholic France; the little catechisms became reading books, comprising an alphabet primer and syllable charts, followed by prayers (Pater, Ave, Credo), the ordinary of the mass, and psalms. The publication of diocesan catechisms started growing between 1680 and 1720, and the little schools then became the customary place where children acquired a Christian education, which was part of an elementary initiation into writing-related skills. Children had to learn how to read there, as well as acquire a minimum of Catholic culture by constantly reciting and rereading passages. It was indeed "much easier to educate a child who [could] read, and to ensure it acquire[d] virtuous values than [to work with] those who kn[e]w nothing, especially as the books act[ed] as permanent masters to those who kn[e]w how to use them" (Batencour 1645). The religious Reformation, initially Protestant, then Catholic a few decades later, therefore introduced the first attempt at universal literacy. Within this project the church did not, however, make literacy a value in itself. Being able to read, or rather to reread a limited corpus of texts pronounced ritually many times, seemed a good way of making a mark on young children's minds; the earlier the process started, the stronger the influence would be. In the seventeenth century, several heterogeneous models of interaction with writing therefore coexisted in towns, whereas illiteracy was still the norm in rural areas (Bardet 1993).

In the eighteenth century, by creating the Institute of the Brothers of the Christian Schools, Jean-Baptiste de La Salle created a new elementary school model, where the use of catechetics (reading and reciting) was linked with the traditional education of a mercantile culture (writing and reckoning). The school founded by Jean-Baptiste de La Salle was a modern, Christian, free school.

It was a modern school because the teaching program was organized so gradually that children had to attend over several years. Structured as a strict linear curriculum, the learning of reading-writing-reckoning placed a strong emphasis on the French language. Jean-Baptiste de La Salle thus clearly expressed his decision to favor the trade and shopkeeper culture over that of the clerk's, through his astonishing decision to forbid the teaching of Latin: "The Brothers will not be allowed to teach the Latin language to anybody, either In the home or outside" (La Salle 1993). Children still continued to learn Latin texts by heart in order to serve at mass, but the first reading texts were the *Notre Pere* and not the Pater Noster, the *Je vous salue, Marie*, and not the Ave Maria. This choice by the Brothers had several consequences. It highlighted from the early learning stages the utilitarian value of learning: French is the spoken and written language of social life, unlike church Latin. As for the prayers read over and over again in French, they were explained in catechism classes, like witness-bearing texts in the reformed forms of worship.

It was a Christian school because "The aim of this Institute [was] to give children a Christian education, and it [was] for that reason that we [ran] schools there." Children were taught to recite the catechism and say prayers, to serve at mass, to take the sacraments, to know the liturgy, and to behave at any moment in a way true to a Christian upbringing. The *Conduite des Ecoles Chretiennes* (Conduct of Christian Schools), written "in order to promote uniformity amongst all schools" (La Salle 1993) covered both the program for Christian teachers and the learning of reading-writing-reckoning.

And finally, it was a free school because the Brothers could have introduced a system of free education for the poor, and paying education for the others, as did other schools, but this option was rejected. They wanted education to be free for everybody, in order to mix the urban working and upper-working classes. They used the concept of the day school as a model, and the teaching premises were placed in close proximity to the pupils' homes, so as to be able to exert influence on the families through the pupils.

The continuous progression in the learning of the catechism was not, however, in step with the progression in the learning of school skills. The revolutionaries had understood that they decided to keep the existing structure but with different texts (revolutionary catechisms, the Declaration of Human Rights, the constitution) (Hébrard 1989a&b). Just as it was starting to develop in schools trying to reestablish Catholicism, the "reading-writing-reckoning" trilogy constituted itself in "subjects," each with its own autonomy.

The Genesis of Writing, from Guizot (1833) to Ferry (1880)

Questions concerning instruction changed direction after the revolution. Whereas the Catholic Church had seen universalizing literacy as a way of spreading the catechism, the successive governments of the nineteenth century tried to avoid new disturbances among the people, and to use instruction as a way of civilizing their customs and minds. It is true that there were still people in the "Party of Order" who believed that the less instructed people were, the less likely they were to question the government. How was one to avoid the dangers faced by a society where books were published freely and where the people, if they knew how to read, could read anything? (Chartier and Hébrard 1989). The liberals' view was to retaliate by introducing a higher level of instruction. Ignorant people were thought to form the foundation of tyrannical regimes, and there would be less to be feared from subversive doctrines and dangerous social classes once they had acquired literacy. Through the circulation of good books, edifying and instructive, schools should enable emotions, ideas, and, values that went beyond the confines of the villages, to be shared. They also had to satisfy the social need for writing. At the time when a genuine postal service was being put into place, correspondence, which enabled families to remain in contact from a distance, was no longer seen as an elitist luxury, but as a social need (Chartier 1995). The emphasis in nineteenth-century schooling therefore consisted in promoting teaching practices that did not stop at the reading stage, but that firmly linked reading and writing (Chartier 1993). In order to reach that point, the school model of transmitting basic skills had to undergo three transformations.

The first of these transformations, the simultaneous learning of reading and writing, was probably the most significant pedagogical innovation of the nineteenth century. Initially brought about in 1834 by the new choices in pedagogical practices ("They will be taught simultaneously reading, writing, and the first elements of verbal arithmetic" [Chervel 1992]), it was introduced in all urban and rural classes between 1840 and 1850 through the use of new writing techniques: pen nibs instead of goose quills, ample supplies of cheap paper, and the use of chalk and slates for beginners (Chartier, Compere, and Julia 1976; Grosperrin 1984). What was still exceptional around 1830 became, by around 1880, the standard education pattern. The second innovation concerned the contents of the teaching practices. The curriculum in which reading, writing, and reckoning were taught in succession was abolished. The simultaneous teaching of reading and writing, the inaugural phase of schooling, led to studying "elements of the French language," and spelling and grammar became part of the daily life of millions of children (Chervel 1977, 1986; Chervel and Manesse 1988). Between 1830 and 1880, new exercises appeared that were to last until the twentieth century—dictation, conjugation, and grammatical analysis. Other activities also required the use of writing: exercises around the four basic operations, mathematical problems (the solution had to be written and the "operations put on paper"), copying texts to be subsequently learned (summaries in history and geography), and reciting lessons in writing. The range of writing exercises went well beyond the simple hand-written reproduction of sentences given as examples. From this mastering of the written language came the third innovation: learning to compose texts. Thirty years of trials and experimentation were necessary in order to develop the new exercises that would fulfill this ambition. The first ideas were initiated by civil servants close to the ministry, and ended up less than thirty years later as an official program. The genesis of this program was revealed in a journal which had a semiofficial status, the *Manuel Général d'Instruction Primaire* (Chartier and Hébrard 1994). This is the research we would like to focus on here.

What teaching practices concerning writing did schools have at their disposal around 1830, under the July Monarchy? At the time when Guizot was setting up the network of state schools and reforming the way in which teachers were recruited, nobody could imagine that school children could one day compose texts. This was reserved for secondary school pupils only, who were introduced very early on to the rhetoric of classical humanities through Latin prose and translations. One of the main exercises in learning to write was amplification: the pupils were given a topic drawn from a Latin author (*inventio*), a summary of the author's argument (*dispositio*), and the moral which had to be drawn from it (*applicatio*). Pupils had to write the development (*elocutio*) by trying to copy as well as possible the style and turns of phrase of the texts which they were given as a model. The writing of the literary people was therefore born from a familiarity with the speeches of Cicero, the history of Livy and the poetry of Virgil, through which they learned the common-places and the rhetoric of antiquity. That was indeed the only school tradition on "the art of thinking and writing."

Teachers, who had not gone through the secondary school system and had not learned Latin, were therefore excluded from the art of writing. However, from 1833 on, in order to obtain the brevet simple (basic diploma) giving them the right to teach, candidates had to "write a piece on a specific topic." The results were generally extremely poor and the jury merely assessed the paper according to its spelling. For the *brevet superieur* (higher diploma), which opened better positions, including heads of schools, the requirements were of a higher standard: "We expect a high quality of writing, otherwise the candidate has to resit" (Barrau, 1846). Finally, from 1835, the new regulations enabled the brightest schoolmasters to take an examination to become inspectors and to join the ranks of the educated elite (Edict of 18 November 1835).

To succeed in all these examinations, the candidates had to demonstrate their writing skills, and in the case of future inspectors, "it is obvious that we want them, through the art of combining and expressing their ideas, to rise above those who receive only an elementary education" (Barreau, 1846). In order to create a new corps of teachers, talent and individual reading were not enough, and a new kind of teaching exercise had to be spontaneously devised. The first projects for the development of writing in elementary schools were aimed first at the teachers and those who instructed them. This can be seen in the *Manuel Général* in 1846 and 1847, at a time when the contents of a potential intermediary stage between elementary and secondary school that would not rely on Latin was being sought. The German *Realschule* was used as an example, and the liberal deputy Saint-Marc Girardin pleaded for schools, in which pupils would be taught the rules of composition and style by "being initiated to the country's literature," through the use of summarizing exercises and text reconstitution. By rewriting themselves a text that had been heard or read, the pupils would learn at the same time to memorize the contents and master the art of writing (Girardin, 1846). Those who were opposed to these ideas claimed that it was absurd to make children rewrite French into French, and beautiful literary French into clumsy school-child French. A French-French translation could not equal the efficacy of a translation from the Latin.

A controversy between the *Manuel Général* and its rival journal, the *Bulletin de l'Instruction Primaire*, showed that several paths were possible. The *Manuel Général* suggested writing small moralizing narratives (for example, "Words of consolation to a young man whose friend has just died"), edifying stories (about the mishaps of a careless or lazy child, for example), letters where feelings had to be expressed according to the conventions of the time (for example, a thank-you letter to a friend or a relative). In order for the pupils to find the material needed for these written pieces, the authors suggested that they summarize texts read for leisure, or learn by heart selected pieces in verse. This would provide pupils with examples to copy and a repertoire of French "common-places," since they could no longer draw on the classics.

The *Bulletin de l'instruction Primaire* strongly condemned these suggestions, stating that they detracted from the aims of elementary teaching. It condemned a project that tried to imitate the rhetoric of secondary schooling without however having the means to fulfill its ambitions, and that could only yield pretentious or ridiculous results. In order to train the future elementary elite, the *Bulletin* advocated the use of new modes of expression, pointing to the merits of the simplicity of elementary teaching, and delving into the two sources of the genuine culture of the pupils—everyday life and schooling. "Take great care, when choosing topics for exercises, to remain within the realities of everyday life, and of the pupils' sphere of knowledge and impressions of school; try to make them talk and write only about subjects that are familiar to them, and about which they have had the opportunity to form a precise idea, either through their own experience or through your teaching" (Chervel 1992; Michel, 1854). This pedagogical approach therefore brought about a quiet break with tradition. Unlike what was happening in secondary schools, it encouraged pupils to write freely without trying to imitate great authors and texts, or those unknown to them. Furthermore, it implied a quasi-natural continuity between direct experience, speaking, and writing (in a situation where the mother tongue, often a local dialect, was not always the language used for writing). In order to prepare pupils to write, the teacher should start by making them read their text in French. "In the composition and style exercises that we are concerned with, the best thing [the schoolmaster] [could] do [was] to train [the pupils] to put in writing the thoughts and feelings that he [had] already taught them to express verbally, with the same simplicity, the same clarity and in an equally correct way" (Chervel 1992; Michel, 1854).

The controversy between the two journals ceased in 1857 when the *Bulletin de l'Instruction Primaire*, by then having fallen into political disrepute, was discontinued.[3] In the course of the following ten years, the *Bulletin*'s suggestions were abandoned, but the *Manuel Général* continued to promote its ideas, i.e., adapting to elementary schools the methods used in secondary schools, where the act of writing was always based on a source text that, once read, could be transformed. Halfway between Roman history and the catechism, the story of the Bible, which was part of the schools' curriculum, offered valuable material to delve into. Pupils were asked to write down the tales of Christianity they had been taught, thereby raising the old tradition of reciting catechism to a more formal level; the Christian culture, symbolized by the two testaments, thus became a corpus of humanities that could be used by both elementary and secondary schools, an antique and sacred corpus, a heritage for all Christians, whether they knew Latin and Greek or not.

Alongside these chosen passages taken from the Bible, pupils could be asked to describe scenes of daily work and labor (e.g., the harshness of working in the fields), or to learn the correct way of writing letters (e.g., business letters). This meant that pupils had to be able to summarize texts read by their teacher without misinterpreting them, and had to know the correct expressions that would enable them to write, from a given framework, a letter that respected the rules mentioned in the "Arts of writing" (*les Arts d'ecrire*). This approach made it possible to cover all different literary genres, as the addressees of the written text (friends, relatives, an old teacher, a benefactor or a business connection) could be changed depending on whether the composition was an edifying narrative, an educational presentation, a moral or sentimental meditation, or an exchange of agreed upon information.

Similar exercises were to be found at a higher level, in preparing teachers for the examinations to become inspectors, or candidates for the different diplomas to become schoolmasters. Until 1865, the emphasis was placed on the story of the Bible: "Relate the sacrifice of Abraham and explain in what way this sacrifice was the image of Jesus Christ" (1861); "Summarize the history of the Jews under David and under Solomon" (1863); "the Agony of Jesus Christ on the Mount of Olives" (1864). Letters concerning "the standards and discipline in school" then became favorites: the candidate had to know how to "describe the poverty and misfortunes" encountered during a charity visit, to warn bright pupils against negative influences, to present to a young colleague "their method for teaching to read" or why "state education offers more than private education."

After the Second Empire, the new institutional obligations dictated the way in which educational practices would evolve. The common cultural frame of reference which was starting to prevail was not the history of Christianity, but the history of the nation. In April 1867, the examining board was allowed to include in the brevet (diploma), as an exercise in style, "a chronicle taken from the history of France," instead of "a chronicle taken from the story of the Bible."[4] When schools started the following October, geography and ethics had become compu1sory subjects in elementary school. In December, a composition in French on the following topic: "a narrative taken either from the history of the Bible or from the history of France, or a very simple narrative of a given topic" (Chervel 1992), was introduced as part of the entrance competitive examination for the *école normale* (normal school). As all examinations for teachers and future teachers had by then integrated the same theories of writing and the same pool of references, the way was open to making composition a compulsory subject in elementary school. This was already achieved by 10 July 1868, although only in the Académie of the Seine (district of the Paris education) and not in the rest of the country.[5] The district's director, Octave Gréard, published regulations for a new school curriculum, which recommended that composition should be taught at all levels and not only in the higher classes. The pupils' achievements were evaluated at the end of the course through the Certificat d'Etudes Primaires, for which they had to write a "composition on the subject of a narrative taken either from the story of the Bible or from the history of France, or a simple letter" (Chervel 1992). Under the ministry of Jules Ferry, this avant-garde Parisian curriculum was the inspiration for the rule that would apply to the whole of France.

Therefore, at the very start of the Third Republic, the elementary school was ready to enter a new phase in history: it had established, beyond the reading-writing-reckoning trilogy, a whole new set of basic skills—new exercises to help master the French language (spelling and grammar) and programs of scientific knowledge, making it possible to create a common cultural frame of reference (the history and geography of France) that would replace the religious culture. Finally, through composition exercises, a form of writing instruction had been developed that could be put into practice on a large scale, and that removed the monopoly of the art of writing from the secondary schools. The Certificat d'Etudes Primaires (school-leaving certificate) marked the successful conclusion of a proper education that, albeit elementary, was comprehensive.

Reading in the Secular School—Between Science, Morals, and Literature

In the Third Republic, schools became free, compulsory, and secular. Teachers, who were then working for the state and no longer employed by town councils, were protected from the political pressures that had previously been exerted on them by mayors and priests. The emphasis placed on training teachers by the écoles normales, that is, teacher training colleges and their supervisors (by the écoles normales superieures at Saint-Cloud and Fontenay, aimed at training teachers for the écoles normales and inspectors), was backed up by administrative procedures and financial investments. The skills and values that were soon to become the creed of the republican school were defined and diffused to all teachers through intellectual work tools, such as Ferdinand Buisson's acclaimed *Dictionnaire de pédagogie* (Nora 1984). School programs, established for the five schooling years, which all children between the ages of seven and twelve were entitled to, introduced the teaching of scientific knowledge in a cautious but determined way. What were the new objectives of reading in a situation of increasing conflict between the church and the state? It is possible to establish this by examining the reading books given to pupils towards the end of the curriculum (when they were ages ten to twelve). At the very beginning of the twentieth century (Chartier and Hébrard 1989), several pedagogical ideas, reflecting choices made possible by prolonged schooling, still coexisted, none having achieved predominance in actual practice.

In the 1900s, once they had learned to read in a "primer" the booklet used in the *cours préparatoire,* "preparatory" lessons where the learning process started, pupils usually only had one textbook, the "reader," which contained all the skills thought to be necessary for school children. An example of this was the manual titled *Lectures courantes* (Current reading) (Cuissart, 1894), reedited several times, the aims of which were clearly presented in its subtitle, "The things that have to be known." Its contents (morals, hygiene, history, physics and natural science, traveling, home economics, architecture, sculpture, pottery, painting) seemed a surreal inventory devoid of any logic. It was in fact easy to see how the teaching was organized: every day, a new text would be read, which would also be a new lesson (on Mondays a lesson in morals, on Tuesdays a lesson in hygiene, and so on). The pupils would take turns in reading and rereading, and then in answering the questions put by the schoolmaster, using sentences taken word-for-word from the text itself, with increasing length and difficulty when moving from the *cours élémentaire* ("elementary" class) to the *cours moyen* (intermediate class), and then to the *cours supérieur* ("higher" class).

The following presentation could thus be found in a book for Catholic education: "The commentary and analysis of a text provides its subdivisions. Using the paragraphs, or even the main sentences of a text, the teacher will raise the following questions: Is there a God? How is His existence represented? Is this truth based on proof?" (Alber 1900). For the other secular lessons (such as natural science, agriculture, home economics, and historical and anecdotal narratives), the same method was used. In secular school manuals, the religious contents had disappeared, but the educational practices used remained that of the catechism (reading was taught in order that the student be able to learn and recite). Each lesson became a single unit in itself, like an entry in a dictionary, and the knowledge and skills covered were inspired by various codes of "good manners," as well as scientific and cultural phenomena, which traditionally went back to the eighteenth century.[6] In the nineteenth century, large publishing companies, such as Hetzel and Hachette, used these new developments in books and instructive journals published for children (Glénisson 1985). Having delighted an educated readership, followed by middle-class children, this new literary genre ended up being used quite naturally in school manuals for the children of lower social classes. The division into daily lessons made it particularly easy to link, without necessarily much coherence, instructive knowledge with moral exhortations, advice in hygiene, and the description of habits and customs (e.g. Devinat 1894).

Injunctions from the government, however, went in a totally different direction—they insisted that a combination of a thousand scientific phenomena did not constitute a coherent corpus of knowledge. The description of scientific processes could not be transformed into ways of thinking, and could not become a substitute for direct experience. High authorities in education therefore refused to acknowledge the validity of these lazy teaching methods, and encouraged schoolmasters to go through lessons themselves, rather than read them from a book (Charpak 1996).

The "subjects" (history, geography, natural sciences) had to be organized within an overall program and a teacher "by rote" (*maitre-répétiteur*), who simply checked that the literal reading was done perfectly, was not as proficient as an educated schoolmaster, who would make his pupils think and ask them to observe and undertake experiments. In history or in geography, this did often not go any further than asking pupils to describe a large-scale scene, but for the "practical lessons" the pupils had more concrete tasks, such as cutting open and examining an apple or a walnut, or learning to use scales or a thermometer. These new skills implied new exercises: illustrations and figures in science topics, map drawing in geography, and history, chronological tables of "important events," kingdoms, and reigns of French kings. Specialized books were published to facilitate the schoolmasters' work in which science, history, and geography lessons were grouped in an organized and coherent way, according to the school programs. Where a lesson taken by a schoolmaster ended with the reading of an explanatory text or copying a summary from the specialized book, this was no longer seen as an exercise in reading or in writing in the purely functional sense of the word (Dancel 1996). Writing had become the invisible tool necessary to help the learning of other skills, and "reading" no longer described the process whereby pupils, having examined illustrations in the little Lavisse (Nora 1984), read the accompanying narrative on the battle of Alesia or the portrait of Colbert.

A second kind of reading manual therefore started to appear in classrooms. These new manuals had lost all the scientific texts present in the previous manuals, and only moralizing texts remained, in the form of edifying anecdotes, and narratives based on the pupils' daily lives, written as little stories in prose or in verse. An 1886 preface thus read: "This little reading book contains narratives in prose and in verse, along with many lexical explanations. The narratives in verse, all mostly taken from our great national poet, Victor Hugo, are simple in nature, but of a high standard and edifying. Both types are easy to read and generally entertaining. All concern morals, and their specific aim is not only to teach the pupils their mother tongue, but also to educate their consciences" (Devinat, 1894).

The ideological stakes of this type of moral education were important for the republic; indeed, although the church accepted the secular school's ability to develop children's intelligence, it denied its legitimacy to form consciences and hearts outside the teachings of religion. Republican schoolmasters strongly opposed this stigma, and showed it by choosing, from a secularized range of texts, exemplary narratives very similar to those which by free schools to teach lessons of Christian morals.[7] All reading books could in fact take the example from the typical formative story of the end of the century, *Le Tour de la France par deux enfants* (The Journey through France of two children), which was an immensely popular best-seller (Nora 1984). In a France wounded by the 1870 war and the loss of Alsace and Lorraine, this reading book managed the feat of achieving both aims—to instruct and to educate.[8] Each chapter of this "book of current reading for the *'cours moyen'* containing more than two hundred instructive illustrations for practical lessons," was a real "lesson" in itself (history, geography, science, morals) seen through an adventurous journey through France. André and Julien discovered new monuments, landscapes, and technical inventions, and gradually started to develop a new way of seeing the world: the variety of their country, the harshness of the times, and solidarity among human beings.

Through this educational journey, the author showed that the love of one's nation could introduce morality into schools in a more unified way than had the Christian religion. As they traveled through France, the two children learned to keep faith and to trust in hardship, and to accept the idea of a collective destiny. They "became" French, which meant belonging to a soil, a language, and a history.

A third model was also born in the last decade of the century, when some people were trying to bring the primary culture closer to that of the secondary. Reading books lost informative texts (which had to be learned), but acquired literary texts (which had to be understood). This time, the reference to a heritage concerned not so much the nation but the heritage itself, that of the "mother" tongue as it had been molded through centuries of writing. "These chosen passages taken from French authors do not resemble the books—often excellent—of practical lessons, of instructive reading, etc., which are in use in a large number of our schools. . . . It is above all the ideas and feelings that we wanted to awaken in the minds and in the hearts [of our young readers. . . and the pleasant emotion which will make us sometimes say 'this is well described— or well told.' In this way, reading is totally disinterested, and has the advantage of making readers enjoy their reading, of making them enjoy it fully in itself, and not for the lessons that could be drawn from it, but for the pleasure and the relaxation it provides" (Jost and Cahen, 1896). After the two previous aims of education—memory-writing (the catechism) and tool-writing (the writing and reckoning of tradesmen and shopkeepers)—and after the modern aims of knowledge-reading (the encyclopedia) and of edifying reading (the moralizing narrative)—reading for the sake of reading started to appear, reading for the love of the text itself, which only literature would render legitimate.[9]

It is hard to understand the aims and objectives of such a project, seemingly so alien to the cultural environment of elementary schools, without focusing on the changes occurring simultaneously in secondary schools. Let us therefore leave the models given by reading books, and return to the official texts.

As we have seen, the teaching practices in secondary schools were aimed mainly at arming pupils with the art of writing, which was formed through familiarity with ancient models. All pupils learned the figures of rhetoric—the set of rules that governed all discourse—not only through its principles, but also through its use, as they would translate and copy Cicero, Livy, or Caesar. However, at the end of the nineteenth century, a debate on the different programs started, placing reading at the center of violent conflicts (Jay 1996). Those in favor of rhetoric, who also defended the Latin classics, were against those who wanted to organize the elite's culture around French literature. This was a significant change of direction, as in those times reading was seen by teachers as a frivolous occupation unless it was part of a writing exercise (translation and composition). This point was demonstrated by a circular from the minister for public instruction to headmasters in 1872: "I am told that, for some heads of schools, the reading book is a kind of enemy which has to be hounded, even if it cannot cause any harm. Although the vastly excessive amount of written exercises could, if necessary, explain this, I refuse to believe it. It would be in total contradiction with the most basic principles of pedagogy."[10]

In order to promote reading, an "art of reading," acceptable to teachers of rhetoric, would have to be developed. This "art of reading" had indeed existed in French since the end of the Second Empire, but had the disadvantage of having been invented solely for pupils of lower grade teaching, as they did not learn Latin: this covered special education—the education of girls and the education of future teachers in teacher training colleges. (Chartier and Hébrard 1989). For the pupils being given special education, "reading a text in French has to play the same role and undertake the same functions as the explication of a Latin or Greek text for those studying classics."[11] This form of education was created in 1865 for pupils from trade, craft, or affluent farming backgrounds, where families wanted to see their children attend the prestigious colleges and lycées but for a shorter (five-year) and more vocational (foreign language, accounting, graphics) education. They were therefore taught to read aloud, "in an intelligent, clear and tasteful manner," French texts that had to be explained by the teacher ("to understand the ideas of the author and their articulation"). The reading was followed by an exercise, which was "to reproduce in writing, always from memory, the passage read and explained, to which the pupils have to try and add themselves the thoughts that it trigger naturally."[11] This was the same process, transferred to the mother tongue, as that which had previously been used with Latin (a translation followed by the expansion of a Latin text), as was suggested by the parliamentary deputy Saint-Marc Girardin, following the example of the German *Realschule*. It was therefore possible to establish a way of teaching in French resting solely on the country's literature, combining both reading and writing. Its weakness was to appear as a kind of "second-best" education, using French because it could no longer use Latin, rather than as a pedagogical innovation.

Further innovations could be found in the context of the education for girls set up by the state in order to fight the hold the church had on girls' boarding schools. Indeed, middle-class girls had no need to learn the art of spoken or written discourse (one is in fact tempted to say quite the opposite), but they did need a demanding cultural education, compatible with their social position. Without placing too much emphasis on writing, a list of texts of a high standard was drawn up for them. The selection was made among traditional texts, mostly from the seventeenth century (Mayeur 1975), but the real innovation was the introduction of the art of reading, and it was even mentioned that this could be entrusted to "teachers of reading." The appropriate exercise in learning to understand, know, and communicate the essence of a text was that of reading aloud with feeling. Ernest Legouve inspired the ministry's instructions to link expressive reading, the national literature, and developing understanding of a text.[12] "A good reading class must be, in essence, a literature class." As all great writers have their own style, they must each be read in a specific way. Learning to read properly therefore means learning to penetrate the secret of their talent. Developing reading skills by studying and comparing, In a reflective way, all our great writers in turn, will therefore become a way of studying French genius"[13] (Instructions for Reading Aloud, 1882). This shift was significant as it meant that, for the first time, training in rhetoric was cast aside, to be replaced solely by a literary training.[13]

It was suggested that the same teaching methods be used to train schoolmasters. The requirements in 1851 were far from literary; future schoolmasters learned to read aloud in order to "correct their local accent," and their teachers checked that what was read had been understood. To achieve this, "the students will be taught to immerse themselves in what they are reading, to distinguish the different parts of the text and to break up sentences, to emphasize pauses and to render, through the various inflections of the voice, the ideas and feelings that the author wanted to express."[14] Thirty years later, a change in the overall aims of the exercise brought about a change in its nature: "To understand a text and, when reading it, to make those who listen to us understand it too; to feel the innermost thoughts of an author and to make them clear to others . . . ; to feel and express the beauty of a great scene or of a brilliant passage, . . . are qualities that all teachers must possess to some extent, otherwise they would be unable to undertake the most useful and valuable part of their task."[15]

In 1881, the student-teachers trained in teacher training colleges were no longer unrefined country people as in previous generations; yet, there was no mention of making them read literary texts in order to develop their writing skills. The writing exercises they were given were narratives (historical or based on daily life), and not the tasks of expanding imposed on secondary school pupils of special education. However, the classics they were told to read were those given to young girls of the enlightened bourgeoisie—the priority, similarly, was "to feel and convey this feeling." Young girls read among themselves or within the family, but teachers had to make their pupils "bring out what [was] expressed" in texts. There was no need for rhetoric to achieve this aim. All that had to be done, and there was a genuine art to it, was to provide the author with a voice, to convey through words all the feelings and emotions that would overcome readers when they came into contact with the ideas of the texts. Teachers would absorb these emotions themselves, and simultaneously communicate them almost "physically" to their young pupils. It was therefore possible, through expressive reading, to train the schoolmaster by training the reader.

Such a program was only possible using texts of unquestionable standards both in content and in form, and literature therefore became a necessary choice. "Why do French authors appear in primary teaching programs? This choice responds to three objectives: the first is mainly literary, the second could be described as national and French, and the third is mainly moral" (Hamon, 1889). Young schoolmasters could only gain from reading the great authors. The simple act of reading, by creating a contagion of feeling, could raise the least educated people to the level of the great minds, and, as Minister Léon Bourgeois, who signed the circular, said, it could "reach them in the depth of their souls , and little by little, arouse in them ideas and feelings that they might never have discovered without this distinguished commerce with the élite of our race."[16] Therefore, a pedagogical project was initiated in the 1880s by the ministry, giving literary reading a central place in the training of schoolmasters and, through them, in the training of working-class children (Milo 1986).

This literary reading had yet more to achieve: if the children of the elite, girls as well as boys, read the same authors and the same texts as working-class children, that would represent a decisive factor of national unification, in spite of the differences in conditions, the separate places for studying and the inequality of destinies.[17] "The great classical authors could be found in all programs. . . . Could this not somehow link all children of one same fatherland, from secondary schools to the smallest village school?"[18] State schools had to give a similar "education" to all children, which meant common references and values. At the time, the Catholic Church considered that only religion could constitute this unifying force, which explained why it claimed power over state schools. As the state, "neutral amongst religions," robbed the church of its control of souls and minds, the republican school's religion could become the fatherland, as well as the national literature.

Entrusting literature with this educational mission meant acknowledging the heritage of the past, although it could by then no longer be seen solely as the Christian past of the seventeenth century (Corneille and Racine, Bossuet and Pascal). "It is absurd to use only monarchist and Christian literature for the education of a democracy that does not have any state religion. . . . Writers under Louis XIV, Boileau, La Fontaine, or Madame de Sévigné did not provide any nationalistic or social thought" (Lanson 1905). Texts from the century of the Enlightenment (Voltaire and Rousseau), or even the nineteenth century therefore had to be used for reading. Chateaubriand and Lamartine became "classics," since the high council of the ministry of public instruction "decided that the word 'classic' did not merely refer to seventeenth century writers, but also to those of the eighteenth and nineteenth century" (Chervel 1997). Literature would provide the younger generations with a number of registers of identification and meditation, and reflect all the facets of the nation's literary history, while respecting the reserve required by secularity. Science could form people's intelligence, train their reasoning capacities, and make them believe in progress, but it could not simultaneously shape their sensitivity and their moral conscience.

A new school subject, French, was therefore born from literary reading.[19] This subject encompassed the old methods of teaching French (sight-reading and handwriting), elements of the French language (spelling and grammar), and added to the corpus texts in which the contents and the form could not be dissociated. The subject matter was sufficiently rich to be able to nourish working programs for several generations, since there was still a long way to go before this program would become reality. In primary schools, it was not enough for schoolmasters to be able to read expressively; they also had to find a way of conveying this ability to the children. In secondary schools, the task was even harder, as the idea that the training of the elite could happen through literary reading in French went against the ancient tradition of rhetoric. A new doctrine therefore had to be devised, and relevant writing exercises invented. These two objectives were achieved during the period between the two world wars.

In primary schools, texts from celebrated authors did not have to be explained to the children. It was enough, through expressive reading, to "convey" the meaning that textual commentaries might have spoiled, confused, or rendered uninteresting. Just before the First World War, it had become the norm to turn to "selected passages" from literature, moving further away from the model of the catechism. The Official Instructions of 1923 confirmed this major change: "teaching to read serves two purposes. It provides children with one of the two tools—the other being writing—which are essential to all school education, and it gives them a means to initiate themselves in the knowledge of the French language and literature."[20] The school curriculum could then be organized in a well structured progression: in the *cours preparatoire* (preparatory class), the problems linked to the learning of the code had to be dealt with, using the method chosen by the schoolmasters—the Ministry left everyone free to make the choice they felt would be the most effective (Chartier and Hébrard 1990). The instructions optimistically stated that sight-reading could be acquired between October and Christmas, leaving the rest of the time free for "fluent reading," which was the stipulated aim of the *cours elementaire*. Being able to read "fluently" meant to read aloud without spelling out the words, pronouncing each one fully. At this stage, "children still need to concentrate too much on the complexity of the combination of letters to be able to enjoy trying to discover the meaning of the words. Questions which [would] interrupt their efforts at sight-reading [would] not help them develop a taste for reading." However, while the pupil who was reading was absorbed by his/her task, the others, who were following the text without making the effort of sight reading, were able to recognize the heard words without any difficulty, and could therefore "understand" the text in its literal sense. Only in the *cours moyen* were young readers required to do "expressive reading," proving that they understood what they were reading as they said it by using the appropriate intonation and inflections. In 1938, "silent reading" was mentioned for the first time in an official text, destined for the older pupils who were preparing for the Certificat d'Études. Until the Second World War, "reading" was always understood in schools as meaning "reading aloud," a convivial, slow, and attentive way of reading, inspired by the lecture form of teaching. Learning to read could mean either learning mechanisms (the correspondences between the letters and the sounds), or practicing giving life and a voice to a short written piece (narrative, description) written by a well-known author.

The Third Republic's encyclopedic model of instructive reading thus disappeared from reading manuals. The educational model of moralizing narratives was maintained until the 1960s through books of successive texts telling stories of children's adventures, which became more boisterous and heroic with time. The model that would win out over the others was the cultural model of literary texts. It established itself within the well-structured routine of passages chosen from famous authors, drawn from classics as well as from contemporary or foreign works, which were still forbidden in secondary schools. These texts, arranged according to centers of interest, were no longer used for their literary value, but because each group of texts introduced, within specific themes, the vocabulary and the expressions that would feed the week's dictation (spelling and grammar) and composition (narrative or description) given at the end of a cycle of reading. A balance was therefore found in the 1920s that would enable the official instructions to remain in place until the 1970s. This curriculum, effective in giving a basic education to children who had to earn their living at an early stage, did not prevent the small percentage of brighter pupils from carrying on into secondary education and joining the children from privileged backgrounds. In primary as well as in secondary schools, the emphasis was placed on the reading of short texts, chosen literary passages that children had to read and reread in order to be able to discuss, feel, and understand them perfectly. It was around this ritualized, collective, and intensive reading that all the activities aimed at "learning French" revolved.

Conclusion: Three Profiles of Young Readers

At the outset of the article, we defined our aim as approaching the history of reading in schools from the perspective of cultural history, by questioning the traditional opposition between the spoken and the written word. According to this opposition, a person learning to read would be moving from the world of spoken culture to that of written culture. As schools developed, the culture shared by all started to become that of writing, which was represented on the one hand by the permanence of ancient texts, even though they were constantly overtaken by new output, and by the possibility of sharing texts from various different places, on the other. By reading similar texts and sharing similar interpretations, social groups constitute communities of readers, even if they are dispersed geographically. At the same time, the spoken culture, which covers various aspects such as the memory of people still alive and a direct exchange between people, communicating through spoken language and gestures, and the acts of repeating and forgetting, would slowly disappear, moving into the world of folklore. The return of illiteracy in developed societies would therefore mean that this sharing does not occur as successfully as it used to, and that the minority of illiterate people would be finding themselves marginalized and excluded from society, because of being condemned to using archaic means of communication.

This way of thinking sees the opposition between spoken and written culture as an anthropological invariant, and this is its weakness, as the opposition between the spoken and the written word is not set in stone. Over the centuries, the symbolic status of writing, the social functions of the "literate," and the objectives and practical uses of reading have changed. Not only did the boundaries between writing and speaking shift several times, but the characteristics of the written culture, and consequently, those of the spoken culture, were modified. Why and how did schools teach pupils to read? The regulations and school programs explain the reason why: at each stage, the objectives of teaching had changed. Examining the exercises, the progression, and the texts studied makes it possible to understand how it was done. The corpuses referred to, and the different possible ways of reading represent as many types of readers. Three different reader profiles can therefore be extracted from the three case studies presented in this article.

It is easy, looking back, to understand this lack of vision, as time lags tend to compress our vision of the succession of developments in the past. There is always a delay between the time when a specific lack of knowledge is felt as something missing, and the time when this lack is acknowledged as a social need which has to be dealt with (whether it be attending church, reading the dictionary, or writing a letter). There is also a delay between the time when educational theorists try to meet expressed needs with new teaching ideas, and the time when schoolteachers become familiar with the innovations, thus enabling the large-scale diffusion of the ideas. Indeed, the constraints set by the format of schooling (large groups of children, compulsory as opposed to voluntary education) and its variations (such as the length of schooling, classes covering one or two levels, compulsory and noncompulsory education, trained or nontrained schoolteachers) make it impossible to apply, in the school context, the many learning processes that are so effective in the wider social sphere on a one-to-one basis. The same applies to the learning of handwriting, impossible to universalize when quills were used. Writing could only be developed once efficient stereotypes of school writing were selected and firmly established. Similarly, the corpus of texts read in class always remains limited in number, even if schoolteachers encourage the more motivated pupils to turn to longer reading material (pious manuals, instructive books, or classics for children). Whereas in the social sphere, the increasing numbers of books published continue to widen the universe of signs, when collective reading remains essential in classrooms, there is limited scope for the range of texts used to broaden perspectives.

This approach helps to explain the constancy of certain forms of reading in schools, from Jean-Baptiste de La Salle to Jules Ferry, in spite of the changes described above. The aims of school learning should be to enable the mental processes necessary for all future reading to become ingrained in pupils' memories. It should provide children with the necessary guidance to build up a world of reference texts and their legitimate interpretation. It therefore has to be founded on a slow but certain learning process, involving much repetition and guidance from the schoolteacher, an intensive rather than an extensive form of reading. Reading in school thus characteristically has a somewhat archaic appearance closer to the medieval mode than to the Enlightenment ideal of seeking novelty and innovation. Schools were thus little affected by the change from an oral to a silent and visual form of reading, a change that otherwise constitutes for historians of reading a highly significant historical turning point in the long run (Cavallo and Chartier 1997). As long as an oral approach to texts remained common practice in the surrounding environment, schools did not yet have to worry about inventing specific educational practices for silent reading, which was already used in classes in an informal way (Goodman 1968; Levin and Williams 1970; Smith 1971).

Within their own spatial constraints schools therefore trained people to read, write, and organize the world according to categories that the corpus of texts and the schoolteachers' discourse rendered almost natural. The school, a community of shared initial interpretation, was obliged to produce a shared understanding of texts, for the simple reason that without the certainty of meaning, education and learning would be impossible. Thus knowledge learned at the early stages did not cover, as is often believed, neutral and purely instrumental skills, ready to be used in any circumstances.

What kind of readers or writers would these pupils become once they reencountered, far from the school environment, the social aspects of work, of the family, or of the neighborhood? What would they do with the mental tools acquired in school, with a greater or lesser extent of patience and violence? How would they forget or transform them in order to acquire other skills, more appropriate to the needs of their social life? Between the different variations in the profiles of readers described by cultural history, and the profiles of school children that we have attempted to re-create in this article, there are differences and similarities with underlying forces that we have yet to understand.

Notes

1. The *écolage* (the fee paid by families to schoolmasters) was higher for writing and reckoning classes, as these required a higher level of expertise from the schoolmaster than reading, which was the learning skill for all beginners.

2. The most famous example was Luther's *Petit catechisme* (little catechism), written in 1529 to unify the expression of the reformed faith: "Young and simple people have to be taught using unified and determined formulas, otherwise they easily get confused."

3. The reason was a competition between the two publishers, Dupont (*Bulletin*) and Hachette (*Manuel Général*). In 1851, Hachette opposed the coup d'état that established the Second Empire, while Dupont supported Napoleon II. In 1857, the Empire became liberal, and Hachette had the opportunity to become an official publisher. In return, Dupont lost the support of the Ministry, leading to the disappearance of the *Bulletin de l'Instruction Primaire*. The *Manuel Général* thus regained its monopoly as a journal for schoolteachers.

4. Act of 10 April 1867. During the Second Empire (1851–1870), Christian religion became during a very short period a school knowledge, to the use of secular schoolmasters for all the pupils (Catholic or not). Christianity became a "culture" (more than a religion) with the Romantics. The movement followed Chateaubriand's novels (René Atala) or his essay (Le Génie du Christianisme). The best example is in Victor Hugo's poetry ("La legende des Siecles") and novels (*Notre Dame de Paris*, *Les Misérables*).

5. The Seine Academy consisted of Paris and the surrounding towns. It had a special status (schoolmasters were payed better than in the rest of the country), and therefore played a leading role in educational practices.

6. *Le spectacle du munde* (The show of the world) by the Abbé Pluche (eight volumes, and around twenty editions and reeditions between 1732 and 1770) was the prime example of this type of popular literature aimed at a learned audience, written as dialogues between a learned priest, two curious aristocrats, and a young knight who has to be educated. The first four volumes cover the sciences (natural history, geography, astronomy), and the four others focus on man within society and in relation to God.

7. The role of liberal protestants such as Ferdinaud Buisson, Félix Pécaut, and Pauline Kergomard has often been highlighted in the development of this secular and moral ideology.

8. Two books written with the same aim in mind were also highly acclaimed; in Italy, De Amicis published *Cuore* in 1886. Translated in French as *Grands Coeurs* (Great hearts), it could be found in all school libraries in France until the 1950s. Similarly, Selma Lagerlöf's *Nils Holgerson*, published in 1906, remains as a magical tale and an educational novel. No social satire and little sense of humor can be found in these books, however, whereas both these factors have ensured the long-lasting success of Collodi's *Pinocchio* (1883) and Mark Twain's works, written during the same period, *The Adventures of Tom Sawyer* (1876), and *The Adventures of Huckelberry Finn* (1885).

9. The love of reading was indeed seen as a danger, as it could lead the new reader to read without a master, in a suspicious solitude, to mix reality with fiction, and above all, to be influenced by immoral or subversive texts, such as the novel or the political essay. "The pleasure and the relaxation" that reading provided were therefore only legitimate for texts that were beyond reproach, morally as well as stylistically, such as chosen passsages from great authors.

10. Circular to all head teachers on teaching in secondary schools, 27 September 1872.

11. Study plans and programs of special secondary teaching, 6 April 1866.

12. Ernerst Legouvé (1807–1903) was a playwright, a society speaker, a prolific writer, and a member of the Academy (1855), who published two essays on expressive reading: "Petit traite de lecture a voix haute a l'usage des ecoles primaires" and "L'Art de la lecture a l'usage de l'enseignement secondaire."

13. Order of 28 July 1882, "Instructions for reading aloud," Ministère de l'Instruction publique.

14. Order of 31 July 1851, "Programme de lecture des écoles normales primaires."

15. Order of 3 August 1881, "Réglement des écoles normales."

16. Circular of 16 October 1890.

17. In his lesson on the history of pedagogy at the Sorbonne, Durkheim, the founder of sociology in France, defined a double mission for schools—to unify (by providing references common to all future citizens of one same nation), and to diversify (by adapting the contents of education programs to the social positions and the tasks that the pupils would have to take on when they become adults).

18. Order of 28 January 1890, Bulletin administratif, no. 89, pp. 92–136.

19. The new reading manuals developed for these purposes had in their titles either the adjective "literary" (as in "literary reading," "literary texts," "literary instruction," or "first literary studying"), or the adjective "French" ("French authors," "French texts," "French through texts," "chosen passages in French").

20. Organization pedagogique et plan d'études des écoles primaires elementaires prescrits par arrêtés du 23 février 1923 avec les lnstructions ministérielles, Paris, Delalain, sd.

References

Alber, F. F. (1900). *Livre de lecture courante. Cours Moyen, Fontenay-sur-Saône*. Paris: Hatier et Vitte.

Bachelard, G. (1938). La psychanalyse du feu. (4th. ed.). Paris: Gallimard.

Bardet, M. (1993). La maitrise de l'ecrit ou l'histoire d'une affirmation sociale: le notaire rural en Haute Auvergne XVIe-XIXe siecle. In G. Pompidou (Ed.), *Illettrismes. Variations historiques et anthropologiques. Ecriture IV, sous la direction de Béatrice Fraenkel* (37–50). Paris: BPI-Centre.

Barrau, T. (1846). De l'Etude de la Composition ed du Style pour les Instituteurs. *Manuel Général* IV: 311–12.

Batencour, J. de. (1645). *L'Escole paroissiale ou la maniere de bien instruire les enfants dans les petites écoles par un prétre de Paris.* Paris: Pierre Targe.

Bellost, B. (Ed.). (1994). *La Formation polytechnicienne, 1794–1994.* Paris: Ed. Dunod.

Blair, A. (1990). Ovidius methodizatus: The metamorphoses of Ovid in sixteenth century Paris college. *History of Universities* 9: 73–118.

———. (1992). Humanist methods in natural philosophy: The commonplace book. *Journal of the History of Ideas*; vol. 4, 53: 541–51.

Botrel. J.-F. (1974). Les aveugles colporteurs d'imprimes en Espagne. *Melanges de la Casa de Velazquez* X: 233–71.

Bruneton, G. J. and Moreaux, B. (1997). Un modele épistolaire populaire. Les lettres d'émigrés béarnais. In D. Fabre (Ed.), *Par écrit. Ethnologie des écritures quotidiennes* (79–103). Paris: Editions de la MSH.

Cavallo, G., and Chartier, R. (Eds.). (1997). *Histoire de la lecture dans le monde occidental.* Paris: Seuil.

Canguilhem, G. (1952). La connaissance de da vie. Paris: Librarie Hachette.

Charpak, G. (Ed.). (1996). La Main ala pâte. Paris: Flammarion.

Chartier, A.-M. (1993). Les illettres de Jules Ferry: reflexions sur la scolarisation de l'ecrit entre XIXe et XXe siecle. In B. Fraenkel (Ed.), *Illettrismes. Variations historiques et anthropologiques. Ecriture IV* (81–102). Paris: BPI- Georges Pompidou.

Chartier, A.-M., and Hébrard, J. (1989). *Discours sur la lecture, 1880–1980.* Paris: BPI-Centre Georges Pompidou.

———. (1990). Methode syllabique et méthode globale. quelques clarifications historiques. *Le Français aujourd'hui* 90: 98–109.

———. (1994). Lire pour écrire a l'école primaire? L'invention de la composition française dans l'école du XIXe siecle. In Y. Reuter (Ed.), *Les interactions lectureécriture. Actes du colloque Théodile-Crel* (pp. 23–90). Berne: Peter Lang.

Chartier, R. (Ed.). (1985). *Pratiques de la lecture.* Marseille: Rivages.

———. (1987). *Lectures et lecteurs dans la France de l'Ancien Regime.* Paris: Seuil.

———. (Ed.). (1995). *La correspondance. Les usages de la lettre au XIXe siecle.* Paris: Fayard.

———. (1996). *Culture ecrite et societe.* Paris: Albin Michel.

Chartier, R. and Martin, H.-J. (Eds.). (1982–1986). *Histoire de l'education français* (4 volumes). Paris: Promodis. (Reedited Fayard, Paris 1988–1992).

Chartier, R., Compere, M.-M., and Julia, D. (1976). *L'Education en France du XVIe au XVIIIe, SEDES.* Paris. [Société d'Edition de l'Enseignement Supérieur].

Chervel, A. (1977a). *Et il fallut apprendre a lire et a ecrire a tous les petits Francais, Histoire de la grammaire scolaire.* Paris: Payot.

———. (1986). *Les Auteurs francais, latins et grecs au programme de l'enseignement secondaire de 1800 a nos jours.* Paris. INRP et Publications de la Sorbonne.

———. (1988a). L'Histoire des disciplines scolaires. *Histoire de l'education, 38,* 59–119.

———. (1988b). *La Transposition didactique, Du savoir savant au savoir enseigne.* Grenoble: La Pensée Sauvage.

———. (1992). *L'enseignement du Français a l'école primaire. Textes officiels, tome 1, 1791–1879* (109–12). Paris: INRP-Economica.

———. (1997). L'enseignement de la litterature dans le secondaire de 1800 a nos jours a travers les textes officiels. In M.-F. Chanfrault-Duchet (Ed.), *Les representations de la litterature dans l'enseignement, 1887–1990* (p. 89). Cahiers d'Histoire Culturelle, 1, Université de Tours.

Chervel, A. and Manesse, D. (1989). *La Dictée.* Paris: Calmann-Lévy.

Clanchy, M. T. (1993). *From memory to written record: England, 1066–1307*. London: Blackwell.

Compere, M.-M. and Pralon-Julia, D. (1992). *Performances scolaires de coliegiens sous l'Ancien Regime*. Paris: INRP-Publications de la Sorbonne. (Les Humanités classiques, *Histoire de l'Education, 74*, May 1997.)

Cuissart, E. (1894). *Troisieme degre de lectures courantes. Ce qu'il faut savoir. Cours moyen et supérieur*. Paris: Picard et Kaan.

Dainville, F. de. (1978). *L'education des jesuites (XVIe-XVIIIe siecles), textes choisis et présentés par MM*. Compere Paris: Editions de Minuit.

Dancel, B. (1996). *Enseigner l'histoire a l'école primaire de la IIIe Republique*. Paris: PUF.

Delaporte, F. (Ed.) (1994). A vital reductionist: Selected writings from Georges Canguilhem. (trans. by Arthur Goldhammer). New York: Zone Books.

Devinat, E. (1894). *Livre de lecture et de morale. Cours moyen et supérieurs*. Paris: Larousse.

Febvre, L. (1942). *La Religion de Rabelais. Le probleme de l'incroyance au XVIe siecle*. Paris: Albin Michel.

Furet, F. and Orzouf, J. (1977). *Lire et ecrire. L'alphabetisation des Français, de Calvin a Jules Ferry* (2 volumes). Paris: Editions de Minuit.

Giard, L. (1995). *Les Jesuites a la Renaissance. Systeme éducatif et production du savoir*. Paris: PUF.

Girardin, S.-M. (1846). De l'Instruction Intermédiare et de ses Rapports avec l'Instruction Secondaire. *Manuel Général, VII*, 286–291.

Glénisson, J, "Le livre pour la jeunesse" (1985). In Chartier Roger and Martin Henri-Jean ed. Histoire de l'Edition Française, vol. 3, Paris, Promodis, 417–43.

Goodman, K. S. (1968). *The psycholinguistic nature of the reading process*. Detroit: Wayne State University Press.

Goyet, F. (1996). *Le Sublime du lieu commun*. Paris: Honoré Champion.

Grafton, A. (1981). Teacher, text, and pupil in the Renaissance classroom: A case study from a Parisian college. *History of Universities* 1: 37–70.

Grosperrin, B. (1984). *Les Petites Fcoles sous l'Ancien Regime*. Ouest, France: Rennes.

Hamon, F. (1889). *"Les auteur français de l' enseignement primaire," Ministere de l'Instruction publique et des Beaux-Arts, Recueil des monographies pédagogiques publiées a l'occasion de l'Exposition universelle de 1889* (Vol. 3). Paris: Imprimerie Nationale.

Hébrard, J. (1988). La scolarisation des savoirs elementaires. *Histoire de l'Education* 38: 7–58.

———. (1989a). La Révolution explicu˝aux enfants: les catéchismes de l'an II. In Levy, M.-F. (Ed.), *L'Enfant, la famille et la Révolution française* (171–192). Paris: Olivier Orban.

———. (1989b). Les catechismes de la premiere Revolution. In L. Andries (Ed.), *Colporter la Révolution, Montreuil, Ville de Montreuil et Biblioteque Robert Desnos* (53–81). Paris: Olivier Orban.

———. (1995). Des ecritures exemplaires: l'art du maitre écrivain en France entre XVIe et XVIIIe siecle. *Mélanges de l'Ecole française de Rome, Italie et Méditerrané*, 473–523.

Jay, M. (1996). *La litterature dans l'enseignement secondaire en France de 1880 a 1925*. These pour le doctorat, Universite de la Sorbonne Nouvelle-Paris III. Paris.

Jost, G. and Cahen, A. (1896). *Lectures courantes extraites des écrivains français, pubilées avec une introduction, des notes, des exercices, et de nombreuses gravures a l'usage des écoles primaires et des classes élémentaires de l'enseignement secondaire* (2 vols). Paris: Hachette.

Julia, D. (Ed.). (1994). Aux Sources de la competence professionnelle. Criteres sco-laires et classements sociaux en Europe, XVIIe-XIXe siecles. *Paedagogica Historica* XXX: 1.

Koyré, A. (1957). From the closed world in the infinite universe. Baltimore: Johns Hopkins Press.

Lanson, G. (1905, September 30). La part respective des grands siecles litteraires: XVIIe siecle ou xvIIIe siecle? *Revue Bleue* 14: 422–23.

La Salle, J. B. de. (1993). *Conduite des écoles chrétiennes divisé en trois parties, d'apres le manuscrit de 1706, Oevres completes.* Rome: Ed. des Freres des écoles chrétiennes.

Latour, B. (1987). *Science in action: How to follow scientists and engineers through society.* Cambridge, MA: Harvard University Press.

Le Goff, J. (1985). *Les Intellectuels au Moyen Age.* Paris: Seuil.

Levin, H. and Williams, J. (Eds.). (1970). *Basic studies in reading.* New York: Harper and Row.

Liscoppe, A. (1996). *La formation de la pratique scientifique.* Paris: La Découverte.

Mandrou, R. (1964). *De la culture populaire au XVIIe et au XVIIIe siecles.* Paris: Plon.

Michel, L. C. (1854). Des exercices de compositioin et de style a l'usage des écoles pri-maires. *Bulletin de l'Instruction Primaire.* February–March.

Milo, D. (1986). Les classiques scolaires. In P. Nora (Ed.), *Les lieux de mémoire, Vol.II, La Nation* (517–62). Paris: Gallimard.

Nora, P. (1984). Le Dictionnaire de Pedagogic de Ferdinand Buisson. In P. Nora (Ed.), *Les Lieux de Memioire.* Vol. 1. Paris: Gallimard.

Petit histoire de l'enseignement des sciences a l'école primaire. (1996). In G. Charpak (Ed.), *La Main a la pâte* (115–37). Paris: Flammarion.

Petrucci, A. (1978). Scrittura, alfabetismo e educazione grafica nella Roma des primo Cinquecento; na un libretto do conti di Maddalena Pizzicarola in Trastevere. *Scittura e Civilta, Torino Bottega d'Erasmo* 2: 163–204.

Prost, A. (1968). *L'Enseignement en France, 1800–1967.* Paris: Armand Colin.

Riché, P. (1979). *Ecoles et enseignemeni dans le Haut Moyen Age.* Paris: Aubier.

Smith, F. (1971). *Understanding reading: A psycholinguistic analysis of reading and learning to read.* New York: Rinehart and Winston.

Toscani, X. (1984). Le «scuole della dottrina cristiana» come fattore di alfabetiz-zazione. *Societa e Storia,* 757–81.

12

Teacher Education Reform in the Shadow of State-University Links

The Cultural Politics of Texts

Katharina E. Heyning

Introduction

From the 1960s onwards, higher education throughout the world has been a playground to policy implementation to promote specific social and economic objectives achieved largely through changes in governance arrangements and curricula. This "new" type of university, what Wittrock refers to "higher education in the age of the great programmes," necessitates a rethinking of the role of universities in the modern world (Wittrock, 1993). Instead of a functionalist understanding, it is necessary to have an analytical theory that takes into account the current realities of institutional authority and the relationship between the nation-state and the university.

Starting in the early 1980s reports critical of university-based teacher education programs began to call into question the content and pedagogy of teacher preparation programs in the United States. These reports challenged the quality of teacher education students, along with the orientations and preparation of teacher educators, and asked for alternative institutional arrangements for entry into the profession of teaching. Many universities also began experiencing increased state control over licensure and certification requirements. In Wisconsin, a struggle occurred between the University of Wisconsin-Madison and the Wisconsin Department of Public Instruction over the control of teacher education programs and teacher certification (Prestine 1992).

The Wisconsin Department of Public Instruction in 1986 created a set of administrative standards that mandated courses in pedagogy and specific academic majors and minors, prescribing course content, admission standards, and graduation requirements for all Wisconsin institutions with a teacher education program.[1]

The creation of such formal governmental texts suggests a significant shift in the dynamics of power and control in the governing of the university. Its emphasis within the university gives reference to a reconstitution of university/state relations that has cultural, political, and economic significance (Popkewitz and Brennan, 1994). The current situation involves multiple sites that include universities and research communities, and a continually shifting set of dynamics that guide and manage the governing taking place.

This chapter explores the connection between the University of Wisconsin-Madison and the governing agency for the state-initiated programmatic reforms in teacher education. It does this by examining the "textual residue of a program's creation"—the meeting minutes and memos circulated within the elementary area of the teacher education program during a ten-year period in which the state agency's mandates were being instituted. The text is examined as a cultural object of study subject to specific rules and discursive formations. When related to other texts and events, the administrative documents help to illuminate an apparatus of power of historically formed rules and patterns of regulation inscribed in the texts. This chapter suggests that although the university/state distinction appears to be more clearly delineated when teacher education reform occurs, what seems on the surface to be purely technical and administrative documents of a university department's programmatic organization are also revealed to be part of a governing practice as the documents are read intertextually. A closer examination reveals that the university/state dichotomy dissolves. What may seem to be only "rituals of documentation" in fact become a construction that can yield important information about the historical constructions of the governing of teacher education reform that transverses state agencies and universities.

This chapter proceeds in the following manner. First, it discusses the Foucauldian idea of archaeology as a method for examining historical text as discourse as a way to think about cultural history, that is, how the knowledge of education generates principles to govern people's action and participation. Second, a discussion of Pierre Bourdieu's notion of authorized language is undertaken as a way to understand the caveats of utilizing faculty meeting minutes as textual discourse. Third, this chapter will frame the discussion of the discursive relationship between the state of Wisconsin and the University of Wisconsin-Madison (referred to as the university/state relationship) as a problematics of government by using Foucault's notion of governmentality.

Historical Text as Discourse: Archaeology and Authorized Language

Historical texts are often examined for clues to unlocking the thoughts and actions of those who produced them. Using the "objective" linguistic data of the text, historians attempt to reconstruct the inner thoughts and life of the author. The researcher's objective is to find meaning in some type of underlying framework, metaphorical system, or secret decoding process. The text is seen as a written depiction of "reality" or an experiential account where "truth" is in the eye of the beholder (Bazerman, 1992). The trouble with this type of examination is that it can result in discursive abstractions where texts have no meanings beyond those of the writer. There is the ever-present risk of falling into postmodern rhetoric or textual narcissism (Baker 1990; Cocks 1989).

To avoid this methodological trap, this study utilized the work of Michel Foucault to engage in an archaeological investigation where the text was examined as an *artifact*. In so doing, the statements made in documents were viewed as monuments and objects of study in their own right, subject to specific rules and discursive formation (Gutting 1989). This form of investigation enables the description of discursive formations without temporal relationships (Foucault 1972). An archaeological investigation displaces "man" from his privileged position at the center of thought. Although similar to structuralist methodologies such as linguistics and ethnology, an archaeology differs in its concern for actual occurrences and their effects, rather than for their structural possibilities. The move away from "man" as the fundamental subject places a greater emphasis on the sharp ruptures in a procession of ideas. An archaeological investigation uncovers discontinuities and breaks in the chronology allowing for a more careful examination of how a series of events may become an object of discourse that can be recognized, clarified, and elaborated upon.

For Foucault, "traditional" histories were too deeply saturated with notions of continuity, causality, and teleology, which stem from forms of modern rationalism and ultimately from the Cartesian notion of the constitutive subject. Instead, Foucault's histories typically begin from his perception that something is "wrong" in the present and that to understand the past is to understand the present.[2] Foucault's early works were called "archaeologies," the subsequent ones "genealogies," and the volumes on the history of sexuality that appeared at the time of his death he called "problematizations" (Flynn 1994). Each of these approaches to understanding "history" questions notions such as power relations, truth, and subjectivity as ways to understand problems in the present. In the examination of the teacher education program reform, this project utilized parts of each of these approaches to understand the history of the program and its relationship to present concerns about the university/state relationship during the program's construction.

The use of the faculty meeting minutes and departmental memos as archival texts is taken from Foucault's concept of archaeology. Rather than study the "arche," or origin, an archaeology examines the "archive," to look for "the systems that establish statements as events (with their own conditions and domain of appearance) and things (with their own possibility and field of use)" (Foucault 1972: 128). The archive presents a linguistic understanding modified by reference to discursive practices that make up the "conditions of existence" for other discursive practices (Flynn 1994). In other words, an archaeological approach to history positions the archive as the locus of the rules and prior practices forming the conditions of inclusion or exclusion that enable certain practices and prevent others from being accepted. Texts, such as the faculty meeting minutes and memos, are read for their discursive formations, which are subject to specific rules.

However, examining the faculty meeting minutes and memos as "discourse" presents unique problems because the minutes were records of meetings that were tempered by form, objectivity and an emphasis on parliamentary procedure. They also represented the interpretations of one person (generally the note-taker) but were then circulated among all faculty for review. When circulated as a fair representation of a historical event, they also became more of a rhetorical enterprise centered on persuasion (Brown 1987; Brown 1992a; Brown 1992b). In order to examine these texts as social discourse, I find it valuable to rely on Pierre Bourdieu's concept of *authorized language*.

Bourdieu suggests that the power of authorized language lies in the delegated power of the spokesperson (Bourdieu 1991). Another way to think of this is that the authority of the university is delegated to the departmental texts because they are a product of the institution. The substance of discourse is a guarantee of delegation by the way it represents the authority of the establishment. Its power is limited only to the extent of delegation and the social positioning of the spokesperson or note-taker. The stylistic features that characterize authorized language all stem from the position the spokesperson occupies in the competitive field of the institution. The structure of the field governs the form of expression and access to the text. Bourdieu refers to "structural censorship" to signify how the authorized spokesperson is subjected to the norms of official protocol when reporting events. The meeting minutes and memos are actually a product of a dialectical compromise between the expressive interest of the note-taker and the structural censorship of the field he or she is working within. Unless an event can be recorded in "acceptable" form, it will go unstated in the minutes. The minutes are a physical manifestation of the compromise between what actually happened and what was recorded. Using Bourdieu's notion of authorized language the texts can be examined as a form of socially constructed discourse. This differs from textual narcissism because an emphasis is put on the relationships of the text within the context of the university instead of on trying to find "truth" or "reality" in the *correct* reading of the text. By asking different questions of the text, knowledge about the power and social relationships between the university and state during the program's construction is made clearer.

Problematics of Government: Technologies and Rationalities

Governmentality is a way of conceptualizing the institutions, procedures, analyses, calculations, and tactics that allow the use of power to govern.[3] Governmentality can be conceptualized as a way of understanding the strategies used to govern (Foucault 1979b). It is a mentality of rule—a way of problematizing the way political rule intervenes upon the conduct of knowledge and people. Instead of deploying power over society (sovereign rule) governmentality is a way of thinking about the utilization of power *within* society. Analyzing the meeting minutes and memos for evidence of political and governmental technologies opens up a space to "see" the technologies of rule during the reform period.

One way to make this visible in the text is to examine it for the *rationalities* that order governmental rule. Examining the text for evidence of political rationalities, however, can be difficult because there isn't a way to measure the degree of rationality in practice. Instead, it is more meaningful to examine how rationalities *become* part of practice. Foucault describes it as follows:

> One isn't assessing things in terms of an absolute against which they could be evaluated as constituting more or less perfect forms of rationality, but rather examining how forms of rationality inscribe themselves in practices or systems of practices, and what role they play within them, because it's true that "practices" don't exist without a certain regime of rationality. (1991: 79)

Foucault goes on to suggest that one should analyze rationality for how it forms an ensemble of rules and procedures, that determines a domain of subjects. This can be thought of as the moral or epistemological character of rationality or the way in which the power to rule is attributed as a "proper" or "just" duty for the authority. This can be seen in two ways. First, rule or action is based on some kind of ideal or *principle*. Here language of the text might position the faculty as trying to persuade the state agency to change a ruling because it caused undue hardships for students in the program. The reason for the faculty's action is based in the principle that they should look out for the interests and needs of the students, and it is for this reason that the state agency should change. Second, the epistemological or moral character of rationality embodies some *conception* of the person over whom government is exercised. There is an understanding of the nature of the subjects being governed. An example of this would be looking at the text for the ways in which the faculty perceived how well the state agency responsible for public education understood their program. The textual analysis would look for comments about what the agency said and how rational its conceptions of the elementary program appeared to the faculty.

In looking for the principles and conceptions of political rationalities in the texts, it is important to recognize that they are not general laws or rules that have been "rediscovered" through historical interpretation. It would be inappropriate to say that the faculty acted only in principle when they positioned state agency rulings as a burden to students. The conceptions and principles that make political rationalities visible are complex and involve a large variety of interactions from within the group. Returning to Foucault:

> we are dealing with sets of calculated, reasoned prescriptions in terms of which
> institutions are meant to be reorganized, spaces arranged, and behaviours regu-
> lated. If they have an identity, it is that of a programming left in abeyance, not
> that of a general but hidden meaning. (1991: 80)

In other words, examining the texts for the political rationalities of the state
agency responsible for public education and the faculty situates them as part of
a whole *technology* of regulations. The morality or principle of actions (such
as acting on behalf of the students) needs to be seen as more than ideology.
Such actions signify a discursive mediation that allows a whole range of technologies to be brought to bear on social behavior. The archived minutes and
memos can be seen as an action (or technology) that was meant to persuade
the faculty (and frequently, the state agency) into changing their behavior.

Analyzing the text for the principle behind the political rationalities (or their
moral character) signals ties to a larger technological apparatus. The same can
be said for analyzing the text for the conceptions of the political rationalities
(or their epistemological character). Knowledge of what was being governed
as measured against what is known as "true" gives clues to the "hidden" technologies of government rule. The text signals the discursive relations between
the university and state. This relationship in the text opens up a space to "see"
the technologies of rule within the political rationalities of the state.

A second way to visualize governmentality in the text is to look for the *technologies* of government. It is through technologies that the political rationalities become deployable. In other words, the technologies are the actual things
used in the governing process. These include the calculations, techniques,
apparatuses, and procedures through which authorities seek to embody and
give effect to governmental ambitions. In studying the university/state relationship, the technologies of government to be considered include the methods of
management used by both the state agency and the university. When the new
certification rules were given to the faculty, they came with a newly created faculty advising worksheet to assist them in helping students through the new
maze of regulations. This was a technology used to govern the way in which
information was disseminated to students in an orderly and accurate way.

Foucault discusses the technologies of government as emerging during the
Classical Age with the beginning of a populational economy. For the first time
in history, scientific categories (rather than juridical) were used to understand
the population being governed.[4] With this new understanding came a need for
a new type of discipline:

> . . . clearly its modes of organization, all the institutions with within which it had
> developed in the seventeenth and eighteenth centuries—schools, manufactories,
> armies, etc.—all this can only be understood on the basis of the development of

the great administrative monarchies, but nevertheless, discipline was never more important or more valorized than at the movement when it became important to manage a population. (Foucault 1991: 102)[5]

One way to think about political technologies as they relate to governmentality is to consider how they enable the management of populations. Political technologies develop a "mode of understanding aimed at particulars" (Dreyfus and Rabinow 1983: 134). After the eighteenth century this newer form of government described by Foucault (1979a) aimed to produce a population of human beings that could be treated as productive, "docile bodies." Instead of sovereign rule, new techniques were created that depended upon amassing knowledge about the population, and that rendered such knowledge calculable by turning it into inscriptions that were "durable and transportable, that could be accumulated in the offices of officials, that could be added, subtracted, compared, and contrasted" (Rose 1989). One form of political technology is documentation. When examining the text, the faculty documentation of certification compliance can be thought of as a political technology through which the faculty disciplined itself.

It is important to remember, however, what is meant by "discipline" in this analogy. It is not a chastisement or punishment of the faculty by the state. Discipline, from this perspective, is a specific technique of power that regards individuals both as objects and instruments of its exercise. Political technologies operate differently and precisely on bodies (or those being governed) through a combination of hierarchical observation and the kinds of "micropenalties" in which more and more areas of life become accessible to power—what Foucault (1979a) terms normalizing judgment. By requiring the documentation of certification compliance on course syllabi, the state agency responsible for public education was able to observe how closely aligned the courses were to the new rules. Documentation was a form of surveillance that allowed the state to "know" the university as a subject or docile body. The texts can be examined for evidence of this type of observational documentation.

Again drawing from Foucault, this fascination with detail has historical significance. In times of sovereign rule, the minutiae of everyday life escaped the governmental gaze. With the emergence of governmentality, however, surveillance and observation of the population as individuals became more important. A vast, meticulous documentary apparatus becomes an essential component of governmental power. The accumulation of individual documentation made possible:

> . . . the measurement of overall phenomena, the description of groups, the characterization of collective facts, the calculation of gaps between individuals, their distribution in a given population. (Foucault 1979a: 190)

Many forms of documentation were required by the state agency with the passage of the new certification rules. Each can be viewed as a form of political technology that helped the state "know" and "watch over" the program.

Today's state is a complex mixture of diverse political entities that govern in a multitude of ways. Often the language used to structure oppositions between the state and civil society, in an attempt to get a "fix" on the way the state governs, does not adequately characterize the diverse ways in which rule is exercised. Positioning the state in opposition to the university doesn't recognize the ways in which the university is bound to the state in terms of funding, certification, and governance. In Wisconsin, university programs must meet certification requirements set by the state agency in order for graduates to receive certification. Seen from this perspective, the university is actually part of the system of state government. To speak of the "power" of the state (or a particular state agency) actually minimizes the way in which its power arises from an assemblage of forces. An alternative to this view would see the power of the state as the ability to create citizens capable of bearing a kind of regulated freedom. The state uses its power to create a situation where the university has the freedom to create a program, but must do so in the way that the state education agency stipulates. The university is still "free" to put any type of program together, but the governmental agency concerned with public education regulates this freedom through licensure requirements.

This view of state-as-government positions power as an entity unto itself. The state has the power to "do" or "create" as it wishes. Another option would be to see the power of the state as a multifocal grouping of forces. This is not to say that the state does not exist. We can speak of the power of the state, which actually does exist, but the state itself is not a defined entity. It can be conceptualized as an assemblage of forces by which particular objectives and injunctions can shape the actions of others. In other words, the "center" of the state is multiple. Instead of examining how the power of the state affects those being governed (such as the university), one examines the devices and mentalities that enable various locals to *act* as center.

Using the idea of governmentality, then, the university/state relationship is understood as the ways in which the assemblages of "state" act through the university apparatus. The university is also scrutinized for how it uses power to affect the state; and university/state relations are understood through the circulation of power. The text is examined for evidence of political rationalities and technologies of rule—what Rose and Miller call the "problematics of government" (1992).

Political Rationalities and Governmental Technologies in the Text

As discussed, political rationalities refer to the morals or principles behind political rule. The analysis of the text for evidence of political rationalities—

both the state's and the university's—leads to an examination of the subtleties of language used to describe each entity. Neither the state nor the faculty mentions their authoritative basis outright in the text. However, by examining the "official" minutes through the lens of governmentality, one can see the relations of power and knowledge they encode. Knowledge is examined for its normalcy or naturalness and who is articulating it.

During the years between 1987 and 1992, faculty meetings seem at one level to constitute a relationship between the State of Wisconsin and the University. At another level, the minutes are a way to consider the different discursive relationship through which teacher preparation constitutes its objects of practice— the teacher education student who is to act on the child of the school. Thus, my examination in this chapter of the recording of discussions about such issues as program requirements in creative and performing arts, minority enrollments, and training in human relations to name but a few will probe these relations in which certain discursive rules and standards frame and discipline the discussions about the link between the State and University. Thus rather than two institutions at odds with each other, there are principles about the teacher and the child that circulate among institutions to define the boundaries and possibilities of the reforms.

In the minutes, the changes proposed by the state agency were variously referred to as "rulings," "requirements," "initiatives," "mandates," and "rules." This gives an indication as to the extent of governing taking place, but it does not explore the concrete governing of the program through its pedagogical strategies. One way to do this is to analyze the rules of rationality or reason in the text for their moral and epistemological character. As suggested, the moral or epistemological character of political rationalities can be conceived as the way in which the power to rule is attributed as a "proper" or "just" duty for the authority, often being based in some kind of principle.

One of the first required programmatic changes during the ten-year span of time under scrutiny was the addition of credits in creative and performing arts for students in the program. A memo stated in part: ". . . we want to keep the burden of new state requirements off the students as much as possible and alleviate their scheduling problems . . ."[6]

Because the new state regulations did not mandate the creation of a new program (the students were only to take more courses), no programmatic changes were particularly necessary. Instead, the text indicates a call to action based in *principle*. The memo suggests a call to action on behalf of the students and against the new regulations. "Using this plan the burden is placed solely on the students, along with increased tuition, costs of books and supplies and living expenses. The usual student, unless endowed with a wealthy parent, finishes the teacher preparation program burdened with onerous debts and a low salary. The almost certain requirements for an 'induction year' being imposed by the [state agency] will add to this burden. I am trying to hold the program to nine semesters."[7]

The new regulation was positioned against a principle that the students' needs should be considered when changing the program. The new requirements are described as being a "burden" to the students. The new requirement is positioned in the text as being wrong in principle and suggests readers should "do the right thing" by not allowing this to happen. The state's political rationality governs the willingness to act—to "hold the program to nine semesters."

Another example of action based in principle is recognized during the discussion of the bulging enrollment in the program: ". . . enrollment cuts are necessary because [state education agency] initiatives must be funded out of our current budget and teaching assistant workloads need to be reduced."[8]

In this example the new initiatives are positioned as causing economic hardships that will indirectly increase teaching assistant workloads. The text suggests a principle for action based on the best interest of the teaching assistants by reducing the number of students in the program. The epistemological character of rule, here, is a moral principle that teaching assistant workloads shouldn't be increased, but reduced. In this instance the power to rule is attributed as a just duty for the authority and aligned against the (perceived) political rationalities of the state.

One way to look at the overt principles that were positioned in the text is to examine the persuasiveness of the actions taken. In the first example, the principle behind the persuasive action can be thought of as "We need to consider the undergraduates when we make decisions." The text suggests that the university is positioned as acting against the programmatic changes stipulated by the state agency responsible for public education in Wisconsin. The memo can be seen as an attempt to persuade the university faculty to make a decision while remembering the students' needs (the moral principle) in relation to the actions of the state. In the second example, the principle behind the persuasive action can be thought of as "We need to act in the best interests of our teaching assistants." Here, the text suggests that the university is positioned as being concerned about the increased workloads brought about by reduced funding due to the new initiatives. In both examples, the political rationality behind the persuasive action was in response to an act of governing by the state agency.

A second way to examine the text in relation to the political rationalities of governmentality is to look at how the epistemological character of the text embodies some conception of the person over whom government is exercised. As discussed, this could include a group to be led, a population to be managed, a resource to be exploited, among others. One way that this becomes visible in the text is through a closer examination of how the university faculty were "asked" to respond to the governing of the state agency. The text often suggests a network external to the university that could be called upon to help "persuade" the state agency into changing its ideas: "[Chair] reported on developments related to [the state agency's] proposed certification rules, discussed their impact on the elementary program and encouraged those at the meeting to contact and inform their non-university public school colleagues of the aspects of the rules so that they might express their own opinions about the certification recommendations."[9]

The text suggests knowledge of a governmental "system" exercising power to change the existing program, and faculty are "encouraged" to express their opinions about them to nonuniversity colleagues. This tactic was also suggested in the text when the state began to require certifiable minors in the teacher education program: "It was suggested that if faculty have reactions to the minors guidelines that were distributed they should talk to their colleagues around the state and submit responses to [the agency] as soon as possible."[10]

In other instances the faculty created ad hoc committees to develop responses to state rules as in these examples: ". . . an Ad Hoc committee [is to] be set up to develop an appropriate response to the effect of current [state agency] requirements on minority enrollments."[11] and ". . . the chair of elementary education [is to] appoint an Ad Hoc committee representing elementary education faculty in mathematics, science, and social studies to develop a response to the new [state agency] rules concerning the aforementioned requirement."[12] Or, the department chair would write a response and then ask for faculty feedback: "It was suggested that [Chair] prepare a statement against this change and supporting the continuing of the Adolescent Psychology option."[13] "A summary of responses to these rules has been prepared and is being sent to the elementary staff separately for review and comment."[14]

In each of these instances the faculty *action* represented in the text can be examined in relation to the governmentality. In each case the action is created to heighten awareness of the program in the eyes of the state, either through networking, formal committee responses, or formal responses by the department chair. The textual examination suggests that the faculty was positioned in disagreement with the state's *conception* of their program. This conception or understanding can be thought of as the faculty's comprehension of the state's political rationality regarding their program.

To clarify, the text positions the state as not fully understanding the program (and those being governed) and positions the faculty as responsible for increasing the state's awareness on several fronts by networking and writing formal responses to rulings. Another interpretation could be that the state wanted to change parts of the program that the faculty believed were integral. In either case the faculty *could* have done nothing about the changes and adjusted the program accordingly. Instead, they appear in the text as acting from within their own form of political rationality to network and write formal responses to the rulings.

The textual analysis provides clues to the epistemological character of the political rationalities of both the faculty and the state. Governmentality is a way of conceptualizing the institutions, procedures, analyses, calculations, and tactics that allow the use of power to govern. Political rationalities order governmental rule and are visible in the ways the university and state use power in relation to each other. The persuasive faculty action represented in the text (networking, writing responses, etc.) is examined in relationship to state governing. The various actions are designed to heighten the state's awareness of the program. The epistemological character of the action signals an underlying principle of mis(non)understanding of the program on behalf of the state. This political rationality includes a conception of what and who is being governed.

The political *technologies* of government can be thought of as the strategies, techniques, and procedures through which different forces operate that enable connections between the aspirations of the authorities and the activities of individuals and groups (Rose and Miller 1992). Technologies are mechanisms that allow the deployment of political rationalities. One way they are visible in the text is through a reliance on documentation. In early 1988 the minutes state: ". . . the Department of Public Instruction may require that they be provided with documentation that our lecturers and supervisors have been made aware of those certification requirements specific to each course."[15]

The texts suggest faculty discussion of the documentation obligation that "lecturers and supervisors have been made aware of certification requirements." The text then goes on to state: "The Faculty of each professional methods courses and practicums will meet at least once early in each academic year to discuss the content and experiences to be included in each course. All supervisors and lecturers will be included in these meetings. Provision for instruction in those certification requirements specific to each course will be examined at these meetings."[16]

One way to think about this section of the text is to consider the faculty as responding to imposed political technologies by the state, for example, that they *document* instructor knowledge of the new rules. The creation of the new policy statement can be thought of as a response and amplification of political technologies. The call for documentation was answered with documentation. The documented policy statement would serve (at least figuratively) to guarantee all teaching faculty had been made aware of the new rules.

In another section of the text, the political technology of documentation was evident in the rewriting of course syllabi to explicitly detail course coverage of new rules and regulations. This technology impacted both the students and faculty. The text frequently refers to the confusion over which rules were being covered by existing programs and which were not as with the following discussion of what documentation would be needed: "After discussion it was agreed that the following documentation should be made available by instructors: (a) a list of the (state agency) standards addressed in the course and (b) a core curriculum or core syllabus for each course with the topics or objectives keyed to the (state agency) standards. Core syllabi were deemed particularly important for courses with multiple sections."[17]

The text also can be read for another type of political technology—the technology of *resistance*. Although the text states that all faculty were to provide syllabi with rule documentation, there also appears a form of resistance in the minutes: "[Professor 1] reported that she has received materials from only a few instructors concerning course content to meet the new [state education agency] standards. After discussion it was agreed that each instructor whose course content meets certain aspects of the new [state education agency] standards turn in [proper documentation] to [Professor 1] by May 21, 1987."[18]

The text also suggests some confusion or resistance over whether *all* syllabi had to have recorded standards: ". . . [Professor 1] inquired as to whether syllabi distributed to students need to have [state agency] standards the course meets listed on the syllabus. [Professor 2] replied that he believed only the syllabi on file in the elementary office need to have the [state agency] standards listed on them. A check of previous minutes verified this interpretation."[19]

The text suggests that the faculty resisted, through noncompliance, the political technology of documentation of state standards. One way to think about this is to view their resistance as part of the power relations circulating in the university. Power relationships, such as the associations between state "rule" and production of faculty resistance, are present everywhere in the power network (Foucault 1990). Power is not something possessed or wielded by powerful agents because it is co-constituted by those who support and resist it. The faculty is seen as resisting the technology of documentation through noncompliance (or compliance resistance), but the act of compliance also makes the ruling power possible. In other words, the technology of documentation maintains the technology of noncompliance and vice versa.

The text details a similar form of political technology of documentation in the form of a new program entitled "human relations" via "code points" in eight content areas: "It was the consensus of the faculty that the elementary areas should meet and document code points by course as soon as possible. . . . Documentation is required to be up to date every other year."[20]

The "human relations" program was intended to expose preservice teachers to populations different from themselves. Students in the teacher education program were generally white, upper-middle-class females with little experience working with children of color or children from lower socioeconomic backgrounds. By documenting certain types of experiences with the targeted diverse (minority and poor) populations, students would accrue "code points" towards their degree completion.

The documentation of rule compliance that the faculty compiled regarding the "human relations code point rule" was a new political technology. Governmentality is dependent upon knowledge of the subject of rule and the documentation mentioned in the text can be thought of as a new technique that helped amass information about the university. In turn, the university sought compliance with the new regulations and "disciplined" itself through documentation. Such political technologies help form those being governed into something calculable and easy to discipline. From a Foucauldian perspective, the documentation can be thought of as a form of discipline that helped to create a productive "docile body" of the program and faculty.

Positioned as an issue of governmentality, the disciplinary techniques that operated within the university culminated in an examination—the state education agency's program review. In such a review, the state agency responsible for public education would inspect the university program (generally by examining printed materials) and determine if all state-defined rules for certification had been met. The text suggests that after one such review the political technology of documentation was an issue: "The [state education agency] mandates that did not explicitly appear on syllabi as being covered in a specific course were the ones that were questioned by the [agency] reviewer . . . the department will also need to come up with a way to document school visits by professors who teach methods courses and in the future student teaching supervisors will need to have had three years of teaching experience."[21]

This type of review/examination can be thought of as a ritual of *surveillance*. As discussed, surveillance enables disciplinary power to become part of an integrated system. Although surveillance is organized as a multiple and anonymous power, its power rests on individuals (Foucault 1979b: 176). Surveillance is often manifested in the creation or extension of rituals, such as the proliferating practices of examination or confession. Foucault refers to the examination as a space where the disciplinary power manifests its potency by arranging objects. The examination is the "ceremony of objectification" (1979b: 187). The reference to the documentation "that did not explicitly appear on the syllabi" suggests an objective examination of the university. The university was examined for how well it was complying with the newly defined rules, and the faculty was expected to state (confess) how the new mandates were being met on their syllabi. The text chronicles an ongoing faculty discussion about which mandates would be covered by the courses taught outside the department (such as through the departments of educational policy studies and educational psychology) and, as such, did not need to appear on the syllabi. As a result, not all of the requirements were noted on the syllabi and this fact was recorded in additional text.

The program review (examination) can be thought of as the epitome of university surveillance needed to discipline and objectify the faculty "body" and program. As with the code point authentication on course syllabi, the program review can be thought of as a form of surveillance that allowed the university to be "known" as a subject or docile body. It served to "objectify" the university faculty by making them an individual body to be acted upon through additional forms of documentation and surveillance. Also key to this understanding is that even more documentation would be required in the future to demonstrate that methods instructors were visiting the school and all supervisors had at least three years of classroom teaching experience.

The text also chronicles how such documentation was "passed on" to the students. The minutes record discussion about how the new certification rules stipulated that students in elementary education had to have experience working with ethnic minority and low-income groups. A policy statement was included in a memo as part of a new advising worksheet (written in a format to be handed out directly to students) that accompanied a copy of the state education agency rule DPI code PI 4.14: "The program shall require a minimum of 50 documented clock hours of direct involvement with adult and pupil members of a group whose background the student does not share including at least one of the following designated ethnic minority groups: African-Americans, American Indians, Asian-Americans, Pacific-Islander-Americans and foreign born persons of color; and various socioeconomic groups including low income. At least 25 of the 50 clock hours of direct involvement shall be with representatives of one or more of the designated ethnic minority groups . . ."[22]

The text explains how fifty hours of "human relations field experience" had to be completed over an eight-week period of time and students had to establish a "one-to-one, ongoing relationship with an individual or members of a small group." Additionally, the experience had to occur in an instructional setting with pupil learners. The sheet warned students of the potential problems of not getting fieldwork accepted: "SUGGESTION: It is a frustrating experience to discover after the fact that the fieldwork you have just completed won't count for human relations credit. Consequently, you are *strongly* advised to obtain, submit, and have your Human Relations Field Experiences Application approved by a member of the human relations staff *before* doing the experience."[23]

This technology of documentation was required by the assemblage of state forces through the production of regulatory text. In turn, the university required students to submit documentation of completion. The political technology was "passed on" to the students through the university. In addition, there was a specific procedure (ritual) the students had to follow to document their experiences. The text explains how it involved several steps that had to be documented and submitted for approval and verification including the completion and approval of an application and attending a two-hour "human relations workshop."

Several things are interesting about the way human relations fieldwork is positioned in the text if we think about these rules as part of the technology of governmentality. First, the experiences are listed as being a *state* rather than a university requirement. This is evident in the way the state education agency code (PI 4.14) is quoted at the top of the handout. Second, and related to the first, is the hierarchical construction of the documentation. The "power" to determine whether an experience meets the criteria outlined by the state is maintained by the counselors in the Human Relations Office. Students must also get supervisory signatures at the start and end of their experience. The human relations field experience documentation can be thought of as a form of surveillance which allowed the university (and state) to "know" the student as a subject or docile body. The student had to conform and discipline their "self" to meet the requirements for certification. At first glance, the power structures in both of these examples appear to be traditional and top-down—the requirements come from the state (not the university) and the determiner of what field experience "counts" is in the hands of the Human Relations Office. However, both of these examples can be explained in an alternative way if one thinks of them in terms of governmentality or "the government of the self by the self in its articulation with relations to others" (Davidson 1994). Foucault has said the "modern" governmental rationality is simultaneously about individualizing and totalizing. While the state requirement appears totalizing, it is at the same time individualizing in that every student must document his or her human relations work, thereby becoming more visible and known. While the individual is understood, he or she also becomes part of a society or population of individuals to be governed. "The student" is part of a grouping of people completing teacher certification requirements at the university.

Third, the types of experiences are clearly identified. The field experiences are nested in a populational construction because students must work with specific groups defined by a classificatory norm. The students must work in multicultural settings, with ethnic minorities or with low-income students. Other distinctions, such as those of gender or disability are not mentioned. The distinctions that are made in the text about the types of persons the student is to work with defines certain regulatory categories that can be seen as populational reasoning and as part of a political technology with a particular history.

The reference to "designated ethnic minority groups" in the rules can also be linked historically to an emerging social topography in the 1960s that centered upon the growth of the American population, its concentration in large cities, and the racial class distribution within these cities (Rose 1989). At this time, social scientists investigating urban areas began to find regular patterns of ethnic groupings in ghetto districts, a surrounding ring of white working-class families, and the bulk of the middle-class white population distributed in the outer suburbs. Political concerns centered on the social and economic inequality amounting to racial segregation in the large cities. With this realization came pressure to change teacher education courses to encourage sensitivity to cultural and racial differences among children. Multicultural and ethnic related pedagogies were introduced in teacher education to "correct" inequalities in society (Popkewitz and Pereyra 1993).

These efforts also introduced new patterns of regulations, as the linguistic distinctions made in the text also organize what is spoken about and how that speech is expected to occur. The veneration of certain groupings in society sets in motion decided ways of discerning problems, solutions, and patterns by which progress and failure are to be judged. Stating that the student must have direct involvement with groups of people "whose background the student does not share" also posits the groups as "other." Students in the program would complete human relations fieldwork with the state education agency's "designated ethnic minority groups." Through the enunciation of racial and social categories a form of cultural authority is articulated in the curriculum (Donald 1992). The cultural "other" becomes something to be classified and understood in relation to privileged norms that are presumed to make the canon of school subjects accessible. Although created with the admirable purpose of helping new teachers understand children with backgrounds different from their own, the program also constructed the child in relationship to other members of a population. Individuality was replaced with normativity.

It is also possible to glimpse in the texts the ways in which identity itself is constructed through the technologies of regulation via the discourses of psychology and child welfare.[24] The use of terms such as *cognitive, social,* and *emotional* development in early drafts of the administrative rules given to the faculty to review indicates a strong propensity towards the science of psychology in defining program content: "The program shall require study of the characteristics of play and its contribution to the cognitive, social, and emotional development and learning of children birth through age 8."[25]

In this rule, the program is clearly linked with the "science" of psychology. Child development, as a method of organizing the curriculum of early learning, is unquestioned in the text. Psychological criteria became the basis for scientific decision making in education during the first half of the twentieth century and its influence remains strong in reform texts to date. Theoretical discussions about curricular goals in education are often predicated upon distinctions made within the psychological as opposed to the social, political, or economic realms (Silin 1988). Another example from the text shows an even stronger emphasis on psychology as child development and child study: "The program shall require the study of the principles and theories of child growth and development including a background in biological, cognitive, psychomotor, emotional, and social development and their relationship to learning. The program shall require study and experience in the methods of child study."[26]

The historical influences of psychology can be seen by reference to child study and developmental psychology. Although there are acute distinctions between child study and child development, what is important to this examination is that both forms of study aimed to make the program more "professional" by emphasizing the science of psychology. In both sections there is an overarching emphasis on developmental aspects of learning through psychological categories (biological, cognitive, psychomotor, emotional, social) and through developmental research techniques (child study and child development theory).

Historically, the school was a natural target for psychologists trying to "discover" internal mental processes, such as creativity, perception, thinking, problem solving, memory, and language (Rose 1989). Educational usage of words such as "cognitive," "social," and "emotional" became commonplace in teacher lesson-plans and helped in the diagnosis of children who needed special attention. Teachers of young children in particular were encouraged to incorporate all aspects of mental ability into their lessons to ensure the well-balanced and integrated maturation of the child. The emergence of the child study movement encouraged teachers and researchers to observe children in order to shed light upon human evolution and the characteristics distinguishing "man" from animals. Made popular largely though the efforts of psychologist G. Stanley Hall, the child study movement encouraged teachers to build curricula based upon observation. Throughout the 1920s child study centers sprang up in universities across the country as a way to "make scientific" the education of young children. However, psychologists of the time, while acknowledging the contributions child study made, contested the belief that observation equated a "science" of maturation. By the early 1940s the normative studies of Arnold Gesell at Yale University launched the beginning of a more "scientific" child study approach. It is Gesell who is credited with popularizing the notion that children pass through sequential, unfolding developmental stages.[27]

What is important to recognize about these distinctions is that the use of such psychological language goes unquestioned in the minutes. Child study and child development are given as "scientific" methodologies to gain knowledge about the proper teaching of children. This emphasis on scientific methodology along with the combination of hierarchical observations and normalizing judgements inherent in their use make all individuals in society a potential category for observation and administration.

The text also suggests the importance of child welfare in the program by its emphasis on parental involvement in education: "The program shall require the study and experiences designed to develop skills in promoting parent education and family involvement in the early childhood level program."[28]

Nurturing and child welfare issues were an integral part of the first early childhood programs in America. The role of the early childhood teacher as "parent educator" began in the first half of this century as psychologists began to apply their trade to the problem of "maladjusted" children. Psychologists believed that parents needed help in raising well-adjusted children because of rapid and profound changes in society, caused largely by the influx of immigrants (Napoli 1981). Early-childhood teachers began to adopt the idea that they, too, had a role in producing well-adjusted children.

Both the "science" of early childhood education and its emphasis on child welfare can be contextualized as part of the way society is governed through the lens of professional knowledge. The use of psychology and psychological descriptions of children provide the means for the subjectificaton of the human soul. They enable "human powers" to be transformed into material that can provide the basis for calculation (Rose 1989). By slicing human learning into cognitive, social, emotional, psychomotor, and biological development, techniques of examination are imposed upon the subject in question. The examining mechanisms of the psychological sciences provide a technique for rendering subjectivity into thought as a calculable force. The application of normalizing judgement makes the human subject visible and transcribes attributes into codified forms of documentation. The "soul" becomes thinkable in terms of psychology. Identity itself is governed.

The use of psychological categories in the text ensures certain techniques of organization will take place. Relations of hierarchy in human development epitomized in the use of child study and child development theories locates humans in space and time in order to achieve certain outcomes. The teaching of young children is to direct their conduct to meet certain predefined results. Using the principles of psychology, technologies of subjectivity are established that enable strategies of power to infiltrate the fissures of the human soul (Rose 1989).

The development and academic application of psychology also enables new forms of expertise in the "professional" social sciences. Armed with a "norm" of social behavior, the population can be scrutinized for deviance by the new professional. This sociopolitical approach emphasizes the welfare of the child in terms of a populational norm. Early childhood educators can examine children for their "normalcy" and act accordingly. Instruction in the synthesization of home and school resources as they influence the development of the young child ensures that the teacher will know how to use all available resources to protect the welfare of the child. The emphasis on parent education will also help to transmit psychological norms and pedagogic techniques into the home to ensure the best possible (maximum) development of the child. The new techniques help the private family to become a site where the production of a "normal" child takes form. The family uses the professional expertise of the teacher to examine and regulate their own behavior and apply specific techniques to produce a "normal" child.

The promotion of subjectivities relating the duties of parenthood with the production of "normal" children enables a mechanism of social control. By internalizing the psychological descriptions of normalcy, families become intensively governed. The technologies visible in the text enable a way of viewing children psychologically in an effort to produce a well-adjusted generation. It is through the promotion of such subjectivities that the population at large is governed.

Conclusion

By examining the governmentality of the university/state relationship in the "everyday spaces" of teacher education text, several things became clearer. First, both the university and the state were positioned in the text as acting from a moral or political framework regarding conception of rule. The university faculty, in particular, appeared in the text as acting from within their own form of political rationality to network and write formal responses to state rulings. It was if they felt they had a right or responsibility to try to argue with the state about certain aspects of the new rules and how they affected students in the program. The epistemological character guiding the persuasive actions was based in morality or principles held by the faculty. The fact that the faculty was documented as acting "on behalf" of the students and teaching assistants in the department when they responded to the state provides clues to the types of governing taking place. The actions that the university faculty took when they responded to the state provide clues to the way they perceived the state's understanding of their program. The actions were taken to heighten awareness of the program in the eyes of the state agency responsible for public education, either through networking, formal committee responses, or formal responses by the department chair. The textual examination suggests that the faculty disagreed with the state conception of their program. This conception or understanding can be thought of as the faculty's comprehension of the state's political rationality regarding their program.

It is somewhat paradoxical that although "the state" was not knowable in the sovereign sense, the discernable political rationalities of the state forces (manifested in technologies of documentation) enabled the faculty to visualize a state body to act upon. This action was in the form of more documentation—another political technology. Even though the population was un-knowable in the traditional sense of governing power, the discourses of documentation rendered the reality of government thinkable.

Second, the political technology of documentation served to objectify the faculty by making them an individual body to be acted upon through additional documentation, surveillance, and the program examination (review). In a sense, the faculty disciplined itself and the program into what the state governing agencies wanted. This increase in documentation was often "answered" with additional technologies negotiated by the faculty and "passed on" to the students. Students were soon required to document their work in the community in terms of human relations code points and hand these in for official "credit" to complete the program. The surveillance of students also became an implicit part of the program, and governing takes place at this level as well.

Third, another form of technology was visible through the complexities of changes that were taking place within the department that structured the way in which information was given to the students. Advising packets were created that provided uniform interpretation of the rules and regulations. From the viewpoint of governmentality, the very rules of classifying embodied in the state education agency's regulations were also embodied in the advising packets. In this sense, when examining the governing process, the university/state distinction dissolves. This dissolution of the university/state dichotomy has many implications for the study of teacher education reform and change. Teacher education reform is generally analyzed as an autocratic "event" caused by forces external to the university and its population. As such, little attention is paid to the ways in which university faculty and students act as part of the changing apparatus of power. The various forms of documentation and codification that became part of the "new" program requirements *could* be thought of as something the state "did" to the university. However, using the Foucauldian idea of governmentality, the documentation is thought of as a form of discipline that helped to produce a productive "docile body" of the program and faculty that often culminated in some form of examination. Power was seen as productive (not repressive) and working through multiple points. In light of this, the university/state dichotomy dissolves. The faculty and program are understood as being "governed" through their relationships with each other—relations whose strategies govern action and participation. The faculty operated within the same rules of organization as the state. Neither the state nor the university is understood in isolation, but rather in relation to each other. I believe it is important to explore these "everyday spaces" of teacher education practice. The aim of such exploration is not to discover what we are but to make problematic the ways we have become, and perhaps refuse some of our own individualization:

> The conclusion would be that the political, ethical, social, philosophical problem of our days is not to try and liberate the individual from the state, and from the state's institutions, but to liberate us both from the state and the type of individualization which is linked to the state. We have to promote new forms of subjectivity through the refusal of this kind of individuality which has been imposed on us for several centuries. (Foucault 1983: 216)

Notes

1. The rules were Teacher Education Program Approval Rules and Procedures PI4 (commonly referred to as PI4).
2. For a discussion of Foucault's treatment of history as a concept throughout his work (see, eg., Gutting 1994 and Sheridan 1980).
3. Throughout this section I draw heavily from Rose and Miller's article (1992) and acknowledge their framing of the problematics of government.
4. Foucault states, "In other words, the transition which takes place in the eighteenth century from an art of government to a political science, from a regime dominated by structures of sovereignty to one ruled by techniques of govern-

ment, turns on the theme of population and hence on the birth of the political economy" (1991: 101).

5.   It is also important to recognize that with the creation of governmental technologies came the discursive conditions that enabled them. Foucault states that with the emergence of governmentality resulted ". . . on the one hand, the formation of a whole series of specific governmental apparatuses, and, on the other, in the development of a whole complex of savoirs" (1991: 103). The savoir of a discursive formation provides the objects, types of cognitive authority (enunciative modes), concepts, and themes (theoretical stages) that are necessary for a knowledge of governing (connaisssance) (Gutting, 1989).

6.   Call to meeting attachment in the form of a memo to Elementary Area Staff dated October 31, 1986.

7.   Ibid.

8.   Minutes of special meeting held on February 27, 1989.

9.   Minutes of October 14, 1985. Although the actual text used faculty names, throughout the analysis I refer to the persons named in the text by their title in order of discussion. For instance, if the person quoted was the department chair, they would be listed as (Chair). Professors and other staff are listed numerically in order of mention in the text (e.g., Professor 1, Professor 2). For each quotation I restart the numbering. There is no correlation between quotations in respect to the numbers.

10.   Minutes of May 8, 1989.

11.   Minutes of May 9, 1988.

12.   Minutes of May 12, 1992.

13.   Minutes of April 9, 1984.

14.   Minutes of March 10, 1986.

15.   Call to meeting of March 3, 1988.

16.   Policy statement attached to meeting minutes of March 7, 1988.

17.   Minutes of March 9, 1987.

18.   Minutes of May 11, 1987.

19.   Minutes of October 12, 1987.

20.   Minutes of February 11, 1991.

21.   Minutes of May 8, 1989.

22.   Attachment to advising worksheet given to faculty October 3, 1986.

23.   Ibid.

24.   This has been discussed in Heyning (2000).

25.   Wisconsin Department of Public Instruction PI 4.12 draft given to faculty December 5, 1988.

26.   Wisconsin Department of Public Instruction, 1989. Draft given to faculty in the fall of 1986.

27.   For a discussion of child development theory see, e.g., Braun and Edwards (1972), Brennan (1986), Cremin (1988), and Robinson and Hom (1977).

28.   PI 4.12, Specific Rules, draft of December, 1988 given to faculty.

References

Baker, S. (1990). Reflection, doubt, and the place of rhetoric in postmodern social theory. *Sociological Theory* 8(2): 232–45.

Bazerman, C. (1992). The interpretation of disciplinary writing. In R. H. Brown (Ed.), *Writing the social text: Poetics and politics in social science discourse* (31–38). New York: Walter DeGryuter.

Bourdieu, P. (1991). *Language and symbolic power* (trans. G. Raymond and M. Adamson). Cambridge, MA: Harvard University Press.

Braun, S. J. and Edwards, E. P. (1972). *History and theory of early childhood education*. Worthington, OH: Charles A. Jones Publishing.

Brennan, J. F. (1986). *History and systems of psychology* (2nd ed.). Englewood Cliffs, NJ: Prentice-Hall.

Brown, R. H. (1987). Reason as rhetorical: On relations among epistemology, discourse and practice. In J. S. Nelson, A. Megill, and D. N. McCloskey (Eds.), *The rhetoric of the human sciences: Language and argument in scholarship and public affairs* (184–97). Madison: University of Wisconsin Press.

———. (1992a). From suspicion to affirmation: Postmodernism and the challenges of rhetorical analysis. In R. H. Brown (Ed.), *Writing the social text: Poetics and politics in social science discourse* (219–27). New York: Walter de Gruyter.

———. (1992b). Poetics, politics, and truth: An invitation to rhetorical analysis. In R. H. Brown (Ed.), *Writing the social text: Poetics and politics in social science discourse* (3–7). New York: Walter deGryuter.

Cocks, J. (1989). *The oppositional imagination: Feminism, critique and political theory*. New York: Routledge.

Cremin, L. A. (1988). *American education: The metropolitan experience, 1876–1980*. New York: Harper and Row.

Davidson, A. (1994). Ethics as ascetics: Foucault, the history of ethics, and ancient thought. In G. Gutting (Ed.), *The Cambridge Companion to Foucault* (115–40). New York: Cambridge University Press.

Donald, J. (1992). *Sentimental education: Schooling, popular culture and the regulation of liberty*. New York: Verso.

Dreyfus, H. L. and Rabinow, P. (1983). *Michel Foucault: Beyond structuralism and hermeneutics*. (2nd ed.). Chicago: University of Chicago Press.

Flynn, T. (1994). Foucault's mapping of history. In G. Gutting (Ed.), *The Cambridge companion to Foucault* (28–46). New York: Cambridge University Press.

Foucault, M. (1972). *The archaeology of knowledge and the discourse on language* (trans. by A.M. Sheridan Smith, Trans.). New York: Pantheon Books. (Original text published 1969).

———. (1979a). *Discipline and punish: The birth of the prison* (Alan Sheridan, Trans.). New York: Vintage Books. (Original text published 1975).

———. (1979b). Governmentality. *Ideology and Consciousness*, 6 (Autumn): 5–22. (Original work published 1978).

———. (1983). Afterword: The subject and power. In H. L. Dreyfus and P. Rabinow (Eds.), *Michel Foucault: Beyond structuralism and hermeneutics*, (2nd ed) 208–25. Chicago: University of Chicago Press.

———. (1990). *The history of sexuality, Volume I: An introduction* (trans. by Robert Hurley). New York: Random House (Original work published 1976).

———. (1991). Questions of method. In G. Burchell, C. Gordon and P. Miller (Eds.), *The Foucault effect: Studies in governmentality* (73–86). Chicago: University of Chicago Press.

Gutting, G. (1989). *Michel Foucault's archaeology of scientific reason*. Cambridge: Cambridge University Press.

———. (1994). Michel Foucault: A user's manual. In G. Gutting (Ed.), *The Cambridge companion to Foucault* (1–27). New York: Cambridge University Press.

Heyning, K. E. (2000). The early childhood teacher as professional: An archaeology of university reform. In J. Jipson and R. Johnson (Eds.), *Resistance and representation: Rethinking childhood education*. New York: Peter Lang.

Napoli, D. S. (1981). *Architects of adjustment: The history of the psychological profession in the United States*. Port Washington, NY: National University Publications.

Popkewitz, T. and Brennan, M. (1994). Certification to credentialing: Reconstituting control mechanisms in teacher education. In K. Borman and N. P. Greenman (Eds.), *Changing American education: Recapturing the past or inventing the future?* Albany: State University of New York Press.

Popkewitz, T. and Pereyra, M. A. (1993). An eight country study of reform practices in teacher education: An outline of the problematic. In T. Popkewitz (Ed.), *Changing patterns of power: Social regulation and teacher education reform* (1–52). New York: State University of New York Press.

Prestine, N. A. (1992). The struggle for control of teacher education: The University of Wisconsin-Madison. In H. D. Gideonse (Ed.), *Teacher education policy: Narrative, stories, and cases* (159–80). New York: State University of New York Press.

Robinson, P. A. and Hom, H. L., Jr., (1977). Child psychology and early childhood education. In P. A. Robinson and H. L. Hom, Jr. (Eds.), *Psychological processes in early education* (23–36). New York: Academic Press.

Rose, N. (1989). *Governing the soul: The shaping of the private self.* New York: Routledge.

Rose, N. and Miller, P. (1992). Political power beyond the state: Problematics of government. *The British Journal of Sociology* 43(2): 173–206.

Sheridan, A. (1980). *Michel Foucault: The will to truth.* New York: Tavistock Publications.

Silin, J. (1988). On becoming knowledgeable professionals. In B. Spodek, O. N. Saracho and D. L. Peters (Eds.), *Professionalism and the early childhood practitioner* (117–34). New York: Teachers College Press.

Wittrock, B. (1993). The modern university: The three transformations. In S. Rothblatt and B. Wittrock (Eds.), *The European and American university since 1800* (303–62). Cambridge: Cambridge University Press.

13

Dewey and Vygotsky

Ideas in Historical Spaces

Thomas S. Popkewitz

Introduction

The assumptions behind turn-of-the century discourses about childhood, the state, and schooling were based on a concept of social administration. Proper planning, it was thought, would produce a New Citizen/"New Man" [*sic*] who could perform competently in changing social, economic, political, and cultural contexts. Pedagogy would rescue the child so that the child could become an adult who was self-disciplined, self-motivated, and would function as a productive participant in the new collective social projects of the day. Similarly, modern pedagogical practices involve the social administration of the child through the inscription of calculated systems of self-inspection and self consciousness.[1] But today's governing principles are different from those of the past. One central terrain in the debate about governing the child in mathematics and science teaching, among other school subjects, is a "constructivism" whose premise is that the "reasonable" teacher (and, as a corollary, the new child) should find his or her own solutions through problem-solving strategies.[2] Central to the constructivist pedagogies is the revisiting of the ideas of the American John Dewey and the Russian Lev Vygotsky, who wrote during the early part of this century.

To explore the governing principles in contemporary pedagogical discourses, I focus on the social contexts in which Dewey and Vygotsky wrote, and the reception of their ideas in current U.S. pedagogical research."[3] On the surface, the research literature assumes an apparent continuity and evolution between the ideas of these past writers and current reform efforts. My argument here is different. While the names of the authors are the same in both periods, contemporary school reforms exist within an amalgamation of institutions, ideas, and technologies that is significantly different from those of the turn of the century.

This history that I speak of is a history of the present. It aims to understand how the contemporary principles of reason in pedagogical practices are historically constructed as the effects of power (see, e.g., Foucault, Dean 1994, for discussions of this view of history in curriculum). But this history of the present also seeks to understand the ironies and paradoxes of pedagogy. Pedagogy is a practice of the social administration of the individual. Since at least the nineteenth century, pedagogical discourses about teaching, children, and learning in schools have connected the scope and aspirations of public powers with the personal and subjective capabilities of individuals.[4] This administration of the child embodies certain norms about the inner capabilities from which the child can become self-governing and self-reliant. It is through examining the changes in the administration of the child that the theories of Dewey and Vygotsky can be understood in the past and the present. These changes in the principles of administration of the child, however, are not only changes in rules of pedagogical "reason" but in the strategies by which systems of social inclusion/exclusion are constructed. While my discussion focuses on certain historical registers that are prominent in pedagogical practices, I recognize that this history is not straightforward, that it involves multiple transactions and trajectories, and entails intense struggles.[5]

This essay emerges from a particular oddity in contemporary literature written from the standpoint of constructivist pedagogy. That literature draws on Vygotsky and Dewey to state the need for a cultural and social historical perspective, but does not make any serious attempt to understand how thought is *culturally and historically* constructed. This paper extends and historicizes previous discussions concerning the social linguistic limitations of constructivism (see, e.g., Gee in press; Martin 1992; Smagorinsky 1995; also see Bowers 1993a).

The Governing of the State, the Governing of the Individual, and the Invention of Modern Psychology

While there are important theoretical distinctions between Dewey and Vygotsky, there are also historical homologies in the construction of their ideas; that is, a historical relation in value and structure that is not reducible to the other[6] The ideas of Vygotsky and Dewey were shaped and fashioned within a period of intense modernization that involved the industrialization, urbanization, and rationalization that we now associate with modernity and the modern Western welfare state (see, e.g., Berger et al. 1973; Carnoy 1984; Evans et al. 1985; Skocpol 1985; Wagner 1994; Zolberg 1991). The psychologies written during that period embodied a particular doctrine of modernity that linked an Enlightenment belief in the potential for reason to produce social progress with a faith in the rationality of science. But these two scholars recognized that science involved more than changing material conditions. It also implied efforts to produce a citizen who would act wisely and autonomously in the new political and social institutions of the times.[7] The social sciences would not only provide a cognitive knowledge, but also discipline the capabilities, values, dispositions, and sensitivities through which individuals problematized their world and individuality. This assumption was part of a larger, profound, reshaping of social life in Europe and the United States during the early years of the twentieth century.

A Historical Homology between Vygotsky and Dewey[8]

In this historical context, Dewey and Vygotsky are quintessentially modern in the sense that they believed that science could contribute to strategies that constructed "New Man." Their sciences, however, were different from the prevailing views of social and psychological theories that universalized and essentialized the problem of change and the subject of change (also see the work of Dewey's colleague, George Herbert Mead, e.g., discussed in Joas 1985). Their theories emphasized a historically contingent notion of individuality. Wood (1932: xi) argues that there was a general affinity between the Russian concern with creating a new unity of "community" and Dewey's belief that "disintegrated individuals can achieve unity only as the dominant energies of community life are incorporated to form their mind." Dewey visited the Soviet Union during the 1920s at a time when many Soviet intellectuals considered pragmatism to be important for the construction of the democratic citizen that was to be an outgrowth of their revolution.

While Dewey and Vygotsky were interested in constituting self-governing citizens as part of a nation-building project, each ordered the problem differently from the other. Where Dewey's central focus was on "community," Vygotsky focused on language as the instrument that would transfer social experiences to the individual.[9] Drawing on the ideas of Russian Symbolism (Davydov 1995), Vygotsky rejected the functionalist proposition that thinking involves innate patterns of action that undergo processes of maturation—that thinking is discovered anew by individuals. In a Marxian tradition, he argued for a democratic individuality by focusing on thought that arises through the individual's "absorption" of social experience. Thought was viewed as an activity rather than as a passive, idealized process. He saw language as a means to individual knowledge, and the interiorization of language was one of the key ways individuals developed self-governing behaviors that guided actions and developed the individual's will to know.

Dewey and Vygotsky both rejected a Cartesian mind/body dualism as well as the separation of methods of inquiry from the substantive knowledge produced about the world (Bowers 1993a, 1993b; Newman and Holzman 1993). Each grounded his ideas in a belief in the radical potential of knowledge, as well as in the variability of human societies and cultures. Both were "pragmatic" theorists in the sense that they saw all teaching and learning as conditional and contingent. Davydov (1995) says that for Vygotsky, teaching and learning (and upbringing) were collaborative activities in which there are no uniform methods.

Yet at the same time, Dewey and Vygotsky each assumed a certain universalism that linked their construction of the "reasoned" person to the particular social/political contexts in which they worked.[10] Vygotsky joined science and progress with the desire for a new social-political order in Russia. The context was one in which Marxism sought to produce a socialist economy from that of a rural, Asiatic mode of production. Vygotsky studied Marx and Engels after the revolution in order to relate psychology to the new social commitments of the state. Vygotsky's universalism tied the Soviet revolution to French Enlightenment beliefs, but circulated within a context of particular Russian nationalism that ascribed a lack of reason among, for example, the minority groups within the Soviet Union (see, e.g., Smagorinsky 1995).

Dewey's notion of community was a hybrid in the sense that it joined together multiple sets of nineteenth-century values and historical trajectories. For Dewey, the capacities and dispositions of the citizen were bound to a particular universalism of Protestant bourgeois society. Dewey's notion of "community" articulated an uneasy tension between nineteenth century U.S. Protestant pastoral images, and ideological notions about human perfectibility, and science as the motor of social progress (Ross 1991). The writing inscribed an American "exceptionalism" that transformed Protestant millennial visions about the United States as a New World into secular ideas about history and human perfectibility (for a general discussion of the religious and pastoral motifs in U.S. thought, see, e.g., Bercovitch 1978; Marx 1964; Ross 1991; West 1989; also see, e.g., O'Donnell 1985). The modern citizen, for Dewey, embodied a Protestant notion of hard work, a commitment to science as a problem-solving approach for a democracy, and an Emersonian notion of citizen "volunteerism" in social affairs. At the same time, Dewey's ideas embedded the ideals of a professional code of ethics that was to challenge the unbridled competition and inequities produced through capitalism (Haskell 1984).

While we might recognize the intellectual power of Vygotsky's and Dewey's ideas, we need to recognize that neither had a major impact on schooling. They wrote in a period of intense nation-building that focused on collective social projects that sought to identify universal solutions to social questions. This focus assured that their ideas, which were based on "problem-solving" and historically contingent pragmatism, would occupy a politically marginal position. The world of business and government was being built upon a type of expertise related to Taylorism, notions of economy of scale, and the formation of a single, collective, universal social identity—the effort to "Americanize" immigrants and marginalized groups in the United States and Sovietization of the individual in the Soviet Union. In the United States, it was the psychology of G. Stanley Hall, Edward Lee Thorndike, curriculum people like Franklin Bobbitt, who merged industrial sociology with behavioral psychology, and William Kilpatrick, who brought a developmentalism into curriculum theory, that provided the directions to classroom practices.[11]

Dewey and Vygotsky are no longer marginalized in contemporary scholarship.[12] However, to say that Dewey's and Vygotsky's ideas are now central to much educational research is not to say that we now are wiser than those who came before us. My argument is very different and related to a sociology of knowledge. The ideas of Dewey and Vygotsky are given value and structure today within a social context that embodies principles of governing the individual and "citizen" quite different from those that existed at the turn of the century.

The Problem of Governing: The Modernization of the "Mind"

Vygotsky and Dewey were part of what current sociological literature refers to as "modernity," a movement of ideas, institutions, and technologies that is historically signalled in discussions of the "Progressive Era" in the United States.[13] The concept of modernity directs attention to massive political, economic, and cultural transformations that occurred in the late nineteenth century and early twentieth century. At one level, these transformations involved the construction of political and social institutions that extended political participation. These institutions produced changes that ranged from the broadening of voting laws to the creation of social welfare institutions that provided for the health, safety, child care, and economic well-being of citizens.

The transformations in institutions also embodied changes in the governing principles by which individuals were expected to participate in society. What is often lost in U.S. educational discussions of progressivism is that the Progressive Era was a political movement that constituted new state institutions to administer social and individual life. (The particular manner in which a central administrative capacity developed in the United States is explored in Skowronek 1982. For a discussion of the state as a dynamic and relational concept, see Wittrock et al. 1991.) Contrary to popular myths about a decentralized political system in the United States, particular systems of governing did emerge to join macro- and micropatterns of social life.

This governing was embodied in the systems of expert reasoning that circulated across institutions (Popkewitz 1996). Expert systems of professional knowledge became paramount in the planning of social change. From the urban reform movements to the administration of the mass school, there was a shift from a normative and philosophical approach to society to a reformist tendency that was grounded in empirical knowledge.

The development of professional knowledge in the late nineteenth century entailed a new relationship between the governing of society and the governing of the individual. This relationship was particularly strong in liberal states,

where individuals were now expected to act with self-discipline and self-moti-
vation. I will call this link between political rationalities and the self-compart-
ment of the individual *governing the self*. Many intellectuals, business leaders,
religious leaders, and politicians believed that social progress was tied to the
development of a "New Man": a term circulating in Europe and the United
States that implied the development of an inner discipline through which individuals could navigate among and control their worlds (see, e.g., Woody 1932;
O'Donnell 1985; Napoli 1981). This new, secular citizen, it was believed,
would shed the previous beliefs and dispositions of religion and an inherited
social order and replace them with a subjectivity that embodied the obligations, responsibilities, and personal discipline embodied in liberal democratic
ideals.[14] The school was a central institution in this form of governance.

While there were ongoing debates and conflict in this period concerning
modernization, there was also a pervasive belief that the democratization of
the individual was a problem of public administration (see, e.g., Wagner 1994).
At one level, the state was to produce the universalization of policies and rou-
tinization of politics that would remove strife and produce harmonious social
development. At a different level, this State targeted the "self" as a site of
administration. The inner dispositions, sensitivities, and awarenesses of the
individual become an object of administration and site of individual salvation,
but now, in the name of individual "freedom."

By the nineteenth century, for example, Enlightenment beliefs about the citizen were made into an entity of political reflection and social administration
(see, e.g., Wagner 1994). Nineteenth-century constitutional doctrines of liberty,
rights, and law that imposed limits on state activities were predicated on the
existence of individuals who were self-governing and took responsibility for
their own conduct (Rose 1989). The state was expected to shape the individual
who would master change through the application of rationality and reason.
From Humboldtian to Hegelian and post-Kantian moral and political philosophy, the state functioned to develop people's faculties and their apprehension
of the good (see, e.g., Hunter 1994).

The social administration of the new citizen, however, should not be construed as a principled argument tied to political philosophy but as a pragmatic
one related to multiple historical trajectories that begin prior to the nineteenth
century. The particular joining of the governing of the state with that of the
governing of civil society (the joining of public/private) emerges in the seventeenth and eighteenth-century European religious wars (Hunter 1995). Distinct
realms of "public" and "private," representing two distinct types of ethical
comportment, were to pacify divided communities through the imposition of a
politically binding conception of the public good. Hunter (1995) argues that
the freedoms associated with liberal societies, religious toleration, and freedom
of worship were produced as part of administrative state efforts to govern frat-

ricidal communities rather than being the expression of democratic institutions or popular resistance. A nonviolent tolerance and pragmatic sphere of political deliberation were created by forcefully separating the civic comportment of the citizen from the private persona of one's conscience, and by subordinating spiritual absolutes to governmental objectives. Schooling was a mechanism used by the state to conceptualize and organize a massive and ongoing program of pacification, discipline, and training responsible for the political and social capacities of the modern citizen (Hunter 1995: 152–63).

The *social imaginary* of liberal thought which divided rhetorically the governing of the state from civil society has had important consequences in the present. Political philosophy and social theory make it seem that certain rights and obligations remained beyond the reach of formal governmental power. The division is embodied in the distinctions of political thought that separate society from the individual, ontology from epistemology, mind from body, the state from civil society, and economy (the entrepreneurial "man") and culture from politics. The separation of state and civil society (the public from private) is embedded in policies about the decentralization of school decision making, about schools-as-markets, as well as pedagogical theories about "voice," empowerment, and emancipation that separate the social and historical from conceptions of the mind (see Popkewitz 1996). Contemporary pedagogies and reforms in teacher education that have defined the dispositions of the child and teacher as the site of change also inscribe distinctions that separate mind and body (private) from the social and historical (public).

But the imaginary of the state/civil society binary obscures the complex webs that cross social and political institutions in the governing of the "self." There was and is no clear demarcation between the state and civil society as the new citizen was administered through multiple institutions of the state and civil society. Schooling merely constituted one of the most explicit of these governing enterprises.

The focus on the inner capabilities and dispositions for self-discipline, a cornerstone of the new social and pedagogical sciences, therefore, should not be seen as "the antithesis of political power, but a key term in its exercise, the more so because most individuals are not merely the subjects of power but play a part in its operations" (Rose and Miller 1992, p.174). Foucault (1979) called this new relationship "governmentality," that is, the art of governing in which the tactics of regulating society would interrelate with the patterns of personal decisionmaking and "reasoning" through which individuals judged their own competence and achievements. Thus, while there is continual talk about the individual being free from government, and culture being separate from political realms, the social administration of the state has aligned political rationalities with the production of an individuality since at least the late nineteenth century.

The Social Sciences and the Problem of Governing

The task of the social administration of freedom is embodied in the formation of the social sciences during the nineteenth and the early twentieth centuries (Haskell 1977; Rueschmayer and Skocpol 1996; Silva and Slaughter 1984; Wagner 1994; Wittrock et al. 1991). In the nineteenth century, it was believed that the social world, like the natural one, could be acted on and changed through scientific practices. Social questions of the day were supposed to be solved through a calculated administration of social affairs.

The social sciences were active factors in the re-visioning of the principles through which individuals were to govern themselves and judge their participation in society. This governing had previously been the domain of spiritual advisors who elaborated the norms of conduct, criteria of self-judgment, and techniques of life conduct for the individual. However, in the nineteenth century, ethical guidance began to draw on the logic of positive knowledge. Achievement, moral deportment, and development/progress of the "self" in childhood were envisioned through the new classificatory systems of scientific reasoning.

The reigning belief was that expert-scientific knowledge could be put into service of the democratic idea. A central site of the production of knowledge and expertise was social science which, in the United States, became housed in the new structures of universities that included graduate training and research, and in the Soviet Union became housed in institutes tied directly to the state. While the institutionalization of the social sciences occurred later in the Soviet Union than in the United States, the Russian state established an institute for educational psychology in 1905. Vygotsky worked there in the 1930s.

The sciences in which Dewey and Vygotsky worked, then, involved more than the organization and the interpretation of social life. The human sciences were expected to spread modernity by giving focus to the microprocesses by which individuals became self-motivated, self-responsible, and "reasonable." The social sciences generated principles for the particular type of childhood, family, citizen, and worker who could operate with the dispositions deemed necessary for liberal democratic societies. While forms of scientific reasoning were contested, social betterment was viewed as dependent upon the rational construction of the "citizens" who could act progressively to control their own circumstances and environment.

In the various arenas of social life, abstract, universal systems of ideas assessed personal competence, achievement, and progress. Bledstein (1976) argues, for example, that the middle classes developed professionalized "communities" through which individuals' life trajectories could be assigned and personal "growth" measured. Concepts such as "career" and "character" tied interpretations of individual success to occupational work in a way that was very different from previous conceptions of the individual.

The invention of social sciences, then, can be viewed as embodying the "modernizing project" of the late nineteenth and early twentieth centuries. Its disciplinary qualities had a double meaning. The systemic, professional knowledge about society functioned as a guide for thinking about institutional reforms and social policy. But the disciplinary knowledge also generated governing principles that related the new political rationalities of a liberal democracy to the construction of individualities. In the above senses, the production of the "individual" through the systems of ideas in the social sciences entailed a profound shift in consciousness.[15] *The social sciences merged what the sociologist Scheler (1924/1980) thought was separate, that is, the interests of power, achievement, and salvation.* The psychology in which Dewey and Vygotsky wrote was an important note in the new disciplinary strategies of governing.

Transferring the Soul to Science: The Modern Invention of Psychology

The psychological sciences in which Vygotsky and Dewey participated were examples of the multiple attempts in the nascent social sciences to spread modernity through *a revisioning of individuality*. While Dewey is considered today as a philosopher, his work crosses philosophy and psychology, and responded to the central currents of ideas in that later field of the human sciences. The construction of modern psychology embodied a commitment to reconstruct society by reconstructing the individual. Psychology would transform Enlightenment beliefs into practical technologies that would construct people's understanding of experience, and form the norms of conduct. Subjectivity was a site of struggle; that is, how individuals thought, felt, talked, and "saw" their selves as actors in the world.

Emerging as an academic discipline during the United States Progressive Era (see, e.g., O'Donnell 1985) and the Czarist regime just prior to the Soviet state, psychology was largely conceptualized and given moral justification by the project to construct the self-governing individual (Herman 1995). Psychology sought to produce the disciplined self that embodied the ethic of self-control and the extension of processes of rationalization into personal conduct (see, e.g., Lears 1981). Demands for social amelioration incorporated the Victorian ethic of self-control and the extension of the processes of rationalization into personal conduct. Industrialization involved a call for "systematic methods of self-control ... beyond the work place into the most intimate areas of daily experience—perhaps even into unconscious wishes, dreams, and fantasies" (Lears 1981: 13; also see Berger et. al. 1973).

Psychology helped to administer the new institutions of governing, and, simultaneously to provide for individuality and reason. It emerged in the United States as a subdiscipline of philosophy to give focus to the natural development of the mind and spirit. By the end of the nineteenth century, psychology was separated from moral and mental philosophy and positioned as the discipline to resolve the theological issues of Protestantism with the material issues of evolution. The presidents of universities, especially private East Coast institutions, embraced psychology as a way of reconciling faith and reason, Christian belief and Enlightenment empiricism (O'Donnell 1985). Psychology would also perform the tasks of dissemination and advancement of practical knowledge in an emerging industrial nation. While the discipline was not monolithic in its outlook, the various approaches shared a goal of organizing liberty and progress through the construction of individuals who could contribute productively to these transformations through their own "self" discipline. Faith was placed in the rational individual as the locus of change.

The disciplinary processes made individual desires, affects, and bodily practices the objects of change. This decentralization and individualization of subjectivities can be thought of as *the governing of the soul* (Foucault 1979; Rose 1989). By soul, I mean that people's desires, attitudes, and bodily practices were made the focus of scrutiny and administration. The social administration of the self was organized within a problematic that transferred the church's pastoral concern with saving the "soul" to secular confessional practices of rescuing of the person by the social planning of the state (see Foucault 1977 1979; Rose 1989).

> The conviction that truth can be discovered through the self-examination of consciousness and the confession of one's thoughts and acts now appears so natural, so compelling, indeed so self-evident, that it seems unreasonable to posit that such self-examination is a central component in a strategy of power. This unseemingness rests on an attachment to the repressive hypothesis; if the truth is inherently opposed to power, then its uncovering would surely lead us on the path to liberation. (Foucault, "Afterword" in Dreyfus and Rabinow 1983: 175)

It was not the ideas of Dewey and Vygotsky that found favor within the educational sciences of both the Soviet Union and the United States. Within the United States, for example, most psychological theories accepted the current social situation as a given. Psychology "would flourish neither as a mental discipline nor as a research science but as the intellectual underpinning and scientific legitimator of utilitarian pursuits, especially in the field of education" (O'Donnell 1985: 37). It focused on the procedural elements through which the institution could bring out what was already presumed to be "natural" and universal in the person (for the United States see, O'Donnell 1985; for the Soviet Union see, Gouldner 1979). United States psychological research provided large scale assessment of groups of students and as indicators of quality of an entire school system. Psychology was to provide school administrators with a way to monitor and control the work of teachers and students. Quantitative measures were used as means "for establishing unchallengeable administrative authority in a time of growing school enrollments and expenditure" (Powell 1980: 10).

The development of psychology was heavily supported by new school administrators centralizing the organization of teaching.[16] The discipline provided a new form of expertise in selecting, organizing, and evaluating institutional and personal knowledge (Danziger 1990). Psychologists believed that they had sufficient knowledge and disinterest to promote institutional change. Acting as an "evolutionary cadre," the psychologists "asked the public to have confidence not merely in their knowledge and skills but in their ability to construct a better world as well" (Napoli 1981: 41). There was a belief that science was the "mainstream of inevitable progress" and that man "could make and remake his own world" (O'Donnell 1985: 212). Promising what utopian thinkers had long sought, Hall (1905/1969) saw psychology as the means to overcome the problems of urban life, family, and inadequate social development.

At the center of the new scientific pedagogy was the expert who could provide the efficiency of science. Thorndike (1910) argued that education should be based upon sound scientific fact rather than opinion. The human mind was considered to be susceptible to exact measurement similar to objects of the natural sciences. However, such measurement was considered to be beyond the capacity of kindergarten or other public school teachers. For that reason, measurement, and the formation of a curriculum based on it, now entered the domain of experimental psychologists (Bloch 1987). Hall asserted that it was the scientifically trained psychologist "who could devise and administer tests such as motor and mental skills, sensual acuity, muscular strength and coordination, speed of reaction, perception of movement and time, and simply memory necessary for the proper functioning of schools" (O'Donnell 1985: 156).

When brought into pedagogical discourses, the psychological categories of "learner" and "development," for example, produced particular discursive practices that replaced the early nineteenth-century construction of teaching that "saw" children as part of a prophetic task of "professing" Christian faith. The child was good or bad, pious or nonpious. Developmental and learning theories, in contrast, opened the child's behaviors, attitudes, and beliefs to scrutiny, such that they could be acted upon to effect change in cognition and affect.[17] The disciplinary discourses were a productive force in which individuals would learn a "self-discipline" to act through "the will to know."

The disciplinary practices that related psychology and pedagogy were instances of the merger of power, achievement, and salvation. While often contested in terms of what forms of scientific reasoning should prevail, social betterment was viewed as dependent upon the rational construction of the "citizens" who could act progressively on their circumstances and environment. In this context,

[t]he school was to act as a moral technology, not merely inculcating obedience, but also seeking to shape personality through the child's emulation of the teacher, through the use of pastoral techniques to encourage self-knowledge and enhance the feeling of sympathetic identification, through establishing the links between virtue, honesty, and self-denial and a purified pleasure. (Rose 1989: 223)

The new systems of social administration in pedagogy to create greater participation, however, also produced systems of exclusion. While learning and child development were supposed to increase individual freedom through education, the psychological notion of childhood ascribed universal character-istics by which to judge development and achievement. But the characteristics assumed to be universal were not. Instead, modern psychology was based on concepts drawn from the values of particular groups in society, and applied in a way that presumed to judge all children. Baker (1998) argues, for example, that particular binaries were inscribed in the concept of "childhood" devel-oped at the end of century. The binaries were: whiteness/blackness; male/female; and civility/savagery. The binaries were part of a scaffolding of ideas that classified and normalized the subjective dispositions of children through conceptions that privileged a particular Protestant view of individuality that was English-speaking, male, and racially charged. The effect of the scaffold-ing was to exclude by drawing discursive maps that designated those children who stood outside the normativity as "noneducable" since they existed out-side of "reason" and salvation.

With this historical horizon of modernity, I can now approach present ped-agogical discourses that draw upon the ideas of Dewey and Vytogsky. I will argue that the site of struggle in contemporary pedagogy is still the *governing of the soul*. The ethical life of the "soul" is spoken about in today's reforms as the capabilities, beliefs, and conceptions/ misconceptions of the child and teacher. The difference today from the past is in the principles of governing in which the struggle for *the soul* is enacted.

Homologies in the Governing Patterns of the "Self": Social Theory, Politics, Economics, the Military, and Pedagogies

As we look at contemporary pedagogical discourses, Dewey and Vygotsky appear within particular educational discourses called "constructivist teach-ing" or "constructivist learning." The picture is painted that the renewed inter-est in Dewey and Vygotsky is part of the evolutionary development of scientific knowledge that will lead to school improvement. My concern here is to explore constructivism as not only an intellectual movement within education but as a historically produced system of reason that embodies more general changes in the governing practices through which individuality is constructed.

The argument of this section (and chapter) is that this rereading of Vygotsky and Dewey in the contemporary reform discourses is part of the recent changes taking place in the governing systems of the "self," which differ in significant ways from those current at the turn of the last century. I explore these changes by examining the various homologies between the images of "the self" in pedagogical discourses and those of contemporary social theory, politics, economics, and the military. I use the notion of homology to explore the generative rules that govern participation within different social fields. These rules are not reducible to one cause or to a single set of origins, but are similar to Wittgenstein's "families of resemblances" in which multiple historical patterns overlap to produce a recognition of likenesses but without signifying causality or the reduction of one social pattern to another.

The homologies that I explore can be summarized as follows: in contrast to social science thought at the turn of the century, which assumed a certain fixed set of relations between identities and institutions, today's "individuality" is presumed to be less stable. The image is of the citizen, worker, warrior, and teacher as "problem-solving" and flexible in responding to multiple and contingently defined contexts. The vehicle through which this image is constructed is through language and "community," which enables a resuscitation of the works of Dewey and Vygotsky. But the use given to Vygotsky and Dewey today involves different principles of governing of *the soul*, to return to the metaphor developed in the previous section. In the last and final section, I pursue the logic of constructivism to consider its irony and paradox. That is, while constructivist knowledge purports to produce a more inclusive practice in schooling, its principles of participation function to disqualify, but this disqualification is produced at the level of "being" or of the dispositions and sensitivities that the child embodies.

The Pluralities of Disciplinary Knowledge and Cartesian Logic

The well-worn phrase that "knowledge is socially constructed" is reiterated in discussions taking place in the disciplines of anthropology, philosophy, political science, psychology, and sociology as well as education (see, e.g., Bourdieu and Passeron 1977; Giddens 1990; Hall 1986; Butler 1993; in education, see Giroux 1992, Kohli 1995; McLaren and Giarelli 1995; Popkewitz and Brennan 1998). These disciplines have begun to engage in a dialogue with linguistic, semiotic, and discourse analysis in the construction of social theory. The emphasis in these discussions is on fluidity, diversity, and the seeming breakup of permanence. Social and psychological theories, for example, no longer speak of identity in terms of universal norms of competence, such as those articulated in early-twentieth-century role theory. Instead, identity is perceived as constructed through norms that speak to the multiple and pragmatic actions through which the "self" is constructed.

The discourses of educational constructivism, then, can be thought of as occurring within the broader conversations in the social sciences that have alternatively been labeled as modernity/high modernity and/or postmodernity. At one level, contemporary social and political theories can be thought of as rearticulating an early-twentieth-century view of knowledge as socially constructed. What is distinctive about current theory, however, is its privileging of language and pragmatism to understand social relations and the construction of subjectivity. Norms of language construction (rules of discourse) are viewed as functioning to form subject-identities (such as those of race, gender, class, sexuality) rather than as a medium to interpret and represent the subject. Postmodern feminist literature, for example, focuses on the concept of women to understand how the knowledge of gender is itself the effect of power— "how difference is established, how it operates, how and in what ways it constitutes subjects who see and act in the world" (Scott 1991: 777; also see, e.g., Butler 1992; Di Stefano 1990; Fraser 1989; Gatens 1991). In this general sense of making language central to theory, the work of Vygotsky is appealing. Furthermore, contemporary social theory is concerned with diversity, flexibility, and contingency as norms for interpreting social life. Revisiting pragmatic philosophy and Dewey's notion of "community" has been pivotal (see, e.g., Rorty 1979).

Within pedagogy, however, a particular type of constructivism appears that is related to cognitive psychology and symbolic interactionalism.[18] The pedagogical discourses have a particular trajectory that is different from that being used in the social disciplines. Within pedagogy, the imagery is of the teacher (and the child) who is expected to collaborate, reflect, and "construct knowledge" in a decentralized system of education. The "new" teacher (and the child) is an "empowered," problem-solving individual capable of responding flexibly to problems that have no clear set of boundaries or singular answers. The teacher is assumed to possess a pragmatic individuality that is tied to the contingencies of situations in which problems arise.

The discourse of the constructivist teacher (and the child) is expressed through discussions of teaching science and mathematics as well as in teacher education reforms where it is asserted that "the generic task of education" consists of "teaching students how to make knowledge and meaning—to *enact culture* ... ," turning away from "a template for a single conception" of reform to "multiple models" (Holmes Group 1986, 1990: 10, 6; also see, The National Council for Teachers of Mathematics 1989).

It is within this pedagogical and psychological literature about pedagogy that the rereading of Vygotsky's ideas about language (communication) and Dewey's pragmatism occurs. Simon (1995: 15), for example, argues that educational constructivism is a pragmatic "epistemological theory" that "derives from a philosophical position that we as human beings have no access to an objective reality, that is a reality independent of our way of knowing it." Pedagogy focuses on the communicative systems employed to construct knowledge and the way these systems emerge and are sustained through community processes of mediation and negotiation (also see, e.g., Cobb et al. 1992; Steffe and Kieran 1994 1995; Cobb et al. 1991; 1992; Cobb 1994).

Constructivist Struggles against the Cartesian Binary

One can read pragmatism, postmodern theories, and the pedagogical constructivism (not necessarily with the same ideological agendas) as concerned with undoing the Cartesian opposition of mind and body and the distinctions between ideas and material existence. This agenda was common to both Dewey and Vygotsky. As is much contemporary thought, they, were critical of twentieth-century European social theory that is built upon Cartesian binaries that separate mind from body and individuality from social relations and history. The binaries, however, are not just theoretical; they also entail practices. This is evident in school pedagogies. Scientific theories of instruction, for example, have been built on binaries: concepts are separated from methods, and the cognitive is separated from the affective. Teacher education courses that separate knowledge about "school and society" from knowledge about learning stand as testimony to the binaries in which the social/personal and mind/body splits are naturalized in teaching.

We can think of constructivist research about teaching as rejecting Cartesian binaries through its pragmatic focus. Instructional strategies to engage children in "challenging problems" and multiple interpretations are viewed as confronting the Cartesian binary of mind/environment. Constructivist pedagogy attempts to "see" a relationship between the practices of knowing and what is known (see, e.g., Cobb et al. 1992; Steffe and Kieren 1994). Knowledge is envisioned as tentative and uncertain, having multiple constructions, and formed through negotiations within community boundaries.

Dewey and Vygotsky are drawn into the pedagogical discussion to establish a relationship between mind and "environment" or context, and the importance of language as a mediation system in the construction of the "self." Dewey's notion of "communities," for example, is deployed to consider the classroom as having the "shared norms" of community. Pedagogical discussions of Vygotsky direct attention to children's linguistic conceptions. Teaching mathematics is likened to Vygotsky's "zone of proximal development" (also called "a zone of potential construction") as teachers use students' mathematical schemata in instructional planning (see, e.g., Simon 1995). The Russian "teaching experiment" is a pedagogical strategy through which teachers can turn students' thoughts into "data" about conceptual development (Cobb et al. 1991; for a general discussion of the teaching experiment in Russian psychology, see Tabachnick et al. 1981).

Reinserting the Cartesian Binary: The Social and Historical as Psychological and Interactional

The undoing of the Cartesian binary in constructivist pedagogy, however, rein-scribes the binary of mind and knowledge at a different level. This occurs through the alchemy of pedagogy. The alchemy of pedagogy, like the attempt to transform lead into gold in the Middle Ages, involves a particular transfor-mation. The alchemy transforms physics, history, and literature, for example, into psychological and social interactional processes. Disciplinary knowledge is treated as having universal structures that are stable, consensual, and fixed.[19] Pedagogical discourses give attention to the flexible processes through which children internalize the stable school subject knowledge. The distinction between disciplinary knowledge and pedagogical processes reproduces a Cartesian-like binary.

The reinscription of a binary world appears, oddly enough, through the acceptance of curriculum as identifying multiple strategies for learning. This flaw in the alchemy relates to the reliance on particular aspects of social psy-chology and psychology in curricululm development. The fixed, logical struc-tures of knowledge form the foundation of a theory of learning. This foundation is assumed when children engage in "problem-solving" practices or for identifying how children develop "conceptions/misconceptions" of cur-riculum problems. "Problem solving" and "conceptions/misconceptions" assume fixed concepts that children are expected to internalize and "master," an assumption of the alchemy that produces a division between knowledge and learning processes.

The alchemy can be examined in constructivism in mathematics education. That literature continually refers to the "nature" and "structure" of mathemat-ics that children learn (see, e, g., Simon 1995: 20; Cobb et al. 1991: 5). The notions of "nature" and "structure" refer to a view of an essential, deep, and underlying core of knowledge that children excavate through pedagogical processes. Learning mathematics becomes learning the logic of mathematical justifications through flexible instructional approaches. Mathematics educa-tion, for example, is "to distinguish between the meanings that students give to representational systems in terms of their current ways of knowing and the mathematical *structure* that the system embodied for adults who know mathe-matics" (Cobb et al. 1991: 5 my emphasis; also see Simon 1995). Cognition is a developmental practice important in understanding the evolving psychogenetic processes related to Piagetian conceptions of stages of learning (see, e.g., Steffe and Kieren 1994; for a critical discussion of this relation, see Bishop 1991).

A consequence of the alchemy is an acceptance of the logical structures of disciplinary knowledge as the foundation of curriculum. The pedagogical struggle for the child's soul is a search for the appropriate strategies that would enable children's internalization of the foundations of knowledge. The communal and social aspects of the production of mathematics or science are restricted to classroom communication patterns and "context" factors that foster or hinder children's learning of disciplinary structures of knowledge. Dewey and Vygotsky, for example, are brought into pedagogical conversations to talk about *principles that govern the soul* or the subjectivities that are required of teachers and students. In what otherwise would seem unproblematic, teachers and students are to be viewed and to view themselves as active constructors of their ways of knowing and as participants in social practices rather than as mirrors of a world independent of experience, history, and culture. Knowing would then be seen as a matter of being able to participate in mathematical practices including the ability to explain and justify those practices" (Cobb, et al. 1992: 15).

In this quote, the references to history and culture are rhetorical flourishes without any systematic reflection about what constitutes the relation of "contexts" and "social" in the production of scientific knowledge other than asserting some notion of communal "shared norms."[20] The socially constructed qualities of science and scientific knowledge are transformed into matters of participating in mathematic practices that "explain and justify one's action." "Community" directs attention to the development of "shared norms" based on an "equilibrium" and "consensus" about knowledge (Cobb et al. 1992; Steffe and Kieren 1995; Simon 1995). "Collaborative learning approach" is used to "arrive at a taken-as-shared interpretation of the problem" (Simon 1995: 120, also Cobb et al. 1991). The "social" is thus presented as a psychological or symbolic interactional process of negotiations to construct knowledge, thus denuding pedagogical practices of any social mooring outside the classroom.

The limitation of the alchemy is further evident when semiotic theory is applied to science. Its structure cannot be taken for granted, but must be seen as a linguistic/semantic practice that is functionally produced in institutional settings. Halliday and Martin (1993), focusing on the semiotics of science, argue that the discourse of science is actively constructed through its structures of related meanings and grammatical forms. The language of science, they continue, does not simply correspond to or respond to human experience. Rather the language of science is an interpretative activity of experience. Martin (1992) then draws semiotic theory into a consideration of pedagogical practices by arguing that children's need to learn the grammatical systems of science through which experience is interpreted. This takes precedence over consideration of their interpretations and constructions of meaning.

If one looks at the history and sociology of science that constructivist literature cites (but which I suspect is read only partially), the alchemy is apparent in the pedagogical celebration of "shared norms," "consensus," and "equilibrium." The studies of science as a communal practice, for example, focus on the multiple layers of scientific work that involve both internal and external questioning and conflict.[21] The social and historical moorings of knowledge, namely the embeddedness of the concepts and methods of science, social science, and literature in historical relations and power structures, are excluded from examination in pedagogical practices (see, e.g., Gouldner 1970; Bernstein 1976; Popkewitz 1977). Historically, the discourses of curriculum have more to do with administering children than with understanding the processes of knowledge production in the sciences, literature, and history (see, e.g., Popkewitz 1987).

The coupling of the stabilization of disciplinary knowledge with the individualization of pedagogical knowledge makes the governing of children *the problem of teaching*, such as how children conceive (or misconceive) what is given and unchangeable. The governing principles of the curriculum go unexamined. What is perceived as children participating in *their* constructions of knowledge is children participating in historically derived systems of reasoning that are themselves the unacknowledged effects of power. In fact, the reinscription of binaries through the alchemy of pedagogy makes the values and norms inscribed in disciplinary fields seem unquestionable as children learn problem-solving methods.

The reinsertion of binaries helps to illustrate the way in which ideas are embedded in the social context surrounding the texts in which they are presented. Both Dewey and Vygotsky argued against Cartesian binaries. However, when used in contemporary pedagogical discourse, the ideas of Dewey and Vygotsky are no longer "their" ideas. Instead they are embedded in, and thus reshaped by, sets of relations embodied within the discursive practices of constructivist pedagogies.

Why is this denial of the social in school knowledge important in pedagogical constructivism? Pedagogical reasoning includes the child in the construction of personal knowledge but excludes the child from the recognition of the social and historical mooring of that knowledge.[22] This determinism is significant as we pursue other homologies with constructivism in politics, work, and the military.

Reconstituting the Relations between the State and Individual

The constructivist images of a problem-solving individual are also embodied in changes in the conceptions of political participation. Although nineteenth-century projects of modernity were concerned with the social and the collective social movements, contemporary political discourses use local and communal metaphors to describe their focus. Today's political landscape with different ideological agendas calls for reforms that emphasize the community—community health, community schools, community-based welfare systems, and so forth (Rose 1994). Current discourses about multiculturalism and the canons of university teaching construct a society of different and disparate groups of people in terms of a "community." Neoliberalist concerns with markets and privatization also revision the political as located within the local, the communal, and the individual. Participation in the local and the community involves a pragmatic agent.

The new pragmatic outlook of social movements entails a form of constructivism that is organized through a particular type of expert knowledge (see, e.g., Laraña et al. 1994). Today's politics embodies:

> a range of other challenges to the mechanism of social government that emerged during these same decades from civil libertarians, feminists, radicals, socialists, sociologists and others. These reorganized programs of government utilize and instrumentalize the multitude of experts of management, of family life, of lifestyle who have proliferated at the points of intersection of socio-political aspirations and private desires for self-advancement. (Rose and Miller 1992: 201)

The pragmatic, communal, and local outlook for change is embodied in current school reforms. The phrase "systemic school reform" is used within U.S. reform efforts to argue for a new set of relations among governmental agencies, professional teacher groups, research communities, and local authorities (see, e.g., Smith and O'Day 1990). The systemic school reform provides the expertise to coordinate and provide coherence in local reform strategies. At one level, discourses of standards and professionalism appear within a context of building strong U.S. government monitoring and steering systems that entail local flexibility, such as national curriculum goals, assessment techniques (e.g., from new achievement tests to portfolio assessments), and a national teacher certification test. At the same time, school shared decision making, site-based management, and reforms concerning the "reflective teacher" and "action research" provide localities and teachers with a sense of autonomy and responsibility in identifying the appropriate strategies to improve teaching.

Inscribed in the diverse organizational strategies of "systemic school reform" is a "constructivist" structuring of the capabilities of the individual who participates and acts. The reform discourses, for example, are based on the concept of a "teacher" who is personally responsible for "problem solving" in a world that is personally unstable. The professional teacher is "self-governing," and has greater local responsibility in implementing curriculum decisions—a normativity also found in the structuring of the new "constructivist" teacher that, as discussed earlier, cites Dewey and Vygotsky as "sources" of its vision (Popkewitz 1991, 1993).

The new political rationalities for the organization of schools are also inscribed in the images of the teacher and the child (see, e.g., Fendler 1998; Hultqvist 1998). Educational reformers assume that the curriculum is "the form of culturally organized experience that is available *as a tool* of governmental policy" (from the educational studies by D. Newman, P. Griffin, and

M. Cole, cited in Cazden 1986: 453, my emphasis). Drawing upon the work of Vygotsky, pedagogy is visioned as administrating individuality through governing the patterns of communication of children. The site of change is now the cognitive and moral compartment of the individual. Instruction is *"regulating* the interaction among children rather than just regulating the individual action"* (Cazden 1986: 450, my emphasis).

A new sense of displacement and the new calculus of intervention reconstitutes the principles of the participatory citizen (see Rose and Miller 1992; also Popkewitz 1996). The centralized/decentralized organization of the teacher and child seems not to have any single center, as all is negotiated within fluid boundaries. In these reform practices, the governing of the individual is not through the explicit definition of procedures but through the deployment of "reasoning" through which the teacher and child construct their capabilities and actions.

The Production of Work and the Worker

The revisioning of work and the worker in the world of business provides other homologies with educational constructivism. According to the business pages of the newspapers and literature about the workplace, a new corporate structure is being formed that is less hierarchical and pyramidal than it was in the past.[23] Furthermore, the Taylorization of mass production instituted in the first half of the century has been challenged because mass production no longer provides an efficient scheme in modern technological industries (Kuttner 1991; Lekachman 1982). Business literature no longer speaks of stable "roles." The new business entails an individual who is "enterprising," with certain problem-solving capabilities—where highly variable customer demands, new technologies, multicentered business structures, and horizontal structures organize workers into groups concerned with specific projects that do not involve the older layers of management (Fatis 1992).

Self-managing teams and individual participation have been given priority in the reorganization of industrial production. The worker is "empowered" and develops flexible, responsive environments that can respond quickly to customer demands.

The changing subjectivities of the worker and their implications to education are discussed in the International Labour Organization's report on metal workers (1994). The desirable worker is conceptualized as one who is not solely competent in skills but one who also possesses certain appropriate capabilities and dispositions. This new worker is reminiscent of the constructivist teacher, and is expressed through the following equation:

"I understand it" + "I can do it" + "I care about it" = "capability" (1994: 23)

A new focus on capability revisits the turn of the century concerns with the social administration of "the soul." But this governing is different from that of Taylorism and Fordism. The focus on capabilities and dispositions of the worker breaks the psychological ties that previously defined individual identity in terms of fixed roles of work and production (Donzelot 1991). The new approaches accent the individual's autonomy, the capacity to adapt, the agency of the individual to make change in a changing world, and individual self-ful-fillment. "Instead of defining the individual by the work he is assigned to, [the new psychology] regards productive activity as the site of deployment of the person's personal skills" (Donzelot 1991: 252).

One cannot ignore the homologies between the subjectivity to govern the citizen, the worker, and constructivist pedagogy (for relations to work, see, e.g., Gee et al. 1996). Each has a similar emphasis on flexibility, problem solving, and contingent, personal, or interactional communication. At the same time, these constructions of identity do not occur on an equal playing field in the sense of the availability of the rules of participation. The identities discussed are not universal as the world of business involves different capabilities of workers. The desirable worker described above differs substantially from the worker constructed by Taylorism and mass production, notions that still dominate a substantial fraction of the labor market. Furthermore, not all workers have equal access to the capabilities associated with the new worker (and citizen). In fact, these constructivist capabilities are not universal traits, but are, instead, specific norms produced within particular social groups. These traits are embedded in power relations, as the specific norms referred to are produced and sanctioned by particular social groups. I will return to this issue later, when I discuss the problem of inclusion and exclusion in the production of participation.

The Disciplining of the Military

It might seem unusual to relate the issue of governing and constructivism to the military, but it should not be. The disciplining technologies of the military have been important in the construction of schools since the eighteenth century. One cannot account for the school testing and measurement industries without paying attention to the problems of recruitment and organization of soldiers during the two world wars (Herman 1995). The systems analysis and budget planning approaches to educational reform that were influential in the United States after World War II were strategies developed in the military and brought into government and the university as research and administrative technologies to guide educational reform (Popkewitz et al. 1982; esp. ch.2). The War on Poverty, subsequent interventions to produce educational equity, and the Defense Department's sponsorship of cognitive psychology are important for understanding the revisions of the strategies of social administration. A particular war expertise was incorporated in the planning, guidance, and assessment of pedagogical practices.

But what is important here are the shifts in the governing principles that underlie the identity in the modern military during the past three decades. I conceptualize these changes as a movement from the traditional role of a "soldier" to that of a modern "warrior"; the latter incorporates much of what we have talked about as a constructivism into the dispositions of combat. Prior to World War II, military discipline was organized by a hierarchy of decision-making that filtered through a "chain of command." Furthermore, the technologies of the soldier involved a relationship with the mechanical hardware of war. The airplane, tanks, and guns were designed through theories of mechanics and physics. The discipline of the fighting person involved learning competence in maintaining and applying the mechanical technologies in a hierarchy of command.

Recent rapid changes that have taken place in military technologies have required performances from personnel that relate the body and mind to systems of communication. It is in this transition that I think of the "warrior" as replacing the "soldier." The modern fighter plane, for example, is inherently unstable and flies only through its monitoring systems. The processing of information is seen as a pragmatic problem in which one must assess the contingent qualities of the context in quickly changing situations that affect the survival of the pilot.[24] The warrior assumes a world of instabilities, pluralities, and a need for pragmatic actions as individuals interact with dynamic communication fluctuations rather than fixed mechanical systems.

In this context, it is significant that American pilot training has depended upon the development of a new expertise. This includes Defense Department sponsorship of artificial intelligence research, and support for the subdiscipline of cognitive psychology in order to prepare pilots for pragmatic and coordinated decision making. (For a treatment of the relation of cognitive sciences and state sponsorship, see Noble 1991). It is interesting that research by the Russian psychologist Galperin, who had been influenced by Vygotskian theory, was first translated into English to help support such research.

The new "constructivist" capabilities of the warrior are evident in command structures. There has been a movement to a different command structure that entails both vertical and horizontal axes. Vertically, the central command is becoming more standardized through weapons procurement and technologies that can control battle information. Horizontally, certain sensitivities and dispositions toward the problem solving of the warrior are stressed that are homologous to what is emphasized in pedagogical literatures about constructivism. The military control structure makes professional flexibility and responsibility a precept of battle discipline. The contingencies of the battle, as determined by the warrior, are the final determinants of operational performance, including, when necessary, overriding prior commands.

Further evidence of the changes in identity is found in current legal investigations about accountability for action in combat. Accountability is no longer assumed to lie with the commanding officer. Now it is regarded as possible that individual pilots and soldiers share personal accountability for decision making in the field. These command structures are similar to the governing patterns found in the centralized/decentralized state patterns of governing as well as in the constructivist pedagogies of the schooling. One can view the military's provisions for greater inclusion of women into battle contexts as well as the recent revision of the hierarchical roles in training as related to the different cognitive structuring that governs the "warrior." One can say that there is a conjuncture between the social and political pressures about gender relationships in the military and the new training requirements for a less hierarchical, more pragmatic, local role in the instruction given to construct the new "warrior."

We can bring together the previous discussions to think about the constructivist discourses in the construction of the citizen and child. The different arenas of politics, work, the military, and the social disciplines overlap and provide a historical specificity to the current discourses about the professional teacher and the child who are self-confident, self-disciplined, and have a capability and willingness to learn. It also enables a historical reading of the changing social relations and governing principles in which Dewey and Vygotsky are read.

Pedagogy as Patterns of Inclusion/Exclusions

While I have pursued the relation of constructivism to the formation of the "self" in different social arenas, these arenas do not operate on a level playing field. This final section, then, examines how the current reading of Vygotsky and Dewey is resituated to produce rules for inclusions *and* exclusions in contemporary pedagogy. The problem of inclusion/exclusion that I speak about is not about what groups are represented or omitted in school decision making or curriculum content. While this notion of inclusion is important, my concern is with the discourses of "problem solving" and "reason" in contemporary pedagogy as generating principles that classify and divide those who have and do not have the appropriate dispositions, sensibilities, and capabilities to act and participate.

This notion of inclusion/exclusion begins with the alchemy that I discussed earlier. Within the alchemy is the construction of "problem solving" and "reflection" that seem to exist outside historical and cultural influences. Reason is discussed in terms of a universalized conception of "problem solving" that is presented as if it were independent of time and place. The idea of context is discussed to focus on the ways in which individuals negotiate differences, or in which the mind "finds" different strategies to engage in the finding of answers to problems. Although certain types of pedagogies are termed "constructivist," then, the constructivist discourses do not systemically examine the way in which knowledge or reason is socially constructed except within psychological paradigms that obscure the historical conditions of reason itself.

To find a way to bridge the relation of social and individual knowledge with the problem of inclusion/exclusion, Bourdieu's (1984) concepts of *social field* and *habitus* are helpful. We can think of the different social distinctions that people make in their daily actions as analogous to players' positions on a "field," such as a baseball field. On the baseball field players occupy different spaces or positions. Each space demands different skills, distinctions, and perspectives that enable the player to be skilled in the game. The distinctions and skills of a pitcher, for example, are different from those of an outfield or a catcher. In a similar manner, we can think of the social world as a field where people occupy different positions and have different sets of skills as they participate in the ordering relations of social life.

The differences among people, according to Bourdieu, are embodied in the *habitus*, the differential systems of recognition and distinctions that divide and organize people's participation. For example, Bourdieu examined the distinctions that different groups have in tastes, such as what people ate, bought for the home, wore as clothes, watched at the cinemas and on television, read, and so on. Bourdieu found homologies in the *habitus* among French primary teachers, secondary teachers, professionals, and engineers in how they "appreciated" art and organized their housing arrangements. These patterns of distinctions and appreciations were different from, for example, office workers and small-shop salespeople.

If we recognize that we live in an unequal playing field, we can use Bourdieu's concepts of *field* and *habitus* to explore how constructivism functions in the production of systems of inclusion/exclusion. We can think of constructivism as "taking" particular, *local* knowledge (*habitus*) of certain groups in the social field and treating that knowledge as the *global* principles of "reason" and "problem solving" related to school success, achievement, and capabilities.[25] The apparently universal norms are brought back into the particular interactions and practices of classrooms as the norms to judge and differentiate among children. This selectivity is not intentional, but subtly embodied in the distinctions and differentiations to order and divide the "things" that are talked about as cognition, "problem solving," and affective development. Educators and researchers refer to problem solving, community, and zones of proximal development as if they were universal processes rather than socially constructed norms related to *habitus*.

The exclusions are produced through the systems of recognition, divisions, and distinctions that construct reason and "the reasonable person." The norms in the pedagogical discourses have no way of accounting for difference except in terms of deviation from certain universal standards. In this way, diverse groups are only seen from the perspective of a "being" that is different from the norm (see, Dumm 1993; Popkewitz 1998b). It is thus implied that the best thing that can happen to such a person is to become "like the normal person." At the same time, the focus on the "subjective" and communicative competence in constructivism, shifts the blame for failure more securely to individuals themselves. This is because such thinking takes little account of differential access to the means for such self expression.

These effects of power to distinguish and divide go unnoticed. They are unnoticed because the norms to discriminate seem to be general, "natural," and unattached to any group. Research by Walkerdine (1988), often cited but systematically ignored within the constructivist pedagogy literature, empirically explores how child-centered pedagogies discursively create a normalized vision of the "natural" child and what is "true." The emphasis on verbalization and justification in the constructivist teaching, she argues, relates to particular *habitus* that embody bourgeois and gendered conceptions. While the ideas of "problem solving" and "community" seem unambiguous and naturally "good" in constructivist research, they can become dangerous when presented as universal principles without social mooring.

The idea of *habitus* helps to understand an anomaly that continually appears in U.S. educational discussions that are often related to issues of inclusion and pedagogy. Research findings continually indicate that parents from different social and cultural groups value education for their children, although there is differential achievement among the groups. If we take the idea of *habitus*, we can recognize that the distinctions available for action and participation in schooling among different groups differ as to the effects of power, including the distinctions given to what is "valued" and understood as education (see, e.g., Sieber 1983; also Fendler 1998). While not the concern of this paper, a limitation of current social policy related to school choice can also be considered through focusing on the available dispositions, sensitivities, and distinctions for generating action and participation. "Choice" assumes erroneously that the available distinctions are the same for all group positions within the field.

Some Concluding Comments

I end where I began this essay. It is easy to laud the conceptual changes in contemporary educational reforms and to accept rhetorical strategies as fact. Contemporary research captures a populist, democratic appeal. The reforms are posited as strategies to make schooling more democratic, more progressive and socially responsive through the making/remaking of the teacher and the child, in a way that I refer to, following Rose (1989), as *governing the soul*. But if we look historically at the knowledge of school reforms as social practices, the logic and reasoning can be understood as having paradoxes and ironies that are the effects of power.

Using Dewey and Vygotsky to develop a historical and comparative perspective, I have argued that there are certain continuities between current and past liberal movements toward the social administration of freedom and the governing of the *soul*. The belief in the disciplined, self-motivated individual has persisted and become part of our current unquestioned assumptions about educational reform. The site of power remains the individual's productive activity and capabilities. Further, my focus on the homologies between pedagogical reforms, social theory, the political governance of education, the economy, and the military explored the complex relations in which contemporary governing patterns are different from the turn of the last century, when Vygotsky and Dewey wrote. When terms such as "community," "zones of proximal development," and so on appear in current reform texts, these terms have no meaning outside of the set of relations in which ideas are located.

Further, the ability of pedagogical practices to open up spaces for individuals to act cannot be assured. In fact, I argued that educational research needs to pose the concepts of inclusion and exclusion as mutually constituted. Within the systems of inclusion are its opposite, as what appears to be a widening of opportunities simultaneously functions to divide and normalize. This inclusion/exclusion is historically tied to the social administration of freedom but given a particular form in contemporary educational reforms. I argued that constructivism "remakes" the problem of inclusion/exclusion through its focus on seemingly universal dispositions and "problem solving" capabilities of the child. But the capabilities are not universal, rather they inscribe norms that disqualify certain children at the level of their "being" rather than through their subject-positions, such as those of group categories of race, class, or gender.

This productive effect of power requires that we rethink not only constructivism but also much of the critical analyses of educational reform that consider the problem of current change as residing in the "conservative restorations" and neoliberal systems of markets, privatization, and school choice. These categories of change miss the substantive and longer term changes in the governing principles that are described here (see Popkewitz 1998a). These analyses still focus on questions of representation and correspondence to social structures rather than on the changing rules by which representation is made possible.

At this point, I return to the earlier paradox and irony of modernity that reappears in current educational reforms. The social administration of freedom was to produce a particular type of disciplined subject who was free from external policing. The situating of Dewey and Vygotsky in contemporary reforms point to the reconstitution of that paradox and irony. The universalizing of reason in constructivism is to produce a greater range of possibilities for teachers and children. But ideas are not merely logical principles to insert into discourses of research and reform. They also produce systems of exclusion as well as inclusion.

My arguments about the pedagogical discourses in which Dewey and Vygotsky are read are intended to historicize the systems of reasoning through which the teacher and child are constructed. As education is a central institution for the production of self-regulating individuals, the discursive principles inscribed in educational research require critical analysis and historical interpretation. Further, while the governing principles in pedagogical discourses are necessarily neither bad nor good, they cannot be taken unproblematically in a paradigm that argues about the "social construction" of knowledge.

Notes

This paper has undergone multiple drafts and comments. Among others who have helped me engage in conversations that have formed this paper are: Ingrid Carlgren, Inés Dussel, Lynn Fendler, Beth Graue, Joanna Hall, Lisa Hennon, Kenneth Hultqvist, Daniel Kallós, Herb Kliebard, Dory Lightfoot, Lizbeth Lundahl-Kallós, Wes Martin, Dienie Nel, António Nóvoa, David Shutkin, Judy Wagener, the Wednesday Group at Madison, and the seminar group in the Pedagogiska Institutionen, Umeå Universitet. I want to thank Bill Tate for helping me identify recent constructivist literature in mathematics education. I also would like to thank the reviewers of *AERJ*, whose comments were helpful in clarifying the internal logic and history of the argument.

1. My use of "modern" and "modernity" refers to the developments in technologies, institutional developments of professionalized knowledge associated with the social sciences, and changes in the state that occur during the nineteenth century. It is important to recognize that the historical trajectories that I speak about involve uneven developments which reach back into the seventeenth century.

2. While there are internal debates about the meaning of "constructivism" (see, e.g., Cobb 1994), my discussion concerns certain general assumptions that structure the debates about the "constructivist" teacher and child. The work of Dewey and Vygotsky appear prominently in this literature. See for example, Cazden (1986), Wertsch (1985, 1991); Moll (1990), and Newman et al. (1989).

3. There has been a lot written about Vygotsky in the United States. Examples of educational literature that focuses on his ideas and on its implications to questions of didactics are Cole & Scribner (1974), Confrey (1992), Davis, et al. (1990), Davydov (1981, 1988, Davydov & Radzikhovski (1985), Driver et al. (1994), Goodman & Goodman (1990), Moll (1990), Newman & Holzman (1993), Van der Verr & Valsiner (1991), Wersch (1985, 1991), and Vygotsky (1962, 1971, 1978, 1985, 1986, 1987, 1994). For discussion of Dewey's ideas, see Blacker (1993), Feinberg (1993), Karier (1986), in a social context, see Ross (1991), and West (1989). My intent is not to replicate these intellectual discussions but to construct a social epistemology through exploring the changes in regulatory patterns as the ideas of Vygotsky and Dewey are brought into contemporary educational discourses. But I can note that the literature tends to view the ideas of the past as part of the evolution of the field. Much of the reform literature celebrates, for example, the movement of the ideas of Dewey and Vygotsky into constructivist reforms (see, e.g., Sperry 1993). That development is seen as more enlightened than previous approaches in identifying what "makes" for a successful school.

4. My assumption is that all scientific discourses are governing ones in the sense discussed here, including my own (I discuss this in Popkewitz 1991 and 1993.

The problem of modern scholarship requires what Bourdieu et al. (1991) call an epistemological vigilance. Also see Bourdieu & Wacquant (1992).

5. I use the concept of "register" as a theoretical concept to recognize that the present is composed of multiple and overlapping records—ideas, events, and occurrences that historically come together as the "rules" of reason. By "registers" I mean different historical trajectories coming together in a single plane but having no single origin or progressive evolution. My traveling among different sets of ideas refers to a grid or overlay of historically formed ideas whose pattern gives intelligibility to today's debates.

6. My use of homology is theoretically to recognize a noncausality in relations (see Bourdieu 1993). My argument about Dewey and Vygotsky is in contrast to Newman and Holzman (1993), who argue for conceptually seeing Dewey and Vygotsky as different. Newman and Holzman focus on the particular logic of their arguments. While I accept this conclusion, my effort is to understand the epistemological and social spaces in which Dewey's and Vygotsky's ideas circulated, what I refer to as "modernity" at the turn of the century, and the textual convergence of their ideas in contemporary pedagogical reform literatures.

7. In light of the eventual repressive conditions of the former Soviet Union, it is easy to lose sight of its unique promise at the time of its revolution and its incorporation of the word "democracy" in its constitution.

8. I use the idea of homology to suggest here a historical relation between Dewey and Vygotsky in the modernization projects of the turn of the last century, and later, to think about the relations among different social sites. In each instance, my concern with homologies is with sets of relations that are not causal but are "families of resemblance."

9. Dewey, in *Democracy and Education*, does connect the idea of community to communication, but does not make communication a central concept. My discussion of Vygotsky was helped by my conversation with Dienne Nel.

10. Vygotsky's scholarship was often viewed with suspicion by those in power within the Soviet government, especially after the initial period of experimentation ended in the mid-twenties. I have heard current Russian scholars say that if Vygotsky had not died at an early age, he probably would have been sent to prison by Stalin.

11. Psychology in the United States, for example, moved away from Dewey's pragmatism and began to treat achievement as if it were institutionally fixed and separate from action, and thus focused on artificially designed experimental situations to understand how learning occurred.

12. One has to look at the development of neopragmatism, where the ideas Dewey are prominent, in the work of Richard Rorty and Richard Bernstein (in education, Cherryholmes 1993), Stone 1999, and St. Maurice 1993, among others), the pages of *American Psychologist*, or constructivist pedagogy, discussed, later to recognize the appeal of Dewey in contemporary scholarship.

13. I use the term "Progressive" as a descriptive historical label to discuss political and social transformations and do not mean to imply a connotation of "progress" (see Popkewitz 1991). The changes have lines of development that are uneven and date back to previous centuries but become clearly discernable in the nineteenth century (see Kaestle 1983, Kliebard 1986). The name "Progressive," does, however, capture a general ideological belief about social change and rationality in bringing social betterment. It mostly refers to political and social movements the northern tier of the United States that initially did not include women, African Americans, or Native Americans. Its assumptions have, over the century, spread more widely, as "Progressivism" is a significant source of the ideology behind the civil rights movements and efforts to check antidemocratic

excesses in the legal/administrative patterns of the state. It is interesting that educational literatures tends not to make the link between the larger political and social transformations and the visioning of schooling in progressive education.

14. Religious systems of authority were also redefined, in part, through the merging of the state with religion, and also through changes in social cosmologies in which religion was constructed (see, e.g., Berger 1969; Luckmann 1967).

15. While we can speak of the development of a modern consciousness as "middle-class" and related to the rise of capitalism, it is important to recognize that the formations of capitalism were not logical necessities, nor can we understand notions of "class" and capitalism as a structural categories that are historically unchangeable (see Boltanski 1982, 1987).

16. Psychology became predominant in pedagogy. Schooling was becoming a major U.S. institution, expanding in numbers and resources at a phenomenal rate. Between 1902–1913, public expenditures on education doubled, between 1913–22, they tripled. More public funds were invested in education than in national defense and public welfare combined during these decades (O'Donnell 1985: 229). Psychological clinics, child study research, and curriculum development projects provided jobs and financial support for psychologists.

17. The treatment of the child as "a learner" has become so natural in the late twentieth century that it is difficult to think of children as anything but learners.

18. As I stated before, my focus is on certain "tendencies" in the production of disciplinary knowledge. I recognize that there are internal debates and struggles about the interpretations and the normative commitments with educational research. My purpose is to consider "constructivist" discourses about teaching reform as a historical problem related to problems of governing. I do not consider the reception of Dewey in critical pedagogical thought but these discussions also contain the pitfalls of not considering ideas as historically positioned (see, e.g., Bowers 1993b, Popkewitz 1998a).

19. There is a relation between constructivism and a prior U.S. Piagetian psychology in education in that they ignore the social construction of disciplinary knowledge and accept a certain biological-evolutionary notion of development. I appreciate Ingrid Carlgren and Joanna Hall for pointing out this legacy of constructivism in education (see, e.g., Hall 1994).

20. Cobb et al. (1992), for example, argue that knowledge is both an individually constructed activity and a communal social practice. They assert a need for an anthropological theory to consider how meanings are constructed within the classroom (see also Cobb 1994). But that interest appears only as a rhetorical flourish, as a psychological-interactional notion of knowledge is emphasized. Mathematics is taken as having logical structures (analytical "things") that function as foundations from which learning is to occur. Works such as Wersch (1991) point to the need to integrate the psychological with the social/anthropological. Lave and Wenger (1991) is also cited but its limitation is in its microethnographic approach that does not go beyond assertions about institutions.

21. This is illustrated in citations that reference the historical and social contingency of knowledge. The literature serves only as icons to justify a narrower psychological and interactional view of knowledge that is devoid of history. For example, the work of Walkerdine (1988) is cited in mathematical education to suggest that activities are "interpreted in the social setting of the classroom and must necessarily differ from everyday interpretations in which people typically invent ways to reduce or eliminate the need to calculate" (Cobb et al. 1991: 13). But what Walkerdine argues is that social practices discursively regulate subjectivities through creating a normalized vision of the "natural" child and what is "true". While constructivist approaches could take issue with her arguments, she is read

selectively to legitimate what she argues against. (For an institutional analysis of mathematics as socially constructed, see Popkewitz 1988).

I find the same selective reading of the history and sociology of science, particularly that of Lakatos (Steffe and Kieren 1995) and Bachelard (Simon 1995). If we look at the work of Lakatos, it was during the 1970s and early 1980s that there was a "soft program" in the history of science. People looked at the "everyday" patterns through which scientists produced knowledge. That "soft" program has been severely criticized, and current work seeks to interrelate the "hard" and "soft" programs to understand the multitiered production of knowledge. The work of Canguilhem provides a different example of a selective reading. His work is part of a tradition of the history of science that considers historical change as tied to the conditions and the manner in which concepts change. It is not a psychological focus but one that places epistemologies into historical and sociological "contexts." The history of science works at a level of analysis that challenges contemporary constructivist assumptions about the socially negotiated "knowledge" of individuals. In both instances, citations provide a selective misrecognition of scholarship and a rereading that justifies rather than scrutinizes the stances taken. For general treatments of changes in the epistemological constructions of science and social science, see Toulmin (1990), Canguilhem (1988), Tiles (1984), Bachelard (1984), Manicas (1987); Brante et al. (1993), Kuhn (1970); for discussion about education, see Popkewitz (1991), the work of Resnick et al. (1991) cited earlier also tries in its way to dissolve such dualisms. Also see Elzinga's (1985) discussion of epistemic drift in the science, focusing on the relation of state and business policies to the forming and reforming of fields within science.

Perhaps when this literature talks about a "radical constructivism" (see, e.g, Steffe and Kerian 1994), we can understand this as nothing "radical," but as a shift from a pedagogy concerned with the consensus and equilibrium outlined previously in textbook conclusions to a pedagogy that now looks to develop consensus and stability through children's and teachers' shared norms. The assumptions about the stability of disciplinary knowledge are obscured through a rhetoric about social interaction and negotiated "knowledge."

22. Where alternative accounts of history, science and mathematics occur in this literature (e.g., Ball and McDiarmid 1991), the discussions give priority to the logical stability of concepts within disciplines *and not to how concepts vary within intellectual traditions and to the interrelation of knowledge, methods, and "social conditions" in the production of social knowledge.*

23. The changes in business organizations have dual qualities. They produce a revamping of such giant international corporations as General Motors, Sears, Roebuck, and IBM. The loss of 25,000 jobs, IBM reflects the changing world of work as smaller units with greater self-management are constructed (Meyerson 1992). To cite another example, the world's microchip makers are regularly able to achieve a fourfold increase in the number of microprocessors that can be placed on a silicon chip every three years, leading to vast increases in power and miniaturization. Each new generation of microchips has created a new computer industry that has overthrown the previous one. Some experts argue that the new model for computer and technological development requires alliances of small, innovative companies, sometimes with government support and sometimes without.

24. For example, the success of the individual fighter pilot is tied to an indefinite coordination with others—on the ground and in the air—a degree of coordination that has disastrous consequences when it breaks down. Thus, when efforts to coordinate air and land forces failed during the Gulf War, errors in target recognition produced some of the heaviest casualties on the Allied side. Indeed,

most Allied casualities in that war were from "friendly fire." U.S. (and NATO) flying tactics are built around the individual pilot's decision-making ability in combat. During the Gulf War, for example, the Allies' tactic was to knock out the Iraqi command posts in their first sorties. The Iraqi air force, in contrast, flew on orders from a central command, and, once that was destroyed, the air force was rendered nonfunctional. This is one of the reasons that the Iraqi air force flew its planes to Iran for safekeeping.

25. It is important to point to the fact that the issues of local knowledge generating principles of inclusion/exclusion are not inherent to constructivism, but a more general theoretical problem of which constructivism is an exemplar in this historical conjuncture.

References

Bachelard, G. (1984). *The new scientific spirit* (trans. by A. Goldhammer). Boston: Beacon Press.

Baker, B. (1998). Childhood-as-rescue in the emergence and spread of the U.S. public school. In T. Popkewitz and M. Brennan (Eds.), *Foucault's challenge: Discourse, knowledge and power in education* (117–43). New York: Teachers College Press.

Ball, D., and McDiarmid, G. (1991). The subject matter preparation of teachers. In W. Houston, M. Haberman, and J. Sikula (Eds.), *Handbook of research on teacher education: A project of the Association of Teacher Educators* (437–49). New York: Macmillan.

Bazerman, C. (1988). *Shaping written knowledge: The genre and activity of the experimental article in science*. Madison: University of Wisconsin Press.

Becker, C. (1932). *The heavenly city of the eighteenth-century philosophers*. New Haven, CT: Yale University Press.

Bercovitch, S. (1978). *The American Jeremiad*. Madison: University of Wisconsin Press.

Berger, P. (1969). *The sacred canopy: Elements of a sociological theory of religion*. New York: Doubleday Anchor.

Berger, P., Berger, B., and Kellner, H. (1973). *The homeless mind: Modernization and consciousness*. New York: Vintage.

Bernstein, R. (1976). *The restructuring of social and political theory*. New York: Harcourt, Brace and Jovanovich.

———. (1992). *The new constellation: The ethical-political horizons of modernity/ postmodernity*. Cambridge, MA: MIT Press.

Bishop, A. (1991). Toward a cultural psychology of mathematics. A review of culture and cognitive development: Studies in mathematical understanding. *Journal for Research in Mathematics Education* 22(1): 76–80.

Blacker, D. (1993). Allowing educational technologies to reveal: A Deweyian perspective. *Educational Theory* 43: 181–94.

Bledstein, B. (1976). *The culture of professionalism, the middle class, and the development of higher education in America*. New York: Norton and Co.

Bloch, M. (1987). Becoming scientific and professional: An historical perspective on the aims and effects of early education. In T. Popkewitz (Ed.), *The formation of school subjects: The struggle for creating an American institution* (25–62). New York: Falmer Press.

Boltanski, L. (1982/1987). *The making of a class: Cadres in French society* (trans. by A. Goldhammer). New York and Paris: Cambridge University Press and Editions de la Mason des Sciences de L'Homme.

Bourdieu, P. (1984). *Distinction: A social critique of the judgment of taste* (trans by R. Nice). Cambridge, MA: Harvard University Press.

————. (1993). *The field of cultural production* (trans. by R. Johnson). New York: Columbia University Press.

Bourdieu, P., and Passeron, J. C. (1977). *Reproduction in education, society, and culture*. Beverly Hills, CA: Sage.

Bourdieu, P., Chamboredon, J., and Passeron, J. (1991). *The craft of sociology: Epistemological preliminaries* (trans. by Richard Nice). New York: Walter de Gruyter.

Bourdieu, P., and Wacquant, L. (1992). *An invitation to reflexive sociology.* Chicago: The University of Chicago Press.

Bowers, C. (1993a). *Critical essays on education, modernity, and the recovery of the ecological imperative.* New York: Teachers College Press.

————. (1993b). *Education, cultural myths, and the ecological crisis.* Albany: State University of New York Press.

Brante, T. Fuller, S. and Lynch, W. (Eds.). (1993). *Controversial science: From content to contention.* Albany: State University of New York Press.

Butler, J. (1992). Contingent foundations: Feminism and the question of "postmodernism." In J. Butler and J. Scott (Eds.), *Feminists theorize the political* (3–21). New York: Routledge.

————. (1993). *Bodies that matter: On the discursive limits of "sex."* New York: Routledge.

Canguilhem, G. (1988). *Ideology and rationality in the history of the life sciences* (trans. by A. Goldhammer). Cambridge, MA: MIT Press.

Carnoy, M. (1984). *The state and political theory.* Princeton, NJ: Princeton University Press.

Cazden, C. (1986). Classroom discourse. In M. Wittrock (Ed.), *Handbook of research on teaching* (3rd ed.) (432–63). New York: Macmillan.

Cherryholms, C. (1993). Reading research. *Journal of Curriculum Studies* 25(1), 1–32.

Cobb, P. (1994). Where is the mind? Constructivist and sociocultural perspectives on mathematical development. *Educational Researcher* 23: 13–20.

Cobb, P., Wood, P., Yackel, E., Nicholls, J., Weatley, G., Trigatti, B., and Perlwitz, M. (1991). Assessment of a problem-centered second-grade mathematics project. *Journal for Research in Mathematics Education* 22(1): 3–29.

Cobb, P., Yackel, E., and Wood, T. (1992). A constructivist alternative to the representational view of mind in mathematics education. *Journal for Research in Mathematics Education* 23(1): 2–33.

Cole, M., and Scribner, S. (1974). *Culture and thought: A Psychological Introduction.* New York: John Wiley.

Confrey, J. (1992). Steering a course between Vygotsky and Piaget. *Educational Researcher* 20: 28–32.

Danziger, K. (1990). *Constructing the subject: Historical origins of psychological research.* New York: Cambridge University Press.

Davis, R., Mahr, C., and Noddings, N. (1990). Constructivist views on the teaching and learning of mathematics. *Journal for Research in Mathematics Education* (Monograph 4).

Davydov, V. (1981). Psychological problems in the education and upbringing of the rising generation. In B. Tabachnick, T. Popkewitz, and B. Szekely (Eds.), *Studying teaching, and learning: Trends in Soviet and American research* (183–99). New York: Praeger.

————. (1988). Problems of developmental teaching (Part 1). *Soviet Education* 30: 6–97.

————. (1995). The influence of L. S. Vygotsky on education theory, research, and practice (trans. by S. Kerr). *The Educational Researcher* 24(3): 12–21.

Davydov, V. and Radzikhovski, L. (1985). Vygotsky's theory and the activity-oriented approach to psychology. In J. Wertsch (Ed.), *Culture, communication, and cognition: Vygotskian perspectives* (35–65). Cambridge: Cambridge University Press.

Dean, M. (1994). *Critical and effective histories: Foucault's methods and historical sociology*. New York: Routledge.

Di Stefano, C. (1990). Dilemmas of difference: Feminism, modernity, and postmodernism. In L. Nicholson (Ed.), *Feminism/Postmodernism* (63–82). New York: Routledge.

Donzelot, J. (1991). Pleasure in work. In G. Burchell, C. Gordon, and P. Miller (Eds.), *The Foucault effect: Studies in governmentality* (251–80). Chicago: University of Chicago Press.

Dreyfus, H., and Rabinow, P. (1983). *Michel Foucault: Beyond structuralism and hermeneutics*. Chicago: University of Chicago Press.

Driver, R., Asoko, H., Leach, J., Mortimer, E., and Scott, P. (1994). Constructing scientific knowledge in the classroom. *Educational Researcher* 23: 5–12.

Dumm, T. (1993). The new enclosures: Racism in the normalized community. In R. Gooding-Williams (Ed.), *Reading Rodney King: Reading urban uprising* (178–95). New York: Routledge.

Elias, N. (1978). *The history of manners: The civilizing process* (Vol. 1). (trans. by E. Jephcott). New York: Pantheon.

Elzinga, A. (1985). Research, bureaucracy and the draft of epistemic criteria. In B. Wittrock and A. Elzinga (Eds.), *The university research system: The public policies of the home of scientists* (191–220). Stockholm: Almquist and Wiskell International.

Evans, P., Rueschemeyer, D., and Skocpol, T. (Eds.). (1985). *Bringing the state back in*. Cambridge: Cambridge University Press.

Fatis, S. (1992). Firms trim hierarchies, empower workers. *The Capital Times*, December 25: 4B-5B.

Feinberg, W. (1993). Dewey and democracy at the dawn of the twenty-first century. *Educational Theory* 43: 195–216.

Fendler, L. (1998). What is it impossible to think? A genealogy of the educated subject. In T. Popkewitz and M. Brennan (Eds.), *Foucault's challenge: Discourse, knowledge, and power in education* (39–63). New York: Teachers College Press.

Foucault, M. (1977). *Power/Knowledge: Selected interviews and other writings, (1972- 1977)* (ed. by C. Gordon). New York: Pantheon.

———. (1979). Governmentality. *Ideology and Consciousness* 6: 5–22.

Fraser, N. (1989). *Unruly practices: Power, discourse, and gender in contemporary social theory*. Minneapolis: University of Minnesota Press.

Freedman, K. (1987). Art education as social production: Culture, society and politics in the formation of the curriculum. In T. Popkewitz (Ed.), *The formation of school subjects: The struggle for creating an American institution* (63–84). London: Falmer.

Gatens, M. (1991). *Feminism and philosophy: Perspectives on difference and equality*. Stanford, CA: Stanford University Press.

Gee, J. (in press). Progressivism, critique and socially situated minds. In C. Edelsky and C. Dudley-Marling (Eds.), *Progressive education: History and critique*. Urbana, IL: NCTE.

Gee, J., Hull, G., and Lanskear, C. (1996). *The new work order: Behind the language of the new capitalism*. Boulder, CO: Westview Press.

Giddens, A. (1990). *The consequences of modernity*. Stanford, CA: Stanford University Press.

Giroux, H. (1992). *Border crossings: Cultural workers and the politics of education*. New York: Routledge.

Goodman, Y., and Goodman, K. (1990). Vygotsky in a whole-language perspective. In L. Doll (Ed.), *Vygotsky and education: Instructional implications and applications of sociohistorical psychology* (223–51). Cambridge: Cambridge University Press.

Gouldner, A. (1970). *The coming crisis of Western sociology.* New York: Basic Books.

———. (1979). *The two Marxisms: Contradictions and anomalies in the development of theory.* New York: Seabury Press.

Hall, G. (1905/1969). *Adolescence: Its psychology and its relation to physiology, anthropology, sociology, sex, crime, religion and education* (vol. 2). New York: Arno and the New York Times.

Hall, J. (1994). *Experience, experiment, and reason: English primary science (1959- (1967).* Ph.D. dissertation, University of Liverpool.

Hall, S. (1986). The problem of ideology-Marxism without guarantees. *Journal of Communication Inquiry* 10: 28–43.

Halliday, M., and Martin, J. (1993). *Writing science: Literacy and discursive power.* Pittsburgh: University of Pittsburgh Press.

Haskell, T. (1977). *The emergence of professional social science: The American social science association and the nineteenth-century crisis of authority.* Urbana: University of Illinois Press.

Haskell, T. (1984). Professionalism versus capitalism: R. H. Towney, Emile Durkheim, and C. S. Pierce on the disinterestedness of professional communities. In T. Haskell (Ed.), *The authority of exerts: Studies in history and theory* (180–225). Bloomington: Indiana University Press.

Herman, T. (1995). *The romance of American psychology, political culture in the age of experts.* Berkeley: University of California Press.

Holmes Group. (1986). *Tomorrow's teachers.* East Lansing, MI: Holmes Group.

———. (1990). *Tomorrow's schools.* East Lansing, MI: Holmes Group.

Hultqvist, K. (1998). A history of the present on children's welfare in Sweden. In T. Popkewitz and M. Brennan (Eds.), *Foucault's challenge: Discourse, knowledge and power in education* (91–116). New York: Teachers College Press.

Hunter, I. (1994). *Rethinking the school: Subjectivity, bureaucracy, criticism.* New York: St. Martin's Press.

———. (1995). Assembling the school. In A. Barry, T. Osborne, and N. Rose (Eds.), *Foucault and political reason, liberalism, neo-liberalism, and rationalities of government* (143- 66). Chicago: University of Chicago Press.

International Labour Organization. (1994). *Consequences of structural adjustment for employment, training, further training and retraining in the metal trades* (Report II ed.). Geneva: International Labour Office, Sectoral Activities Programme.

Joas, H. (1980/1985). *G. H. Mead: A contemporary re-examination of his thought* (R. Meyer, trans). Cambridge, MA: MIT Press.

Kaestle, C. (1983). *Pillars of the republic: Common schools and American society, 1780- 1860.* New York: Hill and Wang.

Karier, C. (1986). *Scientists of the mind: Intellectual founders of modern psychology.* Champaign: University of Illinois Press.

Kliebard, H. (1986). *Struggle for the American curriculum.* London: Routledge and Kegan Paul.

Kohli, W. (1995). *Critical conversations in philosophy of education.* New York: Routledge.

Kuhn, T. (1970). *The structure of scientific revolutions* (2nd ed.). Chicago: University of Chicago Press.

Kuttner, R. (1991). *The end of laissez-faire; National purpose and the global economy after the cold war.* New York: Alfred A. Knopf.

Laraña, E., Johnston, H., and Gusfield, J. (Eds.). (1994). *New social movements from ideology to identify.* Philadephia: Temple University Press.

Lave, J., and Wenger, E. (1991). *Situated learning: Legitimate peripheral participation.* Cambridge: Cambridge University Press.

Lears, J. (1981). *No place of grace: Antimodernism and the transformation of American culture, 1880–1920.* New York: Pantheon.

Lekachman, R. (1982). *Greed is not enough, Reaganomics.* New York: Pantheon Books.

Luckmann, T. (1967). *The invisible religion: The problem of religion in modern society.* New York: Macmillan.

Manicas, P. (1987). *A history and philosophy of the social sciences.* Oxford: Basil Blackwell.

Martin, J. (1992). *Towards a theory of text for contrastive rhetoric: An introduction to issues for text for students and practitioners of contrastive rhetoric.* New York: Peter Lang.

Marx, L. (1964). *The machine in the garden: Technology and the pastoral image in America.* New York: Oxford University Press.

McLaren, P., and Giarelli, J. (Eds.). (1995). *Critical theory and educational research.* Albany: State University of New York.

Meyer, J., Ramirez, J., and Soysal, Y. (1992). World expansion of mass education, 1870–1980. *Sociology of Education* 65: 128–49.

Meyerson, A. (1992). IBM to eliminate 25,000 jobs in 1993 and shut plants. *The New York Times,* December 16: 1.

Moll, L. (Ed.). (1990). *Vygotsky and Education: Instructional Implications and Applications of Sociohistorical Psychology.* Cambridge: Cambridge University Press.

Napoli, D. (1981). *Architects of Adjustment: The History of the Psychological Profession in the United States.* Port Washington, NY: Kennikat Press.

National Council of Teachers of Mathematics. (1989). *Curriculum and Evaluation Standards for School Mathematics.* Reston, VA: National Council of Teachers of Mathematics.

Newman, F., Griffin, D., and Cole, M. (1989). *The construction zone: Working for cognitive change in schools.* Cambridge: Cambridge University Press.

Newman, F., and Holzman, L. (1993). *Lev Vygotsky: Revolutionary scientist.* London: Routledge.

Noble, D. (Ed.). (1991). *The classroom arsenal.* London: Falmer Press.

O'Donnell, J. (1985). *The origins of behaviorism: American psychology, 1876–1920.* New York: New York University Press.

Popkewitz, T. (1977). The latent values of the discipline-centered curriculum. *Theory and Research in Social Education* 5(2): 41–60.

———. (1987). *The formation of school subjects: The struggle for creating an American institution.* New York: Falmer Press.

———. (1991). *A political sociology of education reform: Power/knowledge in teaching, teacher education, and research.* New York: Teachers College Press.

———. (Ed.). (1993). *Changing patterns of power: Social regulation and teacher education reform.* Albany: State University of New York Press.

———. (1996). Rethinking decentralization and the state/civil society distinctions: The state as a problematic of governing. *Journal of Educational Policy* 11, 27–51.

———. (1997). The production of reason and power: curriculum history and intellectual traditions. *Curriculum Studies* 29: 131–64.

———. (1998a). The culture of redemption and the administration of freedom as research. *The Review of Educational Research* 68(1): 1–34.

———. (1998b). *Struggling for the soul: The politics of schooling and the construction of the teacher.* New York: Teachers College Press.

————. and Brennan, M. (Eds.) (1998). *Foucault's challenge: Discourse, knowledge, and power in education*. New York: Teachers College Press.

Popkewitz, T., Tabachnick, R., and Wehlage, G. (1982). *The myth of educational reform*. Madison: University of Wisconsin Press.

Powell, A. (1980). *The uncertain profession: Harvard and the search for educational authority*. Cambridge, MA: Harvard University Press.

Resnick, L., Levine, J., and Teasley, S. (1991). *Perspectives on social shared cognition*. Washington, DC: American Psychological Association.

Rorty, R. (1979). *Philosophy and the mirror of nature*. Princeton, NJ: Princeton University Press.

Rose, N. (1989). *Governing the soul*. New York: Routledge, Chapman and Hall.

————. (1994). Expertise and the government of conduct. *Studies in Law, Politics and Society* 14: 359–97.

Rose, N., and Miller, P. (1992). Political power beyond the state: Problematics of government. *British Journal of Sociology* 43: 173–205.

Ross, D. (1991). *The origins of American social science*. New York: Cambridge University Press.

Rueschemeyer, D., and Skocpol, T. (Eds.). (1996). *States, social knowledge, and the origins of modern social policies*. Lawrenceville, NJ: Princeton University Press.

St. Maurice, H. (1993). Two rhetorics of cynicism in curriculum deliberation, or two riders in a barren land. *Educational Theory* 43: 147–60.

Scheler, M. (1924/1980). *Problems of sociology of knowledge* (trans. by M. Frings). Boston: Routledge & Kegan Paul.

Scott, J. (1991). The evidence of experience. *Critical Inquiry* 17: 773–97.

Sieber, R. (1983). The politics of middle-class success in an inner-city public school. In T. Popkewitz (Ed.), *Charge and stability in schooling: The dual quality of educational reform* (92–108). Geelong, Australia: Deakin University Press.

Silva, E., and Slaughter, S. (1984). *Serving power: The making of the academic social science expert*. Westport, CT: Greenwood Press.

Simon, M. (1995). Reconstructing mathematics pedagogy from a constructivist perspective. *Journal for Research in Mathematics Education* 26(2): 114–145.

Skocpol, T. (1985). *Bringing the state back in*. Cambridge: Cambridge University Press.

Skowronek, S. (1982). *Building a new American state: The expansion of national administrative capacities, 1877–1920*. New York: Cambridge University Press.

Smagorinsky, P. (1995). The social construction of data: Methodological problems of investigating learning in the zone of proximal development. *Review of Educational Research* 65(3): 191–212.

Smith, M. and O'Day, J. (1990). Systemic school reform. *Politics of Education Association Yearbook* (233–267).

Sperry, K. (1993). The impact and promise of the cognitive revolution. *American Psychologist* 48(8): 78–85.

Steffe, L. and Kieren, T. (1994). Radical constructivism and mathematics education. *Journal for Research in Mathematics Education* 25(6): 711–34.

Steffe, L. and Kieren, T. (1995). Toward a working model of constructivist teaching: A reaction to Simon. *Journal for Research in Mathematics Education* 26(2): 146–59.

Stone, L. (1999). Reconstructing Dewey's critical philosophy: Toward a literary pragmatist criticism. In T. Popkewitz and L. Fendler (Eds.), *Critical theories in education: Changing terrains of knowledge and politics* (209- 27). New York: Routledge.

Tabachnick, B. R., Popkewitz, T., and Szekely, B. (Eds.). (1981). Studying, teaching, and learning: Some trends in Soviet and American research. New York: Praeger.

Thorndike, E. (1910). *Educational psychology* (2nd ed.). New York: Teachers College Press.

Tiles, M. (1984). *Bachelard: Science and objectivity*. Cambridge: Cambridge University Press.

Toulmin, S. (1990). *Cosmopolis: The hidden agenda of modernity*. New York: Free Press.

Van der Veer, R., and Valsiner, J. (1991). *Understanding Vygotsky: A quest for synthesis*. Oxford: Blackwell.

Vygotsky, L. (1962). *Thought and language* (ed. and trans. by E. Hanfmann and G. Vakar). Cambridge, MA: MIT Press.

————. (1971). *The psychology of art* (introduction by A. N. Leontiev; commentary by V.V. Ivanov; trans. by Scripta Technica). Cambridge, MA: MIT Press.

————. (1978). *Mind in society: The development of higher psychological process*. Cambridge, MA: Harvard University Press.

————. (1985). *Vygotsky and the social formation of mind*. Cambridge, MA: Harvard University Press.

————. (1986). *Thought and language* (ed. and trans. revised by A. Kozulin). Cambridge, MA: MIT Press.

————. (1987). *The collected works of L. S. Vygotsky*. New York: Plenum Press.

————. (1994). *The Vygotsky reader*. Oxford and Cambridge: Blackwell.

Wagner, P. (1994). *Sociology of modernity: Liberty and discipline*. New York: Routledge.

Walkerdine, V. (1988). *The mastery of reason: Cognitive development and the production of rationality*. London: Routledge.

————. (1990). *Schoolgirl fictions*. London: Verso.

Wertsch, J. (1985). *Vygotsky and the social formation of mind*. Cambridge, MA: Harvard University Press.

————. (1991). *Voices of the mind: A sociocultural approach to mediated action*. Cambridge, MA: Harvard University Press.

West, C. (1989). *The American evasion of philosophy: A genealogy of pragmatism*. Madison: University of Wisconsin Press.

Wittrock, B., Wagner, P., and Wollman, H. (1991). Social science and the modern state, policy knowledge and political institutions in Western Europe and the United States. In P. Wagner, C. Weiss, B. Wittrock, and H. Wollman (Eds.), *Social sciences and modern states: National experiences and theoretical crossroads* (28–85). Cambridge: Cambridge University Press.

Woody, T. (1932). *New minds: New men? The emergence of the Soviet citizen*. New York: Macmillan.

Zolberg, A. (1991). Bounded states in a global market: The uses of international labor migrations. In P. Bourdieu and J. Colman (Eds.), *Social theory for a changing society* (301–336). Boulder, CO: Westview Press.

Contributors

Marta Maria Chagas de Carvalho is a Professor in the Postgraduate Program on Education—History, Politics, Society at the Pontifical Catholic University-São Paulo, Brazil and researcher of Centro de Memória da Educação of Faculdade de Educação of Universidade de São Paulo. She has written extensively about modern Brazilian educational history and pedagogy and the Brasilean Educational Association.

Anne-Marie Chartier is an educational historian at the Service d'Histoire de l'Education (SHE) in the Institut National de la Recherche Pedagogique in Paris. Anne-Marie Chartier and Jean Hébrard's historical research focuses on written culture, the divulgence of reading and writing in society, the schooling process of literacy in basic school, and on teachers' training.

Inés Dussel is the Director of the Education Unit of FLACSO/Argentina and Assistant Professor at the University of San Andres, Argentina. Her academic interests focus on the history of education and pedagogy, postmodern theories of education, and the teaching of human rights. Her current work focuses on the historical construction and disciplining of the body through studies of the wearing of school uniforms in Argentina, France, and the United States.

Barry M. Franklin is a Professor of Education and Public Administration at the University of Michigan-Flint. His research is concerned with the history of curriculum reform policy, curriculum history, and urban education.

David Hamilton is a Professor of Education at Umeå University in Sweden. His research interests are in the origins of modern schooling. He also concentrates on exploring the relationship between research and educational practice.

Jean Hébrard is Inspecteur General at the Ministere de l'Education nationale, and associated researcher at the Service d'Histoire de l'Education in Paris. Jean Hébrard and Anne-Marie Chartier's historical research focuses on written culture, the divulgation of reading and writing in society, the schooling process of literacy in basic school, and on teachers' training.

Katharina E. Heyning is an Assistant Professor at the University of Wisconsin-Whitewater. Her research interests include the reform and change of teacher education, certification and licensure, and the teaching of social studies in elementary schools.

Ingólfur Ásgeir Jóhannesson is an Associate Professor of Education at the University of Akureyri in Iceland. His intellectual interests include teacher professionalism and social and historical issues in education.

António Nóvoa is a Professor of Educational History at the University of Lisbon. He is a historian who is interested in questions of comparative education, methodological traditions in French and American historical approaches, and the study of teaching and curriculum.

Miguel A. Pereyra is Professor of Theory and History of Education at the University of Granada. His research interests are in comparative education, curriculum history, and educational policy reforms.

Thomas S. Popkewitz is a Professor in the Department of Curriculum and Instruction at the University of Wisconsin-Madison. His interest is in the changes in the systems of reason that govern schooling focusing on the relation of knowledge and power in curriculum, teaching, and teacher education.

Heinz-Elmar Tenorth is Professor of History of Education and Dean of the School of Philosophy IV at the Humbold University in Berlin. His research focuses on the history of European education, specializing in the social history of education and educational theory.

Julia Varela is Associate Professor of Sociology and Chair of the Department of Sociology and Communication at the Complutense University in Madrid. Her research interests are in the field of historical sociology.

Antonio Viñao is Professor of History of Education at the University of Murcia in Spain. His interests include the history of the processes involved in the professionalization of teaching intellectual history, the history of school culture and the study of the human mind as a sociohistorical product.

Mirian Jorge Warde is the Coordinator of the Postgraduate Program on Education—History, Politics, Society at the Pontifical Catholic University-São Paulo, Brazil and a senior researcher on the relationship between culture and education in the nineteenth and twentieth centuries.

Name Index

Subject Index

action research 16, 331
actor x, 12, a prior agent of change
  13–14, 18, 20–22, 25, 28, 146,
  151; 156–8; fabrication of 158;
  and paradox 158; and linguistic
  turn 164; 174
ahistorical consciousness 18
alchemy of pedagogy 328–330, 335
"advanced liberalism" 34n11
American exceptionalism: and
  Dewey's writing 316
"antihistory" 10
Annales 7, 8; "mental tools" and 21,
  258n1
archaeology 290, 291–2
Archaeology of Knowledge 107, 110
arithmetic: and statistics as state
  arithmetic 161–2: as social and
  cultural practice 147n5
Arqueologia de la escuela (The
  archaeology of school) 122
arts of governing 160, 319
authorized language 292

black box 51, 86
Boke Named the Gouvenour 193
bodies 17; and cultural codes of
  dress 19; cultural history of
  209–213; and identity 209;
  practices and 210; normalization
  and 210; manners and
  individuation 210–11; as surface

for social inscriptions and
  ambivalence 211; materiality of
  236n2; de Certeau and
  "ungovernability" (slippages) of
  211; as territory of risk 211; as
  caught up in moral and political
  systems of classifications 212; as
  the animate temple of the Holy
  Spirit 222; language of rights and
  changing perceptions of the body
  225; 18th & 19th century shift to
  conception of body as organic
  machine 225–6; shift from
  treatises on manners to textbooks
  on hygiene and pedagogy 225;
  docile bodies 295, 302

capital 244–245
catechisms 266–7; and spreading of
  literacy 268
Catholic Church 91–92, 160; and
  renovating movement in Brazil 92,
  95, 102n17; educational practices
  201–2; and parish schools in
  France 264, 267–8, 274
Centuries of Childhood 124n6
change ix, distinguished from
  traditional intellectual history ix,
  as the history of the present 4–5,
  knowledge as central concern and
  5–6, historizing approach and 7,
  12–3, 18, decentering of the